SOCIALIST REGISTER 2020

D0982249

THE SOCIALIST REGISTER

Founded in 1964

To get online access to all Register volumes visit our website
http://www.socialistregister.com

SOCIALIST REGISTER 2020

BEYOND MARKET DYSTOPIA

NEW WAYS OF LIVING

Edited by LEO PANITCH and GREG ALBO

THE MERLIN PRESS
MONTHLY REVIEW PRESS
FERNWOOD PUBLISHING

First published in 2019
by The Merlin Press Ltd
Central Books Building
Freshwater Road
London
RM8 1RX

www.merlinpress.co.uk

British Library Cataloguing in Publication Data is available from the British
Library

ISSN. 0081–0606

Published in the UK by The Merlin Press
ISBN. 978-0-85036-752-2 Paperback
ISBN. 978-0-85036-753-9 Hardback

Published in the USA by Monthly Review Press
ISBN. 978-1-58367-843-5 Paperback

Published in Canada by Fernwood Publishing
ISBN. 978-1-77363-244-5 Paperback

Printed and bound in the UK on behalf of Stanton Book Services

CONTENTS

CONTRIBUTORS

Amy Bartholomew is an Associate Professor of Law and Legal Studies at Carleton University.

Alyssa Battistoni is an editor at *Jacobin* and a PhD student in political science at Yale University.

Karl Beitel is a Senior Lecturer at the California Institute of Integral Studies.

Michelle Chen writes for *In These Times* and *The Nation*, and is a contributing editor at *Dissent*.

Yu Chunsen was recently awarded a PhD in Chinese Studies Research from King's College London.

Nancy Fraser is the Loeb Professor of Political and Social Science at The New School in New York.

Sam Gindin is the former research director of the Canadian Auto Workers, and Packer Chair in Social Justice at York University.

Barbara Harriss-White is Emeritus Professor of Development Studies at the University of Oxford.

Owen Hatherley is the culture editor of *Tribune*.

Nancy Holmstrom is an Emeritus Professor of Philosophy at Rutgers University.

Ursula Huws is Professor of Labour and Globalisation at the University of Hertfordshire, and founder of Analytica Social and Economic Research.

Roger Keil holds the Research Chair in Global Sub/Urban Studies at York University.

Key MacFarlane is a PhD candidate in the History of Consciousness department at UC Santa Cruz.

Stephen Maher is a PhD Candidate at York University and an Assistant Editor of the *Socialist Register*.

Birgit Mahnkopf is Professor of European Social Policy at the Berlin School of Economics and Law.

Katharyne Mitchell is Professor of Sociology at the University of California, Santa Cruz.

Leo Panitch is Emeritus Professor of Political Science at York University.

Hilary Wainwright is the editor of *Red Pepper* magazine.

PREFACE

This 56th volume of the *Socialist Register* is motivated by wanting to look beyond – while still taking into account – the deep contradictions of neoliberal capitalism that have so far dominated political and economic life in the twenty-first century. These contradictions amount to something of a register of the dislocations and distortions of capitalist markets over the last several decades: the gross income and wealth inequalities of class and nation; the massive global credit expansion in volume and complexity underpinning economic growth; the intricate interconnections between financial markets and global value chains; the ever more limited capacities of states to control economic crises; the breaching of greenhouse gas emission targets under the relentless acceleration of the circulation and accumulation of capital still thoroughly dependent upon fossil fuel energy supplies; and the massive void that now exists between liberal democratic politics deploying policies of social inclusion and the material sources of social polarisation and class divisions. In the Preface to last year's volume, *A World Turned Upside Down?*, we suggested that these developments 'increasingly raise the stark question of whether we should once again be thinking of the options facing the world in terms of "socialism versus barbarism"'... In a world overturning old certainties, soberly expressing the prospects for a way forward for the left requires setting out new left agendas for confronting the corporate powers of capital, and indentifying new hopeful organizational dynamics that could lead to state transformations.'

To look beyond the restricted horizons disciplining the range of acceptable political options today requires overcoming the current limits of vision as well as practice that would allow for other possible political choices. In the past years, we have seen a multiplication of writings on 'alternatives' speaking to 'post-capitalism' but most remain cast in terms of still working within – and most often accommodating – actually-existing capitalism. They too often reflect rather than transcend the contradictions entailed in, for instance, the promise of abundance from automation but also a severe intensification and degradation of work; or in the imperative to address ecological limits in a transformation of the socio-economic system but a seeming inability to reverse the waste economy or climate change; or the sickening over-housing of the few alongside a desperate need to address homelessness, social housing and the new global slums. All this recalls the warning with which Colin Leys, our former co-editor of the *Socialist Register*, persuasively closed his essential text, *Market-Driven Politics: Neoliberal Democracy and the Public Interest* (2001):

> A strong non-market domain, providing various core services, as the common sense of a civilised and democratic society may sound far-fetched in an era of market-driven politics. But it is debatable whether it is really as far-fetched – as hard to imagine or as absurd – as the world towards which market-driven politics is tending, in which more and more of the workforce is absorbed in ever-intensified competition for ever higher output and consumption, while the collective services for which democracy depends gradually decay.

It is precisely this sensibility that informs this volume, *Beyond Market Dystopia: New Ways of Living*. By challenging our contributors to address what are the actual and possible ways of living in this century, we saw this as way of probing how to get beyond the deep contradictions of neoliberal capitalism. We did not want contributors to conceive their remit as future-oriented per se, but rather to see their mandate as locating *utopic visions and struggles* for alternate ways of living in the *dystopic present*. To this end, a number of the essays interrogate central dimensions of 'how we live' and 'how we might live' in terms of educating our children, housing and urbanism, accommodation of refugees and the displaced, and (to lean on that all too common phrase) the competitive time pressures for 'work-life balance'.

These are all key questions, of course, of 'social reproduction', a theme that has cut across many volumes of the *Register*. They are the counterpoint to 'economic reproduction' and 'how we work' at the heart of several essays here. Today, this involves exploring and exposing all the hype and contradictions of the so-called 'gig economy', where automation's potential for increased time apart from work is subordinated to surveillance, hazardous waste, speed-up, and much else that makes for contingent work and precarious living. Finding new ways of living cannot but confront both these obstacles.

Yet even amidst all that appears so new in today's capitalism, classical socialist themes, dilemmas, challenges, and struggles are still very much with us. Indeed, several essays in this volume undertake political archaeologies of the past to find their vestiges providing new meaning for the practices of socialism in the twenty-first century. And we have come to realize that the mandate to seek out strategic, programmatic and even manifesto-oriented directions for socialist futures in the dystopic conditions of the present will need to be stretched out beyond the 2020 volume of the *Register* to the 2021 volume, with this first one more centred on social reproduction, ecology, and so forth, and the next more focused on the tension between 'artificial intelligence' and socialist 'common sense'.

Perhaps the foremost challenge in trying to think beyond the market dystopia of contemporary capitalism is to soberly assess the implications of the alarming ecological conditions we now confront amidst the climate crisis, with its reverberations across the world's ecology, in rising temperatures, the erosion of the polar ice shields, climate refugees, mass species extinctions, and much more. The Preface to the 2007 *Register, Coming to Terms with Nature*, signalled the unavoidable agenda this set for the left while still avoiding a political fatalism and sustaining a socialist vision and practice.

> The idea that environmental problems might be so severe as to potentially threaten the continuation of anything that might be considered tolerable human life has been entertained, but usually only as a fairly remote, if frightening, possibility. It has rarely been treated as something potentially imminent, needing to be considered as a matter of urgency, nor has a legacy of irreversible ecological damage bequeathed to future generations been seriously 'factored in' to our thinking about the problems that any future socialist society will have to cope with ....

This was written at a time when the market dystopias of carbon trading, green commerce, and bio-engineering were just becoming new centres of accumulation, underlining the importance of avoiding, as that Preface went on to caution, 'an anxiety-driven ecological catastrophism, parallel to the kind of crisis-driven economic catastrophism that announces the inevitable demise of capitalism'. Several of the essays in this volume return to confront this challenge, striking a sense of urgency while avoiding entrapment in fatalism. They all underscore the necessity as well as the scale of the remaking of the 'nature-society relation', while insisting on the direct antagonism endless capital accumulation poses for such a remaking and the political obstacles the power structures of capitalism form and, inescapably, need to be confronted. Here, a remarkable range of pathways and struggles for the left are put forward − transforming commitments to ecological restitution and restoration into political actions, transformative linkages between 'Green New Deals' and social reproduction in daily life, and re-establishing an interdependence between liveable ecologies and the democratic provisioning of public goods.

As our lead essay points out, the enthusiasm with which tens of thousands of young people in Britain and the US have embraced the socialist political discourse of Corbyn and Sanders by flocking into Momentum and the Democratic Socialists of America demonstrates the hunger for a new politics to get us from here to there. In probing the limits and possibilities of the class politics and socialist policies they are advancing, this essay points not only to capitalist constraints but also to those embedded in the parties which are the terrain of this struggle for a new socialist politics. Yet as Raymond Williams argued in his essay 'For An Alternative Politics' in the 1981 *Socialist Register*, just as an earlier struggle of this kind was taking place before the Third Way's accommodation to neoliberalism took hold: '[T]hose of us who are committed to the Labour movement, yet who are critics of what has been accurately called Labourism, have an obligation to engage with practical policy, at the levels at which this is ordinarily determined, even when we also insist on discussing those problems of theory and assumption which these processes typically evade.'

We want to thank all the contributors to this volume and are grateful for their willingness to navigate the dual obligations of addressing the dystopic and utopic that we laid on them. Once again we want to extend our thanks to Adrian Howe and Tony Zurbugg of Merlin Press for their efforts on our behalf; and Louis Mackay for yet another innovative and striking image for the cover illustrating the volume's themes. And, as always, we are grateful for the hard work and insights of our assistant editors, Steve Maher (himself a contributor this year) and Alan Zuege, to this volume. They have contributed immeasurably to the quality of the arguments as well as its technical production.

Finally, it is necessary here to note the passing of our long-time editorial associate and collaborator, David Coates. From his successive posts at Leeds, Manchester and Wake Forest Universities, David was a most insightful commentator on British and American politics in an enormous range of articles and books. Among his many contributions to the *Socialist Register*, he co-edited with us and Colin Leys the 2001 survey, *Working Classes, Global Realities*, a volume that maintains a wide readership. And David edited the *Register* anthology, *Paving the Third Way: A Critique of Parliamentary Socialism* (2003), on one of the central themes that has animated this annual since its founding in 1964 by Ralph Miliband and John Saville. We will surely miss him.

GA
LP
July 2019

CLASS POLITICS, SOCIALIST POLICIES, CAPITALIST CONSTRAINTS

STEPHEN MAHER, SAM GINDIN
AND LEO PANITCH

One of the most unexpected aspects of the current conjuncture has been the coming to the fore of socialists at the leadership levels of the British Labour Party and the US Democratic Party. Their class-focused political discourse, directed against the power of the capitalists, of the corporations, of the banks – and the state policies and actions which reflect and sustain this power – no doubt speaks to many of the same popular discontents that have animated the rapid rise of explicitly populist xenophobic politicians on the right. But to dismiss those who advance today's socialist discourse as an equivalent left populism is mistaken in theory and misleading in practice. This is above all because of the political attention they draw to the dynamics, structures, inequalities, and contradictions of capitalism as the systemic core of neoliberal globalization and ruling class privilege and power.

It is significant that this new politics has galvanized tens of thousands of young people into groups like Momentum and the Democratic Socialists of America. Their affiliation thereby to the parties of the centre-left is not only directly concerned with mobilizing support for these socialist leaders and their political discourse, but also using this as a springboard for advancing class struggles in the workplace, the community, and the local state. Nothing like this has happened in at least three generations. It has much to do with the frustrations of two decades of episodic mass protests and the marginality of those socialist parties which provided little strategic perspective beyond direct action, in both cases leaving to the side the matter of how to enter the state to change what it does, let alone to change what it is.

That this should have happened in the UK and US, of all places, is remarkable. It reflects how far political parties are linked to states through electoral systems, which is itself an outcome of certain dialectical historical relationships between states and parties. The resolve, since the early 1980s, of the Socialist Campaign Group of MPs to remain inside the Labour Party – so fundamental to the propulsion of Jeremy Corbyn into the leadership – would never have happened without the barriers imposed by the first-past-the-post system with its bias against new parties to any electorally viable socialist alternative. Nor would the independent Senator Bernie Sanders have contested for the Democratic Party presidential nomination, or socialists at other levels run on the Democratic Party ticket, except for the absence of proportional representation in US elections. On the other hand, the coalescing of socialist forces in recent years outside the mainstream centre-left parties into new parties like Die Linke in Germany, Syriza in Greece, Bloco in Portugal, and Podemos in Spain cannot be understood apart from the openings for their entering the state provided by electoral systems based on proportional representation.

Yet however thin and frayed the electoral base of the old centre-left parties has become, including even the 'classic' social democratic parties of Germany and Sweden, these parties remain the dominant partners in electoral and governmental coalitions that extend from the centre-left to the far left. This suggests that the mobilization of socialist support behind Corbyn and Sanders *inside* the dominant centre-left parties may afford possibilities as radical, at least for the time being, as the mobilization of socialist electoral support *outside* these parties.

The renewed appeal of a socialist political discourse, one hundred years after the Soviet revolution and thirty years after its ignominious endpoint, has astonished the punditocracy. It does indeed appear that socialism in the twenty-first century has finally broken free of the legacy of the Russian revolution which so defined – pro and con – the political discourse of the left through the twentieth century, often weighing 'like a nightmare on the brains of the living'. The emergence of a twenty-first century socialism which neither defines itself by the Bolshevik model, nor abjectly shrinks from advancing a socialist project for fear of being tainted by it, is itself a historic development. This is not to say that the Russian revolution is forgotten, but only that as young socialist activists mobilize against the timidity of career politicians and the machinations of the old centre-left party and media establishment that keeps them in place, they are today far more likely to be inspired by elements of its original revolutionary spirit than its specific revolutionary methods.

Yet even as they do so, the demise of the Communist institutional tradition amidst the impasse of the Social Democratic one also carries with it a legacy which weighs on the brains of the living. This is seen in the tendency to clothe today's socialist agenda in the image of the policy achievements of the

New Deal in the US and of postwar social democracy in Western Europe. The former largely ignores the compromises with capital that prevented the New Deal from ever actually turning into a social democratic welfare state, while the latter plays down how far even postwar European social democracy was itself always limited by its own explicit politics of class compromise. Foremost in mind on the left in recent decades is how far the US Democratic Party and the British Labour Party have travelled down the path to neoliberalism; while largely disregarded has been the fact that this was a common trajectory of *all* social democratic parties.

Indeed, despite the very different economic and social conditions today as compared with the postwar era, there is a tendency to present reforms in terms of merely picking up from 1935 or 1945. That said, there is a sharper awareness among socialists of how far the social democratic welfare state had, by the 1970s, already been beset by the contradictions of being married to the regeneration of a dynamic financial capitalism. Today's leadership of the Labour Party is the self-proclaimed heir to the stifled Bennite agenda of the early 1970s, which was based on the recognition that it would be necessary to go beyond the postwar compromise with capital even to hold on to existing welfare state reforms. Yet the radical reforms advanced today, including the renationalization of the railways and other public utilities, fall far short of the 1973 Labour Party Manifesto's pledge to nationalize the twenty-five leading corporations across the key sectors of the economy alongside the planning agreements which other corporations would be tied to. Also notably absent is the 1976 Alternative Economic Strategy's focus on the need for import and capital controls.[1]

In contrast to the radical proposals for 'taking capital away from capital' that emanated from within European social democratic parties in the 1970s – from the union-led socialization of the corporations in Sweden to the nationalization of the banks in France – the policies being advanced today by socialists inside the centre-left parties look very modest. The emulation of the glory days of the New Deal or of postwar social democracy is inherently limited by the impossibility of restoring the particular social and economic conditions of those days. The past four decades of the internationalization of capitalist states – not least through the removal of capital controls and the free trade agreements that codified their sponsorship of neoliberal globalization – have similarly rendered implausible any notion of merely rebooting the stifled socialist agendas that emerged within social democratic parties at the height of the crisis of the Keynesian welfare state in the 1970s.

This makes it all the more imperative that socialists face squarely, and discuss far more openly than has yet been done, whether the policy proposals that are being advanced in the current conjuncture through an explicitly socialist discourse only amount to the revival of social democratic reformism, or foretell the emergence of a new strategy for structural reform which would create the conditions for taking capital away from capital. This is the remit of this essay. It is not written with the expectation that either Corbyn or Sanders are on the verge of electoral victories that would lead to their forming a government. Rather it seeks to clarify what any socialist-led government in the UK or US in the foreseeable future would have to face. That is, a still deeply-integrated global capitalism, with capitalist economic dominance domestically securely in place, with working-class forces not strong enough, or coherent enough, to sustain a full-blown challenge to that dominance, and with public institutions very far from having the capacity, let alone the orientation, to implement democratic economic and social planning.

Being in no position to take over the 'commanding heights of the economy' – or even to introduce capital controls without immediately inducing more severe economic hardship than the austerity they are pledged to end – such a government would of necessity tread cautiously through piecemeal interventions against capitalist power and advance reforms which risk being overwhelmed in these conditions. All this would sustain the very significant oppositional elements inside the centre-left parties at every level, and especially among the elected career politicians for whom a serious commitment to socialism, however gradualist, is regarded as a dangerous chimera. This poses the questions of how the socialist leadership of such a government could sustain its long-term ambitions, and what would distinguish its policies from the types of reforms advanced by progressive liberals and moderate social democrats today.

A first condition for building on electoral success would be to deliver some material gains for working people. In the context of the massive growth of inequality and high profits in both the UK and the US, there is in fact both the ideological and economic space for delivering improvements in people's lives through programs for social provision. A further step, which could open new paths to future structural reform, would be to expand economic democracy and public investment in infrastructure, transportation, and utilities. The crucial measure, however – one that distinguishes socialists from social democrats – is to develop these plans not in ways that would restore capitalist hegemony, but rather build the power, cohesion, and capacities of the working class to struggle for broader and deeper reforms than what is possible today. A key part of this must be systematic political education based on a sober acknowledgement of the barriers the new socialist movement now faces and what must be done to overcome them to realize that movement's larger potentials. This would, moreover, necessarily involve explicitly recognizing that reforms and education are not enough. Significant gestures towards a post-capitalist future must be introduced and struggled over in the *present*. This requires a politics that is at every step engaged in directly confronting a profound dilemma: giant steps are impossible, small steps risk being swallowed into the logic of the system.

THE LIMITS AND POSSIBILITIES OF ECONOMIC DEMOCRACY

The socialist left on both sides of the Atlantic has emphasized a radical and rapid break with neoliberalism and austerity as the most immediate policy objective. This was the substance of Bernie Sanders' bold call for a 'political revolution' to shift the balance of class forces and reorient politics toward reducing inequality and expanding the welfare state to an extent unprecedented in US history. His wide-ranging platform includes a job guarantee; universal healthcare, pensions, and college education; immigration and police reform; and other policies to increase social provision and limit corporate influence on the electoral system. Additionally, by supporting strikes and other working-class struggles, including using his campaign organization to encourage supporters to march on picket lines in their area and alert immigrant rights activists about impending ICE raids, Sanders has sought to increase the confidence, capacities, and expectations of the working class – not merely working to build a political campaign, but attempting to develop a lasting working-class movement. And as he has repeatedly made clear, his ambitious agenda has little chance of being implemented without large-scale organizing and social mobilization to support it.[2]

Similar concerns have motivated those who propelled and sustained Jeremy Corbyn's leadership of the Labour Party in the UK. The 2017 election manifesto offered to improve the lives of ordinary people in important ways, and included 'landmark' measures whose radical nature was clear. The tax increases to pay for them were to fall on corporations, whose tax avoidance had become notorious, and on the rich who had done well out of both the boom and the crisis. And the long list of measures to restore workers' rights implied a significant shift in the social balance of power, potentially beginning to restore working-class confidence shattered by years of unemployment and trade union decline. Whether either Sanders' or Corbyn's extensive programs of radical reforms, and proposed break with austerity, would prove feasible in practice would depend on whether they could be carried through in the context of a corporate sector highly integrated with global markets; and in the face of predictably intense resistance from shareholders and investors, the City of London and Wall Street, the Treasury and the civil service, the media, and the 'deep state', not to mention the Conservative and Republican parties – as well as the 'moderates' inside their own parties.

In addition to the concern to break with austerity and implement radical reforms to the immediate benefit of working people, the new socialist discourse has focused considerably on the crucial issue of economic democratization. This has created important political space for casting a new challenge to capitalist control over investment, production, and distribution in a positive light. Yet what has been proposed is exceedingly modest, primarily involving various schemes for partial worker ownership and participation in management at the level of the firm. This obviously reflects the current balance of class forces as well as the lack of strategic clarity and political capacities left forces can bring to bear today.

In the American case, this was expressed in Sanders' 2016 call to fundamentally change the 'rigged economy' by 'breaking up the banks' rather than turn them into public utilities.[3] Later, influenced by plans developed in the UK by Corbyn and Labour Shadow Chancellor John McDonnell, Sanders called for workers to be granted seats on corporate boards of directors, along with the creation of a fund that would hold corporate shares and distribute dividends to workers. These plans called as well for state support for the formation of workers' cooperatives. Both were presented as part of a fundamental economic transformation – a challenge to capital and a step toward building a socialist society. Yet they also join a range of proposals that are explicitly – sometimes emphatically – *not* socialist, including a somewhat similar plan by Elizabeth Warren to grant workers seats on corporate boards, limit executives' ability to exercise stock options, and promote 'corporate social responsibility'. Warren's proposed 'Accountable Capitalism Act' is explicitly aimed at rejuvenating capitalism by making corporations more 'inclusive' and 'accountable', while reining in the outsized power of finance.[4] Even aside from her proud declaration that 'I am a capitalist to my bones', the fact that her plan is modelled on German 'co-determination' should serve as a warning as to its limits, given how this has been used in Germany in recent decades to impose relentless wage restraint and competitive restructuring.

Warren's reform proposals are the most detailed of any being advanced among progressive liberal and moderate social democratic politicians today. Her central argument is that in the neoliberal era 'the obsession with maximizing shareholder returns effectively means America's biggest companies have dedicated themselves to making the rich even richer'. This, she argues, has been primarily responsible for the increasing social inequality, declining wages, and economic stagnation that have characterized the neoliberal period. Warren claims financial pressure, combined with their own stock holdings, has led managers to 'short-termist' investment strategies, effectively looting their companies by diverting capital from useful investment to 'buying back' shares of their company's stock to manipulate the share price. As a result, 'good jobs' are disappearing and corporate investment has become a simple matter of handing money out to the super rich. Moreover, this under-investment means companies are 'setting themselves up to fail'. To remedy this, Warren proposes preventing managers and directors from selling shares within five years of receiving them, or within three years of executing a buyback. She also suggests issuing federal corporate charters requiring firms to act as 'benefit corporations', serving a range of stakeholders – including workers, consumers, and communities – rather than just shareholders. This would be supported by granting employees the right to elect 40 per cent of corporate boards of directors, which will 'give workers a stronger voice in corporate decision-making at large companies'. By increasing the autonomy of managers from investor discipline, corporations will supposedly engage in the kind of investment that generated the 'good jobs' and rising standards of living that characterized the postwar managerial period.[5]

Warren's proposal is based on the 'stakeholder capitalism' model, which assumes that the corporation can balance different interests that are not necessarily in conflict. Yet corporations are not impartial arbiters among different 'stakeholders', but crystallizations of capitalist power. Nor is this power merely *economic*, it is also *political*. Corporations pursue state regulatory and tax structures that are conducive to their continued accumulation and competitiveness – policies which worker-appointed directors would be very susceptible to endorsing, even if this came at the expense of other workers or the environment. Should a firm fail to perform the capitalist function, it will suffer higher costs and reduced returns relative to its competitors — and therefore find less capital available for investment and expansion, leading to cutbacks, layoffs, and possibly bankruptcy. Clearly, no directors, no matter who elected them, would favour a strategy inclined to end this way. Rather than profits always appearing as 'too much' (since they are the most obvious sign of exploitation, they can be the most direct source of class-consciousness), profits must be defended, even increased if possible. While worker representatives on boards, as in Germany, have tried to resist profit-driven restructuring at the expense of jobs, these defences have not been able to overcome the relentless pressures of competitiveness.

Warren's concern to fix what existing manufacturing firms do or don't do really requires a much more radical restructuring of the economy, especially the financial sector – which even the nonfinancial sectors would themselves aggressively resist because of the functionality of finance to their domestic and global activities. Managers of non-financial corporations have relied on international finance to integrate the global economy, while managing fluctuating exchange rates and other risks associated with world trade through derivatives trading and other forms of financialization. Non-financial corporations also depend upon finance to execute mergers and acquisitions, and consumer credit markets to maintain consumption to compensate for stagnant wages. These central features of neoliberalism are untouched by Warren's proposals.[6]

Warren's plan aims to reinforce, not challenge, the power of large manufacturing corporations. Throughout the neoliberal period, managers of non-financial corporations have launched numerous failed efforts to defend themselves from financial discipline by setting up anti-takeover defences in the form of golden parachutes, poison pills, and state regulations. Were Warren's bill implemented, it might actually succeed in granting industrial managers the protection from financial investors they have long sought. It has been well documented workers generally side with management in conflicts with outsiders; while the tension between industrial managers and outside investors for corporate control does not negate their unity in seeking to restrain effective worker (or democratic) control over the corporation.[7]

Contrary to those emphasizing the supposed corrupting influence of financial 'short-termism', the rising living standards of postwar capitalism rested on more than merely a specific model of corporate governance. It also depended upon relatively high union density. Though of course highly limited and dependent on capital for jobs, trade unions nonetheless constitute an institutional mechanism for reproducing forms of worker solidarity and agency that, in crucial respects, contradicts the logic of capital, articulating social needs it tends to ignore – including those necessary for its own reproduction, such as a healthy, properly-fed and housed workforce. Without organized workers' struggles against capitalist exploitation, competitive pressure to allocate capital as efficiently as possible, within firms as well as across the economy as a whole, means that downward pressure on wages would continue to produce economic inequality and precarity. A strong trade union movement in many ways represents a more substantial form of economic democracy than granting workers seats on boards, or for that matter extending their ownership stakes in individual firms. While this still begs the question of how to 'take capital away from capital', Warren's plan integrates workers with corporate power in a way that could reinforce the very financialized neoliberalism it seeks to challenge, by undermining the class independence necessary to confront it.

While proposing that workers be allocated 40 per cent of the seats on corporate boards, Warren's plan does not entail transferring stock ownership to them. Sanders goes further than Warren in calling for workers to have 50 per cent of the seats on boards, and places great emphasis on giving workers stock ownership as well. Although promising this would herald a historic shift in class power, this actually risks, like Warren's plan, deepening the embeddedness of workers within 'their' corporations. Giving workers an ownership stake in corporate competitiveness is unlikely to contribute to building the kind of counter-power to capitalist logic that is necessary to bring about a genuinely democratic economy. Sanders has long been a supporter of extending Employee Stock Ownership Plans (ESOPs), at least since the 1980s when he was the mayor of Burlington, Vermont. More recently, Sanders has played a key role in supporting the Vermont Employee Ownership Center, established in 2001 and a model for legislation he has introduced in Congress.[8] With Sanders' decades-long support, Vermont today has the largest per capita employee-owned firms of any state in the US. As he put it in a 2018 speech:

What ESOPs are about … is saying, for a start, that you can have a more productive and profitable company when you listen to all of the people who are working … When you have employee ownership, what you are saying is: 'We are all in this together. Our job is to make this company as productive as we possibly can. What is your idea?' … If you go to work and you feel you are respected … and feel like you are part of the process, guess what? You are going to miss work less often. Absenteeism goes down … productivity goes up, profits go up, morale goes up. People do not bemoan the fact they have to go to work; they feel proud of the company they are going to work for, and they want to do everything possible to make that company better.[9]

This articulation makes the limits of ESOPs abundantly clear: they are not about substantive worker influence, let alone control, over corporate strategies or production processes. Rather, the goal is expanding worker 'voice' to encourage efficiencies, competitiveness, and profitability. As such, ESOPs tend to promote *even deeper* alliances between workers, managers, and owners than is the case with merely granting workers seats on boards.

In a recent interview, Sanders indicated that he would support a plan for worker ownership similar to what has been proposed by Corbyn and McDonnell in the UK.[10] In fact, under Corbyn's leadership, the Labour

Party has been developing strategies for empowering workers and extending economic democracy that go well beyond the limits of ESOPs. In the *Alternative Models of Ownership* report, commissioned by McDonnell and released a few days before the 2017 election, stress is put on the role of municipal public ownership and procurement policies to seed and nurture worker and community co-operatives. But the report was also meant to encourage broad discussion of new socialist strategies.[11] This was a direct descendant of the thinking of the Labour 'new left' about new forms of public ownership which could draw directly on the expertise and insights of workers on the shop floor, along the lines pioneered by the Lucas Aerospace shop stewards in the 1970s and the Greater London Council in the 1980s. The *Alternative Models* report especially revived the concern, voiced by the Labour left ever since the nationalizations of the 1945 Labour government, to avoid top-down corporate management in publicly owned enterprises by encouraging new forms of industrial democracy as well as accountability to 'diverse publics'.

This orientation has exactly characterized McDonnell's own strategic perspective. In an important speech in February 2018, he insisted:

> We should not try to recreate the nationalised industries of the past… we cannot be nostalgic for a model whose management was often too distant, too bureaucratic and too removed from the reality of those at the forefront of delivering services. Taking essential industries away from the whims of the market is an opportunity to move away from profit as the driver of investment and hiring decisions. But just as importantly it's an opportunity for us to put those industries in the hands of those who run and use them.[12]

And in his speech to the September 2018 Labour Party conference McDonnell went even further:

> Democracy is at the heart of our socialism – and extending it should always be our goal. Our predecessors fought for democracy in Parliament, against the divine right of kings and the aristocracy. They fought for working people to get the franchise. Our sisters fought for women's suffrage in the teeth of ferocious opposition and our movement fought for workers to have a voice at work. The trade unions founded this party to take that democratic vision even further. So in 2018 I tell you that at the heart of our programme is the greatest extension of economic democratic rights that this country has ever seen. It starts in the workplace.[13]

This would be enacted through legislation mandating that each year, one per cent of the shares of all large corporations (covering some 40 per cent of the private sector workforce) be transferred into an Inclusive Ownership Fund (IOF), maxing out at a total of 10 per cent ownership accumulated over ten years. Workers representatives would have unspecified voting rights in their company of employment based on the shares allocated, but they could not trade those shares. This fund would pay out dividends to individual workers in each particular firm of up to a maximum of £500 a year each. After the distribution of the dividends to workers, the balance of the funds – an estimated £2.1 billion by the fifth year of the program, totalling one-third of one per cent of the British state's central annual expenditures – would be treated as a social dividend that 'could be spent supporting our public services and social security'. This itself is not substantially different from a modest corporate tax.[14] The cap on dividend payments to employees (under 2 per cent of the average annual income of British workers), as well as the rough equalization of dividend payments across firms and the contributions to universal programs, are intended to prevent the emergence of excessive inequality between workers in different sectors.

One of the most striking features of discussion about these plans has been the assumption that by owning shares, workers will not only benefit from dividend payments, but also gain *control* over corporate strategy. But even if these reforms are a radical departure from the neoliberal fixation on shareholder value, they are clearly limited and would be far from the socialization of capital and economic democratization; their basic thrust appears to be about *distribution* not *democratization*. Worker share ownership does not amount to greater control unless workers are ready to demand it and have the capacity to carry that demand out. There is a tendency to underestimate the complexities of internal corporate decision-making, which extends beyond the level of boards to include various layers of formal and informal decision-making and access to internal and external information. For workers to exert influence within a corporation would therefore demand levels of confidence and capacities explicitly suppressed under capitalism along with access to knowledge and links to sympathetic specialists ('red experts') that cannot be assumed, but need to be systematically developed. Even then, such 'control' would be highly limited, and constrained by the logic of private accumulation unless connected to a broader strategy for socializing the economy. Introducing a new dimension of working-class fragmentation, as these plans risk doing, could make this more, not less, difficult. Despite the radical political vision he has articulated, McDonnell's emphasis on decentralized forms of common ownership skirts the crucial question of how to integrate and coordinate enterprises, sectors, and regions through democratic economic planning processes.[15]

Nevertheless, because they involve transferring shares, comparisons have been drawn between Sanders' and McDonnell's plans and the 'Meidner Plan' of the 1970s. This emerged from a Swedish labour movement that still had the capacities to get it onto the agenda even as the social democratic era was drawing to a close, and the balance of class forces had already begun to shift toward capital. It involved gradually transferring the 'excess' profits secured through the solidarity policy of wage restraint in centralized collective bargaining into wage-earner or community funds that would eventually have *majority* ownership of all corporations with over 25 employees. But in fact it was not only fought tooth and nail by Swedish capital, but also resisted by Palme's Social Democratic government, who contended it had a fatal flaw: if the transfer of ownership is to be announced and highly gradual, why would owners, knowing there is a timetable for their expropriation, continue to invest? 'The capitalists understandably disliked this idea', as Meidner later put in the 1993 *Socialist Register*. Impressive and ambitious though it was by today's standards, in retrospect it can be understood, as Meidner himself did, as an unsuccessful response to the *retreat* of social democratic forces in the face of what he recognized as early as the late 1960s as part and parcel of 'the internationalization of the Swedish economy'.[16]

This points to the contradictions of 'fund socialism'. As the experience with the expansion of worker pension funds in financial markets generally shows, far from becoming a form of 'labour's capital' and democratizing investment as some had hoped, they have served as a major lever for concentrating power in the financial sector and actually increasing pressure on non-financial corporations to maximize 'shareholder value'. As a result, together with the growth of mutual funds, large institutional investors came to either manage or own directly vast concentrations of corporate shares by the 1980s. That the big public sector funds often pushed the neoliberal restructuring of these corporations raises serious doubts about the wisdom of identifying 'socialism' with the creation of financial market funds managed either by the capitalist state or the trustees of union pension funds. In today's intensely competitive global markets, there is little reason to expect worker ownership funds to effect a major – or any – transformation in corporate strategy.

Similar shortcomings are reflected in proposals to extend considerable state support for the formation of worker cooperatives – particularly in the case of plants and facilities capital has decided to abandon. Taking over facilities that capital doesn't want and trying to run them competitively is worthy of support when desperate workers see it as their only alternative, but this cannot be a strategic foundation for democratizing the economy (and without the most comprehensive supports may become an example of 'lemon socialism' and even discredit the effectiveness of worker democracy). External pressures and internal dynamics can reduce coops to sites for achieving a different personal lifestyle or just operating like another business, if perhaps a more egalitarian one. In the worst case, transferring such uncompetitive firms to worker-owners may actually help *facilitate* capital's exit from these assets. Unless co-ops are part of a social movement looking to larger changes – committing a portion of their revenues and energies to political education and class organizing – their *socialist* impact will be marginal.[17]

The fundamental problem with each of these plans is not that they fall short in the proportion of board members or shares allocated to workers, but in the goals themselves. They all tend towards reviving at the firm level a competitive corporatism, whereby workers collaborate with management to enhance the competitiveness of 'their' firm against others. And that in turn reproduces pressures internal to the firm to establish hierarchies that aid competitiveness, rather than develop work relationships that stress equal status and the broadest participation. Democratization can't occur without changing the *context* within which economic units, and thus workers, relate to each other – and it is difficult to see strategies whose horizons are limited to ownership or management of capital by particular groups of workers in a market economy as a step towards socialism.

Moreover, while the emphasis on policies to democratize corporate governance is driven by the more general concern to democratize the economy, the focus of these reforms underestimates the potential of democratizing workplaces that stand, to some degree at least, outside the competitive discipline of profits and competition. So, for example, the commitment to expanding the universal provision of basic social services also opens, or should open, a wide-ranging discussion on how state and para-state agencies in education, health, and social services – where almost twice as many people work as in manufacturing, and where there is a degree of autonomy from market pressures – might be democratically run. To the extent that hierarchies are eroded for workers in these sectors, and to the extent new institutional relationships are established between public sector workers providing these services and the people they serve, examples of alternatives to capitalist relationships and practices are concretized and enthusiasm for their extension can be generated. There are of course pressures and assumptions other than directly competitive ones that limit the democratization of publicly owned companies and state agencies, but deepening workplace democracy in these spaces is a critical opportunity to show what de-privatization can do. And confronting the inherent challenges of how to balance national, regional, local, and workplace goals and democratic practices at this modest scale is clearly critical to developing understandings and capacities for moving to larger scales of economic coordination and collective control.

THE NEED FOR ECONOMIC PLANNING

A socialist strategy should see economic democracy not just in terms of empowering workers within firms, but engaging in a political struggle to transform the *conditions* within which productive units operate, and how they relate to each other. This requires undertaking a class-based rather than a firm-based struggle for democracy, whereby production is oriented to serving social needs rather than corporate interests. Building the democratic capacities of the working class does not revolve around integrating workers more deeply within capitalist finance or corporate structures in the hope for organizational efficiencies, but rather lies in struggling to replace capitalist competition at the national and international levels with solidaristic democratic planning. Worker representation on company boards and cooperatives could play a part in this if they could be leveraged into planning agreements across firms and sectors that aim to fulfill specific democratically-determined objectives – for instance, carrying out a green transition. This would have to be supported by a broader plan, coordinated by the state, to advance the democratic control of investment at national and regional levels of the economy.

This means that any gradual measures to increase worker 'voice' by expanding legal ownership or representation within corporate governance must be backed by structural reforms that extend control over capital assets at the point of production through building state planning capacities. Rather than gearing reforms toward competitiveness, workers and communities could fight to extend social control over production, short of outright seizure of control over capital assets, in each of the three areas discussed above: 1) cooperative production could be locally coordinated and planned, supported by the national state, such that it is not limited to worker ownership of firms producing competitively for the market; 2) national and regional democratic planning structures could be developed to coordinate the extension of universal basic services (housing, education, parks, daycares); and 3) planning agreements could be implemented among major corporations, leveraged across sectors, with national plans linking planning undertaken by workers within individual firms.

In both the US and UK, the proposals for extending economic democracy have in fact been linked with plans for new mechanisms for increasing and expanding long-term public control and planning of investment. Importantly, these proposals transcend some of the limits of firm-level democracy in seeking to deploy the political agency of the state to determine investment priorities across society as a whole. This involves constructing new state capacities to undertake economic planning in order to break with neoliberal stagnation, reverse deindustrialization and regional inequities, boost employment and wages, and address the climate crisis. In the US, this has revolved around the call for a 'Green New Deal', most prominently articulated by Alexandria Ocasio-Cortez since she was elected to Congress. In the UK, Corbyn and McDonnell have advanced plans for a 'green industrial revolution' as a component of an industrial strategy that includes a new role for the Bank of England in supervising private investment. Insofar as these plans are presented in the context of a socialist discourse oriented to fundamentally transform and democratize the economy, it is important to understand whether, and in what ways, they constitute meaningful steps toward replacing the power of capitalist finance over investment with solidaristic democratic planning, capable of overcoming competitive pressures for profit-driven production.

The ambition of these strategies is constrained by the weakness of the labour movement as well as by the much-reduced capacities of state institutions through four decades of neoliberal restructuring. Moreover, extending democratic control over the economy means confronting the central state economic policy apparatuses that were empowered through these same processes of restructuring, and are today the key seats of control for the dominant sectors of capitalist classes. Orienting them to a radically different agenda will require significant conflict, institutional reorganization, and strategic planning. This is reflected in how far each of the above plans has generally been articulated as a *supplement* to, and not a *replacement* for, private investment and capitalist financial institutions. To assess whether, while operating on the margins of the structures of financialized neoliberal capitalism, they could form part of a strategy for a broader project of democratizing the state and the economy, it may be useful once again to examine them alongside the explicitly non-socialist proposals put forward in the US context by Elizabeth Warren.

Warren's emphasis on strengthening US capitalism through public investment, and cultivation of alliances between popular forces and sections of capital to this end, makes her claims to channel Roosevelt rather more convincing than those democratic socialists who invoke FDR. Warren's 'Plan for Economic Patriotism' aims to rejuvenate the US economy through a market-focused state industrial policy to enhance national technology-based competitiveness. In her words, 'economic patriotism is about using all the tools we have to boost American workers and American industries so they have the best opportunity to compete internationally'.[18] As its title suggests, Warren's plan tries to bridge Trump's economic nationalism and Sanders' democratic socialism.[19] Unlike Trump, Warren rejects blaming globalization or immigration for the suffering caused by neoliberalism; like Sanders, she roots popular frustrations in criticisms of corporations, in particular the financial sector.

The trouble, for Warren, is that giant corporations 'wave the flag – but they have no loyalty or allegiance to America', as evidenced by their relocation of production to places like Mexico and China. Rather than catering to the financial interests of such disloyal multinationals, she proposes that 'our government do what other leading nations do and act aggressively' to achieve 'faster growth, stronger American industry, and more good American jobs'. This includes counteracting the role of 'foreign investors' in driving up 'the value of our currency for their own benefit'; boosting R&D expenditure while requiring that the resulting production be carried out in the US and distributed equitably across regions; using government procurements to encourage production within the US; increasing export subsidies through the Export-Import Bank while requiring it to 'focus more on smaller and medium-sized businesses'; and expanding worker training programs.[20]

Warren asserts that unlike other states – including China, Japan, and Germany – the US lacks a centralized industrial policy, with R&D programs fragmented across myriad state agencies. A new Department of Economic Development, which would replace the Commerce Department, would consolidate these efforts and develop a single, coherent, market-oriented industrial strategy. That this agency would also subsume the Office of the US Trade Representative reflects Warren's concern that over the neoliberal period, the power and autonomy of state agencies promoting the internationalization of capital have been consistently enhanced.[21] In Warren's terms, this amounts to the empowerment of 'government agencies that undermine sustainable American jobs'. By consolidating these programs and offices 'in one place', she hopes 'to make it clear that the unified mission of the federal government is to promote sustainable, middle-class American jobs'. Her plan thus seeks to counteract financial short-termism by building the capacity within the state to systematically undertake long-term investment planning. A four-year plan called a 'National Jobs Strategy' would 'guide how the Department of Economic Development prioritizes its investments and direct its programs', enticing corporations to invest at home by offering subsidies for R&D and up-skilling labour to perform high-value added production.

This approach has real and immediate limits, based as it is on continuously competing to supply capital with a favourable 'investment climate' in which to competitively produce high value-added exports. As summarized in *The National Review*, 'Senator Warren's "economic patriotism" consists of calling the bosses at the Fortune 500 a★★holes and then writing them a check for tens of billions of dollars. I suspect the gentlemen in pinstripes will find a way to endure the insult.'[22] Moreover, Warren's decidedly scaled-down embrace of the Green New Deal (GND) proposed by Ocasio-Cortez and supported by Sanders has taken the form of a 'Green Manufacturing Plan' that draws on the experience of the industrial mobilization for the Second World War and the subsequent 'space race'. The plan calls for addressing the climate crisis through massive state investment – $2 trillion by her estimates – to support the development of new technologies that can then be commodified and sold by manufacturing corporations. As Warren sees it, 'over the next decade, the expected market for clean energy technology in emerging economies alone is $23 trillion. America should dominate this new market.'[23] In addition to helping ease the US balance of payments by boosting exports, she claims this would generate over one million new jobs for 'American workers' while targeting investments to reduce regional inequalities.

The Green New Deal introduced in Congress by Ocasio-Cortez and in the Senate by Edward Markey was significantly broader and more ambitious in its intentions.[24] The fourteen-page non-binding resolution called for a 'ten-year national mobilization' to address the climate crisis by 'meeting 100 percent of the power demand in the United States through clean, renewable, and zero-emission energy sources'; repairing and upgrading existing infrastructure while constructing new 'green' infrastructure, including 'smart' power grids; 'upgrading all existing buildings in the United States and building new buildings to achieve maximal energy efficiency'; 'overhauling transportation systems' including building zero-emission vehicle infrastructure and expanding public transportation and high-speed rail; and 'spurring massive growth in clean manufacturing'. It also included a host of radical measures such as a federal government job guarantee ('with a family-sustaining wage, adequate family and medical leave, paid vacations, and retirement security') for everyone in the country; as well as 'high-quality health care'; 'affordable, safe, and adequate housing'; 'access to clean water, clean air, healthy and affordable food, and nature'; and 'training and high-quality education, including higher education'.

That Warren was prepared to sign on to the AOC-Markey bill illustrates just how ambiguous the GND is in today's new socialist discourse. Clearly, beyond the urgent call for doing something dramatic, the actual form a GND would ultimately take would be conditioned by significant class and intra-class struggles. While some firms stand to benefit from such a program, large sections of capital will remain vehemently opposed to a GND, which not only jeopardizes the bottom lines of individual corporations (in the case of the extractive sector, possible expropriation), but also threatens to embolden the left and permanently extend a degree of state planning. Yet while the GND and its socialist proponents have taken a directly confrontational approach to business and explicitly emphasized the need for working-class mobilization, the state lacks the administrative, technical, and fiscal capacities to produce and install the technologies and infrastructures required. This means that private capital will likely be involved – and expect a profit – no matter what version of the GND (if any) is implemented. On the other hand, Warren's entire model of 'responsible capitalism' rests on the emergence of an alliance between popular forces and a section of capital ready to accept stronger state regulation, direction of investment, and redistribution of income.

The push for a GND has created a significant opening for the left to directly challenge the fossil fuel industry, to link climate change to the broader injustices produced by capitalism, and to identify *both* parties' reliance on corporate financing as being responsible for their joint failure to address the problem. Sanders especially has emphasized the need for working-class people to mobilize against corporate power in the fight for climate justice:

> These companies lied to the American people about the very existence of climate change and committed one of the greatest frauds in the history of our country. Just as the tobacco industry was ultimately forced to pay for the fraud they committed, the fossil fuel industry must be forced to do the same … We've got an enormous amount of work in front of us. We've got to educate. We've got to organize. And we've got to fight for political power.[25]

The point of such socialist discourse is to stress that, rather than technological policy fixes to deal with the environmental crisis in ways which strengthen capital, the key objective is to find ways to weaken the power of corporations over working-class lives and challenge the logic of competitiveness and profitability. For socialists, the principal failures of capitalism are its destructive impacts on people's lives, potentials, and on planetary survival – pointing to the need to fight for a radically different way of organizing how we live and relate to nature. In the context of a

GND, this means finding ways to extend solidaristic democratic planning alongside measures to limit corporate control of intellectual property and push for the free transfer of green technologies to other societies (rather than conceiving of this in terms of export sales), while identifying capitalism itself as the problem. Yet while they have called for Congress to spend trillions on infrastructure (green and otherwise), Sanders and Ocasio-Cortez have not, in fact, advanced a specific strategy for transcending Warren's focus on competitiveness, profitability, and commodification. Policies for expanding state investment and using procurement and other regulations to ensure corporate investment occurs at home may have a role, but only as a first step in asserting broader and deeper popular sovereignty over the economy – whereby democratically-determined social priorities, rather than the endless accumulation of abstract value, guide investment decisions.

The same ambiguities about how to challenge finance and overcome the pressures of competitiveness were clearly visible in the Labour Party's 2017 election manifesto, which set out an industrial strategy to create an 'economy that works for all' through the strategic use of public procurement and national and regional investment banks. Much of this was cast as a 'new deal for business' oriented towards making British industry more regionally balanced and internationally competitive – and underpinned by a 'successful international financial industry'. Unlike the early 1970s, when Tony Benn and his new left allies controlled the National Executive's policy committees and were able to formulate a reasonably coherent and comprehensive industrial strategy (which was almost entirely ignored once Labour was re-elected in 1974), Corbyn and his team inherited nothing of that nature. Experts in a wide variety of fields have many creative ideas for progressive policies that a Labour government could use, including on macro-economic policy, banking, taxation, pensions, debt, and ways of restoring the primacy of the public interest in the funding and management of the public infrastructure. The party machine has, however, hardly tapped into them. The 2017 manifesto, hastily drafted when the snap election was called, largely drew on policy proposals the unions had put forward in previous years and there were plenty of omissions and weaknesses, some due to the speed with which it had to be composed. Whole areas of policy clearly needed far more radical measures, and as one astute critic of the manifesto put it, 'the need for a radical reorientation of economic priorities away from the industrial capitalist obsession with economic growth' if ecological catastrophe was to be avoided.[26] Another crucial element missing from the manifesto was any significant move towards democratizing the state.

Since the 2017 election, it has fallen to McDonnell and Rebecca Long-

Bailey in particular, as the shadow ministers responsible for finance and industry respectively, to flesh out Labour's industrial, investment and environmental plans.[27] In March 2018, McDonnell affirmed (notably in a *Financial Times* interview) that 'our objectives are socialist ... [which] means an irreversible shift in the balance of power and wealth in favour of working people ... When we go into government, everyone will be in government'.[28] Important in this regard was his determination, conveyed in his 2018 speeches at the Labour Party conference and Momentum's The World Transformed event, to 'reprogram the Treasury, rewriting its rule books on how it makes decisions about what, when, and where to invest' so as to finally bring to an end its being used 'as a barrier against putting power back into the hands of the people'. This expressly included setting up a 'Public and Community Ownership Unit' in the Treasury which would 'bring in the external expertise we will need'.

More detailed plans for structural changes at the Bank of England were outlined in an independent report, commissioned by McDonnell, which proposed 'restructuring and relocating core Bank of England functions [to] provide a counterweight to the dominance of London'.[29] This would not only involve establishing regional offices 'to ensure that productive lending is geared towards local businesses', but moving some of the main Bank of England offices, even including the Monetary Policy Committee, to Birmingham. There it would sit alongside the offices of a new National Investment Bank and a Strategic Investment Board, which would be responsible for generating and allocating investment under Labour's industrial strategy, along with a National Transformation Fund, responsible for Labour's infrastructure program. This geographic shift was seen as essential for realizing the report's main policy proposals: beyond setting a three per cent productivity growth target, these included establishing credit guidelines to shift private bank lending away from real estate; discretionary corporate bond purchasing to stimulate investment and reduce the cost of the infrastructure program; and aiding the National Investment Board by using the still mainly publicly-owned Royal Bank of Scotland as its banking arm.

In itself, this plan was still far from anything that might be called a socialist strategy for structural change. This was not because of the report's sensible insistence that decision-making must reflect the views of 'scientists, researchers, engineers and technology experts', nor merely because it said that 'private sector investment is critical' and that all the institutions involved 'must encourage an entrepreneurial spirit'. More significantly, the national models it offered for a Labour government's industrial strategy to emulate went so far beyond social democratic Norway or even Germany as to actually include such uncompromisingly capitalist regimes as Singapore, South Korea, Japan – and most notably, even the US itself. Lurking here was perhaps the most problematic aspect of Labour's industrial strategy: its silence on the question of how the promotion of internationally competitive export enterprises, within the framework of global capitalism, relates to the development of a transformational socialist strategy.[30]

Nevertheless, McDonnell's subsequent proposals for dealing with the climate crisis, in particular, revealed the extent to which his strategic thinking on these questions surpassed his counterparts in the US. After praising the 'Extinction Rebellion' protestors and even inviting them to brief his policy team, McDonnell pledged support for a 'Sustainable Investment Board' comprised of the chancellor, business secretary, and Bank of England governor to oversee private investment and ensure compliance with the government's environmental standards and directives, with the goal of achieving net zero carbon emissions by 2050. This would be a potentially highly important step in democratizing the central bank, forcing it to serve social and ecological needs gearing its oversight of private investment toward enforcing social priorities beyond merely limiting financial market volatility. In order to enforce these priorities on private investors, McDonnell pledged that Labour would delist from the London Stock Exchange companies that fail to meet environmental standards. The City of London reacted with predictable shock and horror to the proposal, referring to it as 'financial totalitarianism' that 'could undermine the entire financial system'.[31] Yet the proposal actually highlighted the limitations on the policy options of nation-states in a world of global financial integration – and the importance for socialist strategy of imposing limits on the free movement of capital.[32]

Notably, McDonnell actually signalled to Momentum's participants at The World Transformed in 2017 that plans were in hand to deal with capital flight or a run on the pound.[33] His public silence since then on the difficult question of how and when to introduce controls over the movement of capital was entirely understandable, given its political sensitivity and the importance of the financial sector's foreign exchange earnings. But policies on this issue were no less necessary than industrial policies if a socialist-led government was to be able to direct investment where it was needed and prevent capital flight. The logical response to a refusal by companies to invest for long-term productivity growth would be to introduce capital controls and investment planning. But this could not be done without developing the state's capacity to transform financial services, Britain's dominant economic sector, into a public utility – even taking advantage of the possibility of starting with the

Royal Bank of Scotland, still largely in public ownership after having been rescued in the wake of the 2007-2008 crisis.[34]

It makes sense to concentrate on thinking through expanding social ownership where openings exist, such as in radically democratizing the provision of social services and, as Corbyn and McDonnell have emphasized, in running the renationalized companies in exemplary democratic ways that balance worker participation, community interests, and the larger national interests. This holds the promise of inspiring and mobilizing workers behind the expansion of public investments, especially those needed to implement a Green New Deal defined in terms of 'a public-led society-wide mission shaped by workers, unions and communities ... through a transformational change in the forms and directions of investment, ownership, planning and control in society'.[35] Moreover, the Monbiot Report's proposals for the gradual but potentially large scale transfer of land into various forms of common ownership – explicitly presented as the type of 'non-reformist reform' first advanced in the UK by Andre Gorz in the 1968 *Socialist Register* – could have more transformative implications than did the 1945 Labour government's adoption of the Beveridge Report's welfare measures.[36]

Building on various proposals advanced by policy circles supportive of McDonnell to deploy the substantive procurement weight of the goods and services provided or at least paid for by state and para-state institutions (e.g. health, education, social care, public transportation, water, electricity, perhaps the internet down the road), planning agreements might well be forced on companies anxious to get public contracts in what has been recently been defined as this 'foundational' sector of the economy.[37] This could represent a meaningful step toward the socialization of these companies and more substantive democratization, while working to establish exemplary standards of transparency, product quality, and working conditions that could influence expectations in other workplaces. Similarly, there is an opportunity in state and para-state social services and programs – a very significant part of the economy – to not only deliver needed programs, but also to show that reforms inspired from a socialist perspective could involve participatory planning structures at the local level. The goal would be to make such programs more democratic and constructive of organic social relationships among unions, users, and communities.[38]

Though the independence such initiatives could have from the forces of capitalist competition should not be exaggerated, they could have a modicum of protection from capital outflow by virtue of their insulation from financial markets and the pressures of private accumulation, as well as their new popular mandate. The autonomy from capital secured in these spaces could then be used to validate the benefits and possibilities of social ownership, running workplaces in a far more democratic manner and balancing the needs of the workers and communities most involved with broader societal interests. But as vital as such reforms could be, what cannot be set aside is how all this would relate to developing greater working class coherence and confidence – what needs to be seen today in terms of the *remaking* of the working class – to the end of facilitating its commitment to sustaining a long term socialist strategy.

CONCLUSION

This brings us back to the profound political dilemma this essay has tried to confront: that for a socialist-led government in the current conjuncture giant steps would be impossible, but small steps risk being swallowed into the logic of the system. Even meeting the first condition for being able to build on electoral success, i.e., immediately delivering material gains for the working classes, entails being honest about the obstacles in the way. Taxing the 1 per cent – or the top 5 per cent or top 10 per cent – is a good idea for all kinds of quite obvious reasons. The potential gains from undertaxed and untaxed corporate and financial income and assets, not to mention personal wealth taxes, inheritance taxes, luxury taxes, and so forth, are enormous. But the capacity to do this without effective capital controls needs to be faced squarely. Moreover, the idea that taxing the 'billionaire class' would be sufficient to pay for the impressive range of policies proposed by socialists today is clearly fanciful – and tends to underestimate the need for weaning the working class itself away from the anti-tax propaganda of the neoliberal era.

In addition to taxation, state borrowing through the issuance of bonds can finance short-term spending. But as a long-term mechanism for raising indefinite sums, it is constrained by the interest payments these bonds must pay to creditors (generally those with higher incomes), and it leaves social programs vulnerable to financial markets or central banks raising interest rates. Dipping into the very large pools of bargained pension funds is another alternative bandied about; but the particular workers whose deferred wages were placed in these funds will not take kindly to what they will see as their paying for universal benefits without similar returns being earned. At a minimum, the pool would have to be supplemented by a levy on every financial institution (not just pension funds, but also banks and insurance companies). Similarly, 'quantitative easing for the many' through relying on central bank powers to issue money credit sounds attractive, but avoids the hard questions of what is entailed in changing the structures and functions of central banking, let alone the constraints that international financial markets would impose on this through the impact on exchange rates and the outflow of capital.[39]

There is no simple technocratic means to raise government revenues either through taxation or the monetary financing of budgetary deficits. The redistribution of society's resources is inseparable from the redistribution of power. An over-riding limit in all the steps towards taking control over economic life, even in the case of relatively modest expansions of social provision, is the power of capital to exit and invest abroad (along with the refusal of capital to keep coming in). Overcoming that threat and getting control over the funds to complete the socialist project must, at some point, raise the necessity of imposing controls on finance. It is, however, critical to see this not as merely 'keeping capital at home' along the lines of 'economic patriotism'. If such controls are to be meaningful, they must extend to *what happens to this capital* even if it is forced to remain.

This is where the second condition for building on any socialist electoral successes comes in, requiring the opening of new paths to structural reform through expanding economic democracy, public investment – and economic planning. There is no escaping the fact that radically different priorities imply not just a redistribution of income and control over money, but a real redistribution of how society's labour, equipment, and resources are used, and to what ends. And we must be fully aware that this redistribution not only involves severe impositions on capital, but also includes a cultural shift within the working class between individual consumption and an egalitarian collective consumption. This requires nothing less than a transformation of working-class consciousness alongside the development of new political capacities, whereby workers go beyond expanding their control of 'their' workplaces to extending democratic control of the economy. The limits we have identified in this essay in current proposals for economic democracy and investment planning actually reflect the limited abilities of working classes to struggle for broader and deeper reforms than what is possible today.

Though the 'Green New Deal' and 'just transitions' for working people have become central parts of the lexicon of today's socialist discourse, these well-intentioned calls to action and promises of secure transitions remain, for 'the many', mostly abstract slogans – reflecting the distance between policy and grounded participation. Yet the dynamics of capitalist restructuring create new possibilities for linking the need to address the environmental crisis with practical and immediate struggles. Understanding the regular drumbeat of closures as a loss of essential collective productive capacities raises the possibility of struggles to socialize and convert these facilities to the production of 'green' products and infrastructure by combining workers skills with the equipment capital has rejected to manufacture products of social and ecological value.

Working-class mobilizations at the community and plant levels could be linked to the initiatives of a socialist-led government to institutionalize a wide range of supports led by a new 'public conversion agency'. Placing the abandoned facilities and equipment in the public domain rather than leaving them to groups of workers 'owning' their workplaces would allow for the establishment of research units in each community or region staffed by working teams engaged in exploring both the technical and social dimensions of conversion, with higher environmental standards in turn increasing the demand for 'green' goods. Local conversion councils would take on the task of developing environmental/industrial literacy and strengthening community engagement. And as such capacities develop, the facilities targeted could extend from those that corporations no longer want to new or existing facilities that can make critical contributions to addressing the environmental crisis, and eventually – and organically – to taking on the 'commanding heights' of the economy. What is central here is the link between concrete everyday struggles in communities with the politics of environmental transformation.

What would need to be strategically addressed, first of all, by a socialist-led government would be how to most constructively transform public institutions – not only so as to render them capable of fully supporting such reforms, but to combine this with continuing to build a politically coherent working class. In other words, the key strategic challenge would be how to link policies of reform to the development of the sorts of state and class capacities that together could realize socialist possibilities. This requires moving beyond alternative policies to an alternative *politics* concerned with developing worker and community solidarity, strategic coherence, and socialist commitments reflected in a growing popular self-assurance to push ahead.

This needs to be linked to the priority a socialist-led government would have to give to strengthening unions institutionally. Labour law reforms are being advanced to re-establish and extend legal requirements for union recognition and dues check-off. But such state support for restoring union density – as opposed to removing barriers to unions actively organizing new members – raises serious questions about the *kind* of unionism that will emerge. Numerically stronger unions will indeed be critical to sustain the most significant policy initiatives of any socialist-led government. But the expansion of unions in their present form would not necessarily mean unions oriented to building the class and advancing socialism, as opposed to making particularistic gains within capitalism. Building the class is not the same as increasing union density. Approaching this in terms of class formation leads to an emphasis on particular kinds of changes in labour law: easing secondary boycotts to strengthen solidarity; access to corporate information as an alternative to granting workers seats on boards and thereby compromising class independence; raising minimum wages and labour standards for the weakest sections of the class, not only because it is the egalitarian thing to do, but also because reducing inequalities within the class is a condition for easing tensions that stand in the way of unity.

The severely limited internal democratic practices, organizing capacities, and political ambitions of unions today underlines what must be a key strategic conclusion: that really advancing economic democracy *and* planning also requires substantial transformations in working-class organizations themselves. The emergence of new socialist forces in both the Democratic Party and the British Labour Party cannot be understood except in relation to the longstanding linkages between the unions and these parties. But this also has much to do with the manifest limitations of the US Democratic Party and even the British Labour Party in sustaining, rather than undermining, the new socialist forces that have entered these parties. It is to be hoped, however, that this experience will help lay the ground for finally discovering what kinds of unions and parties can give coherence to the socialist project in the twenty-first century.[40]

NOTES

1   See Leo Panitch and Colin Leys, *The End of Parliamentary Socialism: From New Left to New Labour*, London: Verso, 1997, chs. 3 and 4 *passim*, and Ch. 6, pp. 118-24; and the forthcoming *Searching for Socialism: The Project of the New Labour Left from Benn to Corbyn*, London: Verso, 2020.

2   In this regard, DSA members have worked to take advantage of the opening this has created to rebuild the labour movement. See Eric Blanc, *Red State Revolt: The Teachers' Strike Wave and Working-Class Politics,* London: Verso, 2019.

3   Matthew Yglesias, 'Bernie Sanders's plan to break up the banks, explained', *Vox*, 21 January 2016.

4   *Accountable Capitalism Act*, S. S. 3348, 115th Congress, 2018.

5   Elizabeth Warren, 'Companies Shouldn't Be Accountable Only to Shareholders', *Wall Street Journal,* 14 August 2018.

6   The argument that finance is starving non-financial corporations of funds for investment doesn't tally with the fact that high corporate profits and low interest rates indicate there is no shortage of potential funds. On the other hand, a corollary of the relative dominance of finance within the US and UK is that both economies are skewed not only to finance but to related business services like consultancies, accountants, lawyers,

and real estate and so manufacturing output and employment are a smaller part of their overall economic activity.

7   See Michael Useem, *Executive Defense: Shareholder Power and Corporate Reorganization*, Boston: Harvard University Press, 1993; Jesse Fried, 'Trump and Warren offer the wrong diagnosis of short-termism', *Financial Times*, 27 August 2018.

8   Rachel M. Cohen, 'Could Expanding Employee Ownership Be The Next Big Economic Policy?' *The Intercept*, 26 December 2018.

9   Bernie Sanders, Speech at 2018 Vermont Employee Ownership Conference, available at: www.youtube.com.

10   Jeff Stein, 'Bernie Sanders backs two policies to dramatically shift corporate power to US workers', *Washington Post*, 20 June 2019.

11   *Alternative Models of Ownership,* Report to the Shadow Chancellor of the Exchequer and Shadow Secretary of State for Business, Energy and Industrial Strategy, 2017.

12   John McDonnell, speech at 'Alternative Models of Ownership' conference, London, 10 February 2018, available at: www.john-mcdonnell.net/john_s_speech. The way this speech was reported in the mainstream media illustrates the extreme difficulty faced by the Labour leadership in getting heard. The only 'broadsheet' to give it reasonable coverage was the (online) *Independent*. The BBC's coverage was minimal and negative: 'John McDonnell: Labour public ownership plan will cost nothing', BBC, 10 February 2018.

13   John McDonnell, speech to Labour Party Conference, 24 September 2018.

14   In some ways, it is less desirable than a conventional tax, since corporations are able to decide on the level of dividends they pay out – and thus their contribution to this flexible 'tax'.

15   Labour's 2016 *Digital Democracy Manifesto* might have been expected to address this, but it was instead characterized by 'a rather narrow image of technology that concentrates on the internet, end-users and "networked individuals"… an image of publicness in the form of networks that nevertheless has security and privacy at its heart'. Nina Power, 'Digital Democracy', in Leo Panitch and Greg Albo, eds., *Rethinking Democracy: Socialist Register 2018*, London: Merlin Press, 2017, p. 174.

16   Rudolph Meidner, 'Why Did the Swedish Model Fail', in Ralph Miliband and Leo Panitch, eds, *Socialist Register 1993: Real Problems, False Solutions,* pp. 217, 225.

17   Sam Gindin, 'Chasing Utopia', *Jacobin*, 10 March 2016.

18   Elizabeth Warren, 'A Plan for Economic Patriotism', *Medium,* 4 June 2019, available at: medium.com.

19   Warren's strident nationalist rhetoric led hard-right Fox News commentator Tucker Carlson to proclaim 'she sounds like Trump at his best'. Isaac Stanley-Becker, '"She sounds like Trump at his best": Tucker Carlson endorses Elizabeth Warren's economic populism', *Washington Post*, 6 June 2019. Daniel Drezner of the Fletcher School in Law and Diplomacy at Tufts, has similarly – and with equal exaggeration – characterized Warren's program as 'Trumpism with a human face'. *The Economist,* 18 February 2019, p. 23.

20   Warren, 'A Plan For Economic Patriotism'.

21   As discussed in Leo Panitch and Sam Gindin, *The Making of Global Capitalism*, London: Verso, 2013, chs. 10 and 11.

22   Kevin D. Williamson, 'Colbert Reports', *The National Review*, 9 June 2019.

23   Elizabeth Warren, 'My Green Manufacturing Plan for America', *Medium*, 4 June 2019, available at: www.medium.com. This relies on the support of the Department of Economic Development in implementing a 'Green Apollo Project' by investing $400 billion over ten years in clean energy development (more than ten times what was invested over the last decade), a $1.5 trillion procurement commitment over ten years to purchase 'American-made' clean energy products, expanded export subsidies through the Ex-Im Bank, and a 'Green Marshall Plan' that entails 'a commitment to using all the tools in our diplomatic and economic arsenal to encourage other countries to purchase and deploy American-made clean energy technology'.

24   116th United States Congress H. Res.0109 (1st session), *Recognizing the duty of the Federal Government to create a Green New Deal*. See: Myron Ebell, 'Green New Deal Launched with Support from Democratic Presidential Candidates', Competitive Enterprise Institute, 11 February 2019; and Rex Santus, 'AOC's Green New Deal has the backing of every major 2020 candidate', *Vice*, 7 February 2019.

25   Miranda Green, 'Sanders and Ocasio-Cortez join up to preach Green New Deal, take jabs at Biden', *The Hill*, 13 May 2019.

26   Jeremy Gilbert, 'Leading Richer Lives', in Mike Phipps, ed., *For the Many: Preparing Labour for Power*, London: OR Books, 2017, p. 175.

27   For a good overview, see: Robin Blackburn, 'The Corbyn Project: Public Capital and Labour's New Deal', *New Left Review*, 111(May/June), 2018, pp. 5-32. See *Labour's Fiscal Credibility Rule*, 2017; *Richer Britain, Richer Lives: Labour's Industrial Strategy*, 2017; *A National Investment Bank for Britain: Putting dynamism into our industrial strategy*, 2017; and '*The Green Transformation: Labour's Environment Policy*', 2018, all available at: www.labour.org.uk.

28   Jim Pickard, 'John McDonnell interview: is Britain ready for a socialist chancellor?' *Financial Times*, 2 March 2018.

29   Graham Turner, et al, *Financing Investment: Final Report*, GFC Economics and Clearpoint Advisors, 20 June 2018, p. 102. Although the report was careful to make clear that it did not represent the views of the Labour Party or the Shadow Chancellor of the Exchequer, it appeared on the Labour Party's website as soon as it was completed. See also: Josh Halliday, 'Labour would break up Treasury and create northern No 11, says McDonnell', *The Guardian*, 7 July 2019.

30   The *Financing Investment* report's conception of such enterprises as part of 'high-tech clusters', does not begin to address this problem. And although it was praised by McDonnell in his speech to the 2018 party conference, the final report of the IPPR's Commission on Economic Justice (*Prosperity and Justice: A plan for the new economy*, London: IPPR, September, 2018), did not begin to do so either, especially with its notions of 'industrial clusters' operating amidst 'more open and competitive markets' under the rubric of a 'partnership economy' between capital, labour and the state.

31   Owen Bennett, 'City voices anger at John McDonnell's "financial totalitarianism" climate change plans', *City A.M.*, 25 June 2019.

32   Though the importance of the City of London in global financial markets makes the threat to delist companies far from insignificant, the possibility for capitalists to raise capital on other stock exchanges around the world, especially in New York, would mitigate the impact of such a move. In fact, the uniqueness of Wall Street in the global economy suggests that such a strategy could have a more significant impact if implemented in the US – though neither Sanders nor Ocasio-Cortez have gone so

far as to suggest anything like this. This is part of a more general avoidance of directly addressing how to transform the financial system and deal with the power of the Federal Reserve.

33   'Labour plans for capital flight or run on pound if elected', *Financial Times* 26 September 2017.

34   Christine Berry and Laurie Macfarlane, 'A New Public Banking Ecosystem: A report to the Labour Party commission by the Communication Workers Union and the Democracy Collaborative', 2019.

35   As has it been defined in the *Road Map to a Green New Deal: From Extraction to Stewardship*, London: Common Wealth, July 2019, p. 12. Notably this report traces its roots back to the path charted by the original Green New Deal group's first report, *A Green New Deal*, published by the New Economics Foundation (NEF) in 2008.

36   *Land for the Many: Changing the Way Our Fundamental Asset is Used, Owned and Governed*, London: Labour Party, June 2019, p. 44, available at: labour.org.uk. See Andre Gorz, 'Reform and Revolution', in Ralph Miliband and John Saville, eds., *Socialist Register 1968*, London: Merlin Press, 1967. The Monbiot Report cites Gorz's book of the same year: *Strategy for Labor,* Boston: Beacon Press, 1968.

37   This is at the root of the argument made by the Foundational Economy Collective. The 'providential foundational economy' is defined as comprising mainly public sector (but increasingly outsourced) activities providing universal services, such a health, education, social care, police, public administration, plus their close private suppliers; while the 'material foundational economy' comprises the infrastructure of everyday life, such as pipes and cables providing electricity, gas, water, sewerage, and telecommunications to households, in addition to railways, roads, filling stations and auto services, as well as the public/social vehicles that use them such as buses and trains. Once public postal services and private retail banking (also defined as essential to everyday life) are included, the foundational economy as a whole accounts for almost 44 per cent of employment in the UK as well as in Germany, and at least a third in other high incomes countries. See: *Foundational Economy*, Manchester: Manchester University Press, 2019, pp. 23-4, 40-41.

38   An essential first step in this direction is: *Democratising Local Public Services: A Plan for Twenty-First Century Insourcing*, A Labour Party Report, Community Wealth Building Unit, 2019. In introducing this report, McDonnell said: 'Local government is a key site for building a socialist society, and today is another step on the road to giving local councils the powers they need to contribute to that society … Insourcing is an essential part of a programme for practical socialism, which delivers people's basic needs and improves people's everyday lives.' John McDonnell, speech at the launch of Democratising Local Public Services, 20 July 2019, available at: labour.org.uk.

39   See the important critiques of such proposals coming from 'modern monetary theorists' by Doug Henwood and James Meadway: Doug Henwood, 'Modern Monetary Theory Isn't Helping', *Jacobin*, 21 February 2019; James Meadway, 'Against MMT', *Tribune*, 6 March 2019.

40   See Leo Panitch and Sam Gindin, 'Class, Party and the Challenge of State Transformation', in Leo Panitch and Greg Albo, eds., *Socialist Register 2017: Rethinking Revolution*, London: Merlin Press, 2016; and *The Socialist Challenge Today: Syriza, Sanders, Corbyn*, London: Merlin Press, 2018 (updated and expanded edition forthcoming with Haymarket Press, Spring 2020).

MAKING THE WORLD A BETTER PLACE: RESTITUTION AND RESTORATION

BARBARA HARRISS-WHITE

'We have two choices: to abandon hope and ensure that the worst will happen; or to make use of the opportunities that exist and contribute to a better world. It is not a very difficult choice,' says Noam Chomsky.[1] But how? If we are to understand political responses to the degradation of our natural habitat and their need for socialist action, we must first seek to understand what is currently happening in our environment and why. This is the objective of the first part of this essay, while the possibilities and obstacles faced by the question 'what is to be done' and the projects for a therapeutic politics of restoration form the second.

THE SCIENCE OF THE ECOLOGICAL CATASTROPHE

In science, nature is conceived as a complex interconnected set of bio-physical sub-systems, 'a tightly coupled dance, with life and the material environment as partners'.[2] This dynamic coupling provides the conditions of existence for our species. Overwhelming evidence points to the approaching collapse of these conditions. While cumulative man-made gaseous waste *up to the present* is unlikely to cause temperature rises to exceed 1.5 degrees,[3] unless physically unprecedented and revolutionary measures are taken from now onwards the biophysical conditions for existence of many human beings are likely to be destroyed within the lifetime of anyone under the age of twenty. In the view of one distinguished scientific team, the 'safe operating space' in at least three major physical sub-systems (of their set of nine) had quite likely already been exhausted a decade ago by material developments 'eating away at our own social support systems'.[4] These three are:

(1) Climate change. On top of the heating already under way – the product of global economic activity using fossil fuels (which Trump's Energy Department now deigns to call 'freedom molecules') is heading,

under business-as-usual assumptions, for a rise in global temperature that will put paid to most kinds of business. Half the world's man-made atmospheric carbon dioxide (CO_2) was emitted in the last thirty years, during which time the twenty companies that produced a third of world-historical emissions[5] (from energy and cement) have been hard at work defending, and grabbing ever-increasing subsidies for, fossil fuels.[6]

(2) Losses of biodiversity and of redundancy[7] are accelerating at a rate not found in any record since the cretaceous extinction some 66 million years ago.[8]

(3) Vast excesses of nitrogen and phosphorus from fertilizer run-off and fossil fuel combustion already compromise the resilience of soil and water sub-systems, pollute the oceans and risk anoxic extinctions.

Three further planetary sub-systems currently thought to be approaching dangerous thresholds of destabilisation are:

(1) The oceans, where acidification due to carbonic acid is dissolving the calcium in corals, shellfish, and planktonic species, threatening substantial portions of marine ecosystems, and the fishing industry which depends on them.

(2) Fresh water, whose diversion for agricultural, industrial, and domestic use is causing pollution, droughts, and water scarcities.

(3) Land: land-use change for the expansion of agriculture is reducing biodiversity, releasing greenhouse gases, inviting destructive weather events, and redistributing species, sometimes with disastrous consequences.[9]

In addition, other activities threaten natural eco-systems in ways which are less well measured – 'known unknowns'. The team behind the science of safe operating spaces for mankind, cited above, identifies three:

(1) Persistent organic pollutants, plastics, endocrine disrupters (such as oestrogen-mimicking chemicals), heavy metals and nuclear waste are all compromising ecosystems.[10]

(2) Atmospheric aerosols, an increasing proportion of which are man-made, penetrate deep into animal tissues including lungs and may aggravate respiratory, cardiovascular, and allergic disease.[11]

(3) Atmospheric ozone depletion is allowing carcinogenic ultra-violet B-rays to damage life. The Montreal Protocol (which started to be implemented in 1989) has reduced the ozone depletion rate, but success of this treaty has diverted attention from the special conditions which

enabled it to succeed and encouraged an unfounded faith that similar political actions of a kind which will not disrupt the global economy can avert environmental threats.[12]

This summary of trends in the planet's physical sub-systems jolts us into realising that most writing about climate change and global heating is severely reductionist. First, the huge regional variations in the processes that are under way are airbrushed out.[13] Second, climate change, which everyone talks about, is only one of many major interacting threats to our planetary ecosystems. Third, the factors causing climate change also contribute and feed back to these other threats – both directly (e.g. oil pollution in the Caspian sea) and indirectly through causing climate change (which is set to overtake land-use change as the major driver of biodiversity loss). Many parts of this complex interactive system are being damaged, in some cases irreparably, by activities which policymakers and publics have often not even identified as problems.

Despite the enormous environmental damage previously done to regions under communist rule, it is capitalism that now bestrides the narrow world like a colossus – pace Shakespeare's *Julius Caesar* – yet it is capitalism which is studiously not identified in the stream of scientists' assessments. Instead, UN agencies list 'countries' as causers of gaseous emissions in terms of their cumulative stocks and current flows of green-house gases: gross, net, per capita, and per megawatt hour. And the problem, weakly called 'pollution', is further categorised by criteria such as the toxicity of industrial waste for the immediate area, or by economic sectors, or by the types of consumption involved. Conceiving the problem in these ways identifies and ranks the 'national' perpetrators differently. This generates agendas of response for each kind of problem, the signal result of which is that they have all failed to arrest the march of planetary society toward or beyond safe environmental thresholds. So the question of what is to be done has become increasingly urgent.

In line with the reductionism noted above, the UN has framed the urgency in terms of a 'window of opportunity' before we have used up the planet's atmospheric 'budget' for the concentration of CO_2 at a level that will keep the increase in temperature below 1.5 degrees above the average level of the years 1850-1900.[14] While according to some estimates the 'window' is already closed, in 2018 the IPCC declared it still open, giving us anywhere between two and twelve years before planetary self-reinforcing feedback processes kick in. Other scientists reckon we may have ten to thirty years. But no serious scientist thinks we have longer than this.[15] Scientists also imagine targets that would need to be met within these time frames – e.g. national targets for shifting to renewable energy[16] – and dates are set. But as targets proliferate, they become increasingly draconian, while the deadlines set for them recede into a future when the windows will have closed and the discursive frame becomes fantastic.

This sense of urgency has been criticized as amounting to 'catastrophism'.[17] Insofar as the dire findings of science are used to generate a political mobilising response driven by fear, one version of this might be what Greta Thunberg famously said at Davos in 2019: 'I want you to panic … I want you to act as if the house was on fire.'[18] Another version would be Richard Smith's and other ecological Marxist's claims that capitalism will shortly collapse through the combined weight of its internal contradictions and its rift with nature.[19] The critics respond that catastrophism is a counsel of despair on several counts.[20] First, anxiety is a weak driver of radical social change. Second, the crisis revealed by science is not a crisis of nature, or even of humanity versus nature;[21] it is produced by the co-evolution of capital with nature. Capital constantly internalises constraints, responds to the price signals they cause, and dynamically reinvents itself. Wartime planning, carbon trading, bio-engineering, geo-engineering, GMOs, and dematerialisation are frequently cited examples.[22] Despite the evident limits to resource availability, '(t)he idea of the limit is aesthetic' explained David Harvey in conversation with Leo Panitch.[23] For Harvey, the only limit of consequence is the limit to social alienation; reaching that limit will trigger revolutionary political action.[24]

However, as John Bellamy Foster observed about the *Socialist Register's* 2007 issue on the environment: '(t)he very fact that capitalism is not likely to collapse of itself and may 'prevail' for some time to come is precisely why the planet is in such absolute peril … (T)he advent of a more barbaric form [of capitalism] is no longer the worst of our worries. It is the threat to the planet itself that constitutes our most dire challenge.'[25] The British Labour Party's recent policy paper on the environment puts it differently: 'winning slowly on climate change is the same as losing.'[26]

HUMAN DEVELOPMENT AND RESTITUTION
UNDER SOCIALISM

If we accept the dire nature and urgent timeframe of the challenges posed by what science tells us about the ecological impact of capitalism, it is useful to revisit the early materialists' concepts of physical metabolism and human development. There are two reasons for this: first, because of their implications for 'the way we live now', and second, for their insights about social responses to our environmental crises – and about socialist responses.

These concepts were developed by Marx and his peers in a radically different context in the mid-nineteenth century.[27] Their question was man's relations to nature.[28] Out of the attempt to apply to society 'developments in the science of physiology that were derived from agricultural thought',[29] came the concept of metabolism (*Stoffwechsel* in German).[30] For Marx, social and ecological metabolism is the process of material exchanges in which nature is appropriated 'for the satisfaction of human needs'.[31] Nature and society co-evolve: nature through the laws of irreversible physical processes, society through historically 'institutionalised norms governing the division of labour and distribution of wealth'.[32] 'Man *lives* on nature – means that nature is his body, with which he must remain in continuous interchange if he is not to die.'[33] It follows that while we are united with nature, in the sense that we are materially a part of it, we also cannot exist without continual struggles with nature to shape it to our needs and wants.

Under capital, struggles take a particular shape.[34] Nature, in the form of matter and energy, is continually transformed through competition. The 'natural resource' of labour is also commodified, exploited, and alienated from the conditions of production. In so doing, a 'whole gamut of permanent conditions of life required by the generations' is encroached upon, conditions of social reproduction whose commodification threatens the conditions of life.[35] Capitalist production relations open up a fourfold social-metabolic rift:

(1) Through the privatised ownership and extraction of natural resources and ever-greater spatial relocations of the commodities produced, they disrupt the natural stocks and flows of material and energy.

(2) Through the exploitation of labour, they transform the inseparability of labour and nature, thereby ensuring that nature is objectified as a set of resources for human exploitation.[36]

(3) Through competition and commodification, they encroach on the very existence conditions of non-human life forms, as well as those needed by humans.

(4) Capitalist production, distribution, and consumption of commodities also re-shape metabolism through the ever-increasing generation of waste material. The depletion of energy and materials due to the dumping of most waste has been accepted because it has not been an immediate obstacle to the production of surplus value. Although the planet is an open energy system and part of the solar system, the physical and social processes of degradation, dissipation, decomposition, and reconstitution of waste operate at (slow) speeds that neither the capitalist system, nor the planet, can use or cope with.[37]

Marx envisaged an alternative dialectical process, one that was impossible under capitalist production relations.[38] He invoked the systematic application of science to govern 'the human metabolism with nature in a rational way … with the least expenditure of energy … and the re-use of waste … under collective (social) control … as associated producers'.[39] These are the social and ecological conditions in which fully emancipated individual 'human development'[40] unfolds and in which science is to be used neither to dominate nature nor to assume nature is inexhaustible.[41] It is noteworthy in this respect that Marx ended the longest chapter by far in volume one of *Capital*, 'Machinery and Modern Industry', with this crucial argument:

Capitalist production completely tears asunder the old bond of union which held together agriculture and manufacture in their infancy. But at the same time it creates the material conditions for a higher synthesis in the future, viz., the union of agriculture and industry on the basis of the more perfected forms they have each acquired during their temporary separation. Capitalist production, by collecting the population in great centres, and causing an ever-increasing preponderance of town population, on the one hand concentrates the historical motive power of society; on the other hand, it disturbs the circulation of matter between man and the soil, i.e., prevents the return to the soil of its elements consumed by man in the form of food and clothing; it therefore violates the conditions necessary to lasting fertility of the soil … But while upsetting the naturally grown conditions for the maintenance of that circulation of matter, it imperiously calls for its restoration as a system [N.B. the German term in the original is 'restitution' – BHW], as a regulating law of social production, and under a form appropriate to the full development of the human race … In modern agriculture, as in the urban industries, the increased productiveness and quantity of the labour set in motion are bought at the cost of laying waste and consuming by disease labour-power itself. Moreover, all progress in capitalistic agriculture is a progress in the art, not only of robbing the labourer, but of robbing the soil; all progress in increasing the fertility of the soil for a given time, is a progress towards ruining the lasting sources of that fertility … Capitalist production, therefore, develops technology, and the combining together of various processes into a social whole, only by sapping the original sources of all wealth – the soil and the labourer.[42]

That Marx actually used the concept of 'restitution' here, which is quite different from 'restoration', as it has usually been translated into English, is important. For Marx makes it clear that human development, while being bound to relations with nature and with collective work, is not a matter of restoring nature to a status quo ante: restitution is different. This difference is not only because the metabolic status quo ante (before either capitalism or settled agriculture) is irretrievably altered and 'spoiled'.[43] Nor is it just because the processes and sequencing of restoration are not understood[44] or because biophysical processes are dynamic not static, and the very notion of the status quo is inappropriate. Nor is it because any kind of compensation cannot be other than physically dislocated. Nor does the difference between restoration and restitution even arise because social relations with nature have spun out of capital's control. Rather the activity of ecological restitution is a collaboration with nature involving collective work through which individuals also achieve and practise human development.[45]

Understanding Marx's concept of human development as implying the relation to nature which he called 'restitution' – akin to what we might perhaps now call ecological trusteeship – helps to appreciate why he thought this was something which only a socialist society could achieve. 'Societies are not owners of the earth, they are simply its possessors, its beneficiaries, and have to bequeath it in an improved state to succeeding generations as *boni patres familias*'.[46] Our full, free and rich development requires we *improve* the earth.[47]

The idea of restitution did not originate with Marx, although the composite project of human-ecological development did. Restitution as an ecological idea – one originating long before the concept and discipline of ecology – seems to have been communicated in the influential mid-nineteenth century *Letters on Modern Agriculture* of German soil scientist Justus von Liebig, with which Engels and Marx were very familiar.[48] Liebig researched agriculture but his argument is equally valid for all of the material imbalances within and between all sectors of an economy – what Thompson and Medel called the web of life.[49] In his critique of the 'spoiliation system of farming', which constantly robs the soil of nutrients, Leibig writes that 'rational agriculture is based on the principle of restitution'.[50] Here he means restoring soil fertility. It is not land as territory, but the constituents of the soil, which provide for the nutrition of plants and through which wealth is constituted, that requires restitution. In letters about the conditions needed for minerals to do their nutritional work for plants, Liebig's *erlass* (which can also mean 'enact' and 'adopt') is again translated in terms of restitution, a process of returning to the soil minerals and manures in the form of plant, animal, and human waste.[51] Even more relevant to twenty-first-century conditions, Liebig uses the concept to cover the restoration of a disturbed agricultural equilibrium while providing sustainably for sustenance.[52] Restitution would now have to be extended to addressing rifts of nutrients, matter, and energy which have interactive and disruptive effects ranging from the microbiome inside our bodies to the entire planet's lithosphere, biosphere, and atmosphere.

Today the concept of restitution survives only in philosophy and law where it means both compensation for loss and the act of returning something stolen – as in movements for the 'restitution of silenced histories, repressed subjectivities, subalternized knowledges'.[53] As a political concept it tends to be avoided – even in socialist thought. There are a few exceptions. Distinguishing social restitution from metabolic restoration, the environmental-political philosopher Peter Critchley theorises the former as a condition of the latter. Citing Istvan Meszaros, he sees 'socialism ... presented in its true form as a project of restitution ... restored to the social body and exercised by the associated producers as social powers'.[54] South African land policy provides a contemporary example of restitution understood as a project of economic justice and territory, involving the transfer of land to groups of African farmers.[55] Yet as the anthropologist Lesley Green explains, if restitution is confined to the ownership of the means of production, even if this involves the collective ownership of land by 'associated producers as social powers', the relationship of people to land in a capitalist agrarian economy in which 'partnership with the ecosystem is replaced by mastery over soils' is inadequately addressed. He explains: 'the breaks imposed in soil ecology under industrial agriculture' need a fuller concept of restitution to stop. 'Farmers need to be supported to work with the partnerships that make healthy soils for free: partnerships with plants, soil microbes, insects, cows, earthworms, burrowing animals – and time! Because these partnerships take time to make soil.'[56]

We see in this example that the concept of restitution has survived, if at all, in a form dis-integrated from the processes of collective work for human development through the improvement of nature as a general objective of social and political existence. It is now coterminous with a set of less ambitious concepts: notably restoration – used by most environmental scholars and defining entire sub-fields of economics and of biology – but also 'conservation', 'repair', 'compensation', 'recuperation', 'reparation' (a branch of ecology),[57] 'halting degradation',[58] and not forgetting the IPCC's negative emissions scenarios, of which more anon.

Reducing nature to land and soils, as we have done so far, also ducks the fact that a rapidly expanding proportion of the global population – at least 55 per cent – is not involved directly in the work through which the kind of nature referred to so far in this essay is subjugated. Most people are involved in consuming – and creating waste from – the result of this process. Yet our production and consumption of (fuel) energy, cement, iron and steel, aluminum, minerals, chemicals, and paper exceed man-land-livestock relations in their consequences for metabolic rifts.[59] Not only is it impossible to restore the natural world to its condition prior to the capitalist and communist metabolic rifts – let alone to its condition in perhaps 200,000 BCE when humans first started using fire to modify vegetative cover.[60] It is also impossible to restore what is being destroyed now. Capitalism is destroying nature irreparably.

RESTITUTION AND RESTORATION IN THE TWENTY-FIRST CENTURY

Over time the spectre of planetary peril has belatedly coaxed responses at a planetary scale: from the Pentagon's basing of its military planning and technologies on the assumption that global warming will not be halted; to massively detailed scientific assessments (including the Vatican's apostolic academies' weighty volumes of evidence and the Pope's denunciation of greed and indifference); the adoption of market mechanisms to abate CO_2 emissions, the institutional conditions for which cannot be met;[61] and regular rounds of conflictual deliberations and inadequate voluntary pledges by the planet's 196 nation-states.[62] There is no lack of blueprints. Faced with the disparity between the evidence and the social reaction, with cognitive dissonance and insufficiency of will on a global scale,[63] some people take to cycling and shop for vegan food with cloth bags, avoid single-use plastic, segregate and recycle waste and buy renewable electricity and 'green gas'. Determined local groups invest in solar panels on school roofs, cities tax and try to ban diesel vehicles, and frequent fliers get trees planted. But extreme weather events and climate-change-related migrations and conflicts mean that already more and more people are dying. With restitution as the object of human development nothing but a utopian vision, socialists have to confront the limited but nonetheless imperative question of figuring out how the destruction of the remaining ecological space for human life can be halted in time. The first steps towards what Richard Smith has called 'post-capitalist ecological democracy',[64] a move towards human development in harmony with nature, cannot avoid an engagement with the conditions of actually existing capitalism.

In full awareness that I am practising the reductionism I have criticised above, gyrating between the abstract and the concrete and historical, reviewing literatures trapped in disciplinary silos which carve nature into special – often mutually incomprehensible – fields, and being unavoidably forced, for reasons of space, to try to summarise extensive fields of knowledge, I turn now to looking at restorative initiatives for just one of the nine planetary sub-systems on which life depends: air. Although each subsystem has its own specific material and political problems, the dimensions of all of them are clear enough from what is known about air;[65] and the drivers of gaseous pollution and atmospheric heating are also driving crises in the other physical subsystems. Following the template for full human development, I ask three kinds of questions about the initiatives on offer: how is science being used; how is it proposed that the use of materials and energy will be minimised, and waste re-used; and what forms of social organisation and control are envisaged for them?

Restoring the Earth's Air

What we inhale when we draw our first breath has become invisible garbage. Our ways of living in the twenty-first century have finally confronted us with a phenomenon first identified in the early nineteenth century: the effect of waste gas on atmospheric temperature, and on the health of everyone. Making the world a better place means both stopping the (rate of) rise in global temperature and lowering the pollution in our atmosphere. Despite wars of denial and scepticism, the atrophy of US research funds, and the disappearance of websites, science has been mobilised for the ecological crisis across the board.

Here we take one iconic text as the example of the collective work of science. In 2016, the UN's climate change body, the IPCC, set about organising 91 climate scientists (and 188 contributing authors) from 40 countries in a particularly focused way to assess the prospects for damage-limitation.[66] Organised into working groups for physical science, impacts and adaptation, and mitigation, they painstakingly reviewed about 6,000 research papers and fielded 42,000 peer reviewers' comments. All the while, the voluntary pledges from the 195 national signatories to the Paris Accord of 2015 were adding up to a total which suggested their target of a maximum rise in global temperature of 1.5 degrees above the 1850-1900 average was going to be overshot by 100 per cent – i.e. the pledges implied an increase of 3 degrees. In late 2018 the scientists estimated and extrapolated the damages that could be expected to result from a global temperature rise of 2 degrees over the 1850-1900 average, and compared them with those resulting from 1.5 degrees. On the assumption that business-as-usual continues, the scientists estimated that the temperature would hit the 1.5-degree threshold somewhere between 2030 and – a strangely specific date – 2052. They also asked how global temperature rise could be kept under 1.5 degrees by 2100 and how to halt the rate of change of atmospheric gases.[67]

The IPCC accepted a brief that covered the whole planet. Its thirty background chapters are extensive, detailed, the opposite of hubristic – and rarely read. Its conclusions are carefully qualified with references to the varied dynamics of regional ecosystems – especially the most vulnerable coastlines and drylands, the Arctic, small islands, and poor agrarian populations. And throughout its argument, general statements drag around their balls and chains of confidence levels and probabilities. The 'carbon budget' – the amount of CO_2 that can be released into the atmosphere – that remains if temperature rise is to be kept under the 1.5 degree target is subject to substantial uncertainty – between 580 and 770 Giga tonnes (Gt) – due to there being several accepted definitions and measurements of global temperature. To make things worse, without controls, gases other than CO_2 could reduce this budget by anywhere from 100 to 250 Gts.

The IPCC responded to the need for action by producing some 90 complex integrated assessment models generating planetary emissions pathways, four of which are published as illustrative simplifications, replete with wide margins of probability. They reveal what is at stake. Pathway number one simulates an immediate start to the process of restoration, by banning fossil fuel, lowering energy demand while increasing the standard of living in the 'south', investing heavily in afforestation, and decarbonising rapidly – indeed completely by 2050. Pathway two involves the UN's sustainable development goals which require investment in contemporary versions of human development, changes in land use and consumption, aid for a global convergence in sustainable development, comparatively limited use of bio-energy and carbon capture and storage technology (BECCS), and considerable low carbon innovation. Pathway three assumes historical patterns of fossil fuel and nuclear technology with emissions reductions from decarbonised energy and drops in demand, with BECSS intensifying dramatically over time. Pathway four represents GHG-intensive lifestyles, *overshooting* 1.5 degrees[68] and with a delayed response requiring correspondingly greater compensation by intensive carbon dioxide removal (CDR) and BECCS.

The IPCC's report makes clear the great difficulty of making a single conclusion for the planet. But its banner headline is that to limit heating to the 1.5 degree target would require global annual net human-caused emissions of CO_2 to fall by about 45 per cent from 2010 levels by 2030, reaching 'net zero' around 2050.[69]

Minimising energy, materials and waste

All four extrapolations into the future involve rapid 'far reaching', 'unprecedented' transitions in energy, land use, infrastructure, and industrial systems. These are not transitions in the sense in which lay people understand the term. Although it is commonly said that the technology exists, none of the major carbon-reducing mechanisms required by these pathways exists at scale. It is climate scientists with their economists who are assuming there is a can-opener. If it exists at all, how the carbon draw-down technology is to be scaled up, whether it could work in varied conditions across the world, and whether land exists sufficient for the scale of bio-energy production required are unproven questions. However, the later the process of restoration is initiated, the steeper the reduction gradient and the greater the need for these imagined technologies. Overshoot is modelled, perhaps reassuring politicians, but the technical problems with atmospheric cooling technology (let alone the effects on the earth) suggest that overshoot should be avoided at all costs.[70]

The IPCC excludes 'solar radiation modification measures' from its technological armoury (speculative geoengineering, at present including clouds of sulphur dioxide, orbiting sunshades, injections of aerosols in the stratosphere, pan-oceanic fertilisation by iron filings to stimulate carbon sequestration by phytoplankton, etc.). But the transformation of energy systems, the extraction and storage of carbon, the slashing of the output of other greenhouse gases, the development of new ways to lower the materials intensity of production-consumption systems, and the scaling up of bio-energy sources, would all affect the biosphere in ways currently unknown. For ecosystem restoration, the estimated range in the quantities of livestock pasture needing conversion, mostly to forests of 0.5-11m. sq. km. is extraordinary; just as the accompanying vegetarian revolution in global diets is far-fetched in its authoritarian assumptions.[71] And while the IPCC sees gaseous waste as *the* problem, it overlooks the handling of other waste gases and other waste in the production-consumption system.

The mind-boggling amount of new inventions assumed for all four pathways casts precaution to the winds, while their compatibility with the incentives and requirements of the (unmentioned) capitalist economy is simply assumed.

Social and political control

Although time is of the essence, the IPCC report's planetary scope means the pathways to emissions reductions have to be ahistorical and asocial. Yet they cannot avoid being political projects. The IPCC's depoliticised politics speaks of 'emissions portfolios' that are imagined to be held by, or assigned to, each national state. These can vary in energy and resource intensities, rates of decarbonisation, and permutations, combinations, and sequences of CO_2 removal technologies.

The IPCC report is far from an encomium to neoliberalism. Conventional market-mechanisms such as carbon trading (which have so far failed) go unmentioned, while calls for effective governance (as well as governance systems and multi-level governance) and transformational adaptation are strewn about the report. So are repeated warnings about 'barriers': socio-economic, financial, institutional, technological, and environmental barriers. Delay is another obstacle – escalating costs, locking-in polluting infrastructure, stranding assets and reducing flexibility.

For the IPCC, state capacity and competence is paramount in overcoming these barriers and obstacles. States are assumed able to direct and control capital. Since individual national projects of restorative environmental action will churn indiscriminately in global atmospheric currents,[72] states are assumed capable of acting in the planetary interest and of suppressing temptations to free ride. There is more. Remarkably, the IPCC calls for careful management of poverty reduction and careful consideration of ethics and equity. It expects achieving the 1.5 goal to generate 'synergies in excess of trade-offs' in technocratic swathes of sustainable human development: in health, food and human security livelihoods, cities, and economic growth – all delivered, by implication, through 'green capitalism'. Is this less utopian than Andreas Malm's ecologically sensitive reformulation of the communist manifesto,[73] or than the collective work of restitution achieved though the rich human development envisaged by Marx?

In subsequent discussions, some of these scientists have shown that they see politics as 'ideology', something they seek to avoid. When calling for unprecedented transformations, they mean unprecedented technologically, not politically. Politicians just lack 'political will'. What their 'pathways' clearly call for is a powerful planetary political authority, yet there is no call for it.

'OUT OF THE MOUTHS OF BABES'

At first sight, nothing could be more different from the IPCC's report than a single iconic child. 'School Strikes for Climate' was initiated as a protest by fifteen-year-old Greta Thunberg in August 2018, struggling, as she explains, with her inability to live in a state of cognitive dissonance between the climate science and daily social life.[74] After her address at the Katowice COP 24 meeting, by March 2019 an estimated 1.4 million children in 112 countries had joined the Friday School Strikes for Climate. They were joined by many parents and by an independently mobilised, militant and effective mass movement of civil disobedience, Extinction Rebellion.[75] In the May EU parliamentary elections the 'Greta effect' on adult voters was widely credited with the one-third increase in the number of Green Party MEPs across the EU.[76]

Thunberg is consistent in her desire to restore. She protests about popular ignorance, official silence, political apathy about the climate science, political concealment, denial, and hostility. She appeals to states to fulfil the (inadequate) Paris Agreement pledges and to ban fossil fuels. She demands that the EU lives within planetary boundaries, doubling the target rate of emissions reduction (from 1990 levels) from 45 per cent to at least 80 per cent by 2030, and including the reduction of pollution from aviation and shipping. She exemplifies individual lifestyle environmentalism as a vegan, an austere consumer, and a 'flight-shamer' who uses public transport and electric cars.

Three aspects of the movement she has triggered are noteworthy. First, Thunberg reads the science as implying a catastrophe and sees the IPCC report as arguing that 'we are less than 12 years away from not being able to undo our mistakes', or 'from an irreversible chain reaction'.[77] Whatever its faults, and although the document stresses urgent action, we have seen here that this is not exactly what it says. However, the twelve-year time-frame has been seized on by the media and in popular consciousness either as counting-down to the end of the world (i.e. the sixth extinction, including of humanity), or alternatively as a useful political escape hatch in electoral democracies currently unwilling to address the seriousness and complexity of climate change where politicians are 'decision averse'.

Second, Thunberg concretises a politics of generational responsibility. 'You are stealing our future.' And public figures as varied as Pope Francis, Antonio Guterres, Prince Charles, George Monbiot, and Michael Gove have confessed guilt at the profligacy of their generation, at their procrastination, and at the failure of their efforts to counter climate change. Naming and blaming a generation may make a useful case for rapid action. But climate change is not the work of a generation but the manifestation of a metabolic rift caused by global capital, energised by fossil fuel, devouring material resources, unfolding in historical time and victimising those least responsible – in terms of regions,[78] of nations, and of their constituent labouring classes. Let's not forget that some of the aged have fought life-long inside and outside their workplaces against capital and its waste. If the ideas of young people not yet in the workforce were to prevail over capital – without identifying it

– and if they could mobilise economic and political force where trade unions and many other civil society and politically activist organisations have failed, this would be an achievement unique in world history.

Third comes the question of state competence, for Thunberg's call for action is directed – as is that of the IPCC – to politicians and officials. Her point is that gesture is not action. Decades ago, the legal scholar Philip Alston argued that signatures and intentions are but the first step in any process of action.[79] Public interest commitments have to be codified; provision and claim need to be institutionalised; mechanisms for redress of non-provision established and enforcement empowered. Each of these processes embodies a political struggle against opposition. Without these institutional mechanisms in place, intentions cannot be operationalized. At national levels, the unprecedentedly complicated policy processes for restoring merely the air and transforming global society have barely started and are not coordinated.[80] Meanwhile a considerable scholarly literature questions the competence of the now commodified and captured state to do anything much other than capital's bidding.[81] And, as Aeron Davies reveals, even capital's bidding is compromised by the 'precarious, rootless and increasingly self-serving' elites permeating the state. After twenty years of research, he concludes they are 'reckless opportunists'.[82] Joseph Stiglitz, the 'within-system' dissenting economist who earlier computed the costs of the disastrous Iraq war, and is expert at the arts and sciences of global accounting, calls for a 'war footing' on climate change.[83] But as the civil servant credited with sensitising Thatcher to climate change, Crispin Tickell, warned exasperatedly in 2010, 'we have lost the capacity to plan'.[84]

A NATIONAL RESPONSE: THE UK LABOUR PARTY

The British Labour Party's 2017 Manifesto champions the environment in brief, dense paragraphs which outline an anti-market, pro-state policy and commit to 60 per cent renewable energy by 2030. Yet as Jeremy Gilbert observed, nothing in the manifesto suggested an ecosocialist vision unhitched from industrial capitalism and growth.[85] In late 2018 the Labour Party consolidated its commitments in an Environment Policy paper, which was explicitly grounded in the IPCC science plus a wider science and technology literature, but focused on preventing the tipping points and feedback loops which the IPCC had pointedly steered around in its report.[86] The paper is evidence-based and – following Keynes and Samuelson – commits to revising policy in the light of changes in knowledge. Reducing materials and polluting energy are prominent priorities in its stresses on renewable energy, ultra-low emissions vehicles, and energy efficiency in buildings and industry.

Labour will also reverse bio-diversity decline. Tree planting and conservation are principles for policy in agriculture and fisheries. Atmospheric and non-atmospheric waste is to be reduced through public transport and an assault on plastics.

The politics of this environment policy are complicated. Like the IPCC, Labour calls for transformational change and the rebalancing of economic power away from markets (proven to be inadequate for the task) and towards coordinated planning. It mainstreams livelihoods in such planning, building on the 'just transition' of international labour movements.[87] Unlike the IPCC, Labour is also able to be quite specific about banning fracking, and about the renationalisation of electricity transmission, distribution and grid connectivity,[88] railways (including an extended Hi-speed2 to Scotland) and water. To enable this, Labour would create a National Transformation Fund of £250 billion over a decade. The policy also recognises the principle of subsidiarity through local government control over home insulation to high performance standards, zero carbon affordable new building, and cycle networks. Local government already controls waste disposal and recycling. In agriculture and fisheries, subsidies for small-scale sustainable practices are proposed, and the routine use of antibiotics in livestock rearing would be banned.[89]

Labour's internationalism will shape an environmental foreign policy; development aid will avoid fossil fuel investments and encourage low carbon and SDG convergence worldwide. Vagueness may be encouraged by the IPCC demonstration effect. Labour is unspecific about the redistribution of resource control, e.g. whether and how the ultra-low emissions vehicles will be manufactured – or imported, as well as how future airport and aviation expansion will be 'severely' regulated. Several of IPCC's central concerns are conspicuous by their absence: the phase out of (imported) coal, the controversial future of nuclear energy, and the holy grail of carbon capture and storage. Like the IPCC report, Labour's policy is not conflictual. The social preconditions needed for it to work are not identified, nor are its workforce implications, nor is opposition to it. Buying opposition out, bypassing, or destroying it are tactics not incorporated into the party's policy.

Labour's policy for a green transformation is noteworthy for three related reasons. First it bears a close family resemblance to several other prominent blueprints, some over a decade old: not just the Green New Deal legislation Alexandria Ocasio-Cortez has presented to Congress,[90] but also the UK's Green Party's 2009 Million Jobs Green Recovery Package, and the Campaign against Climate Change (CACC) Trade Union branch's Million Climate Jobs project (updated between 2009 and 2014) which put work central.[91] Second, all these projects embrace the need for social and political transformations both as necessary in themselves and as preconditions for the technological project to restore the damaged atmosphere.[92] Third, reluctantly or with conviction, explicitly mentioning capital or euphemising it, all these projects argue that the crisis can be addressed through reforms within the system. Though the UK has joined the declarations of a 'climate emergency', this never threatened the Conservative Government's neoliberal worldview. 'No special powers have been put in place.'[93] Labour's radical reforms, such as ending fossil fuel monopolies and redistributing control over resources, themselves co-exist with anything but transformative sounding competitive commitments to develop export markets for green technology and access to the EU's internal energy market.

CONCLUSION

This has been a hard essay to write, first, because of the vast variety and accelerating pace of activity throughout the world demanding action; second, because even so the project of restoration has yet to be paid the attention it requires; third, because of the inexorable and unremitting degradation of the planet's physical sub-systems as the metabolic rift deepens and becomes more complex; fourth, because of the need to contain the scope of this essay by being selective in the choice of sub-system and sources. It does not help that the science is organised in proliferating sub-fields and sometimes has to operate with wide margins of probability.

What does the science say? Almost all the findings point in the same direction. For a blueprint to restore the atmosphere, there is no planetary alternative to the IPCC's. The longer an unprecedented global assault on the causes of GHG emissions is delayed, the less likely the planet will be habitable in ways we recognise.

What does it mean we need to do and by when? The IPCC 2018, representing 195 governments, is indeed at pains to stress the urgency of the growing ecological crisis. To have a chance to keep the rise in global temperature below 1.5 degrees, global emissions have to be halved by 2030. How? It's not our department said IPPC. It involves technologies for materials and energy efficiency, land-use change, and carbon extraction that are currently unproven and at scales that are currently imaginary.

Can it be done in time under the assumption that the world remains capitalist? The project is without historical precedent. But the IPCC, the School Strikes, New Deals, and Extinction Rebellion, not to mention the Pentagon, all assume the need to work extremely fast, through competent states, and within capitalism – without explicitly considering its nature and mechanisms. Concerned individuals are pitted against the energy majors, so it will be left to these corporations to self-destruct, which at present is highly unlikely.[94] Even restoration needs growth, materials, and energy. Paul Burkett has visited this issue, arguing that such solutions as 'recycling and waste management, restoration of forests, strip mined lands and plundered maritime eco-systems, all become ecologically impoverished constitutive parts of the problem, requiring a fresh expenditure of energy and materials rather than being ecologically restorative'.[95]

What can be done in any one country? The British Labour Party plan confronts some of the obstacles but, like all the national movements involved in the problem, operates under capitalism and also faces the free rider objection. An exception to the latter though not the former, Costa Rica has a lot to lose from the impact of climate change on its mountain-cloud forests, while the results of its commitment to carbon neutrality by 2021 will pass unnoticed in the troubled atmosphere.[96] Will its refusal to free ride have ripple effects, just as the butterfly does in chaos theory?

How should socialists act given these constraints? Marx proposed a relationship with the material world, one of restitution, that would require a socialist society to develop and maintain, and which would at least not degrade that world further but would try to improve it. This is however a utopian dream, especially given the non-existence of socialist forces and the time-scale of the threat.[97] Even restoration has no counter-hegemonic politics.

So, given that the problem is capitalism, are socialists defining the ecological crisis as one of restorative class struggle? The Labour Party, even under its current socialist leadership, does not do this. Can it be afforded politically? Can socialists engage practically with the science? Is the time frame of a focus on socialist education, organisation, and agitation consistent with the time frame of essential action to keep human life on earth viable? If not, then what?

NOTES

For the memory of Delys Weston, whose 2012 thesis see (note 56 below) is very useful. And with thanks to Greg Albo, Maryam Aslany, Arndt Emmerich, Alfy Gathorne-Hardy, M. Ali Jan, Colin Leys, Leo Panitch, Xu Huijiao, and the Oxford Institute for Science, Innovation and Society's 2019 seminar on modelling, evidence, and truth in science and policy.

1   Noam Chomsky interviewed by Scott Casleton, 'Choosing Hope', *Boston Review*, 4 June 2019.

2   James Lovelock, who named it Gaia. See: Lawrence E. Joseph, 'James Lovelock, Gaia's Grand Old Man,' *Salon*, 17 August 2000.

3   Intergovernmental Panel on Climate Change (IPCC), *Global Warming of 1.5°C. An IPCC Special Report on the impacts of global warming of 1.5°C above pre-industrial levels and related global greenhouse gas emission pathways, in the context of strengthening the global response to the threat of climate change, sustainable development, and efforts to eradicate poverty: Summary for Policymakers,* Incheon, South Korea/IPCC, 2018.

4   Johan Rockström, et al., 'A Safe Operating Space for Humanity', *Nature,* 461, 2009, pp. 472-75; updated by Will Steffen, et al., 'Planetary Boundaries: Guiding Human Development on a Changing Planet', *Science,* 347, 2015, pp. 1-10. Steffen, et al. respond to challenges about the definition and comprehensiveness of these nine sub-systems, as well as the ecological significance and measurement of thresholds beyond which development is not bio-geo-physically safe.

5   Richard Heede, 'Tracing anthropogenic carbon dioxide and methane emissions to fossil fuel and cement producers, 1854- 2010', *Journal of Climatic Change,* 22(1-2), 2014, pp. 229-41.

6   To this, David Schwartzman would add the military industrial complex: David Schwartzman, 'Beyond Eco-catastrophism: the Conditions for Solar Communism', in Leo Panitch and Greg Albo, eds., *Socialist Register 2017: Rethinking Revolution,* London: Merlin Press, 2016, pp. 143-60.

7   Redundancy involves the co-existence of similar species, known to support ecosystem resilience. Marten Scheffer, et al. 'The Evolution of Functionally Redundant Species; Evidence from Beetles', *Plos One,* 10(10), 2015.

8   Elisabeth Kolbert, *The Sixth Extinction,* London: Picador, 2014.

9   For fuller referencing and many examples see the review in: Barbara Harriss-White, 'Globalisation, Development and the Metabolic Rift', *SOAS Lecture,* 2015, available at: www.southasia.ox.ac.uk/sites/default/files/southasia/documents/media/general-south_asia_wp21_soas_globalisation_lecture.pdf.

10   Rockström, et al., 'A safe operating Space for Humanity', p. 473.

11   Ulrich Poschl, 'Atmospheric Aerosols: Composition, Transformation, Climate and Health Effects', *Angew. Chem. Int. Ed.,* 44, 2005, pp. 7520-40.

12   Annie Gabriel, 'Saving the Ozone Layer: Why the Montreal Protocol Worked', *The Conversation,* 9 September 2012, available at: theconversation.com.

13   Robert Wills, et al., 'Extracting Modes of Variability and Change from Climate Model Ensembles', *Seventh International Workshop on Climate Informatics,* 20-22 September 2017, available at: atmos.uw.edu/~david/Wills_etal_2017a.pdf.

14   No records exist for 1750, established as the key pre-industrial date. See Gwyn Prins and Steve Rayner, *'The Hartwell Paper: A New Direction for Climate Policy After the Crash of 2009',* LSE, 2010, available at: eprints.lse.ac.uk/27939/1/HartwellPaper_English_version.pdf.

15   Bojana Bajzelj and Keith Richards, 'The Positive Feedback Loop Between the Impacts of Climate Change and Agricultural Expansion and Relocation', *Land,* 3, 2014, pp. 898-916.

16   Ibid; and see Barbara Harriss-White and Elinor Harriss, 'Unsustainable Capitalism: the Politics of Renewable Energy in the UK', in Leo Panitch and Colin Leys, eds., *Socialist Register 2007: Coming to Terms With Nature,* London: Merlin Press, 2006, pp. 72-101.

17   Sasha Lilley, et al. *Catastrophism: The Apocalyptic Politics of Collapse and Rebirth,* Oakland: PM Press/Spectre, 2012.

18 Greta Thunberg, *No-One is Too Small to Make a Difference*, London: Penguin Random House, 2019.

19 See Richard Smith, 'Capitalism and the Destruction of Life on Earth: Six Theses on Saving the Humans', *Truthout*, 10 November 2013, available at truthout.org; Rupert Read, 'Climate Catastrophe: The Case for Rebellion,' 2019, available at: www. youtube.com.

20 See Doug Henwood quoting Engels in the 'Foreword' in Lilley, et al. *Catastrophism*.

21 Royal Society, *People and the Planet,* London: Royal Society, 2012, available at: royalsociety.org.

22 For examples see Leo Panitch and Colin Leys, eds., *Socialist Register 2007: Coming to Terms with Nature*, London: Merlin Press, 2006.

23 Leo Panitch and David Harvey, 'Red Talks, Episode One', 2014, available at vimeo. com.

24 Harvey's use of alienation encompasses the day-to-day lack of care of socially alienated people and the condition of the subsumption of work and 'many aspects of daily life' under the power of capital – at the limits of which anti-capitalist movements will rise up. David Harvey, 'Universal Alienation and the Real Subsumption of Daily Life under Capital: A Response to Hardt and Negri', *Triple-C*, 16(2), 2018, pp. 449-453.

25 John Bellamy Foster, 'Marxism versus 'Anxiety-Driven Ecological Catastrophism'?' *Climate and Capitalism*, 12 March 2007, available at: climateandcapitalism.com.

26 The Labour Party, *The Green Transformation: Labour's Environment Policy*, London: Labour, 2018, available at: www.labour.org.uk.

27 Paul Burkett, 'Marx's Vision of Sustainable Human Development', *Monthly Review*, 57(5), 2005. Michael Lebowitz, 'The Unifying Element in All Struggles Against Capital Is the Right of Everyone to Full Human Development', *Monthly Review*, 63(6), 2011.

28 Throughout this essay, 'man' refers to man and woman. The gendering of the argument cannot be covered in the space here and is for another essay.

29 Karel Ludenhoff, 'Marx, Socialism and Ecology', *Logos*, 17(2), 2018, available online at: www.imhojournal.org.

30 Ecological references in Marx's published writings have been criticised as scattered and incoherent. John Bellamy Foster has put paid to that notion in his *Marx's Ecology: Materialism and Nature*, New York: Monthly Review Press, 2000. Now both Kohei Seito and Peter Critchley have published significant and meticulous evaluations of the ecological contributions of his notebooks translated in the MEGA project. See Kohei Saito, *Karl Marx's Eco-Socialism: Capital, Nature, and the Unfinished Critique of Political Economy*, New York: Monthly Review Press, 2017; Peter Critchley, *Social Restitution and Metabolic Restoration in the Thought of Karl Marx,* 2018; and see http://pcritchley2. wixsite.com/beingandplace/publications.

31 Karl Marx, *Economic Manuscript of 1861-63: A Contribution to the Critique of Political Economy*, translated by Ben Fowkes, Lawrence & Wishart, 2010; Karl Marx, *Capital: A Critical Analysis of Capitalist Production, Volume I*, translated from the third German edition by Samuel Moore & Edward Aveling, London: George Allen & Unwin, 1938 [reprint of 1889 English edition], Chapter 7, pp. 283-90, available at www.marxists.org.

32 Tim Hayward quoted in: Foster, *Marx's Ecology*, p. 159.

33 Karl Marx, 'Estranged Labour', *Economic and Philosophical Manuscripts of 1844*, available at: www.marxists.org.

34   Elmar Altvater developed this analysis: Elmar Altvater, 'The Social and Natural Environment of Fossil Capitalism', in Leo Panitch and Colin Leys, eds., *Socialist Register 2007: Coming to Terms With Nature*, London: Merlin Press, 2006, pp. 37-59.

35   Karl Marx, *Capital*, Volume 1, p. 638; Volume 3, p. 754 (quoted in John Bellamy Foster, *Marx's Ecology*, p. 164).

36   For an extended analysis of the concept of unity with nature in Marx see John Reid, 'Marx on the Unity of Man', *The Thomist*, 28(3), 1964, pp. 259-301.

37   Heather Rogers, 'Garbage Capitalism's Green Commerce', in Leo Panitch and Colin Leys, eds., *Socialist Register 2007: Coming to Terms With Nature,* London: Merlin Press, 2006, pp. 231-53; and on growth and on entropy as waste see Robin Hahnel, 'The Growth Imperative: Beyond Assuming Conclusions', *Review of Radical Political Economy*, 45(1), 2012, pp. 24-41.

38   See Critchley, *Social Restitution*, p. 265.

39   Karl Marx, *Capital* Volume 3, New York: International Publishers, 1981, Chapter 48, available at: www.marxists.org.

40   The modern project of human development is attributed to Pakistani economist and GDP heretic Mahboob Ul Huq while working at UNDP from 1988, and involves the provision of a series of basic needs and standards for a decent life.

41   This is the starting point of the critique by Saito of critics of Marx's promethianism (eco-socialism).

42   Marx, *Capital* Volume 1, pp. 513-15. The German term in the original is 'restitution' as in Systematische Restitution der Stoffwechselbedingungen'.

43   Marx and Engels wrote as early as 1845 in the *German Ideology* that '(t)he nature that preceded human history ... today no longer exists'; See Karl Marx and Friedrich Engels, *The German Ideology*, 1932, available at www.marxists.org.

44   For example low or zero weight is given to microbial relationships which humans cannot see.

45   The extent to which this is embedded in energy is very rarely acknowledged either by mainstream advocates of human development or by socialists.

46   Marx, *Capital* Volume 3, Chapter 46.

47   This is an obligation stronger either than that of contemporary 'sustainable development', which now stresses at best the maintenance of stocks of material and energy for future generations, or that of human development, which is now sliced into seventeen technocratic subfields.

48   Justus von Liebig, *Naturwissenschaftliche Briefe über die moderne Landwirthschaft*, Leipzig: C. F. Winter, 1859, available at: catalog.hathitrust.org.

49   John Thompson and Rodrigo Medel, 'Coevolution and the Web of Life', *Evolution: Education and Outreach,* 3(1), 2010, p. 6.

50   Justus von Liebig, *Letters on Modern Agriculture*, 1859, pp. 175-77, available at: archive.org.

51   Liebig, *Letters*, pp. 111, 144, 186, 217, 255.

52   Liebig, *Letters*, p. 245.

53   Walter D. Mignolo, 'Delinking: The Rhetoric of Modernity, the Logic of Coloniality, and the Grammar of De-Coloniality', *Cultural Studies*, 21(2-3), March/May 2007, p. 451.

54   Critchley, *Social Restitution*, p. 35.

55   Delys Weston, *The Political Economy of Global Warming*, PhD Thesis, Curtin University, Australia, 2012, available at: espace.curtin.edu.au.

56   Lesley Green, 'Towards a Politics for Soil Restitution', *Daily Maverick*, 5 February 2019, available at: www.dailymaverick.co.za.

57   'Redistributing care, land and work so that everyone has a chance to contribute to the improvement of their lives and to that of the ecology around them'. See Jason Moore and Raj Patel, 'Unearthing the Capitalocene: Towards a Reparations Ecology', *Resilience*, 4 January 2018, available at: www.resilience.org.

58   Jean-Marie Baland and Jean-Philippe Platteau, *Halting Degradation of Natural Resources: Is There a Role for Rural Communities?*, Oxford: Oxford University Press, 2000.

59   For air pollution statistics see: 'Statistics Explained', *Eurostat*, December 2018, available at: ec.europa.eu. See also Intergovernmental Science-Policy Platform on Biodiversity and Ecosystem Services (IPBES), *Global Assessment Report on Biodiversity and Ecosystem Services*, 2019.

60   Juli Pausas and Jon Keeley, 'A Burning Story: The Role of Fire in the History of Life', *Bioscience*, 59(7), 2009, pp. 593-601.

61   Jon Hilsenrath, 'Cap and trade's unlikely critics: its creators', *Wall Street Journal*, 13 August 2009.

62   The UK has cut emissions to nineteenth-century levels by a rapid switch to renewable energy, but also by slow growth, the exclusion of activities like aviation, and 'exporting' emissions to countries from which commodities are imported. Agricultural, residential and public sector/government emissions are up. See: David Hendry, 'First-in, first-out: Driving the UK's per capita carbon dioxide emissions below 1860 levels', *VOX CEPR Policy Portal*, 12 December 2018, available at: voxeu.org.

63   Patrik Sorqvist and Linda Langeborg, 'Why People Harm the Environment Although They Try to Treat It Well: An Evolutionary-Cognitive Perspective on Climate Compensation', *Frontiers in Psychology*, 4 March 2019.

64   Richard Smith, 'Beyond Growth or beyond Capitalism?', *Real-world Economics Review*, 53, June 2010, available at: www.paecon.net.

65   For soil, see the review by Peter Betary, et al., 'The role of agri-environment schemes in conservation and environmental management', *Conservation Biology*, 29(4), 2015. For biodiversity, see Benjamin Phalan, 'What Have We Learned from the Land Sparing-sharing Model?', *Sustainability*, 10(6), 2018, 1760.

66   To which some signatories are known privately to object. See: Suzanne Goldenberg, 'Governments reject IPCC economist's "meaningless" climate costs estimate', *The Guardian*, 28 March 2014.

67   IPCC, 2018.

68   Though 81/90 models involved overshoot 1.5.

69   IPCC 2018 reduces atmospheric GHGs to CO_2, but where possible adds separate analyses of the additional physically significant non-CO_2 radiative forces (variously methane, nitrous oxide, black C, fluorinated gases and ozone precursors).

70   Though additional energy investment between 2016-2050 is estimated at roughly $850 bn per year, IPCC also appeals to 'knowledge gaps' in cost benefit analysis which are in fact filled: Simon Dietz et al., 'The Economics of 1.5°C Climate Change', *Annual Review of Environment and Resources*, 43, 2018, pp. 455-80. In June 2019 the British Chancellor of the Exchequer put the cost of net zero at £1tn for the UK and was roundly criticised for scaremongering.

71 EAT-Lancet Commission, *Food in The Anthropocene: the EAT-Lancet Commission on Healthy Diets from Sustainable Food Systems,* 16 January 2019, available at: thelancet.com/commissions/EAT.

72 Wills, et al., 'Extracting Modes of Variability and Change from Climate Model Ensembles'.

73 Andreas Malm, 'Revolution in a Warming World: Lessons from the Russian to the Syrian Revolutions', in Leo Panitch and Greg Albo, eds., *Socialist Register 2017: Rethinking Revolution,* London: Merlin Press, 2016, pp. 120-42.

74 Greta Thunberg, 'The disarming case to act right now on climate change', *TEDxStockholm,* November 2018, available at: www.ted.com.

75 For Extinction Rebellion see rebellion.earth. Extinction Rebellion was downgraded to a 'climate change protest' by BBC Radio 4 in April 2019.

76 From 52 in 2014 to 74 in 2019.

77 Greta Thunberg speech to EU, Brussels, 21 February 2019. Available online at https://www.youtube.com/watch?v=CWQPDsHJ0gc

78 Marcus Taylor, *The Political Ecology of Climate Change Adaptation: Livelihoods, Agrarian Change and the Conflicts of Development,* London: Earthscan, 2015.

79 Philip Alston, 'International Law and the Right to Food', chapter 11 in Barbara Harriss-White and Raymond Hoffenberg, eds., *Food: Multidiscplinary Perspectives,* Oxford: Blackwells, 1994, pp. 205-16.

80 France's new development law and programme, being codified in 2019, is an attempt to step in the right direction (not without flaws). Available at: www.diplomatie.gouv.fr.

81 Colin Leys, 'The Cynical State', in Leo Panitch and Colin Leys, eds., *Socialist Register 2006: Telling the Truth,* London: Merlin Press, 2005, pp. 1-27.

82 Aeron Davis, *Reckless Opportunists: Elites at the End of the Establishment,* Manchester: Manchester University Press, 2018.

83 Joseph Stiglitz, 'The climate crisis is our third world war. It needs a bold response', *The Guardian,* 4 June 2019.

84 At the then-LSE director Tony Gidden's Climate Change conference, LSE, 2009.

85 Jeremy Gilbert, 'Leading richer lives', in Mike Phipps, ed., *For the Many: Preparing Labour for Power,* London: OR Books, 2017, pp. 163-80.

86 Labour, Green Transformation.

87 See documentation on the just transition at: www.ituc-csi.org/just-transition-centre.

88 Not production.

89 Bowing to special humane single-interest groups and showing their power, hunting and wild animals in circuses are also both to be prohibited. It does not propose a phase-out of livestock production.

90 Alexandria Ocasio-Cortez, 'Recognizing the duty of the Federal Government to create a Green New Deal'. *H. RES. 109,* 7 February 2019, available at: www.congress.gov.

91 Jonathan Neale, et al., *One Million Climate Jobs: Tackling the Environmental and Economic Crises,* Campaign against Climate Change, 2014, available at: www.cacctu.org.uk.

92 See also a most interesting Leeds University research project about human development within bio-geo-physical thresholds: goodlife.leeds.ac.uk.

93 Ed Miliband, 'How to Save the Planet', *Prospect,* 10 June 2019, available at: www.prospectmagazine.co.uk.

94 British Petroleum, *BP Energy Outlook,* 2019, available at: www.bp.com.

95   Paul Burkett, *Marxism and Ecological Economics*, London: Haymarket, 2009, p. 170. As Alvater already warned in 2007, Jason Hickel and Giorgos Kallis have also recently shown with evidence the proposition that growth cannot be decoupled from material resources is not possible under capitalism: Jason Hickel and Giorgos Kallis, 'Is Green Growth Possible?', *New Political Economy*, 17 April 2019.

96   Yessenia Funes, 'Costa Rica Lays Out Plan to Zero Out Carbon Emissions by 2050', *Gizmodo*, 26 February 2019, available at: earther.gizmodo.com.

97   For Critchley, the real contradicts the ideal, *Social Restitution*, p. 12.

BEYOND THE 'BARBED-WIRE LABYRINTH': MIGRANT SPACES OF RADICAL DEMOCRACY

AMY BARTHOLOMEW
AND HILARY WAINWRIGHT

In 1951 Hannah Arendt famously analyzed the 'calamity' of rightlessness that accompanied the crisis of statelessness, within which she included migrants and refugees, as the 'deprivation of a place in the world which makes opinions significant and actions effective'. The stateless, she argued, are treated as the pawn of politics and are 'forced to live outside the common world'. She also identified camps – the 'barbed-wire labyrinth into which events' had driven those who were stateless – as the 'routine solution for the problem of domicile of the "displaced persons"'. The stateless were treated *everywhere* as the 'scum of the earth', a condition which would go on, she contended, to threaten politics itself.[1]

Today, the UNHCR identifies 70.8 million people as 'forcibly displaced' in the world, a figure that includes 41.3 million internally displaced people, 25.9 million refugees, and 3.5 million asylum seekers, but not the over 10 million officially stateless persons, most of whom live in the so-called 'developing world'.[2] The only Western country to appear in the top ten list of refugee-hosting countries is Germany. The remainder are, in descending order of number of refugees, Turkey, Jordan, Lebanon, Pakistan, Uganda, Iran, and Ethiopia.[3] Yet as in Arendt's time, we in the West are again fixated on the 'migration' or 'refugee crisis' on the borders of Europe and now between the US and Mexico.

Despite a 'Eurocentric' myopia, however, we certainly are in, if not a migration crisis, then a crisis of borders. These figures, and the lives they indicate that go effectively unlived, are the calamity that we have produced through wars, civil and international – often the results of imperialism today and colonialism yesterday. They are also the disasters that have accompanied climate change, instability, and reverberating violence in states that are not officially at war but are wracked by the consequences of past and present imperial interventions and the brutality of dispossession by accumulation driven by the de-regulated global market. All this has been accompanied by the rise of authoritarian and racist right-wing forces across the globe, much of it fuelled by migration. The impact of these forces, in combination, means that virtually all states and all regional 'governance' regimes will have to face the 'crisis' of migration and borders for a very long time to come. So far, they have chosen to cope by the externalization of borders, walls, tracking, prolonged detention in appalling conditions, the toleration of death at sea, the closing of ports to rescue ships, the criminalization of those who seek to aid migrants, all connected, of course, to *refoulement*, the illegal and forcible return of refugees or asylum seekers to a country where they are liable to be subjected to persecution.

This is the dystopian nightmare of dehumanization, the treatment of migrants everywhere as the 'scum of the earth' in the twenty-first century. Almost seventy years after Arendt issued her warning on this, the mayor of Lesvos in Greece, Spiros Galinos, echoed her words: 'Europe's future is at stake', pointing to the policies now pursued by the EU, including border closures and deportations to Turkey, which 'create fear, xenophobia and racism, which in turn leads to fascism'.[4] Indeed, what is widely reported erroneously as the 'refugee crisis' in Europe today has played out most intensely on its periphery in Greece (and Italy). Confronted with a double crisis – the economic and the 'refugee' crises – Greece became the 'hotspot of Europe'.[5] Focusing on the case of Greece starkly illuminates the injustices of the international and regional regimes of refugee law and politics, and the failures of the international human rights system to protect the rights of all persons (just as Arendt recognized). But it also illuminates the complexity of state responses and their reduced room for manoeuvre (as they see it); given the EU's position, it especially speaks to the inadequacy of relying even on a left political party, such as Syriza, in government to protect migrants and their rights. It has become clear that we cannot expect such a party to develop solidaristic policies aimed to address the fracturing politics of the rightward move that has been fuelled by the continuing presence of immiserated migrants and the right-wing's electorally opportunistic 'ugly dog whistle' that the country is losing its 'ethnic identity due to migration'.[6]

This essay will juxtapose the Greek state's continuation and, indeed, intensification of the dystopian regime of border control and refugee camps to migrant-citizen-solidarian spaces and practices, illustrated by the now-famous City Plaza hotel squat as a 'Refugee Accommodation and Solidarity Space' in Athens.[7] This provides at least a glimpse of the promise of autonomous, solidarity, prefigurative practices that challenge all the 'routine solutions' for mass migration.[8] We will argue that solidarity initiatives like City Plaza hotel show that it could be otherwise, thus challenging both the EU's near imposition of camp life on Greece and also Syriza's 'realpolitik' in the context of migration. It will go on to argue, however, that, to build on transformations achieved through prefigurative practice and achieve systemic change, action is required at the level of the state and therefore of political organisation. This in turn requires a strategy that recognises in practice the importance of supporting, spreading, and sharing power with those engaged in prefigurative transformative initiatives like City Plaza.

GREECE AND THE BORDER CRISIS

In the run up to the election in 2015, Syriza promised to end the 'deterrence regime' of migrant detention, 'to radically overhaul Greece's immigration policies by providing citizenship to second-generation migrants born in the country', and to close migrant detention centres.[9] After gaining office it opened the borders, in part by ending the illegal pushback of migrants by the coastguard, reduced detention time, and limited police repression. The Greek Coastguard is credited with saving 240 migrants when a boat capsized in fall 2016.[10] The government also moved on the promise of citizenship, encouraging the early optimism that Syriza would pursue 'advanced political experimentations in the field of migration, including a stop to deportations and a steady dismantling of detention structures'.[11] Not long after its entering office, however, after more than a million migrants transited through Greece to Northern Europe, and with the impending closure of the Macedonian border,[12] Greece invited NATO to patrol the Aegean for the first time on a European 'migrant mission', along with Frontex, the EU border control agency, and the German, Greek, and Turkish coastguards, providing intelligence to the latter returning migrants to Turkey. The US defense secretary, Ashton Carter, joined the head of NATO in cynically proclaiming the 'humanitarian' nature of this mission to address 'human trafficking'.[13]

Since Syriza became the government, Greece has also charged humanitarian workers with human trafficking and other offences for saving migrants, although the courts have pushed back against this.[14] It has recently been accused of systematic pushbacks at the Evros River, although here, too, a Greek prosecutor has begun an investigation.[15] It has also evicted autonomous solidarity groups, who had been the backbone of support to migrants and refugees up to that time from the 'hotspots' and camps in favour of registered NGOs.[16] And far from closing refugee and migrant camps, under the pressure of the border crisis, the government has increased the number of camps and the numbers of migrants in them, and their deplorable conditions have become the norm. All this has led one observer to comment that under Syriza there has been a return to the 'policies of the past right-wing governments who deployed border fences, detention centers, and the coast guard to push back some migrant boats in the Aegean'.[17]

Several factors can be broadly identified in accounting for these regressive steps. First is the double crisis of the economy and migration which made Greece, the 'laboratory of neoliberal shock therapy … also Europe's entrance gate for the millions of people leaving countries devastated by war and poverty'.[18] The crippling mandatory public sector cuts required by the EU left the Syriza government initially ill-placed to rapidly prepare for and respond to the dramatic increase of migrants in the 'long summer of migration' of 2015-16 when a million people, mostly from Syria, Afghanistan, and Iraq, landed primarily in the Greek islands of Lesvos, Chios, and Samos, seeking to transit on to Northern Europe. Second, it is no secret that the European Union pressured Greece on migration and the borders much as it did on the economy.[19] In addition to adding NATO to the 'deterrence' scheme, the infamous 'EU-Turkey' deal and the establishment of 'hotspot' reception centres on the Greek islands were fundamental to Europe's objectives and the Greek state accepted all of these. Why Syriza gave into Europe's pressure is murky, but the explanation seems to run parallel to the argument about Syriza's 'capitulation' to the memoranda. With respect to the border crisis, the EU threatened Syriza with removal from the Schengen zone if it did not take a leading role in the deterrence objective to 'save' the rest of Europe from the 'burden' of the refugees. Just as on the economic front, it was threatened with removal from the eurozone; this additional threat was issued 'precisely because Greece has been increasingly deemed incapable of fulfilling its role as a premier watchdog at the EU's border with Turkey.'[20] Yet as with the overall trajectory of the Syriza government, a third factor in Syriza's participation in the EU deterrence objective may have been its succumbing to the limits and contradictions of social democratic politics.

The Greek state under Syriza linked the two crises itself: without European assistance, due to the economic crisis, it could not adequately address the refugee 'crisis'. But it also used the unprecedented 'crisis' – with scenes of desperate migrants attempting to enter Northern Europe – as a negotiating chip with Europe.[21] As part of the 'most expensive humanitarian response in history', estimates of how much was sent to 'care' for and process the migrants in Greece and address the enormous demands of developing an adequate asylum system range from $800 million to 1.6 billion euros, while the actual figures of who received the money, and where it has gone, all remain matters of bitter dispute between the Greek government, on the one hand, and the EU and NGOs, on the other. Furthermore, Greece's top court has ordered a fraud investigation into the use of EU funds paid to Greece.[22] But no matter where the truth lies in these disputes, as one sympathetic Syriza insider on the islands emphasized, the party has treated the refugee camps and the enormous NGO presence in the crisis as bringing in money to the islands, thus stimulating an 'economy based on the pain of others'.[23]

The EU-Turkey deal is fundamental to the containment of migrants in the islands where that 'economy of pain' is borne by them. Presented by the European Commission in April 2015 as part of its 'European Agenda on Migration', the hotspot 'approach', according to a brief by the European Parliamentary Research Service, involves the establishment of 'first reception facilities – [that] aim to better coordinate EU agencies' and national authorities' efforts at external borders of the EU, on initial reception, identification, registration and fingerprinting of asylum-seekers and migrants.'[24] Hotspots illustrate how the European institutions, namely the European Asylum Support Office (EASO), Frontex, Europol, and others, combine to 'collaborate' with 'frontline' states. In the Greek case, this involves the return of migrants to Turkey, their containment in Greece as they wait for return, asylum in Greece, or acceptance by another European state. Controlling and fingerprinting any who seek asylum, hotspots are also aimed at 'safeguarding' the EU by providing biodata that can be used should they slip into Europe undocumented.[25]

With the closing of the border between Macedonia and Greece, the EU–Turkey deal announced on 18 March 2016 (with the Greek government well aware it was in the works) was designed to ensure that all new 'irregular migrants' who crossed from Turkey to Greece would be returned to Turkey.[26] While treating Turkey as a 'safe third country' and giving it, initially, six billion euros plus promises of visa-free travel to Europe the deal has, in fact, had the consequence of trapping around 15,000 on the Greek islands.[27] Thus was Greece transformed 'from a space of transit to a space of containment' with the hotspots and other camps holding many of the migrants.[28] According to the European Council, the EU-Turkey deal was meant to be a 'temporary and extraordinary measure' to put an end to 'human suffering' (caused by 'human trafficking') by breaking 'the business model of the smugglers and to offer migrants an alternative to putting their lives at risk' as well as to 'restore the public order'.[29] Of course, the dominant humanitarian justification here, too, is as ludicrous as it is transparent in its real aim of returning migrants to Turkey and 'deterring' future desperate migrants from getting close to Europe. The official camps and 'hotspots', too, function very differently. Although justified as humanitarian by the EU (and also the Greek state),[30] the hotspots have resulted in long-term stays and created 'some of the most appalling, mismanaged, and dangerous refugee camps in the world'.[31] Meanwhile, the islands themselves were also transformed into spaces of indefinite detention for, under the deal, migrants who arrived after 20 March 2016 are also denied the freedom to move from the islands until they are returned or receive status, if they do, except in 'exceptional cases' such as receiving a positive 'vulnerability' assessment.[32] The key point of this was – and is – to keep them from getting to the mainland where they might be able to travel to Europe undocumented, and to corral them for return to Turkey. All of this has made Greece 'a field of experimentation for European policies aimed at locking the borders and deterring migration'.[33]

A common argument among former and even current Syriza supporters is that Syriza accepted the EU-Turkey deal and hotspots because Tsipras wanted to move to the centre, to occupy a more social democratic space partly because some supporters had left the party for PASOK, others for the right wing. And this, more than one averred, was partly a consequence of its estrangement by that time from the solidarity movements.[34] The fact that the Syriza parliamentary group has been in coalition with a right-wing party, the Independent Greeks, may also be counted as a factor explaining its participation. The Greek Ministry of Defence plays a key role in overseeing the migrant camps and, after the election in 2015, Panos Kammenos of the Independent Greeks was made head of Defence by Syriza, a position with which he was reportedly 'rewarded' for supporting Syriza in the election.[35] Not only was he from a right-wing party, but during the bail out negotiations he also threatened to 'flood' Europe with migrants including 'some jihadists', evidence of his racist conception of migrants early on as both political pawns and harbouring dangerous elements.[36] Since then he has been the subject of an EU anti-fraud investigation involving funds for food for migrants in camps, and accused of funnelling contracts to friends with little evidence of upgrading the camps for which they were funded.[37] In any case, whatever the full balance of responsibility for its original imposition, Syriza has enforced, as Aspasia Velissariou has put it, 'the harsh model of regulation, control and segregation of refugee populations, the logic of which ironically reproduces precisely the biopolitics imposed on the Greeks by the EU austerity agenda'.[38]

'A WAREHOUSE OF SOULS'

In February 2016, Tsipras complained that the EU was leaving Greece to be 'a warehouse of souls'.[39] This is obvious in Greece in myriad ways, from migrant homelessness to the confinement of migrants in Greece and in the conditions of the camps. The degrading conditions of the migrant camps in Greece – state-run camps, hotspots, and NGO-run camps alike – are stark.[40] The former are notorious for treating asylum-seekers as abject, disposable life while the latter are marked by the infantilizing practices of treating 'vulnerable' others through the disempowering logic of humanitarianism.[41] The hotspots and other state-run camps and detention sites have been very widely criticized. For example, the Greek Council for Refugees maintains the camps on the islands are 'extremely alarming' and the conditions in the hotspots 'may reach the level of inhuman or degrading treatment in certain cases'.[42] In April 2018, the coordinator for the Greek office of Amnesty International reiterated what a myriad of NGOs and UN reports have also concluded about the conditions of detention and containment: 'This situation causes distress, violates people's rights, and insults the dignity of some of the world's most vulnerable people. It's an open wound for Greece and human rights.'[43] Of course, Amnesty should have included Europe in this evaluation as Médecins Sans Frontières has done. Criticizing the bitter fruit of the EU–Turkey deal three years on, MSF pointed to the fact that it has 'trapped thousands … in overcrowded, unsanitary, unsafe and degrading conditions with little access to basic health services, which has resulted in a deterioration of their health and well-being and caused widespread misery … Greece has become a dumping ground for the men, women and children that the European Union has failed to protect'.[44]

Consider the refugee camps on the islands. They not only suffer from right-wing racist attacks, but also from violence within the camps between different populations and factions of asylum seekers. Widespread sexual assault is so threatening that women only go to the restrooms at night in groups out of fear, or have resorted to adult diapers so they need not make the dangerous journey. Sewage spills into the flimsy tents of the overcrowded camps, which are also subject to extreme heat, cold, and flooding. Above all, there is the indignity of being treated *at best* as mere objects of humanitarian aid, amid the grinding purposelessness that comes with the long-term waiting and worrying, with little information forthcoming about what they are waiting for, what their future might entail.[45] These lives of abjection, these disposable lives, have resulted in hunger strikes, self-hangings, and self-immolations by asylum-seekers. That migrants are left to die not only in the Aegean (and the Mediterranean) but also in the camps is starkly borne out by the rampant mental health crises, avoidable illnesses, lack of physicians and psychologists, as well as the high rates of suicide and attempted suicide in them, the 'riots' and fights in the camps, hunger strikes and other means of resisting the relations of domination within them as well as of the larger asylum system and borders.[46]

The non-hotspot camps handed over to official NGOs (like Souda camp, on Chios, now closed, and Kara Tepe on Lesvos) are based on humanitarian conceptions of aid and they may be marginally better (more adequate) than the former, yet they remain debilitating. Functioning as part of what Zygmunt Baumann has called the state's contracted-out 'gardener' engaged in sifting migrants from refugees, and the officially 'vulnerable' from the rest, they, too, produce superfluousness, with the effect of depoliticizing asylum-seekers and migrants alike. The 'life of lines' led there is no life – 'time is suspended; it is time, but not history'.[47] Aid is given as charity and camps are run through 'technocratic management' with refugees treated as beholden beneficiaries rather than as equal subjects with consequently little regard for the actual subjective needs, desires, or agency of the migrants, and life, such as it is, is typically controlled in myriad, intricate ways. Material life can either deny or eliminate the conditions necessary for action, and kill transformative agency, or it can ignite it, and prompt us to begin something new. The camps of both types, of course, predominantly do the former.

One could multiply references to reports by human rights and lawyers organizations that detail the degrading and dehumanizing conditions in the camps both on the islands and the mainland.[48] But perhaps the domination and suffering in the camps is better illuminated with a story. On 30 March 2017, yet another asylum-seeker threatened suicide in the Vial hotspot on the island of Chios. This time it was through self-immolation. He was horribly burned while holding a flammable liquid and a source of flame when he was tackled by a security officer and, whether he intended it or not, he was set alight. Anyone who has seen the video of the immolation shared on Facebook will not doubt the reports that this 29-year-old Syrian was burned over 85 per cent of his body, nor that he died from his injuries some days later.[49] In response to that tragedy, which followed in the wake of other suicides in the camps, Wassim Omar, also an asylum-seeker fleeing war in Syria, posted an extremely moving poem on Facebook. (Wassim had left with his young family and, after braving people-smugglers demanding more money than agreed to and holding his young son hostage for yet more, he had the bad luck to finally arrive on Chios the day after the EU-Turkey deal went into effect, and subsequently led a thirty day hunger strike protesting the lack of information available to asylum-seekers regarding their status in the NGO-run Souda camp on Chios.) The poem, posted on March 30, 2017, deserves to be read, and re-read. It is a missive to the world:

> To be a killer or murderer, it isn't necessary to have a gun or bloodshed.
> To be a thief, it isn't necessary to steal or rob money or property.
> Killing has many faces and robbery has more, too.
> What you have been doing, is worse than what the war has done to us.
> When the EU opened its gates and borders to welcome refugees, it gave them hope, will, and life.
> If it hadn't done it, they would have been living with death and facing it too.
> After it opened its doors and borders, it helped poor people – refugees – to come back to life and will again.
> But because of this disastrous EU-Turkey deal, they lost their hope, will, and life again.
> The EU gave poor people – refugees – hope and then it stole it and took it away.
> So that was harder, harder than bullets from guns for these poor people, the refugees.
> March 20, 2016 was a black date and day in refugees' lives, it killed their hopes, ambitions, aspirations, goals, and humanity.
> We refugees are no longer treated as human, we are just numbers, politicos are playing with us like pieces on a chessboard.
> We are living a life as one who doesn't have a life.
> You politicos do not ever have the right to rob us of our life.
> Return to us what we have lost, our lost life here waiting on beaches.

The same day that Wassim posted this poem of grief, Greece's then Minister of Migration, Yiannis Mouzalas, also responded to the situation on Chios. A Syriza MP, Mouzalas underlined that 'the situation on Chios is exceeding its limits'. What did he suggest to address this? 'The establishment of a closed reception center for migrants is a condition for asylum to operate. We must reconsider the issue.' He thus backed away from Syriza's stated position against closed detention sites for asylum-seekers, and is reported to have added: 'We will undertake additional measures to prevent [the] abuse of asylum. We will restrict privileges for return to their home country. If they do not voluntarily request it [asylum] within five days of their arrival, they will not be entitled to request it.'[50] Adding insult to injury, Syriza put Mouzalas forward for 'Europe's top human rights job' in the Council of Europe not long after.[51]

One might wonder how Mouzalas thought the tragedy of self-harm, suicide, and violence in the camps undertaken by desperate asylum-seekers would be addressed by supporting more camps, and more *closed* camps. But addressing the conditions that drive migrants and asylum-seekers to desperate actions is clearly not what the purportedly socialist minister was aiming at. Rather, he sought to continue the conditions that Wassim so eloquently describes, the conditions that rob human beings fleeing war of their life, of their meaningful life. 'We are living a life as one who doesn't have a life.' There may be no more evocative description of what Giorgio Agamben calls 'bare life', mere biological existence, than this. Nor is there likely a better or more evocative description of what Michel Foucault called the state's just 'letting die' than Wassim's hard-won knowledge that there is more than one way to murder.[52] And that is precisely what a Syriza Minister, in the government of a party that claims to stand for democratic socialism, was proposing to do *more of*.

The recognition that, in government, Syriza has participated in this 'architecture of coercion' is sobering.[53] Having become embroiled in Fortress Europe's strategies of deterrence and containment, it left the camps in dehumanizing conditions. A Syriza MP, in late night bar-talk during the run-up to the May 2019 European elections, actually boasted about just how much better the island hotspots are in 2019 – making special reference to Moria – with not a word about the international condemnation of them, no explanation that decried a recalcitrant state apparatus to explain their conditions. They are, according to him, and ignoring all the other camps, actually a victory that Syriza can be proud of, as it has decreased the overcrowding in Moria. The latter is true; under the pressure of international and European criticism, Moria and some other camps on the islands have been, to a certain extent, decongested. But easing overcrowding in a handful of camps should hardly be considered a victory.[54] Camp conditions remain dire while containment drags on, refugees remain far too often uncertain of their future, and violence in the camps seems to increase.

The Syriza government was, as we have argued, in a difficult spot, threatened as it was by the EU to accept and implement the hotspots and the EU-Turkey deal and, thus, to be Europe's Manus Island.[55] But were there really no alternatives to participating in the extension of bare, meaningless life and creating camps that would merely 'let die'; to excluding solidarity groups from the camps in favour of official NGOs; or, to extending avoidably repressive actions including evicting some of the refugee squats, criminalizing aid to refugees, and so on? The argument here is that there were.

'WE, THE PEOPLE OF CITY PLAZA'[56]

City Plaza hotel illustrates the character of this alternative in day-to-day practice. We now turn to explore how its principles could have been the basis of a wider strategy had Syriza been willing to collaborate with the positive initiatives of those Greek and international 'solidarians' working side-by-side with refugees, even in the face of being forcibly evicted in police raids, threatened with eviction in lawsuits, arrested and prosecuted for their solidarity actions, or attacked by neo-fascist groups. On 15 April 2019, the director of the Moria hotspot, Greek army general Giannis Balbakakis, who was appointed director two years before, stated in response to international criticism of the camp, 'anyone who thinks they can do better than us is welcome to try'.[57] The irony is that there were much better alternatives right under the general's nose.

As Olga Lafazani, of the self-organized refugee-solidarian squat, City Plaza hotel in Athens, has rightly said, solidarity initiatives like this one show by their very existence that the state's use of camps is, in fact, a 'political choice' for, if solidarians and refugees can organize initiatives like City Plaza, so, too, could the state if it chose to do so.[58] If encampment is a dystopian experiment, refugee-solidarity housing initiatives like City Plaza are another kind of experiment – of a more utopian kind.

The solidarity movement in Greece goes back to even before the 'squares movement' emerged as a powerful force in the context of the Greek economic crisis.[59] This long history has provided much of the material and ideological basis and the networks the refugee solidarity movement draws upon. One of a number of refugee squats and broader refugee solidarity efforts in Greece,[60] City Plaza's occupation and establishment as a 'Refugee Accommodation and Solidarity Space' was particularly close to DIKTYO, a Network for Social and Political Rights that describes itself as 'part of the anti-capitalist, internationalist, and democratic Left', the associated Solidarity Initiative for Economic and Political Rights, the Solidarity Initiative for Economic and Political Refugees, and broader anti-racist initiatives.[61] Many of those involved in the movements were also Syriza members, although the movements remained autonomous of the party.

A seven-story hotel shuttered for seven years, City Plaza was occupied in April 2016 by one hundred refugees and one hundred and fifty solidarians shortly after the EU-Turkey deal went into effect.[62] The occupation was envisioned as an anti-racist and anti-capitalist challenge to the border regime, 'to the entrapment of tens of thousands of refugees', 'the mass detention of refugees in the border regions and the disastrous living conditions for homeless refugees in the cities and the huge, state-run camps'.[63] The squat did not spring up spontaneously. Rather, it had long been planned and prepared for through the anti-racist and solidarity networks. It was first proposed by the Solidarity Initiative for Economic and Political Refugees in September 2015. When the borders closed and the EU-Turkey deal was sealed in 2016, with migrants stuck in Greece, often in camps, decent housing became critically important, and the hotel was occupied following a month of intense meetings of solidarity activists. As 'solidarity groups were increasingly forbidden from entering the camps, and control over the volunteers was enforced, even in informal spaces such as the Port of Piraeus', the group decided it was crucial to have a space that could be both a 'housing project and hub of struggle'.[64] City Plaza was chosen, in part, because it is located in the heart of Athens and thus its presence claims the 'right of visibility' of refugees that is denied and repressed in far-flung camps and also because it is in a neighbourhood known to be home to right-wing and anti-migrant fascists including Golden Dawn who have a strong social base there.[65] It was conceived, as Lafazani has put it, as a

'radical answer', activating a multi-scale response to the re-establishment of borders. What we proposed – namely, co-habitation in dignified conditions in the heart of the city – went against the social and spatial exclusion of the camps. It was also a counter-attack against the illegalization of the antiracist movement by mustering an excess of solidarity and grassroots self-organization.[66]

Perhaps one-half of the original group of solidarians who squatted City Plaza were Syriza members, many of whom were deeply alienated by the 'capitulation' of the Syriza government to the EU memoranda, its participation in the Turkey-EU deal, and its position on the border regime and refugee camps more broadly.[67] In addition to the Greek solidarians and refugees who occupied the hotel, the initiative also depended on international solidarity efforts, in particular in Germany, from the beginning, especially for raising funds for City Plaza.[68] Because it refused state, EU, or NGO funding on principle, the financial support coming from international networks was crucial to City Plaza. In addition to providing dignified housing for refugees it was important to the project to cover the basic needs of the residents for food, medication, personal and baby items, cleaning supplies, and so on in order to provide for the residents' material security, especially after having lived in dehumanizing conditions of extreme insecurity for so long. It also collaborated with social pharmacies and relied to some extent on donations of food and, more generally, the network of solidarity initiatives present in Athens. A visit there, as virtually all of the press on City Plaza confirms, quickly revealed the fundamental differences between it and the camps.

Despite being oriented toward meeting the needs of refugees, City Plaza has consciously rejected the often degrading and infantalizing humanitarian model of assistance or charity in favor of one borne out of the solidarity movements. While accommodating up to 400 refugees at a time (and some solidarians and a few needy Greeks, plus one dog, for a time), it is run on the principles of horizontal 'self-organization and autonomy', anti-racism, radical democracy, equality, freedom, and inclusiveness. It is organized on the 'principle of unity' under the banner of 'We live together. We work together. We struggle together.'[69] Indeed, at City Plaza solidarians and refugees live, work, and struggle together in adequate and safe accommodations, with good and plentiful food, and decent bathroom facilities. Children play and go to school, residents have privacy, relative autonomy, and community; there are foreign language classes, women's groups, and groups meet together to discuss politics, create small fund-raising strategies, address issues of organization, and devise political campaigns.[70] The radical orientation of the squat is extended to the common tasks required of such a project; it depends on the residents' active participation in daily tasks. In these ways it rejects the bare life of the camps marked as they are not just by terrible material conditions and violence but also utter boredom and dejection. Life is worth living at City Plaza, even precarious life in transit or in waiting.

Drawing on the broader philosophy of the solidarity movement and in keeping with its commitment to radical democracy, City Plaza is deeply committed to the political inclusion of the refugee residents in decision-making in the squat. This is extended to determining the common tasks required of such a project. Collective decision-making ranges from the mundane, everyday, but crucial, decisions 'to determine who will serve and who will eat' (as Leonard Cohen once memorably put it), all the way to how to address conflicts in the squat. The squat is organized on the basis of general or 'house' assemblies which strive to make these decisions on the basis of consensus. For example, after a period of voluntary participation in housekeeping chores, and after complaints followed that some residents did not participate in them, the squat decided through the house assembly that adults in each room had to take up one agreed upon task each week.[71] Over time, it has struggled, as well, to address some of the pitfalls of the public consensus model of decision-making, particularly with regard to questions of sexual and domestic violence, matters that may threaten women if aired in complete publicity. It has also developed a system of smaller working groups to organize everyday tasks like the kitchen, reception, schooling, security, and the café.[72]

Of course, City Plaza cannot open its doors to everyone who needs accommodation and must, therefore, in a painfully ironic twist, select who may stay there. Doing so operates as an acknowledged factor of exclusion and it recognizes this as one of its most compelling problems. But, as a political project, City Plaza does not seek to house all in need but, rather, to be a specific challenge to state practices of encampment, what Lafazani calls a 'counter-example of coexistence'.[73] While it continually faces unmet needs for adequate housing, it refuses to make decisions about who may stay based on status or 'vulnerability'. Instead, a reception group of solidarians (including refugees) meets to decide who to admit by attempting to balance the needs of those hoping to be admitted and the needs of the squat.

The radically democratic model of living together that City Plaza has struggled to develop attempts to reclaim the rights that migrants have been deprived of (the rights to safety, 'right to visibility' and integration in the city). It demands rights (a right to decent accommodation, social rights, including rights of education, the right to freedom of movement, the right to remain, etc.) and it enacts rights by living 'as if' migrants had the rights they do not in reality have as a matter of state practice, and thus, in some sense, it produces rights.[74] It also contests private property rights as the primordial right against which all else must be measured by engaging in this formally illegal, ongoing act of disobedience.[75] In doing all of this, it furthermore demands and enacts a 'right to have rights' as Arendt put it – that is, a right to belong, to membership, and to a place where one's words and actions may actually have effect because one is treated as an equal.[76] As an appeal for support put out under City Plaza's name puts it:

> We do not, of course, believe that the problem can only be solved through squatting, as the provision of shelter is a fundamental obligation of the state and local authorities; we do, however, believe that squats can act not only as a means of claiming rights, but also as a factual exercising of rights precisely by those who are deprived of rights; the illegalized and excluded economical [sic] and political refugees.[77]

The squat enacts rights by struggling to practice equality and freedom in its everyday relations and tasks, and with the radically democratic organization of the space and community always being built there; it is as much a process as a place. The residents struggle to develop their political capacities to democratically organize their everyday lives. This seems especially remarkable given the highly gendered societies from which most of the asylum-seekers come, the differences of language, ethnicity, and long-standing ethnic and political enmities as well as new resentments about some being more privileged than others in the asylum system. In its organizational practices, City Plaza struggles to develop the capacities of both the migrants *and* the solidarians (who rather problematically in this context are usually considered to be the Greeks and internationals) to live otherwise, to think otherwise, and to struggle in common. In doing so, City Plaza tries to identify and meet needs in respectful, non-dominating ways, and consciously proceeds on the basis of the communist principle of 'to each according to his needs, from each according to his ability'.[78]

As the idea of being a 'hub of struggle' implies, the solidarians or 'commoners' of City Plaza have also been developing a 'culture of resistance' that goes beyond the space itself. Not only is it run democratically and autonomously of both state and official funding structures, but it has also become a key organizing point of and for the struggles of asylum-seekers and migrants in Athens and beyond. Migrants, Greek, and international solidarians organize protests, publicize them, develop creative alternative media campaigns, and the space functions as a social space in the heart of the city for political discussions about the 'refugee and migrant crisis'. Formulating challenges to borders and migration policies that presuppose nation-states premised on the relatively free movement of capital but not human beings, they are at the same time challenging nation-states to reflect on the meaning and implications of borders, demanding rights that include the right to free movement for all and a right of non-citizens to remain. In doing so they are contesting not just border regimes and camps but also, even more radically, who the 'we' is, whose democracy, whose anti-capitalism, whose socialism we are imagining and trying to develop. In these respects, it challenges settled conceptions of the 'worth of life' and contests freedom understood merely as 'the freedom to compete' by contesting the competition for residency, refugee-status, and citizenship but also all that lies at the core of neoliberal capitalism.[79]

We do not want to depict City Plaza as a perfect 'concrete utopia'.[80] There are contradictions and internal struggles, to be sure, as are recognized when Lafazani acknowledges it should not be considered an experiment undertaken in 'laboratory conditions'. She forthrightly recognizes that City Plaza, even apart from its own exclusions, is not devoid of troubles, of power differentials, inequality of statuses, or of hierarchies both between refugees and between refugees and solidarians. They recognize in a clear-eyed fashion that 'objectively we are not all equal'.[81] For example, that Greek solidarians speak the language and are far more familiar with the political and legal context; that they are connected to networks of solidarians in the city and beyond; that they are not haunted by questions of citizenship status or lack of it; and that they are far better placed to negotiate that context. Refugees also typically come from the camps where they have learned to be submissive, or only to ask for services rather than seek to participate in them; the solidarians must convince them to take an active part in the project. Furthermore, insofar as most of the refugees view their stay as temporary, it is, as Lafanzani acknowledges, a 'bit like building in sand'.[82] Lafazani also admits that, against their principled commitments, the local solidarians take 'primary responsibility for its functioning' and have a 'stronger influence' in the project. Despite, or rather, because of this honest recognition, it continues to relentlessly try to 'manufacture through a community of everyday life, a levelling process'. Indeed, City Plaza shows that it could be otherwise. By its very existence (and as is also the case with the existence of other, less famous, occupations and squats), it also contests private property as the primordial 'human right' and hegemonic claims that camps and 'hotspots' are the only viable means of 'accommodating' migrants and asylum-seekers.

Thus, migrant spaces of radical democracy like City Plaza seek to provide the conditions that contest this world of borders and camps, with their participation in 'global apartheid' and their fundamental violations of human dignity and human rights.[83] They challenge the Syriza government's realpolitik and the claim that it can't be otherwise. They do so in ways that may nurture agency while developing a left universalism and internationalism based on respect for (and a reinterpretation of) human rights and solidarity across the national and ethnic cleavages that are exacerbated by the system of asylum (and result in resentment and violence in the camps between national and ethnic groups). By producing a 'new imaginary and a practical alternative' filled with life, even life in waiting, and solidarity across differences and forms of inequality (across precariousness and precarity, as Squire puts it),[84] such prefigurative experiments in radical democracy also contest many of the conditions that provide the groundwork for the 'ugly dog whistle' for racist and right-wing reactions. As Lafazani has recognized, communities of struggle like City Plaza are:

> … initiatives and projects that take place with conditions of inequality, partitioning of rights, and antagonisms between the oppressed. This contradiction cannot be overcome voluntarily, just because we willed it to be so and invited others to join us. In other words, a belief does not exist in the existence of 'islands of freedom' within the wider relations of exploitation and domination, within the world of capital and the state.

The belief that does exist, however, is that between the cracks created by social struggles, moments of emancipation grow and come to light, the horizon of our possibilities expands, and we can catch glimpses of a society of freedom and equality.[85]

SHOWING IT COULD BE OTHERWISE

All of this raises two sorts of questions. First, if Syriza had maintained and further developed close ties with social solidarity networks in Greece, might it have been able to resist Europe's coercion on privileging deterrence, supporting the EU-Turkey deal, and accepting the hotspots; might the actually existing alternatives created by the solidarity networks have provided the basis on which it could have avoided the large-scale encampment across Greece in favour of alternatives? Or, even if it had not ejected solidarity actors from the camps in favour of NGOs, might a different model of encampment have developed, or at least been struggled for, within the camps themselves? Second, and less speculatively, if initiatives like City Plaza are not merely to function as 'islands of freedom', but for their prefigurative form of politics to expand the 'horizon of our possibilities', what sort of wider political relations, structures, and institutions are necessary? Or, as Christos Giovanopoulos, who was one of the national coordinators of the 'Solidarity for All' network, has put it: what would it take for such 'incubator[s] of self-management structures and transformative policies and politics' to 'scale up' politically?[86]

It is useful to explore more deeply what a prefigurative practice such as City Plaza involves and ask what is the source of its transformative potential. Prefiguration begins from a refusal to accept and to be complicit in reproducing the status quo. Through solidarity and collaboration which stimulate sparks of imagination and mutually reinforcing self-determination, this refusal leads on to experimentation with an alternative solution, an alternative way of living, surviving, and being social. So whether refugees in City Plaza or feminists who helped create centres for women facing domestic violence in the early 1970s (when the concept of 'prefigurative politics' started to be widely used), victims of oppression exert their agency through which they create, in a context of refusal and sometimes resistance, a solution to their oppression. This both gives them autonomy from the social relations of oppression and develops a capacity to continue on a daily basis to sustain an alternative. And when alternatives are based on emancipatory values, their action can inspire both support and emulation from others. Prefigurative practices embody both material power enabling a group to be resilient and gain a degree of self-determination (albeit precarious and limited) and a symbolic political power that breaks with the dominant ideology. This is the basis on which we can assert that the balance of power can be shifted through concrete prefigurative practices rather than through humanitarian appeals.

Giovanopoulos argues rightly that the famous Solidarity for All network of health, housing, and food groups that addressed the problems of everyday life imposed by EU austerity:

> … could have been a means to solidify the political will and perspective of the people. It could have also produced its material backing, had Syriza, as opposition and government, taken it seriously since 2012. Even in the case of being forced into a deal [with the EU], this movement could have provided Syriza with a wider margin to negotiate and move … [as a] generator of policies designed on the basis of its practices through the deepening of democratic processes and popular participation.[87]

This relates closely to the two distinct kinds of power that need to be mobilised as a condition for systemic change.[88] On the one hand, power as transformative capacity building that City Plaza and other such solidarity groups practice; and on the other, power as domination, including power over the state. The latter has been the traditional instrument by which the left has sought to achieve social justice, 'delivering it to the people' through the party's domination over state spending legislation. Power as domination can be, under certain conditions, a resource for power as transformative capacity – change through self-organisation 'by the people' or 'with the people'. Many movement initiatives to refuse and then to transform oppressive social relations, while being able to change relations that previously depended on their complicity, face institutional, structural, and material constraints over which they have no power. In these circumstances, they conclude that for their transformative power to be sustained and contribute to wider systemic change, they need to gain control over the resources of the state: public funding through a redistributive taxation system; legislative action to restrain and contain the power of private and corporate capital and create public and social spaces in which civic driven alternatives can thrive.

This distinction between power as transformative capacity and power as domination, and the recognition of the necessity of both for any successful project of social and political change, challenges the political party's long-standing monopoly over progressive social change. It implies a party working for social justice which recognises explicitly and self-consciously that to achieve its goal, it has to share power with other social actors of a different kind, autonomous from its control and patronage. City Plaza provides an example of how the two kinds of power could have been combined but were not. City Plaza activists identified four large buildings in Athens that could have provided 200 apartments for refugees and migrants, and suggested to Syriza that it should take over these buildings and make them available for refugees on a similar basis as City Plaza. Lafazani tells what happened:

> Syriza said 'yes, yes, for sure we will do it. Thank you for the proposals.' When approached again three months later they said, 'Yes we want to do it, but there was a small bureaucratic problem, in three months it will be done.' After three more months: 'yes we want to but we could not solve the bureaucratic issue. We are working on it.' And they don't do anything. They never say no. They say 'yes we are with the anti-racist movement. We are with workers' rights. We are a left government.' But they always have an excuse.[89]

Behind the excuses, though, is a deeper problem: the presumption that they, the party, are the only actors that really matter. Movements, solidarity initiatives, and radical campaigns are auxiliary to the party; at best a source of support. Syriza is not alone in this congenital inability to share power and recognize that legislative office is not the only kind of power involved in achieving fundamental social and political transformation. Syriza was one of several parties (others included Rifondazione Communista in Italy, Podemos in Spain, Bloco Esquerda in Portugal) which, in the early twenty-first century, claimed to break from the twentieth-century Social Democratic and Eurocommunist left, both in their initial declarations of opposition to the pressures of the corporate-driven global market and the imperatives of US imperialism, and in their efforts to be 'the electoral voice' of social movements and to open up their organisation to movement activists and leaders. They made strong claims to be the party of the social movements, especially the anti-capitalist, alter-globalisation movement that grew up at the turn of the century against the corporate-driven market, and the threats it posed to democracy, workers' rights, human rights more generally, and the planet. While many movement activists did indeed join or support these parties hoping that they would in practice support the movements, in reality, the party leaderships understood the political potential of social movements as sources of electoral and cultural support in the service of their overriding priority of electoral success. There was little or no recognition of these movements and their associated prefigurative practices as being a distinct source of power. The result was that in practice, in the absence of alliances that provided material counter-power, these parties tended to make many of the same compromises as the traditional Social Democratic left and, in the process, severely undermined themselves.

Andreas Karitzis, an ex-member of Syriza's leadership, has argued that once in power, Syriza viewed itself and acted as the 'active factor that made decisions and political choices, while the movements could simply express their support ... an essentially extrinsic relationship that limits the potential for integrating them into the social and political struggle on terms in which they can substantively participate'. What is needed instead, Karitzis insists, 'is a substantive change in the traditional imaginaries and patterns of relations between movements, forces in government, and the state'.[90] The experience of City Plaza gives practical relevance to Karitzis' argument for the 'need to go beyond electoral politics, not against it'.[91] It illustrates what could have been – a micro-illustration of an alternative response to the 'border crisis' – and points to the importance of other prefigurative practices too often treated with indifference (if not contempt) by the Syriza leadership. Similarly, the union of water workers in Thessaloniki were working with local citizens and sympathetic experts – through 'SOS Nero' – to develop plans for improving the public efficiency of a public utility. They assumed they would get support from Syriza, not only to bring water fully under public ownership, but also to support the nominee of the campaign against privatization, for general manager. As in Lafazani's account of trying to get Syriza to support other refugees' centres, they got many 'Yeses' but in practice a constant 'No'. The alternative proposal for improving the public water service would have given Syriza a stronger basis to refuse the Troika's privatization plan, countering widespread criticisms of state companies as corrupt and inefficient, and backed by the political mobilisation against privatization in such a major region as Thessaloniki.

These experiences have resulted in a deep alienation from Syriza, but an experience like City Plaza, or the radical campaign to defend and improve public water, even if defeated or finally unsustainable, leaves all those involved in no doubt that such activity is political. And this is true in all those countries where parties of the radical left attracted many idealistic young people determined to create political change rather than just talk about it. Large numbers of such activists are in different ways deepening their knowledge and practice of prefigurative forms of organisation, whether it is theories and experiments in the commons, including the digital commons, new communications and cultural infrastructures, international anti-racist, pro-migrant networks in the face of the rise of the right across Europe, or the new kind of trade union organisation reaching out to precarious workers, left unsupported by many of the traditional trade unions organizations. They are in effect creating a new landscape of radical politics, spreading, and perhaps systematizing, power as transformative capacity so that it has an infrastructure and support system rather than being simply an occasional shining example that is no match for the overwhelming powers of the state and ruling class.

To gauge the destructive strength of the gravitational pull of the existing political system, it is salutary to remind ourselves that Syriza, as an alliance of radical left organisations like other parties of the European left, was initially oriented to break free of the logics of this system. And yet they could not. They were sucked into its gravitational vortex, with all their movementist culture and participatory organisation shattered. The turn of social democratic parties to an increasingly anti-immigrant stance today (justified as 'realistic') is aimed, hopelessly, at pulling voters away from hard-right parties at the expense of migrants and human rights. Coupled with the ominous threat of splits in radical left-wing parties like Die Linke over immigration, this speaks directly to the failures so far to build left political party solidarity between resentful national voters who bear the brunt of neoliberalism, and fearful and oppressed migrants.[92] This speaks all the more to the lesson we need to draw from the Greek experience with Syriza, on the one hand, and City Plaza, on the other. No political organisation of a genuinely different kind, one able to resist the destructive, self-serving capacities of power as domination, can be built exclusively within the political sphere itself. It has to have its live roots nourished and stabilised by a strong infrastructure of power as transformative capacity. The experience of three years of City Plaza demonstrates that the capacity is there. The problem that we face now, when every space for democratic self-organization has to be fought for, is how to continue building the infrastructure which will allow that transformative capacity to flourish and have the impact on the political sphere that is so greatly needed today.

CODA

In the 8 July 2019 election, Syriza was defeated by New Democracy. The City Plaza hotel occupation ended two days later. Although Syriza's share of the vote did not collapse to the extent predicted, its 31.5 per cent of the vote was almost 5 per cent less than in the election of September 2015 when it won 36.2. Notably, abstentions reached 44 per cent, a record high since the 1974 elections held immediately after the end of the dictatorship, yet before fully, formally, democratic politics had been established. Indications are that many young people abstained. The defeat was thus a serious setback but not a collapse, and there is little sign, at the time of writing, of a radical rethink among the Syriza leadership that would reverse its repositioning as a social democratic party. Another very significant feature of the election was the reconfiguration of the right. The openly fascist Golden Dawn failed to win enough votes to pass the three per cent threshold for seats in the parliament, but many of its themes have now become part of the platform of New Democracy, whose election campaign was based on an explicit appeal to win support from voters from the far right; with attacks on every minority, a contempt for anyone in need, and a prioritization of security over human rights, with migrants defined as the major security problem. The ruthless dismissal of human rights in their campaign propaganda proved to be an election winner. No time was lost before turning this into a brutal reality. Ten days after the election, a presidential decree merged the Ministry of Migration policy with the Security Ministry into the new Ministry of Citizen Protection. As the Hellenic League for Human Rights reports, 'the design and implementation of national immigration policy by this ministry symbolizes its treatment as a matter of security and public order'.[93] In fact, the new minister's first meeting, after promising 'better border control and migration management', was with officials of the Greek Police. He then toured Moria camp, with its barbed-wire entrance festooned with flowers, and lauded 'the comprehensive management of the refugee problem by the country's services here on the island'.[94]

In light of New Democracy's other campaign promises to restore law and order by confronting 'anarchists' in Athens, it was perhaps not surprising that one of the first reactions by solidarity initiatives to its election was the closure of City Plaza. Yet, as the project's closing statement indicates, in May 2018, more than a year prior to the election, City Plaza's solidarians had in fact made the difficult decision that the occupation would come to an end after all the resident refugees found decent alternative accommodation or were able to leave otherwise. At that time it was already 'decided that, despite it being a difficult choice, City Plaza should rightly close the way it began and operated: as a political project, by protecting the central element which turned it into a[n] example, that is organisation from below, safe and dignified living, community of struggle, and addressed to society as a whole.'[95]

New Democracy's victory was, therefore, not the reason for the closure though it definitely hastened its pace. City Plaza's closing statement identifies the exhaustion of energies and the depletion of resources as the underlying reasons for making the decision in 2018. In this difficult context it faced the agonizing decision of whether to 'legalize/normalize' the squat, effectively turning it into an NGO-run and government-directed organization, or to close. The first option would fundamentally contradict its status as an autonomous political project of cohabitation and radical democracy. And so, in keeping with its commitments, it decided to close down on its own terms, with closure itself a political choice – 'to begin and end as a squat'. The moment of closure, like all such choices, though, was taken under conditions not of its choosing: in the context of two ongoing eviction orders and New Democracy regularly denouncing its illegality – its 'destruction of private property and 'lawlessness'. It appears that eviction was imminent. The City Plaza statement, again, points to the difficult decision of whether to 'heroically' wait for this moment to come, but in keeping with its commitment to refugees and migrants, it recognized that that would be a far more threatening event for those without legal status than for its Greek solidarians, and that eviction would be a negative precedent rather than the memory it sought to bestow.[96] Very honestly, too, it identified the squat's end as:

> linked to the wider movement's inability to develop effective forms of organization, mobilization, and discourse on the refugee questions, which match the demands of the time. It is true that many parts of the wider social movement decided on different degrees of involvement, being unable to support the project and/or develop similar ones, which would [have] galvanise[d] our efforts through a new dynamic. This position is not apportioning blame, but highlights the project as part of a wider social and political process, reflecting the ideological-political and organisational crisis within the movement, with which we will have to deal in the next phase.[97]

As this clearly recognizes, it is not only left political parties like Syriza which need fundamentally to rethink their purpose and organization but also the social movements themselves in order to develop their transformative capacities through renewed efforts of solidarity across struggles. Room for optimism in this regard can be taken from City Plaza's closing statement: 'We say goodbye to *Spiti* (home) Plaza with one promise: to transfer this rich experience, to continue to enrich and broaden the ways and the places of common struggle.'

NOTES

We would like to thank Wassim Omar for his poem, and Olga Lafazani, Christos Giovanopoulos, Michalis Spourdalikis, Aris Spourdalakis, and several anonymous interviewees for discussions in the preparation of this essay.

1   Hannah Arendt, *The Origins of Totalitarianism*, New Edition with Added Prefaces, New York: Harcourt, 1968 [1951]. The quotes here are at pp. 296, 302, 292, 279, and 269.

2   UNHCR, 'Figures at a Glance', 19 June 2019, available at: www.unhcr.org.

3   Amnesty International, 'The World's Refugees in Numbers', 2019, available at: www. amnesty.org. This does not include the over 5 million Palestinian refugees recognized by UNRWA.

4   Benjamin Dodman, 'Greece's Tale of Two Crises', *France 24*, ND, available at: webdoc.france24.com/greece-migrants-refugees-crisis-austerity-lesbos. What to make of this given Galinos was an MP for New Democracy before leaving it to found the Independent Greeks in 2012 is unclear. But the sentiment is widely expressed by solidarity groups, as well.

5   Anna Carastathis, Aila Spathopoulou, and Myrto Tsilimpounidi, 'Crisis, What Crisis? Immigrants, Refugees, and Invisible Struggles', *Refuge*, 34(2), 2018, p. 30.

6   Aris-George-Baldur Spourdalakis, Dionysia Pitsili-Chatzi, Leo Panitch, Hilary Wainwright, and Jodi Dean, 'New Democracy Against Democracy', *Jacobin,* 16 January 2019. Also see '#RefugeesGr #Athens: 3 Years #City Plaza', 25 April 2019, available at: enoughisenough14.org/2019/04/25/refugeesgr-athens-three-years-cityplaza.

7   Refugee Accommodation and Solidarity Space City Plaza, 'Three Years #City Plaza,' Facebook, 23 April 2019.

8   On prefigurative politics see, for example, Athina Arampatzi, 'Constructing Solidarity as Resistive and Creative Agency in Austerity Greece', *Comparative European Politics*, 16(1) 2018, pp. 50-66; on viewing City Plaza as commoning, see Charalampos Tsavdaroglou, 'The Newcomers' Right to the Common Space: The Case of Athens During the Refugee Crisis', *ACME: An International Journal for Critical Geographies*, 17(2) 2018, pp. 376-401.

9   Daniel Howden, 'Greece: Between Deterrence and Integration', *News Deeply,* May 2017, available at: newsdeeply.com; and Patrick Strickland, 'Greeks Protest Government Crackdown Refugee Squats', *Al Jazeera*, 23 June 2017.

10   Niki Kitsantonis,'Greece Saves 240 as Boat with Migrants Capsizes', *New York Times*, 28 October 2016. Frontex was also involved in the rescue. Even Theodoros Karyotis, a left critic of Syriza, credits Syriza with rescuing migrants from the sea early on. 'Greece Criminalizing Solidarity: Syriza's War on the Movements', *ROAR Magazine*, 31 July 2016.

11   Sandro Mezzadra, 'In the Wake of the Greek Spring and the Summer of Migration', *South Atlantic Quarterly*, 117(3) 2018, p. 927.

12   See Amnesty International, 'Trapped in Greece: An Avoidable Refugee Crisis', 2016, available at www.amnesty.org.

13   'Migrant Crisis: NATO Deploys Aegean People-Smuggling Patrols', *BBC*, 11 February 2016; and Adam Withnall, 'NATO Orders Fleet to Deploy in Aegean Sea "to Help End Europe's Refugee Crisis"', *The Independent*, 11 February 2016. On initial contradictory statements about whether NATO would be directly involved in pushbacks, see Ewen

MacAskill and Emma Graham-Harrison, 'NATO launches naval patrols to return migrants to Turkey', *The Guardian*, 11 February 2016. On Turkish coastguard returns, see Lisa Gross, 'Disobedient Border Crossings', *Harekact*, 30 July 2018, available at: harekact.bordermonitoring.eu.

14   See, for example, Niki Kitsantonis, 'Volunteers Who Rescued Migrants are Cleared of Criminal Charges in Greece', *New York Times*, 7 May 2018; Piper French, 'Rescue a Refugee: Get Charged with Trafficking?' *The New Republic*, 5 March 2019; and Sarah Hucal, 'Sister of Olympic Swimmer and Syrian Refugee Facing 25 Years in Greek Prison for Volunteering to Help Migrants', *ABC News,* 5 December 2018.

15   Lizan Nijkrake, 'Greek Prosecutor Investigating Allegations of "Systematic" Violence Against Migrants at Evros River', *CBC*, 6 March 2019.

16   'A key concern of the Ministry of Migration policy was the removal from refugee camps and the hotspots of all volunteers and organizations whose presence was considered an obstacle to the implementation of detention, restriction of movement, and deportations to Turkey. Therefore, a strict process of registration of "recognized NGOs" was implemented, excluding all independent volunteers and antiracist groups from the field.' Giorgos Maniatis, 'From a Crisis of Management to Humanitarian Crisis Management', *South Atlantic Quarterly*, 117(3), 2018, p. 908. Also see Leonidas Oikonomakis, 'Solidarity in Transition: The Case of Greece', in Donatella della Porta, ed., *Solidarity Mobilizations in the 'Refugee Crisis: Contentious Moves'*, Cham, Switzerland: Palgrave Macmillan, 2018, pp. 65-98; and Marienna Pope-Weidemann, 'Refugee Crisis: The EU Cracks Down on Volunteers', *Red Pepper*, 17 March 2016.

17   Howden, 'Greece: Between Deterrence and Integration'.

18   Mania Barsefski and Thanassis Kourkoulas interviewed by Stathis Kouvalakis, 'Europe's Border Guards', *Jacobin*, 2 May 2016.

19   See, for example, Gabriela Baczynska and Tom Korkemeier, 'Greece Threatened with Expulsion from Schengen over Migration Crisis', *Reuters*, 25 January 2016.

20   Carastathis, et al, 'Crisis, What Crisis?', pp. 33-4. Also see Baczynska and Korkemeier, 'Greece Threatened with Expulsion'; and Katharyne Mitchell and Matthew Sparke who maintain the EU 'dictated' the hotspot approach to Greece. 'Hotspot Geopolitics versus Geosocial Solidarity: Contending Constructions of Safe Space for Migrants in Europe', *Environment and Planning D: Society and Space,* online first, 2018, p. 8.

21   On the border, see Helena Smith, 'Macedonia forcibly returns thousands of migrants to Greece', *The Guardian,* 15 March 2016. On using refugees as bargaining chips, see Oikonomakis, 'Solidarity in Transition'.

22   The first cited figures are from Daniel Howden and Apostolis Fotiadis, 'Where did the money go? How Greece humbled the refugee crisis', *The Guardian*, 9 March 2017. The second figure is a quote by Dimitris Avramopoulos, European Commissioner for Migration, cited in Pavlos Zafiropoulos, 'EU's Mishandled Millions Not Reaching Refugees', *Deutsche Welle*, 25 January 2017. Also see Jennifer Rankin and Helena Smith, 'Immigrants in Greece face winter crisis after public sector cuts', *The Guardian*, 27 November 2018. While figures differ, perhaps due to the complexity and overlapping bureaucracies involved but also perhaps due to the numbers games that Europe and Greece play, it was reported in 2017 that the 'Greek migration officials have had access to one of the largest money pots administered by the European Commission'. Howden and Fotiadis, 'Where did the money go?'. Also see John Psaropoulos, 'Greek official

blows the whistle on refugee costs', *Al Jazeera*, 15 October 2018.

23   Anonymous, authors' interview, May 2019, echoing Karyotis who, early on, criticized 'the creation of lucrative new markets out of human misery' in relation to the reliance on NGOs in the Greek border crisis. See also 'Greece Criminalizing Solidarity', *ROAR Magazine*.

24   European Parliamentary Research Service, 'Hotspots at EU External Borders: State of Play', June 2018, available at: www.europarl.europa.eu.

25   By February 2016, Greece was pressured to quickly construct its five hotspots (in Lesvos, Chios, Samos, Leros, and Kos). See Carastathis, et al., 'Crisis, What Crisis?' p. 34.

26   Howden and Fotiadis, 'Where did the money go?'. Taking all of Greece into account, the Greek Minister of Migration, Dimitris Vitsas, claimed over 70,000 migrants in Greece in early 2019. Nick Kampouros, 'Number of Migrants Rises in Greece as EU Fails in Relocation Efforts', *Greek Reporter,* 12 March 2019, available at: greece. greekreporter.com.

27   Tania Karas, '"Warehouse of Souls": How the EU Abandoned Greece', *World Policy Journal*, XXXIII, 4, 2016/2017, pp. 55-60. This chapter does not address the important question of treating Turkey as a 'safe third country' or the fate of migrants returned to Turkey. For one report, see Deportation Monitoring Aegean, 'Surrendered to Harmandali Removal Prison – How EU Policies Lead to Expulsion and Maltreatment of Migrants Deported to Turkey', 4 June 2019, available at: dm-aegean.bordermonitoring. eu.

28   Martina Tazzioli, 'Containment through Mobility: Migrants' Spatial Disobediences and the Reshaping of Control through the Hotspot System', *Journal of Ethnic and Migration Studies*, 44(16), 2018, p. 2769.

29   European Council, 'EU-Turkey Statement: 18 March 2016'.

30   Mitchell and Sparke, 'Hotspot Geopolitics versus Geosocial Solidarity'.

31   Greek Council for Refugees, 'Limits of Indignation: The EU-Turkey Statement and its Implementation in the Samos "Hotspot"', 10 April 2019, p.16 (www.gcr.gr/media/ k2/attachments/Report_Samos.pdf), quoting Bill Frelick, of Human Rights Watch, 'Déjà vu on the Greek-Turkey Border', 20 December 2018, available at: www.hrw. org.

32   Howden, 'Greece: Between Deterrence and Integration'.

33   Projet Babels, 'De Lesbos a Calais: Comment l'Europe Fabrique des Camps', Neuvy-en-Champagne, 15, 2017, quoted in Stathis Kouvalakis, 'Borderland: Greece and the EU's Southern Question', *New Left Review*, 110(Mar/April), 2018, p. 18.

34   Anonymous authors' interviews and discussions in Greece.

35   Howden and Fotiadis, 'Where did the money go?'

36   Bruno Waterfield, 'Greece's Defence Minister Threatens to Send Migrants Including Jihadists to Western Europe', *The Telegraph*, 9 March 2015. https://www.telegraph. co.uk/news/worldnews/islamic-state/11459675/Greeces-defence-minister-threatens-to-send-migrants-including-jihadists-to-Western-Europe.html

37   Jennifer Rankin and Helena Smith, 'Immigrants in Greece face winter crisis after public sector cuts', *The Guardian*, 27 November 2018; and 'Refugee Found Dead in Lesbos Camp, Protests over Living Conditions', *The National Herald*, 8 January 2019.

38   Aspasia Velissariou, 'Refugees in Greece: The Greeks as 'Refugees', *Global Discourse*, 8(2), 2018, p. 283.

39   Tsipras describing Greece in the 'migration crisis,' quoted in McVeigh and Smith, 'Double crisis deepens despair in Greece's "warehouse of souls"', *The Guardian*, 27 February 2016.

40   Patrick Kingsley reports, 'the conditions [in Moria] have fueled accusations that the camp has been left to fester in order to deter migration and that European Union funds provided to help Greece deal with asylum seekers are being misused.' '"Better to Drown": A Greek Refugee Camp's Epidemic of Misery', *New York Times,* 2 October 2018.

41   See Vicki Squire, 'Mobile Solidarities and Precariousness at City Plaza: Beyond Vulnerable and Disposable Lives', *Studies in Social Justice*, 12(1), 2018, pp. 111-132. For a classic critique of humanitarianism, see Didier Fassin, *Humanitarian Reason: A Moral History of the Present,* Berkeley: University of California Press, 2012.

42   Greek Council for Refugees, 'Conditions in Reception Facilities', 2019, available at: www.asylumineurope.org. Also see Greek Council for Refugees, 'Limits of Indignation', which describes (p. 6) the overflow area of the Samos hotspot as 'a habitat for insects, rodents, and various other types of wildlife (e.g. snakes and scorpions). It has no access to running or clean water – an issue also occasionally encountered in the facility itself – no access to electricity and lighting, and no protection from the weather.'

43   Derek Gatopoulos, 'Lesbos: Europe's Migrant Barrier Nears Breaking Point', *AP*, 11 May 2018.

44   Médecins Sans Frontières, 'Turkey-EU Deal Continues Cycle of Containment and Despair', 18 March 2019.

45   See: Patrick Strickland, 'Refugees in Greece feel like prisoners and hostages', *Al Jazeera*, 3 October 2017. Daniel Boffey and Helene Smith, 'Oxfam condemns EU over "inhumane" Lesvos refugee camp', *The Guardian*, 9 January 2019; Janice Dickson speaking of Moria camp, 'Refugee Women Live in Fear, Avoiding Washrooms Because of Sexual Harassment', *CTV News*, 15 October 2018; Human Rights Watch, 'Greece: Dire Conditions for Asylum Seekers on Lesbos', 21 November 2018. These conditions were witnessed or reported to one of the authors of this paper in 2016 and again in 2019. In 2019, the smell of sewage in the 'overflow' area of Moria camp was overpowering. Interviewees, both Greeks and migrants, often deplored the violence in the camps, sexual assaults, squalid conditions, and the more recent rise, they say, of prostitution and drugs organized by 'gangs'.

46   'In an open letter published on MSF's website in September, Dr. Alessandro Barberio, a psychiatrist working at the MSF Lesbos Project, wrote: "In all of my years of medical practice, I have never witnessed such overwhelming numbers of people suffering from serious mental health conditions, as I am witnessing now amongst refugees on the island of Lesbos. The vast majority of people I see are presenting with psychotic symptoms, suicidal thoughts – even attempts at suicide – and are confused. Many are unable to meet or perform even their most basic everyday functions, such as sleeping, eating well, maintaining personal hygiene, and communicating."' Quoted in: John Vassilopoulos, 'Brutal Conditions at Greek Refugee Camps Condemned', *World Socialist Website*, 9 October 2018. Also see Lizzie Dearden, 'Child Refugees Attempting Suicide Amid Increasing Desperation Among Thousands of Trapped Migrants in Greece', *The Independent*, 16 March 2017.

47   Respectively, see Zygmunt Bauman on the 'gardening' state' in *Modernity and the Holocaust*, Cambridge: Polity, 1989, p. 12; and Claudio Minca, 'Geographies of the

Camp', *Political Geography*, 49, 2015, p. 76. On 'technocratic management', see Maniatis, 'From a Crisis of Management to Humanitarian Crisis Management', p. 911. On the 'life of lines', see Patrick Kingsley, '"Better to Drown". According to Oxfam, in Moria camp on Lesvos, asylum seekers line up for 3 hours to get food: Oxfam Media Report, 'Vulnerable and Abandoned', 9 January 2019. The Greek Council of Refugees echoes this in Vathy, on Samos, as well, in 'Limits of Indignation'. On time but not history, see Zygmunt Bauman, 'In the Lowly Nowherevilles of Liquid Modernity', *Ethnography*, 33(3), 2002, p. 345.

48 See as just one recent example: 'The Case of Oinofyta: From One Hell to Another', *Medium*, 2 January 2019. For a compelling video, see Valérie Gauriat and Apostolos Staikos, 'Migrants and Greeks in Samos Share Anger and Despair', *Euronews*, 14 May 2019, available at: www.euronews.com.

49 Teo Kermeliotis, 'Chios: Syrian refugee critical after "self-immolation"', *Al Jazeera*, 30 March 2017. Also see Wesley Dockery and Naser Ahmadi, 'Doctors without Borders: Children Attempting Suicide at Greece's Moria Camp', *Info Migrants*, 31 August 2018, available at: www.infomigrants.net.

50 A. Makris, 'Closed Reception Centers will Reinforce Asylum Procedures, Says Migration Policy Min. Mouzalas,' *Greek Reporter*, 31 March 2017, available at: greece. greekreporter.com. He is reported to have acknowledged just two months prior, in January 2017, that 'the situation in the hot spots is very bad' and that 'conditions on the islands are awful'. Scenes of flimsy tents in snow and cold weather on the islands, prompted a spokeswoman for the European Commission to admit that 'the situation is untenable'. But she quickly added, 'ensuring adequate reception conditions in Greece is a responsibility of Greek authorities'. Helene Smith, 'Greece: severe weather places refugees at risk and government under fire,' *The Guardian*, 10 January 2017.

51 Kostis Papaioannou and Vassilis Papadopoulos, 'Europe's top human rights job deserves better', *The Guardian*, 3 November 2017.

52 Giorgio Agamben, *Homo Sacer: Sovereign Power and Bare Life*, Stanford: Stanford University Press, 1998; Michel Foucault, *'Society Must be Defended': Lectures at the College de France 1975-1976*, trans. David Macey, New York: Picador, 1997, pp. 249-63.

53 Vicki Squire, 'City Plaza: A Way Forward for the European "Migration Crisis"?' *Open Democracy*, 14 June 2016, available at: www.opendemocracy.net.

54 Moria went from an estimated 9000 in late 2018 to a reported 5000 in early 2019, yet its capacity is 3100.

55 See Baczynska and Körkemeier, 'Greece Threatened with Expulsion'; Ian Traynor, 'EU migration crisis: Greece threatened with Schengen Area expulsion', *The Guardian*, 25 January 2016; and Amnesty International, 'European Leaders Must End the Humanitarian and Human Rights Crisis at Europe's Borders', 14 March 2019.

56 'Three Years #City Plaza'.

57 See Claire Paccalin, '"Anyone who thinks they can do better than us is welcome to try," Says Director of Moria Camp on Lesbos', *Info Migrants*, 15 April 2019.

58 Olga Lafazani, '1.5 Years City Plaza: A Project on the Antipodes of Bordering and Control Policies', AntipodeFoundation.org, 13 November 2017; also see Maria Margaronis, Chloe Hadjimatheou (producer), BBC Sounds Documentary, 'Greece's Haven Hotel', *BBC News*, 5 April 2018.

59   In particular, the anti-racist movement. Authors' interview with Lafazani. For one account see, Costas Douzinas, *Philosophy and Resistance in the Crisis*, Cambridge: Polity, 2013.

60   Of the other estimated twelve refugee squats in Athens, Notara26 (which describes itself as the 'first housing squat for refugees and migrants' claims that, by July 2017, 6000 refugees/migrants had passed through it), alongside 5th School Squat and Onioro, may be counted among the longest lasting and successful. Of the many broader refugee solidarity initiatives one might name the 'No Border Kitchen' (Lesvos), Solidarity Farms (associated with 5th School Squat), and PIKPA, on Lesvos (which became a registered NGO in 2016). On the latter, see: lesvossolidarity.org/en/who-we-are/history. On Notara26, see 'Greece's First Housing Squat for Refugees and Migrants', *Unicorn Riot*, available at: unicornriot.ninja/2018/greeces-first-housing-squat-for-refugees-migrants-notara-26. On Oniro, see Qusay Loubani, 'Small, Illegal Refugee Paradise', *Open Democracy*, 13 October 2016. On squats in Thessoloniki: Sophie Dicker, 'Solidarity in the City: Platforms for Refugee Self-Support in Thessoloniki', in *Making Lives: Refugee Self-Reliance and Humanitarian Action in Cities*, eds. Juliano Fiori and Andrea Rigon, London: Humanitarian Affairs Team: Save the Children, 2017, p. 73.

61   Mara Scampoli and Mattia Alunni Cardinali, '"Welcome to Greece" – DIKTYO, a Network for Political and Social Rights', *Melting Pot Europa*, 23 October 2017, available at: www.meltingpot.org; and Lafazani, '1.5 Years City Plaza'.

62   Lafazani, '1.5 Years City Plaza'; and 'Three Years at #City Plaza'. The distinction between 'solidarians' and refugees or migrants is highly problematic, of course, but we follow the language of the movement here.

63   'Support the City Plaza Refugee Accommodation and Solidarity Center in Athens, Greece', 13 June, 2016, available at: solidarity2refugees.gr/support-city-plaza-refugee-accommodation-solidarity-center-athens-greece; also see Olga Lafazani, 'Homeplace Plaza: Challenging the Border between Host and Hosted', *South Atlantic Quarterly*, 117(3), 2018, pp. 896-7.

64   Lafazani, '1.5 Years City Plaza'.

65   Patrick Strickland, 'Greek leftists turn deserted hotel into refugee homes', *Al Jazeera*, 3 July 2016.

66   Lafazani, '1.5 Years City Plaza'.

67   According to Oikonomakis, 'Half of the ex-SYRIZA-youth branch who left the party after the referendum and were for some time demobilized, eventually joined City Plaza.' Oikonomakis, 'Solidarity in Transition', p.75. In personal discussions, others have told us that perhaps 1/3 of the original solidarians at City Plaza were from Syriza.

68   Authors' interview with Lafazani.

69   'Support the City Plaza Refugee Accommodation and Solidarity Center in Athens, Greece'. Also see Alexandra Koptyaeva, 'Collective Homemaking in Transit', *Forced Migration Review Online*, available at: www.fmreview.org/shelter/koptyaeva.html.

70   Refugee Accommodation and Solidarity Space City Plaza, 'Three Years #City Plaza'.

71   Lafazani, 'Homeplace Plaza', pp. 901-2; and authors' interview with Lafazani.

72   Ibid, p. 897. Also see Mezzadra, 'In the Wake of the Greek Spring'.

73   Lafazani, 'Homeplace Plaza', pp. 898 and 900; and authors' interview with Lafazani.

74   Alexander Kolokotronis, 'Building Alternative Institutions in Greece: An Interview with Christos Giovanopoulos', *Counterpunch*, 11 March 2016. Also see Mara Scampoli

and Mattia Alunni Cardinali, '"Welcome to Greece" – DIKTYO, A Network for Political and Social Rights', 23 October 2017; and Lafazani, '1.5 Years City Plaza'.

75   Lafazani, '1.5 Years City Plaza'.

76   Arendt, *Origins of Totalitarianism*, pp. 296-301; Lafazani, 'Homeplace Plaza', p. 900.

77   'Support the City Plaza Refugee Accommodation and Solidarity Center in Athens, Greece'.

78   Authors' interview with Lafazani.

79   Leo Panitch, *Renewing Socialism: Transforming Democracy, Strategy and Imagination*, Pontypool: Merlin Press, 2008, p. 181.

80   On 'concrete utopias' in Bloch's sense: Uri Gordon, 'Prefigurative Politics between Ethical Practice and Absent Promise', *Political Studies* 66(2), 2018, pp. 521-637.

81   Lafazani, 'Homeplace Plaza', pp. 902-3; authors' interview with Lafazani.

82   Authors' interview with Lafazani.

83   Patrick Hayden, 'From Exclusion to Containment: Arendt, Sovereign Power, and Statelessness', *Societies Without Borders*, 3, 2008, p. 262.

84   Squire, 'Mobile Solidarities and Precariousness at City Plaza'.

85   Lafazani, '1.5 Years City Plaza'.

86   Christos Giovanopoulos, 'More than Self-Help and Organization: From Solidarity For All to a Strategy of Consolidating Material Power', *KOMVOS*, 2016, available at: komvoshub.org.

87   Kolokotronis, 'Building Alternative Institutions in Greece: An Interview with Christos Giovanopoulos'.

88   Hilary Wainwright, *A New Politics From the Left,* Cambridge: Polity Press, 2018.

89   Authors' interview with Lafazani. This sort of response was also reported widely among solidarity groups and humanitarian actors in the islands.

90   Andreas Karitzis, *The European Left in Times of Crisis: Lessons from Greece*, Amsterdam: TNI, 2017, p. 49.

91   'Creative Resistance: An Interview with Andreas Karitzis', *Jacobin*, 4 November 2015.

92   See Lea Ypi, 'The secret by which the capitalist class maintains its power: The effect of anti-immigration rhetoric', 12 April 2019, available at: blogs.lse.ac.uk/politicsandpolicy/the-effect-of-anti-immigration-rhetoric; Karina Piser, 'The European Left's Dangerous Anti-Immigrant Turn', *The Nation,* 7 June 2019; and David Adler, 'Meet Europe's Left Nationalists', *The Nation*, 10 January 2019. See also 'Germany: New Aufstehen movement of Sahra Wagenknecht is shaking up leftists', *Die Weltung*, 11 August 2018, available at: www.dw.com.

93   Hellenic League for Human Rights, 'Press Release on the Posting of Asylum, Immigration and Prisons to the Ministry of Citizen Protection', 17 July 2019, available at: www.hlhr.gr.

94   Philip Chrysopoulos, 'New Greek Government to Deploy More Police on the Streets', *Greek Reporter*, 12 July 2019, available at: greece.greekreporter.com; 'New Minister Positively Impressed by Moria Camp', *Are You Syrious?* 10 July 2019, available at: medium.com.

95   Economic and Political Refugee Solidarity Initiative, 'Greece: 39 Months at City Plaza for Refugees Ends', *The Bullet*, 15 July 2019, available at: socialistproject.ca.

96   Authors' interview with Lafazani.

97   'Greece: 39 Months at City Plaza for Refugees Ends'.

BEYOND THE EDUCATIONAL DYSTOPIA: NEW WAYS OF LEARNING THROUGH REMEMBERING

KATHARYNE MITCHELL
AND KEY MACFARLANE

For youth, the last several decades of market capitalism have accelerated a process through which children are perceived and educated as either mini entrepreneurs and 'human capital', or surplus populations and human waste. These twin forms of hell are articulated through an increasingly fetishized view of human development, with success measured in relation to individual potential and productivity, and the latter measured by the creation of economic value. This is occurring within a larger global context of dispossession, privatization, and market conformance, with corresponding pressures to produce children who can perform well in this system. Forty years on from the initial shock of Reaganomics and Thatcherism, summer camps now teach eight-year-olds how to interview CFOs, monetize their hobbies, and become successful business leaders and innovators – or 'biznovators'.[1] Meanwhile, charter school management organizations actively recruit higher achieving students and their more attentive parents from under-resourced neighborhoods, leaving the 'surplus' children and deracinated public schools ever further behind.[2]

This was graphically captured in Season Four of David Simon's TV series *The Wire* (aptly set, as we shall see below, in Baltimore), which depicted the stunted lives and non-existent opportunities for students of a racially segregated public school. But the stunting of the lives of children extends all the way to the erstwhile social democratic Valhalla of Sweden, where today hundreds of children remain in bed. Some haven't gotten up for months, others for years. They are all the children of refugees, afflicted with what is being called *uppgivenhetssyndrom* (resignation syndrome).[3] *Uppgivenhetssyndrom* occurs when refugee children react to their precarious situations by completely giving up on life, falling into coma-like states in which they are unable to move, drink, eat, or speak, let alone go to school. Faced with the dangers of racialization, surveillance, and deportation, they choose sleep.

Uppgivenhetssyndrom is symptomatic of a larger global dystopia in which certain children are rendered as 'waste', whether dead or asleep. Global capitalism creates a world of disposable child subjects, absorbing and concealing the ongoing violence of exploitation and extraction.[4] Turning children into waste means interrupting their life course – it involves processes of arrested development. Uneven global development is usually discussed at scales above the individual, often in terms of geopolitics. But for refugee children suffering from *uppgivenhetssyndrom*, geopolitical rhythms – such as those of transnational migration – are reflected in, and cast a spell over, biological rhythms. These children face a double deceleration: not only are they, as migrants, held up at borders and subject to greater scrutiny and surveillance on the part of the state; their bodies themselves are arrested. For in sleep, metabolism slows down. When dreams occur, during REM cycles, muscles experience paralysis.

Arrested development converges today in the landscapes of education. Neoliberal market incursions into both public and private schools have produced multiple forms of dislocation, where children are increasingly separated from close social relations and local communities so as to more effectively 'accumulate' their individual human capital. In today's market-mediated world, acquiring the skills of personal and professional calculation is assumed to be a necessary first step in developing one's 'human capital'. Education is seen as key in this process, providing ever-increasing forms of value to the figure of *homo economicus*. Further, as this figure is perceived as an autonomous being hampered by the sticky particularities of the grounded and the social, the unmooring of place and time is understood and promoted as freedom – a gift to the child.

In his book, *Powers of Freedom,* Nikolas Rose introduced the concept of 'responsibilization' to highlight both the choice and the necessity of opting *in* to the responsibilities of individual freedom, calculation, and self-development. 'Numbers, and the techniques of calculation in terms of numbers', he wrote, 'have a role in subjectification – they turn the individual into a calculating self, [one] endowed with a range of ways of thinking about, calculating about, predicting and judging their own activities and those of others'.[5] Freedom to is also freedom from – a separation from the people and places that hold one's personal calculations and human development back. While these processes have had vastly different ramifications for the children of the wealthy and those of the impoverished, they have nevertheless contributed to the overall undermining of childhood and to an unsustainable future of atomized, responsibilized, and asocial adults.

In this essay we explore this dystopic world of neoliberal education, while at the same time giving examples of how teachers and students are taking back classrooms and pedagogic practices throughout the United States. The key to contesting dislocation, we suggest, is quite literal: bringing back time and place in radical ways that resonate with young people. Walter Benjamin explored possibilities of the revolutionary past in his concept of *jetztzeit*.[6] Rather than relying on any vulgar Marxist teleological or evolutionist notion of history (made up of 'homogenous, empty time'), he favored a more kaleidoscopic approach – one in which a 'tiger's leap into the past' opened up possibilities for revolutionary thought and action in the present. For Benjamin, as for his friend Ernst Bloch, one place where these possibilities expressed themselves is in the figure of the child. Both writers were drawn to, and at times deeply enchanted by, the spaces and rhythms of childhood – its toys, fairytales, and colorful dreams. While often overlooked, Benjamin's[7] and Bloch's[8] writings on childhood provide a microcosm of their political projects more generally. As Bloch once argued, the moment of youth is always also a moment of radical political potential.[9] To be young, for Bloch, is to have one foot out of the present. It is to be open to other pasts and other futures, an idea with rich pedagogic possibility. This essay is inspired by the radical pedagogical potential of Benjamin's and Bloch's work, highlighting in particular how new configurations of political possibility are formed through spatially situated practices and modes of learning.

EDUCATION AND SOCIETY UNDER CAPITALISM

Early scholarship on the articulation of educational systems and economic modes of production related primarily to examining how public education was developed largely for the purpose of sustaining capitalist systems of accumulation. This body of work explored the relationship between production and social reproduction, defining and articulating some of the ways in which national systems of public education are imbricated in the formation of capitalism. Initially, a linkage between the rise of industrial capitalism and the training of a new workforce was suggested, but later empirical work indicated that what was actually taught in the early classrooms could not be connected directly with the kinds of skills that were becoming desirable in the industrial workforce. A second wave of thought emphasized the reproduction of the social conditions of capitalist labour rather than the actual production of capitalist labourers. In this literature, schooling was depicted as a key controlling mechanism, a tool of social management that had the capacity to defuse explosive class relations. As an institution intimately involved in the reproduction of consciousness, education was perceived as being used by dominant elites to achieve a subordinate class-consciousness, thus aiding in the maintenance of unequal class relations.[10] Abjuring the deterministic tone of this argument, others have sought to find a balance between the structuring forces of the economy and the agency of individuals and groups in asserting their own socio-cultural positions. Paul Willis's *Learning to Labor: How Working Class Kids Get Working Class Jobs* became the classic text in this genre.[11]

Following these lines of enquiry, critical education researchers began to emphasize the ways education was also tied to state formation. Andy Green argued that modern education systems in Europe and North America were an important means of furthering state development with respect to its mercantilist aims and its training programs for bureaucratic positions and state manufacturing projects.[12] State schooling was not just about the creation of a literate population or a trained workforce, he argued, but was implicated more generally in the creation of a particular kind of state subject – one schooled in the norms of behaviour related to state formation and national citizenship.

Although Green and other educational historians investigated the shifting practices of individual nation-states, few examined state formation in spatial terms. In the contemporary moment, schooling and school change is linked not just with changes in the nature of labour-capital relationships or the internal formation of the nation-state, but also with spatial changes related to the state's connections with the global economy.[13] One of the ways geographers have understood these shifting state and economic imperatives is through David Harvey's concept of the 'spatial fix'.[14] A spatial fix is the idea that capitalism's periodic crises of overaccumulation can be temporarily resolved through the creation of new spaces of investment, which are able to soak up stagnant pools of capital and labour. According to Harvey, this strategy became especially important in the US in the 1970s when, after a long post-war boom, the economy showed signs of stagflation. As nationally bound systems of production became outmoded, states began rolling out neoliberal free-market policies in an attempt to jumpstart the economy. These paved the way for new 'fixes' globally, as deregulation and privatization enabled capital to flow rapidly across borders, seeking out cheap labour and resources worldwide. Over the years, this economic flexibility and geographic expansion led to massive increases in uneven global development.

Recent changes in education can be understood as part of these geographic shifts. Capitalism's tensions are played out on the mind and body of the schoolchild. Education is a site where new economic strategies can be explored, tinkered with, and internalized. It is also one node through which these strategies can proliferate globally. New generations of students provide direct opportunities for fresh cycles of capital investment, as is evident in the billions of dollars of total student debt among college graduates in the US today. At the level of society, education systems work to bind the development of youth to the development of a larger social body. While the latter has long included nationalist trajectories of 'progress', increasingly students are being mapped onto the jagged rhythms of global capitalism as well. On the individual level, the *telos* of childhood development ends with the 'free-floating' global entrepreneur, investing where they think best. But for every entrepreneurial child there are many more who are rendered 'surplus' or 'waste' through the failures of educational systems and other institutions.[15] When they get older these children will provide formal and informal economies with cheap, expendable sources of labour, including within the prison system itself. It is this ongoing criminalization that reveals youth as a true moment of danger for capitalist society. Youth provides a source of new energy and growth; it is the living conduit through which existing social relations are renewed (or not) from one generation to the next.[16]

THE KIDPRENEUR AND THE MICROSOCIETY

With student loan debt in the US now totalling over $1.5 trillion, the system of higher education is clearly unsustainable. But the future is not necessarily any brighter. There are early signs of a movement away from traditional loan structures to what are known as Income Share Agreements or ISAs, in which recipients pledge a share of their future earnings against debt.[17] If ISAs are successful, children will need to spend their formative years building profiles to attract lenders; child-ranking algorithms will single out risky 'subprime' students, who will be encouraged by parents and educators to improve their investment grades and financial projections, or else pay higher interest rates on their lives. Childhood will be transformed into one big start-up opportunity.

While its algorithms are still under construction, this future is already with us. All across the world, children are being encouraged, at increasingly young ages, to become 'kidpreneurs'. New educational products, services, and programs purport not only to boost a child's intelligence, as the edutainment industry has done since the 1970s, but also their financial savviness. Baby

Einstein has given way to Baby Milton Friedman. There are, for instance, a growing number of organizations dedicated to cultivating financial literacy in children. Brain Arts Products offers a program that teaches toddlers (ages three to five) what money is and 'how to play at shopping'.[18] Similarly, 'My Classroom Economy' professes to 'teach children financial responsibility through fun, experiential learning'.[19] The program, which is free to download for any K–12 teacher, is designed to simulate a real-world economy. At all grade levels 'students need to earn school "dollars" so that they can rent their own desks', and once in middle school, to pay electricity bills and taxes. It's a fully functioning market that requires very little outside tinkering. 'The beauty of the program', the website boasts, 'is that you don't need to teach [financial] lessons; rather, the children will experience them and learn for themselves.'[20]

Today, kids are increasingly taught financial responsibility by being thrust into a 'microsociety'. George Richmond first developed the microsociety approach to education in the late 1960s while he was struggling as a fifth-grade teacher in Brooklyn, New York. Richmond found that turning the classroom into a scaled-down model of adult society – complete with money, jobs, and a market system – helped motivate his students to learn, while living out their professional fantasies.[21] In 1973 he published a book about his experiment, called *The Micro-Society School: A Real World in Miniature*. Later, in 1991, Richmond and his wife started MicroSociety, Inc., which continues today in 'helping kids create their own worlds within school'.[22] The website describes the microsociety as a 'thriving, modern-day, mini-metropolis' that includes 'a government center, entrepreneurial hub, non-profit organizations, consumer marketplace, university and community gathering spaces'.[23] The result is a carefully controlled environment that is thought to 'simulate the inherent performance motivators in real-world economic systems'. By shrinking things down, the microsociety strives to mould students into 'responsible global citizens, and dynamic collaborators and communicators', able to succeed in a hypercompetitive global economy.

In recent years the microsociety has become especially entrepreneurial. In 2015, Austin's David Crocket High School and its feeder elementary and middle schools launched Student Inc., the first K–12 public school entrepreneurship track in the US. The program is based on the microsociety idea, with students from each grade level running various kinds of businesses.[24] In elementary school, even arts & crafts is marketized. One teacher at Cunningham Elementary describes how her class made 'leaf people': 'We get the leaves off the tree, real leaves, and then we glue them on to a paper, and then we make their faces, and then we sell them.'[25] By the time high school rolls around, students are made to compete for investment. In a setting similar to ABC's *Shark Tank*, they pitch their ideas to a local venture capitalist firm, before taking a senior-year 'accelerator class' to run their businesses.

Training kidpreneurs occurs outside the classroom as well. There are now several financial literacy apps designed specifically for children. Apps like PiggyBot, iAllowance, and Bankaroo encourage kids to keep track of allowances, spending, and saving, while enabling parents to monitor all transactions. Some even allow parents to send the kids reminders and create incentives. As the app FamZoo (which is marketed to preschoolers and up) tells parents: 'you are the "banker", and your kids are the "customers"'. The purpose of this, it proudly claims, is 'preparing kids for the financial jungle'. This includes making responsible investment decisions. The app BusyKid, for example, allows children to invest in real stock and to donate to charities with the allowance they earned through chores, which they receive each week on payday.

Similar to in-school programs like My Classroom Economy and Student Inc., financial literacy apps create a kind of incubator microsociety, but one that is virtual and with even fewer 'real-world' consequences. Some like Star Banks Adventure, Green$treets: Unleash the Loot, and Renegade Buggy create new worlds altogether, teaching entrepreneurship through interactive gameplay. In the latter, players zoom through an urban terrain on a 'supercharged' shopping cart, grabbing various items, coins, and coupons. Be sure to use 'smart consumer strategies', says the app's website, and to 'compare unit sizes, buy in bulk, and use coupons and promos along the way'. By saving money, you can become a 'checkout hero', all while 'racing down a high-speed track'.

The fast pace of app games like Renegade Buggy manifests the acceleration as well as commodification of childhood. Through apps, education programs, and loan structures, children are nudged into entrepreneurial adulthood, while their attention is divided by a high-speed economy of information and games. Most of the groups promoting the kidpreneur stress just how fun and rewarding business development can be. At the same time, the kidpreneur is framed as an economic necessity. 'The world is changing', says the website for the book *Kidpreneurs: Young Entrepreneurs with Big Ideas!*, 'can your child keep up?' Kids must accelerate or else fall behind and out. Viewed in economic terms, the kidpreneur and the microsociety quickly lose their playful sheen. They appear as what they are: hellish strategies for addressing an ongoing crisis of capital accumulation. They reflect the persistent need to annihilate – or rather *miniaturize* – space and time in order to extract and realize surplus value. This space includes the space of the classroom and this time includes the time of childhood. But the compression of time and space comes at a cost. While a few children make their (parents') dreams come true as fast-track entrepreneurs, many more are arrested, stalled, banished, or worse.

THE DISPOSABLE CHILD: VIOLENCE IN MINIATURE

In Baltimore's public schools, where 53 per cent of the students registered as low income, and 79 per cent are black, only 13 per cent of fourth- and eighth-graders are reading at a proficient level.[26] For years, Baltimore has been a hotspot for childhood lead poisoning, especially in the poor, predominantly black neighbourhoods where houses and infrastructures are crumbling, their neighbourhoods redlined and renovations long overdue. Although numbers have declined in recent years, Baltimore has nearly three times the national rate of lead poisoning among children.[27] This became national news in 2015 when it was revealed, just after he was killed by police, that Freddie Gray had been exposed to large amounts of the heavy metal in his childhood home.[28] Gray was one of the 65,000 children in Baltimore found to have dangerously high blood-lead levels between 1993 and 2013.[29] Early lead exposure is associated with a wide range of mental and behavioural impairments in children, including disruptions to neurodevelopment, attention, and memory formation.

In this way, racialized bodies in Baltimore are subject to yet another kind of arrested development – on a cellular level. Lead exposure in Baltimore occurs not only at home but also at school. In 2007 officials shut down water fountains across the city's schools due to high lead levels in the water.[30] Most public schools in Baltimore today continue to rely on bottled water for drinking, creating the feeling of a permanent humanitarian crisis or warzone. This is just one example of the decrepit state of Baltimore's educational facilities. Sometimes failing infrastructure has led to scenarios that are truly post-apocalyptic. For example, in January 2018, heating systems across one-third of the city's schools broke down. In classrooms children huddled together in winter coats trying not to freeze, before schools eventually shut their doors.[31] Just a few months later, several schools were closed again, this time due to excessive heat and lack of air conditioning.[32]

This form of racialized educational dystopia has a long history. Going back to suburban white flight, disinvestment, blockbusting, race riots, runaway manufacturing, and gentrification, Baltimore, like many other rust belt cities, has never really recovered. Intense racialization and chronic underinvestment continue to shape the urban landscape. It is the youth who are forced to relive this hell each generation, as decades of racialized and class-based violence permeate the landscape itself in dilapidated school buildings and contaminated water supplies. One place where these legacies intersect is the classroom. Rather than a cosmopolitan microsociety as envisioned by Richmond, public schools in Baltimore are sites where expansive histories of violence are condensed. They play out in miniature within the spaces of learning and the bodies of children.

As history is buried in flesh and the built environment, Baltimore's education system can appear as a 'natural disaster', and thus somehow inevitable. In the case of lead poisoning, since it can occur *in utero*, these disasters are essentially passed down between generations. Structures of racialized violence are extended to the biological level, reproduced in 'nature' itself. This has been a boon for capital. Especially in post-industrial cities like Baltimore, the health risks associated with widespread toxicity and infrastructural decay provide momentum for growing industries such as health care and environmental services.[33] In Baltimore, and across the world, continued capital accumulation increasingly relies on making certain bodies – especially children's bodies – vulnerable to ill-health and death.[34]

RECLAIMING CLASSROOMS, COMMUNITIES AND CHILDHOOD

The attacks on children and young people come from many directions but they are being met with an increasingly widespread network of well-organized and determined parents and teachers. In January 2019 over 30,000 teachers and staff in Los Angeles went on strike to protest the working conditions in classrooms, including inadequate numbers of counsellors, nurses and librarians, as well as burgeoning class sizes. 'We work with students every day who face trauma and face hardship', one teacher noted, 'So we're doing this as a life passion to improve our community'.[35] Equally impassioned teachers in New Zealand and the UK went on strike in their respective communities in the spring of 2019, indicating similar problems of large classes, excessive paperwork, inadequate service staff, and low pay. Noting that 'teachers are overwhelmed', a primary school teacher in Auckland demanded government investment in schools and communities for 'the future of teachers and the country's children'.[36] These actions followed multiple teachers' rebellions on four continents in 2018.[37]

The link between working conditions for teachers and life conditions for children is apparent to most parents, who have joined teachers in contesting the steady erosion of the workplace and the local community. The national movement 'Parents Across America', for example, was formed by parents to contest the top-down imposition of educational 'reforms' now impacting the spaces and lives of both children and teachers. This social movement actively links up parents in state 'chapters', working collaboratively to challenge school privatization as well as deskilling processes such as packaged curricula.[38] Meanwhile, parents, teachers, and students have also joined forces to contest so-called high stakes standardized tests, where American students are forced to spend increasing amounts of time preparing for an ever growing number of federally mandated examinations in English, math, social studies, and science (and other subjects as well in a number of states). Not only do these tests affect children's ability to graduate up to the next grade level, they are also used to evaluate teachers and determine their pay, as well as to sweep up schools – often those in poor and minority neighbourhoods – into a vortex of 'failure', frequently leading to school closure. The ensuing processes of dispossession and gentrification following these school closures have been well documented for cities such as Chicago, Detroit, Newark, Oakland, and Philadelphia.[39] Tens of thousands of teachers and students opposed to these tactics have engaged in public acts of civil disobedience by banding together in a 'United Opt Out' movement, where they refuse to participate in the standardized testing regime, taking to the streets and social media to proclaim their opposition. Not only are the tests opposed, but also the inequitable, often horrific conditions in which the schools, and the children in them, are located. As one teacher noted, 'Why are the standards – the first ones we set – not, all kids will come to school not hungry, not sick and with access to books? Those are some great standards, but yet those standards we're not allowed to go after'.[40]

Opposition to the acceleration and commodification of childhood can be found in an equal number of venues and forms. In countries like the US and UK, homeschooling is on the rise. While the flexibility of the homeschool provides the opportunity for some parents to craft a more entrepreneurial curriculum for their kids,[41] it allows others to challenge kidpreneurialism altogether. For parents like Claire Mumford, homeschooling provides an alternative to the 'oppressive' environment of school, where children are forced to sit 'at a desk all day, with fluorescent lights, computer screens, barely able to see outside'.[42] Leaving this dystopia behind, Mumford's children now have 'time to relax and to be kids – to go to the woods, build dens and to learn what they're excited about'. In a similar vein, the growing 'free range parenting' movement in the US seeks to give children more independence and outdoor freedom, away from the attention economy of digital advertisements, phone apps, and social media.[43] Similar campaigns in the UK are fighting for 'children's right to play' outside of adult supervision.

In creating spaces for kids to 'do nothing', these struggles directly challenge an accelerated view of childhood according to which all actions and gestures are judged on the basis of future economic 'usefulness'.[44] Rather than spending time on financial literacy apps or drafting business plans, childhood time is freed up. Deeper forms of attention are unfolded and expanded, allowing children to better orient themselves in time and space. This temporal and geographical grounding enables them to challenge the present as active political agents, as we see in the following study.

MAPPING THE EMANCIPATORY PRESENT

Childhood, Ernst Bloch argued, is never fully caged by its moment of conjuncture. Rather, as a site of historical sedimentation, childhood provides a potential space for experimentation, play, and escape – a sandbox where buried pasts can be dug up, collected, and reshaped as material for an emancipatory present. We have found that teaching critical geography to young people creates the sandbox where the past can be sifted to inform the present. This type of pedagogy can broaden understandings of how spatial production is a critical part of uneven development – from resource extraction and gentrification to the exploitation of labour and people's emotional connections to place. It can also provide knowledge about historical commitments to community building and resistance through time. Learning about the construction of neighbourhoods and activist actions over the production of space can provide the foundations for present and future forms of resistance to spatial injustice.

In the late 1920s, Walter Benjamin began experimenting with the new technology of radio broadcasting as a tool for childhood education.[45] The radio scripts he wrote for children include numerous stories, some of which have explicitly geographic themes, from 'toy tours' around Berlin to reporting on the Mississippi Flood of 1927, which ends with a warning about the Ku Klux Klan. It is in the pedagogical spirit of Benjamin that we turn our attention to a different technology: digital mapping. Three decades ago the cartographer and map historian Brian Harley noted that maps and mapmaking should always be viewed critically as tools that are generally at the disposal of dominant groups in society, and whose fundamental purpose is to 'codify, to legitimate, and to promote the world views which are prevalent in different periods and places'.[46] But although maps frequently uphold and advance dominant spatial and social norms and interests, they can also be produced in alternative ways for counter-hegemonic purposes.[47] Much critical research, for example, has demonstrated the usefulness of geographic information systems (GIS) in mapping populations usually rendered invisible and unacknowledged, such as recent immigrants and the homeless.[48] When tools such as GIS are in the right hands, populations such as these can benefit from being seen and counted in assessments of vulnerability and/or the need for social services. These types of studies recognize the embeddedness of maps in histories and geographies of power. They challenge the notion of objectivity and neutrality in any mapping project. But by the same token, they take into account the political possibilities inherent in modern geospatial technologies, actively and reflectively employing these tools in applied realms to further a critical politics of mapping against the grain. Additionally, a significant amount of research in critical cartography has focused on the possibilities of an increasing democratization of knowledge and decision-making through the use of what has become known as participatory GIS.[49] This body of work emphasizes facilitating access to publicly available information so that shared knowledge can enable marginalized groups to participate freely in promoting their own interests.

The effect of this can be readily seen in the case of a middle school in a poor but rapidly gentrifying area of south Seattle, where a geography colleague and a social studies teacher, working with twenty-nine seventh-grade girls (ages thirteen and fourteen) over a period of several weeks, collaborated in a research project designed to develop in what ways a greater understanding of spatial production and management – such as through processes of mapping and counter-mapping – might provide the knowledge and skills to challenge inequitable resource allocation, segregation, gentrification, and other forms of spatial injustice.[50] The students explored the cultural histories of women and different ethnic and racial groups in the city as part of a class project. The girls formed teams of four students and each team researched and mapped an ethnic group or women in Seattle. The teams conducted interviews with local people who had been active in community-building and resistance projects over the past half century. They also used online and library-based resources to augment their knowledge. Additionally, all of the students produced oral history video documentaries and interactive multimedia maps of important sites and spatial processes affecting the groups that they researched.

Research sessions were initiated with a discussion of the political importance of space, including teaching about how much of politics is often quite literally played out through the 'taking' of space. For example, women and those categorized in the various racial or ethnic groups the students were studying often furthered their own political agendas through practices such as taking to the streets to demand the right to vote, or taking seats in buses, classrooms, and at lunch counters demanding the right to be served. Helping young people understand the power of space is best initiated through discussions and practices related to how communities have lost or won space through the course of political struggle. Additionally, students can be made more aware of how often marginalized communities have held space in a manner affirming group identity through time. This kind of approach advances a social justice or emancipatory agenda, but it does so through the relatively simple means of calling attention to certain kinds of spatial patterns, processes, and relationships through time.

Questions about broader processes and patterns of spatial production and control, and why particular events happened at particular locations, elicit larger conceptual frameworks involving rights of association, property, *habeas corpus*, and other civic and legal rights integral to belonging and citizenship in the United States. For example, when mapped and discussed within a historical framework, students are able to see the abrogation of key aspects of rights around citizenship and space, such as the internment of Japanese Americans during the Second World War, or spatial patterns of institutionalized racism such as the redlining of minority neighbourhoods. At the same time, they can better visualize how subjugated communities might be enhanced or protected through spatial proximity or access to critical resources. Through discussion and further research, they can also become aware of changes through time – changes that are often the result of the activism of key figures, groups, or institutions asserting their rights to particular spaces and resources.

The students involved in the research project investigated institutions such as immigrant enclaves, benevolent societies, student unions, women's centres, and community headquarters as spaces of social, political, and economic safety for historically marginalized or terrorized groups. They also looked at evidence of exclusion and discrimination against these groups in processes such as redlining, steering, internment, quarantining, and incarceration. The mapping project was rooted in the proposition that place – specifically a reflective and critical knowledge about the places that are experienced in everyday life – could be a central catalyst in the development of political subjectivity and a commitment to political engagement. The study thus explored the link between a critical awareness of shared concerns and the development of a collective social awareness that might enhance civic agency and commitment to social and political action.

In each digital map created by the different teams, the students placed pins on areas of historical significance to their group. One of the teams investigating the historical geography of African-Americans in Seattle, for example, pinned the location of a second Black Panthers headquarters on their map. When the mapping platform was active, a viewer could click on a pin or on an area, and a comment box would pop up to the right. In this box the students would often add some textual description of the place, a photograph, a question, or another related site for the viewer to visit. The conversations the students held about these pinned sites and corresponding text and photographs were mostly oral, but the researchers encouraged them to write some of their ideas into the comment box as well.

One student responded to a verbal question as to why there was a 'second' Black Panthers headquarters by noting, 'I think that the BPP [Black Panther Party] got evicted from some of their buildings and that's why they have multiple headquarters'. This spurred another 'why' question, followed by a response from the teacher. In these types of exchanges, the written comments were used to stimulate more oral dialogue, but they also provided a record of ideas, exchanges, and teaching moments that other students could see and react to at a later time or from a different place.

In another example from the team working on the Japanese immigrant community in Seattle, a student mapped the Seattle Courthouse and explained why it was important to a university student named Hirabayashi. She noted how Hirabayashi 'refused the evacuation', and in his legal defence invoked the Fifth Amendment in court. Students offered supportive comments after viewing the post. They also added additional information to the post, including a related website of interest. Significantly, one of the more advanced students in the class answered a direct question posed by the teacher about the Fifth Amendment's relevance to the internment struggles of Japanese-Americans. She showed her own understanding of the concept of due process, and at the same time helped the other students make further connections between the historical event of the internment and the idea of due process as a right purportedly guaranteed by the American Constitution.

In a third example, a student located a general area of the map (the International District) by using the line tool. She uploaded a photo from a main street in that neighbourhood as a vehicle for talking about the practice of redlining. In her text, she introduced redlining in a somewhat confusing way: 'Many Filipino people lived in the international district because it was the only place that wasn't redlined. Redlining is when basically an invisible line is put dividing where Filipinos can buy land.' This prompted an oral question from a student outside the team, who had heard about it in relation to her own group's spatial formation and identity. The students' comments that appeared in the text box following this dialogue demonstrated the collaborative, spatially oriented learning process that occurred in the classroom as a result of this exchange. One student indicated her initial confusion about redlining with the question, 'How did redlining actually work if it was like an invisible?' This was answered by the teacher, who used the student's question as a way of introducing the concept of restrictive covenants. Another student then brought in her own understanding of the process, which she had learned from her research on the Chinese experience in Seattle. She noted authoritatively, 'Filipinos were not the only people who got redlined'.

The maps picked up on the role of civic institutions as a locus for activism or resistance and as sites for reinforcing cultural practices and community ties. Most of the teams' maps included a cultural or community centre such as the Japanese American Citizens' League, the NAACP (National Association of Advancement for Colored People), the Filipino Community Center, or a women's association in the greater metro area. Several members of the teams were also passionate about demonstrating their knowledge of public space and public events as critical sites of protest.

Many of the students used the mapping exercises as a way to inform themselves about both the geography and history of their own neighbourhoods in the city. Marking areas and sites of importance on their maps brought the cultural history of Seattle home to them, and helped them to add to their existing knowledge of the city. They began to see relationships between places, including where people live and where they work. On a broader regional scale, they began to see what it must have been like to be quarantined or interned so far away from family and friends. This form of learning can help to render space and place socially contextualized, bringing geography to life and making it complementary to a broader project of subjectivity formation around political activism.

The students' growing interest in their own neighbourhoods was manifested in some of the civic engagement worksheets that the researchers had them fill towards the end of the research project. Here the research team posed a number of questions related to social and spatial problems that the ethnic groups or women had faced in Seattle. Three members of the African-American team responded to these questions by noting 'redlining' as a key problem. Among the insights that the students derived, an important one was the understanding that both discriminatory actions such as redlining and the creation of affirmative locales such as the black student union are profoundly spatial processes critical in both scope and impact for historically subordinated groups. Literally placing people, institutions, and events in the students' own neighbourhoods through locating them on a map of the city and attaching historical and contemporary documents to each mapped space helped them to graphically and visually connect both geography and history to the present time and place, and make it relevant to their own lives.

The researchers employed the students' growing neighbourhood awareness to draw out their own sense of place. On the whole, a growth in spatial awareness was observed among the students as well as a strong concern about 'spatial politics' related to the positive and negative geographical processes affecting group identity. Bringing together history, geography, and emancipatory politics through a collaborative mapping project helped the students to understand how minority communities are formed in and through space, and how important space is for maintaining solidarity and resisting oppression by dominant groups.

Further, through the process of researching, mapping, and talking with each other about their own city and neighbourhoods, the students showed a greater awareness that history is not necessarily a set of seemingly abstract events but rather is something that happened here, to us, in 'our' space. Mapping 'our' culture and 'our' history rendered events and processes more immediate, visceral, personal, and potentially alterable in terms of their seeming trajectory. Collectively visualizing and discussing historical acts such as the quarantining of Filipinos (there were two girls of Filipino descent in the class), or redlining in the African-American neighbourhood where several of the girls lived, for example, galvanized a sense of collective responsibility for these spaces and the people who inhabit them.

In a similar way, the students used strategies of counter-mapping to resist hegemonic ways of representing space. They uncovered absences in the historical record and celebrated the multiple ways that women and minority groups had demanded and taken space in times past. Through this process, the students learned about and represented new spatial narratives of the city, becoming energized political activists on the way.

RECLAIMING THE PAST

From summer camps where the children of the elite dream of becoming successful entrepreneurs, to bedrooms where the children of refugees are trapped in their dreams, we live in a dystopian world. It is a world we must both reject and reframe, and it is children who are pointing the way. This was equally true eighty years ago when Ernst Bloch was writing during the rise of fascism in Europe. Children, he argued in 1935, always manage to 'escape' the world of their parents.[51] What the playing child is able to grasp, Bloch says, are spaces and times that are 'long past for the adult' but that remain rife with both 'terror and magic' and simultaneously 'full of hope'.

Walter Benjamin likewise saw seeds of potential in childhood. His 1930 essay 'Program for a Proletarian Children's Theater' outlines a revolutionary pedagogy organized around childhood theatre performance. The goal of the performance is to create a space for the radical unleashing of play. Such play works, in turn, to release in children 'the most powerful energies of the future'.[52] Benjamin wanted to harness these energies as a revolutionary force, one that turns bourgeois society 'upside down', such that it is adults who learn from children. If Benjamin's theatre can be thought of as a microsociety, it is a miniature version, not of the existing world but of 'what is to come', a global society envisioned through the improvised gestures of the young.

While Benjamin's revolutionary pedagogy is concerned with liberating the future, this is only possible through a radical reclamation of history and geography. Childhood is where the spaces, memories, and dreams of the past are discovered anew each generation, where they experience, as Benjamin says, an 'awakening'.[53] What this means, and what we have argued here, is that the figure of the child is an *elementary* site of political struggle. In order for global capitalist society to reproduce itself over time, certain histories must be recollected while others are actively buried.[54] Spatially situated educational practices, those that draw attention to the geographies of selective memory, help to break this dystopian violence. They point to radical spaces and legacies that have been paved over or interred, but which can be seized and recovered in ways that challenge the revolving tyranny of the present. As part of a larger emancipatory project for the future, this reclaiming of the past, with and for children, is paramount.

NOTES

1   Brendan O'Connor, 'Starting Them Young with Capitalism', *New York Times*, 26 May 2019.

2   Diane Ravitch, *Reign of Error: The Hoax of the Privatization Movement and the Danger to America's Public Schools*, New York: Alfred Knopf, 2013.

3   Rachel Aviv, 'The Trauma of Facing Deportation', *The New Yorker*, 27 March 2017.

4   It is not just children who are rendered 'waste' within global capitalism. See for instance Melissa Wright, *Disposable Women and Other Myths of Global Capitalism*, London: Routledge, 2006.

5   Nikolas Rose, *Powers of Freedom: Reframing Political Thought*, Cambridge: Cambridge University Press, 1999.

6   Walter Benjamin, *Illuminations*, Translated by Harry Zohn, New York: Shocken Books, 1968, p. 261.

7   For an overview of Benjamin's writings on childhood see Carlo Salzani, 'Experience and Play: Walter Benjamin and the Prelapsarian Child', in A. Benjamin and C. Rice eds, *Walter Benjamin and the Architecture of Modernity*, Melbourne: re.press, 2009, pp. 175–200.

8   For an overview of Bloch's writings on childhood see Nina Cemiloğlu, 'Between Marxism and Romanticism: Childhood and Education in the Works of Ernst Bloch', *folklor/edebiyat*, 24(94), pp. 217–26.

9   Ernst Bloch, 'Nonsynchronism and the Obligation to Its Dialectics', *New German Critique*, 11(Spring), 1977, pp. 22–38.

10 Samuel Bowles and Herbert Gintis, *Schooling in Capitalist America: Educational Reform and the Contradictions of Economic Life*, Chicago: Haymarket Books, 1976.

11 Paul Willis, *Learning to Labor: How Working Class Kids Get Working Class Jobs*, New York: Columbia University Press, 1977.

12 Andy Green, *Education and State Formation: The Rise of Educational Systems in England, France and the USA*, New York: St. Martin's Press, 1990.

13 Katharyne Mitchell, 'Educating the National Citizen in Neoliberal Times: From the Multicultural Self to the Strategic Cosmopolitan', *Transactions of the Institute of British Geographers*, 28(4), 2003, pp. 387-403.

14 David Harvey, *Limits to Capital*, Oxford: Blackwell, 1982.

15 Cindi Katz, 'The Angel of Geography: Superman, Tiger Mother, Aspiration Management, and the Child as Waste', *Progress in Human Geography*, 42(5), 2018, pp 723-40.

16 Key MacFarlane, 'Children of the Grave', *Human Geography*, 12(1), 2019, pp. 73–77.

17 Malcolm Harris, 'What's Scarier Than Student Loans? Welcome to the World of Subprime Children', *The New York Times*, 11 May 2019.

18 Brain Arts Productions, 'Programs', brainartsproductions.org/programs.

19 My Classroom Economy, 'What is My Classroom Economy?', available at: www.myclassroomeconomy.org.

20 My Classroom Economy, 'Grades K −1', available at: myclassroomeconomy.org/grades/gradek-1.html.

21 Cary Cherniss, *Social Change and the MicroSocietyÒ Program*, Thousand Oaks: Corwin Press, 1973.

22 MicroSociety, available at: www.microsociety.org.

23 MicroSociety, 'The Microsociety Model', www.microsociety.org/the-microsociety-model.

24 Tom Foster, 'Inside the Schools That Want to Create the Next Mark Zuckerberg – Starting at Age 5', *Inc.*, March 2017.

25 Kate McGee, 'Austin High Schoolers to Practice Life Skills As Entrepreneurs-in-Training', *KUT*, 11 November 2015, available at: www.kut.org.

26 Liz Bowie, 'Baltimore Students Score Near Bottom in Reading, Math on Key National Assessment', *The Baltimore Sun*, 10 April 2018.

27 Anna Maria Barry-Jester, 'Baltimore's Toxic Legacy of Lead Paint', *FiveThirtyEight*, 7 May 2015, available at: fivethirtyeight.com.

28 Key MacFarlane, 'Rites of Passage', *Ultra*, 12 May 2015, available at: www.ultra-com.org.

29 Maryland Department of the Environment, 'Childhood Blood Lead Surveillance in Maryland: Annual Report 2013', July 2014, available at: mde.maryland.gov.

30 Liz Bowie, 'Water From a Fountain? Not in Baltimore City Schools', *The Baltimore Sun*, 9 April 2016.

31 Christine Hauser, 'Baltimore City Schools Are Without Heat, Prompting Protests From Teachers and Parents', *The New York Times*, 4 January 2018.

32 Liz Bowie, 'Baltimore City, County School Systems Working to Install Air Conditioning at Every School', *The Baltimore Sun*, 6 September 2018.

33   Key MacFarlane, 'Time, Waste, and the City: The Rise of the Environmental Industry', *Antipode*, 51(1), 2019, pp. 225–47.

34   James Tyner, *Dead Labor*, Minneapolis: University of Minnesota Press, 2019; Matthew Sparke, 'Austerity and the Embodiment of Neoliberalism as Ill-Health: Towards a Theory of Biological Sub-Citizenship', *Social Science and Medicine*, 187, 2017, pp. 287–95.

35   Holly Yan, 'The LA Teachers' Strike Ends after Union Approves Deal with School District', *CNN,* 22 July, 2019.

36   Eleanor Ainge Roy, 'New Zealand Schools Hit by 'Mega-Strike' as 50,000 Teachers Walk Out', *The Guardian,* 28 May 2019.

37   Eric London, 'Teachers' Rebellion Spreads on Four Continents', *World Socialist Web Site,* 28 March, 2018, available at: www.wsws.org.

38   See Parents Across America, parentsacrossamerica.org.

39   Pauline Lipman, *The New Political Economy of Urban Education: Neoliberalism, Race, and the Right to the City*, London: Routledge, 2011.

40   Allie Bidwell, 'Opt-Out Movement About More than Tests, Advocates Say', *U.S. News,* 10 March 2015.

41   Andreas Widmer, 'Why Homeschoolers Make Great Entrepreneurs', *The Stream*, 10 January 2019, available at: stream.org.

42   Sally Williams, '"School is Very Oppressive": Why Home-Schooling is on the Rise', *The Guardian*, 3 November 2018.

43   Charles Duncan, 'What is "Free Range Parenting?" New SC Bill Could Change the Way You Raise Your Kids', *The State*, 9 January 2019.

44   Cf. Jenny Odell, *How do Do Nothing: Resisting the Attention Economy*, Brooklyn: Melville House, 1999.

45   Walter Benjamin, *Radio Benjamin*, London: Verso, 2014.

46   Brian Harley, 'Deconstructing the Map', *Cartographica*, 26(2), 1989, p. 429. See also, Jeremy Crampton, 'Maps as Social Constructions: Power, Communication and Visualization', *Progress in Human Geography*, 25(2), 2001, pp. 235-53.

47   Leila Harris and Helen Hazen, 'Power of Maps: (Counter) Mapping for Conservation', *ACME: An International Journal for Critical Geographies*, 4(1), 2005, pp. 99-130; Manissa Maharawal and Erin McElroy, 'The Anti-Eviction Mapping Project: Counter Mapping and Oral History toward Bay Area Housing Justice', *Annals of the American Association of Geographers*, 108(2), 2018, pp. 380-89.

48   Rob Fiedler, Nadine Schuurman, and Jennifer Hyndman, 'Hidden Homelessness in Greater Vancouver', *Cities*, 23(3), 2006, pp. 205–16.

49   Sarah Elwood, 'Critical Issues in Participatory GIS: Deconstructions, Reconstructions, and New Research Directions', *Transactions in GIS*, 10(5), 2006, pp. 693-708.

50   The research in this section was conducted by Katharyne Mitchell and Sarah Elwood at the University of Washington and supported by the Spencer Foundation and the National Geographic Education Foundation. The overall discussion in this section draws on Katharyne Mitchell, *Making Workers: Radical Geographies of Education*, London: Pluto Press, 2018. See also Katharyne Mitchell and Sarah Elwood, 'Mapping Children's Politics: The Promise of Articulation and the Limits of Nonrepresentational Theory', *Environment and Planning D: Society and Space*, 30(5), 2012, pp. 788-804; Sarah Elwood and Katharyne Mitchell, 'Another Politics is Possible: Neogeographies, Visual Spatial Tactics and Political Formation', *Cartographica*, 48(4), 2013, pp. 275-92.

51 Ernst Bloch, 'The Colourful Escape', *Heritage of Our Times*, Cambrige: Polity Press, 1991, pp. 151–2.

52 Walter Benjamin, 'Program for a Proletarian Children's Theater', in M. W. Jennings, H. Eiland, and G. Smith (eds.), *Walter Benjamin: Selecting Writings Volume 2, Part 1: 1927–1930*, Cambridge, MA: The Belknap Press of Harvard University Press, 2005, pp. 201–6.

53 Walter Benjamin, *The Arcades Project*, Cambridge, MA: The Belknap Press of Harvard University Press, 2002, p. 390.

54 Key MacFarlane and Katharyne Mitchell, 'Hamburg's Spaces of Danger: Race, Violence, and Memory in a Contemporary Global City', *International Journal of Urban and Regional Research*, in press.

THE FUTURE OF WORK IN THE ERA OF 'DIGITAL CAPITALISM'

BIRGIT MAHNKOPF

In many countries, government agencies, business and employers' associations, CEOs from big corporations, and even trade union leaders seem to be convinced that a fourth wave of industrial revolution is under way which will reconfigure the global production system and even societies at large. In the Anglo-Saxon context, this wave is often referred to as the 'internet of things', while in Germany and other European countries, where the digitalization of production and distribution is at the centre of the debate, this operates under the term 'Industry 4.0'. These terms not only describe the digitalization of horizontal and vertical value chains of companies, but also formulate a vision of the future that promises new market and export opportunities as well as a new ecologically sustainable way of doing business. It is assumed that a 'new spirit of capitalism' will allow for a certain margin of autonomy and non-hierarchical cooperation not only between firms and workers but also with the so-called 'prosumers', a term designed to catch the convergence of boundaries between consumers and producers, and referring to the unpaid – and usually unaware – work of the internet user.

Some pundits like Paul Mason go so far as to imagine that the fourth industrial revolution might provide not only a technologically inspired route out of fossil fuel dependence, but would more generally free us from capitalist imperatives.[1] Others are more sceptical about the promises of digitalization, either pointing to various technological bottlenecks that stand in the way of a widespread use of digital infrastructure, or stressing the corporate crusade against data governance (just getting started), or questioning whether the digital economy can be placed at the service of ecological sustainability. This essay attempts to subject the digitalization hype, especially how far digitalization can be linked to societal goals in favour of workers, to a critical assessment.

THE PROMISES OF INDUSTRY 4.0

Those promoting a brilliant new world of 'smart factories' and a 'greener future', for both the advanced industrialized countries and developing countries alike, tell us that digital infrastructures could open new value creation potential. The argument is that a decrease in average cost of production due to automation would boost output and exports, translating into increasing labour demand. The generation of data, and its subsequent use in the different parts of the value chain and across the entire economy, is expected to allow for a merger of the physical and the virtual world. Such a system of physical-to-digital technologies embodied in machines and equipment (such as robots, scanners and actuators) would enable sensing and monitoring of the entire economy. Artificial intelligence and algorithms would help to determine the optimal size of production runs, and even the makeup of working teams performing tasks that cannot be digitalized/automated.

In addition to increased efficiency and flexibility of manufacturing, a new wave of mass consumption is expected: new 'smart' products will be produced, such as wearable tech, autonomous vehicles, biochips, biosensors, involving all kinds of new materials. At the same time, a more human world of work appears on the horizon – through an upgrading of jobs, better cooperation and participation between groups of employees, a substitution of stressful and unattractive tasks, comprehensive training opportunities and upward mobility of workers. This is the main reason why, in Germany, not only government and business but also trade unions are very much in favour of the new industrial revolution whereby intelligent machines interacting self-reliantly with the physical world will profoundly change the future of work. Representatives of industry expect substantial improvements in production agility and flexibility, on the one hand, and the mitigation of production errors, on the other, both with highly positive effects on productivity and profitability. With the help of a cyber-physical production system (often coined the 'smart factory'), movable, modular production machines, as well as 3D-printers, could dynamically reconfigure a company's entire network of operations.

Insofar as manufacturing still accounts for 22 per cent of GDP in Germany and the tradable manufacture sector accounts for 80 per cent of German exports, expectations that the digitalization of manufacturing might lower prices, increase demand, and create employment in automation-producing firms makes all this look especially promising. Indeed, IG Metall, the metal workers union, is actively engaged in an alliance between government and business associations on 'Industry 4.0'. This is despite the fact that two-thirds of all workers, according to a survey conducted by the DGB, the German national trade union congress, say they have no influence on how digital technology is used at their workplace, while half complain about increased workload due to digitalization. The metal workers union appears unconcerned about this, apparently sharing the views of management that German companies could – and should – be the vanguards of ongoing technological change, and that the expected job losses could to a large extent be compensated for by the new jobs that will be created by increasing exports. And there is no concern that this export-oriented competitiveness strategy also means exporting unemployment abroad, insofar as workers elsewhere will lose their jobs in the process.

What also sustains this positive orientation to 'Industry 4.0' is the belief that the 'dematerialization' of production and consumption will reduce our 'ecological footprint', and that digitalization through apps, electronic platforms and other technological innovations will also contribute to solving social problems. It is claimed this would benefit the countries of the Global South in particular: better integrating them into global commodity chains, enabling electronic access to education, encouraging 'good governance' through improved transparency and online citizen participation, and contributing to increasing agricultural productivity through the targeted use of fertilizers and economical irrigation.[2] All this is in fact very dubious. But before discussing some of the much less positive foreseeable consequences the digitalization of manufacturing will have on workers in different parts of the world, it is necessary briefly to address the technological limits of today's 'digital revolution'.

BOTTLENECKS FOR A 'DIGITAL REVOLUTION'

Fibre optics are commonly regarded as the future of digital networks, as they enable significantly higher transmission speed than their copper-based counterparts. However, these networks are hardly to be found in many parts of the world. And we are still very far away from meeting a number of crucial technological preconditions for 'smart factories' in the form of a standardized application programming interface, common data language, and the integration of still largely self-sufficient systems in the logistics, energy supply, and building management areas of production. Finally, the transition of companies to the digital landscape exposes them to the dangers of cyber-attacks not only by individuals, inside or outside the firm, but by computers, social networks, the 'cloud', and by nefarious organizations operating at a global level. Not surprisingly, proponents of the digitalization process assume that most of these technological challenges will be addressed successfully – no matter what this would cost individual companies and governments – even though no solution is in sight. But for both high-income countries and the developing world, ordinary cybercrime, cyber-attacks against the financial sector, and data breaches are a growing problem. This is the case particularly in Africa, as customers often conduct financial transactions over insecure mobile phones and transmissions lines that are not designed to protect communications.[3]

Problems with digitalization in developing and emerging countries are almost exclusively addressed as a technical challenge and as question of investment in the development of digital infrastructures. When risks of digitalization are mentioned, they are often confined to the 'digital divide', meaning the lack of internet access for almost four billion people in the Global South. The 'digital divide' does indeed remain extensive: at the end of 2018, only a bit more than half of the global population was using the internet, more than 80 per cent in developed countries but only 45.3 per cent in developing countries. Even though the strongest growth of all regions was reported in Africa, only about a quarter of its population is using the internet and the proportion of households with access to a computer is still very low.[4] (South Africa is an exception; however, most of its communication infrastructure is concentrated in the hands of the affluent white population, which has both access to computers and the internet and the skills required to use them.)

Occasionally, the rapid spread of smart phone usage in countries of the Global South is seen as an indicator of their openness to innovation and an imminent 'digital revolution'. Many studies refer to the widespread use of electronic purses in Kenya since 2007, and argue that this has made banking services more accessible to the poor. In Kenya, as in other developing countries, many people have mastered English as the *lingua franca* of globalization; offshore call centres and other ambitious large-scale projects are expected to create many new jobs in the long term. However, most African internet users still must go to internet cafes, where access is slow and expensive. Indeed, access to advanced technology in Africa is constrained by infrastructure parameters such as the lack of electricity, IT penetration, tele-density, internet density and broadband penetration. The technological bottleneck in broadband expansion and the deficits in education and vocational training represent an even greater obstacle for developing countries than for the countries of the Global North.

Even more skewed is the position of developing countries with respect to so-called 'artificial intelligence' programs and applications. These neural networks, which can be deployed in both monitored and unsupervised modes, are programmed to learn through algorithmic regulations that process huge volumes of structured data (such as measured values, names, addresses) and unstructured data (such as images, films, texts, language files) to turn huge volumes of information into usable patterns and classification. In the US and China, billions are being invested in AI research from public and private sources in order to apply AI to a multitude of functions, including image identification, voice recognition, and self-driving vehicle technologies. Indeed, as announced in its 'Made in China 2025' and 'Internet-Plus' agendas, China would like to outperform the US as the leader in the high-tech sector and become the world champion in AI by 2030, and plans to pump some $60 billion a year into the industry.[5] With potential domestic access to the data of more than a billion people, the country's high-tech trio of Baidu, Alibaba, and Tencent has a certain advantage over their Silicon Valley rivals Google, Apple, Facebook, and Amazon. But Russia, Japan, and South Korea are also trying to establish their own AI systems. Even France, Germany, the UK, Canada, and small countries such as Estonia, Finland, and Iceland have developed AI-initiatives in order to improve national productivity, while the goal of greatly increasing R&D investment in AI at the EU level is linked to the further development of Europe's 'single market' and its greater industrial pre-eminence globally. Still, the global competition for supremacy in this key technology of the twenty-first century is essentially between a handful of US and Chinese companies.

Today, technological 'sovereignty' can only be found – if it can be found at all – in the economic arena, to the extent that a country can form a closed value chain – from chips, to computers, batteries, and software. The greater or lesser degree of technological sovereignty of a country or region will ultimately also determine where the greatest gains in employment will come from digitalization and who will bear the negative consequences of its economic deployment. Digitalization in all its forms, from 'smart homes' to electrical cars and the new merging of the physical and virtual worlds through data-based production organized through the 'cloud', is associated with the expectation that good quality and high-paying jobs can be attracted almost anywhere, provided that basic technical infrastructure exists. However, even many 'best-case' examples of high-tech production yield more ambiguous conclusions. Foxconn's 'green plant' in Wisconsin where displays are built, Apple's data center in Iowa, or Teslas's lithium-ion battery factory for electric cars in the desert of Nevada, all indicate that local authorities can often attract high-tech firms (which create very specialized and very few permanent jobs as well as generate toxins) only by exempting these firms from sales, property, and general business taxes for ten or even twenty years. The tax breaks embedded in these deals often soak up most of the additional tax revenue from local budgets, while at the same time the influx of new tech workers drives up rents, as well as causing overcrowding in schools and hospitals.[6]

EMPLOYMENT AND THE NEW WAVE OF AUTOMATION

Initially, digitalization appeared to mean nothing more than a new level of automation. But the use of robots paired with AI means its impact has been of another order altogether in almost all economic sectors, whether in auto and electrical manufacturing, metal processing and metal engineering, plastic and chemical industries, the beverage and food sectors, and not least, the arms and security industries where AI is already integral to many operations. Many jobs will also be impacted in sectors such as agriculture, retail trade, and banking and insurance; while labour intensive work in administration, law, radiology, and telemarketing will also be transformed. Robots and software systems can replace virtually all activities that are measurable and repetitive. In short, in the years ahead not only blue-collar but also white-collar jobs can and will be automated, to one degree or another.[7] In the future, taxi, courier, and freight forwarding companies will increasingly use autonomous driving systems. This also applies to many activities that require thinking along with others, whereby computers take on cognitive performance for such tasks, reorganize and restructure them. In banking, for example, it will be software applications and not individual bank employees who will be decisive in who receives a loan and on what terms. Even in the area of care, there is already an increase in robotization; machines support the transfer of patients and ensure that medicines are taken in regulated schedule. In the US and even in Germany, it is permitted that computer algorithms make personnel decisions with respect to hiring. Even the activities of teachers and social workers are also likely to change considerably as a result of the use of learning programs.

Many scenarios today assume that, in the short run, at least one third, and in the longer run, far more than one-half of all the job activities carried out by people today will no longer exist. New occupational fields will emerge for tasks such as social media management, the interior design of virtual rooms, or the insurance of algorithms. This might fit into the dreams of many young people in Europe, Africa, or other places who prefer to become 'influencers', 'You-Tubers' or 'gamers' rather than waiters, administrative employees, or skilled metal workers. Lower paid positions requiring the least amount of education are more likely to disappear, while higher skilled servant jobs (i.e. in the care sector) for which there is a growing demand, will not necessarily be paid decently. At the same time, skilled work in technology companies (from content moderation to software testing) is embedded in a two-tier system of employment, as a growing share of the workforce, employed by outside agents and without any job security, receives a fraction of the wage benefits of full-time employees.

One important reason why the development of AI and robots is being driven forward, particularly in China, can be found in the demographic development of a rapidly aging population which is exerting corresponding wage pressure on Chinese companies. Robots are supposed to be used in the manufacturing industry and many other sectors of the economy to keep company costs low and increase profits in times of slower economic growth and increased competition. But so far only every fourth robot is manufactured by a Chinese company. In 2017 there were just 97 robots per 10,000 employees in China, far fewer than the 710 in South Korea. In Singapore, Germany, and Japan, the deployment of robots is also quite high, with the peak ratios in the German automotive industry already at more than 1000 robots per 10,000 employees at the end of 2017.[8] This is the basis for the strategic calculation of the German mechanical engineering industry; it views itself among the winners of 'Industry 4.0' because it already produces the robots that will substitute for human labour elsewhere. China is, however, catching up quickly. With the help of the Swiss industrial group ABB, a state-of-art production facility will be built in Shanghai in the next two years in which robots, together with workers, will produce robots. In this facility, AI is projected to assist in the production of approximately 100,000 robots per year, representing a quarter of the previous robot production of the whole world. The International Federation of Robotics expects that in only two years, nearly 500,000 robots will be in use in Asia, while in Europe there will be less than 100,000 and only 64,000 in the US. It is plausible to suggest that soon most of all robot sales will be concentrated in the five markets of China, South Korea, Japan, the US, and Europe (with Singapore likely to be a sixth). The use of robots in developing countries as a whole will continue to lag behind, even though digitalization in the form of e-commerce is growing quite quickly, especially in Africa. As a result of the few robots deployed so far in developing countries, the impact of digitalization on the labour markets in these countries might be expected to be comparably lower than those in the advanced capitalist countries.

In principle, companies all over the world expect the digitalization of all production and business processes to reduce costs by savings in manpower, energy, and raw materials. As with technological changes in past decades, it might be argued that in terms of the disappearance of jobs in the companies affected by the restructuring, 'the pace, scale and impact of change was nowhere near as catastrophic as initially feared ... if technology is accompanied by investment in training, education and compensation, its worst effect can be much reduced ... New technology will lead to change in the bundles of tasks that make up many jobs. Some will go, and new ones arise.'[9] So far, the quantitative effects of digitalization on the labour market are hard to estimate and thus figures presented in different studies vary. While a first influential 2013 study of Benedikt Frey and Michael Osborne claimed that nearly 50 per cent of all occupations across all sectors in the US were at risk of being automated by 2030, a 2017 McKinsey study argued that this would likely not happen until mid-century. A similar study carried out for EU countries by Jeremy Bowles concluded that in the less competitive economies such as Romania, Bulgaria, Greece, and Portugal, up to 40 to 60 per cent of all jobs might be lost due to digitalization.[10] But the results of more recent studies on the potential impact of digitalization on labour markets of advanced industrialized countries suggest wide divergences between countries.[11] In Germany, significant job losses, estimated at approximately 60,000, might occur over the next ten years due to digitalization, especially in the manufacturing sector. However, at the same time, it is also expected that the high export quota of the German metal industry can be maintained and that almost as many new jobs with an IT and a scientific profile will be created as will be lost to digitalization. Unlike in the US, capital investments in robots in Germany have so far not led to a reduction in total employment.[12]

For developing and emerging economies, available assessments of employment trends are far less promising. In its *World Development Report for 2016*, the World Bank assumed that two-thirds of all jobs would be susceptible to automation, and that since most countries will only be using and not producing robots and other automation machinery, huge employment losses in developing and emerging economies might be expected. Although it saw some evidence for 'smart production' processes in a few emerging markets such as Brazil, India, Indonesia, Malaysia, Mexico, Thailand, and Turkey, the report showed that most developing countries were constrained by a scarcity of trained technicians and engineers and by infrastructure issues such as reliable electricity supplies. Combined with a continued slowdown in trade and global value chains remaining concentrated amongst a small number of countries, this Word Bank report afforded a bleak future. As AI becomes embedded as the newest vintage of the capital stock, manufacturing might well no longer offer a pathway to growth in low- and middle-income countries.[13]

The World Bank's sobering picture of digital capitalism on a global scale is supported by numerous studies undertaken by private consultancies such as McKinsey Global Institute and PriceWaterhouseCoopers.[14] All these studies suggest that job destruction is likely to accelerate under the pressure of technological change, and therefore machines, robots, and computers will increasingly have an absolute cost advantage over labour.

The most severe impact of digitalization in manufacturing is expected to be in South-East Asia, where during the last decades export production in sectors such as clothing, footwear, textiles, and electronics have become a backbone of economic development. Automobile assembly and parts manufacturing in the region are also at risk from automation. More than 50 per cent of all manufacturing jobs in Cambodia, Laos, Vietnam, the Philippines, and Thailand are at risk, with approximately 137 million people in the region impacted.[15] Some companies, such as the shoe company Adidas, have already re-established manufacturing in Germany, with the extensive use of the new automation processes. Indeed, the dynamic of 're-shoring' industrial production back to the core capitalist countries has recently been linked to an even more shocking development for employment. The *Human Rights Outlook* for 2018, produced by Verisk Maplecroft, shows that in Vietnam and Cambodia, over 85 per cent of jobs in the garment, textile, and footwear industries are at high risk of automation. Most of these jobs are held by women, and they will have to look for work further down the supply chains, where abuses are more likely to occur, and where regulations as well as workers' rights are more easily ignored.[16] This report suggests that the risk of slavery and human trafficking becoming more prominent in global supply chains will spiral, particularly in the five Asian countries mentioned above, as these countries are already rated as 'high risk' countries in the Modern Slavery Index.

THE 'NEW NORMAL' OF WORK

The foremost contention of the proponents of 'Industry 4.0' is that routine processes and physically strenuous activities will easily – and soon – be carried out by machines. Humans are expected to become machine supervisors rather than direct producers. For high-skilled workers, digitalization will presumably go together with a further blurring of the boundaries between working time and lifetime, less controls over the pace and intensity of work, more stress, and new challenges for work-life balance. At the same time, companies are likely to rely less than today on a workforce permanently attached to the company and to hire on demand a flexible workforce. For many workers, the employment relationship will become a series of work assignments, and the new jobs created will lack a clear allocation to specific organizations. The ties to the firm will be cut and trade unions will have even larger difficulties than today in communicating with and organizing employees, and representing their interests. All routine work, including standardized and anonymous processes, but particularly digital services, will become subject to contingent labour and further efficiency pressure. Although those activities which involve direct human interaction are foreseen as becoming more highly valued, this will be more than offset by digital services being divided into ever smaller parts and delegated to 'virtual labourers' performing tasks which can be done in a few seconds and remunerated, in a piece rate fashion, at a few cents per task. In this context, 'cloud' and 'crowd-working' (via Amazon Turk, Clickworker, Crowdflower, Microtask), and forms of work-on-demand (such as Uber, Lyft, TaskRabbit, Handy, Wonolo), are all expected to flourish. Such online technologies used to link 'labour supply' and 'labour demand' can be expected to increase the trend towards the casualization of work and further informalization of the economy.[17]

Like other sorts of casual work, 'crowd-' or 'click-workers' are largely isolated and often even invisible; and as today's pieceworkers providing their services 'on-demand', their earnings are often lower and erratic. The misleading designation of these workers as independent contractors is not a new phenomenon as it occurs in comparable terms in other sectors such as the garment, construction, and trucking industries. But the misleading categorization of workers as independent contractors permits the avoidance of labour laws as well as the payment of benefits and taxes. In addition, the transnational character of 'crowd-work', across countries such as China, India, the Philippines, and Indonesia, makes it harder to rely on the regulation of working time, salary, and social security provisions in any given national jurisdiction. Furthermore, a division between work and private life vanishes with the on-demand calls on workers repositioned as contractors, adding new stress factors to life in neoliberal capitalism. In a sense, the emerging world of digital work bears resemblance to the 'putting-out system' of early capitalism, which allowed workers – especially women – a certain amount of flexibility and balance in their lives while at the same time constraining daily life by the constant pressure to produce. This is aggravated by those aspects of neoliberal ideology that encourage such work§ to be seen as 'just for fun' or even, more simply and misleadingly, to overcome boredom. Insofar as neoliberal ideology has been able to capture the minds of ordinary people, especially of young ones, they understand themselves as 'micro-entrepreneurs' or as being 'their own boss' even though only in rare cases are they working autonomously. Moreover, their self-employment is typically not associated with an upward career trajectory or even with an escape from poverty. Working as a formally independent contractor is often little more than a trap for young people who are in an endless cycle between self-employment and often poor-quality jobs with bad working conditions and low pay (and sometimes just an unpaid family member). In fact, since digital workers have very different social backgrounds and professional experiences, it is entirely possible for students to be competing with single mothers, and pensioners from the core capitalist countries with programmers in India whose income feeds an entire family with young children.

This is indeed a new feature of the so-called 'gig economy', where working on-demand via apps threatens to become an even more severe problem in the future, not least for trade unions. There are good reasons to assume that irregularity, flexibility, uncertainty, unpredictability, and different sorts of risk will be the 'new normal of work' in the era of digital capitalism. It does not matter whether these workers will be classified as 'precarious', as 'informal' or 'own account' workers. In the global marketplace, they are subjugated to unstable employment, lower wages and incomes, and even more dangerous working conditions; they will not receive regular social benefits; and they will often be denied the right to join a union. The labour controls enabled by the algorithms of digital platforms make the labour disciplines of capitalism even more rigid as they impose seemingly 'scientific' measures and evaluations. But in contrast to the old manufacturing compromises of Fordism where workers exchanged, at least in part, their submission to factory discipline for social benefits, regular wage gains, and political representation, these are all gone. Many digital workers who fill permanent or temporary job needs are denied the protections of permanent and formal work contracts, including the legal rights of employees (often being classified as independent contractors). Only a tiny fraction of the total workforce – at the global, regional, and national levels – will succeed in finding access to regular and regulated, higher skilled, and better paid jobs. It is increasingly apparent that the growing disorder of the present modes of neoliberal capitalism is closely linked to the fading away of the state as a 'broker', under pressure from unions and left parties, between capital and labour.

The job and social security that workers in the advanced capitalist economies – a small share of the world population – achieved for a few decades after the Second World War is fast disappearing. This is a development that contributes to the dynamics of escalating disparity and progressive inequality in all parts of the world. In a world of 'oligarchic globalization', where only the economically strong nations and the wealthiest 20 per cent, and in particular the richest one per cent, can have realistic positive expectations, liberal welfare policies of progressive inclusion are no longer on the political agenda. Even in those countries where labour rights remain comparatively strong for the core work force in the leading companies of the manufacturing sector, millions of workers are already trapped into a low-wage cycle with very little chance to advance. Those still working in factories and offices will increasingly be controlled by apps and algorithms. Algorithms are the equivalent of the old assembly line – but much harder to disrupt and more difficult to locate as spaces for organizing.[18]

MANY QUESTIONS, UNCERTAIN FUTURES

Digitalization is changing the world of work, with noticeable consequences for workers. As a recent study of the entire service sector in Germany shows, as physical stress decreases, work stress and psychological pressure increase significantly: surveillance, control of work, and increased workload are all experienced by many employees.[19] Job profiles are changing: in the transport sector, truck drivers are becoming transport managers who must do more and more accounting work in their cabins; in the auto and steel sectors, it is very likely that in the future more people will be working alongside or directly with robots on the assembly line. Nobody knows how humans will deal with the permanent pressure for work efficiency emanating from soulless machines. Some companies will certainly go so far as to use robots instead of workers to reduce labour costs. But not everything that can be automated will be automated. In capitalism this always depends on which option proves to be more 'favourable' to those social forces that can command people as well as machines.

Despite ongoing controversies about the quantitative implications of digitalization for employment in the different regions of the world, there is enough evidence that workers will find it increasingly difficult to compete against machines and raise their stagnant wages. Due to the newest wave of automation, it will be possible to produce (even) more (useless) commodities with fewer people, which will increase structural unemployment at least in some, and likely in many, countries and lead to further pressure on wages. In contrast to earlier waves of automation, today not only unskilled workers are affected by economic and social insecurity, but also the skilled working class in what have been 'good jobs' with union protections. It is plausible to expect, therefore, that the drive towards digital technologies, robots and AI goes hand-in-hand with the development of labour markets that are characterized by even more flexibility then today, by one-day or zero-hour contracts and discrete tasks on digital platforms, all leading to ever-more precarious and insecure forms of work and thus livelihoods. And we have already seen how far right wing and xenophobic parties and movements have exploited workers' justified concerns about their employment futures.

Trade unions in Germany are now demanding an extension of co-determination in the workplace, both about the length and the distribution of working time over the week and the permissible amount of work to be done in the context of digital capitalism. It remains to be seen whether this will be successful or not, but in countries without a comparable regulation of co-determination at the company level, trade union representatives will find it very difficult to defend even a shrinking core workforce and what they have previously negotiated in terms of protection mechanisms for their members in the past. That said, even as regards the challenging fight for workers' rights in the 'platform economy', there are some positive developments that might give hope. Food delivery couriers in Italy, the Netherlands, Belgium, Germany, and France have formed their own unions and are contesting the disastrous 'freelance' schemes in the growing goods transport sector through strikes and militant protest actions, organizing even cross-border solidarity and support.[20] And in Silicon Valley at least some of the engineers, designers, and product managers have begun to see themselves as tech workers whose interests are in opposition to the Silicon elites; they have started to build alliances with the shuttle drivers, security guards, janitors, and cafeteria staff that make up the industry's invisible workforce.

What is certain, however, is that neither the 'masters of the algorithms' who possess the intellectual property rights, nor the owners of the means of production, will convert productivity increases that can be achieved with the help of digitalization into a reduction in weekly working hours. The 'disruptive technologies' of digitalization, robotics, and AI also further challenge, as neoliberalism has already done, the existing regimes of national welfare states (in the Global North) with a social security system built on full-employment and stable and localized jobs. Consequently, in many countries of the European Union a vivid debate has emerged around the old idea of a 'machine tax' and new modes of financing social and economic security for all citizens, including free-lancers and gig workers 'working on-demand'. The core idea of a 'machine tax' is to tax companies according to their deployment of robots, PCs, and other machines relative to employees. With the revenues from such a tax, either an 'unconditional basic income' (UBI) could be introduced, or 'universal basic services' (UBS) expanded, by financing the education sector more generously or significantly reducing social security contributions. It is not surprising that CEOs of relatively labour-intensive companies, like the German manufacturer Siemens, are sympathetic to the UBI concept. There are, however, pros and cons about the proposal of a UBI as an effective answer to the dilemmas posed by advancing robotization. Most obviously, within capitalist economies as they actually exist, replacing current social security systems completely by a *high* UBI would be a neoliberal project which is neither fundable nor desirable.[21] But a UBI of a *low* amount, as an extension of existing social benefits and services financed by taxes on capital and the consumption of nature, might fit into the most promising proposals to address the employment effects of digitalization. This is the progressive proposal for a shorter working week and the sharing of paid wage labour. Addressing the distribution of work, in terms of total weekly hours and by occupation, is not only necessary for compensating job losses due to automation, but could also allow a fairer distribution of unpaid work in the private sphere. Further, it could help to engage in the work of maintenance, repair, and refurbishing commodities in the 'circular economy' (an economy minimizing waste and maximizing the reuse material resources) that is necessary to address cumulative, and prevent further, ecological damage.[22]

For many civil society organizations and activists striving for a socio-ecological transformation of capitalism, the 'digital age' is seen as facilitating decentralization, encouraging horizontal collaboration and sharing knowledge between local initiatives and individual users in a global network, and as the vital precondition for peer-to-peer production and a new 'commons' as building blocks of a new postcapitalist society. Certainly, the internet enables 'crowd-sourcing' of funds and ideas, and at the same time allows small producers, including farmers, to communicate easily with customers. The distribution of 3D printing technology could facilitate efficient production of a range of items people need in micro factories on a local scale, and thereby reduce the need for transport, marketing, and assembling. There are many quite sensible areas of application for the digitization of communication, exchange processes, and transport systems.

But digital capitalism is also formed through – and dominated by – the enormous concentration of political and economic power in the few companies that dominate the internet. The enormous surveillance potential of digital infrastructure, for example, is as important as the implications for production and employment. And it goes without saying that the societal dependence on a few 'global monopolies' threatens to further narrow the political scope for alternative policies and social projects at the national and even regional or local levels, especially for the countries of the Global South. However, there is no technical or social necessity that profit-driven platforms dominate the economy. If existing governments decided that internet platforms are infrastructures of a general 'public interest', more alternative platforms could operate and emerge, and more cooperative projects and small-scale initiatives of all kinds would have a chance to develop. There is also the simple necessity for campaigns to tax the exorbitant profits of BIG DATA, to intervene against the intellectual property rights protections in national and international trade law for data collectors and brokers, and to gain collective and democratic control and ownership of data.[23]

So, even current governments could do a lot within existing regulatory capacities without any radical rupture at the level of the state. They could restrict access to and trade of data by the GAFAM complex of companies (Google, Amazon, Facebook, Apple, Microsoft); they could refuse to sign international trade agreements which deprive governments of instruments to regulate the digital economy;[24] they could develop their own (regional) digital infrastructures as 'collectively' owned ones; they could ban autonomous weapon systems, which are based on robotics and AI as the proverbial 'dual-use' technologies; and they could sanction companies such as Amazon Web Services (AWS) that through their service platforms facilitate the violation of UN human rights norms. Most importantly, in our times of 'peak everything', governments could establish a multilateral regime of resource governance in order to contain geopolitical competition over the scarce raw materials necessary not only for digital technologies and AI, but also for renewable energy technologies.

If these are all possible reforms worth campaigning for today, more fundamental change will be required insofar as the promises of the 'fourth industrial revolution' are not consistent, above all from an ecological point of view, with the limits which must be introduced in all spheres of life against productivism and endless accumulation. Soon the 'internet of things', which will interconnect devices, robots, factories, offices, infrastructures, autonomous and semi-autonomous driving systems, will also extend to autonomous weapon systems. This is already developing very rapidly in the US, China, Russia, Israel, and South Korea. These networks are all controlled by AI, and will multiply data flows thousands of times over across the globe. But with faster and massively increased volumes of data flows, the greater will be the consumption of computers, raw material, energy, and, as part of the data expansion, the production of toxic electronic waste. The AI for speech recognition alone, as well as the algorithms being developed as 'smart' and environmentally-friendly solutions for our everyday lives and industry alike, also consumes huge amounts of electricity.[25] The energy demand for crypto-currencies is enormous. (In 2018, Bitcoin alone is estimated to have required at least 46 terawatt hours of electricity for its computing system, with this causing the release of around 22 megatons of carbon dioxide.)[26]

Much the same could be the result if the proposed Facebook digital currency 'Libra' goes ahead. This is yet another example of the ecological and material costs of digital capitalism.

The prospects of 'digital capitalism' will be deeply intertwined with the future prices and physical availability of both oil and critical metals. As economies across the globe transition to renewable energy, decentralized electricity production and electric mobility, while consumer demand for all kinds of mobile devices rise and governments push ahead with their spending on modern military systems (including autonomous drones), the demand increases for the resources on which these depend – not only oil and water, but also 'critical metals' such as copper, nickel, silver, uranium, lead and so called 'rare earth metals' (such as indium, gallium, germanium, lithium and many others). The future of digitalization, robotics, and AI thus depends not only on the geopolitical conditions for securing access to the corporate traders in digital data that are concentrated in the US, China and, to a lesser extent, Russia. Their future depends even more on securing the access to the energy and raw materials that are needed to produce the smart products and sell the associated services.

As with every other technological advance of capitalist production, digitalization and AI will not resolve pressing social problems, let alone the underlying economic and political contradictions of global capitalism. Above all today, there is a pressing imperative to debate the unavoidable trade-offs that are looming between economic purposes and ecological constraints. 'Industry 4.0' will make sure that we are buying goods and services we neither need nor want, seduced by the incessant marketing of social media. But the ecological and social sacrifices we will have to make for this type of 'digital progress' are simply not acceptable. Ultimately, it is people who determine the further development of technical systems. Consequently, they can also set limits for technical – and self – optimization, which should not be exceeded. In this context, socialists should be insisting on the urgent need for the broad public debate that is required to answer questions such as: Why is it good to replace humans in so many functions? And why should we make ourselves redundant, not only as workers but also in other senses? What does it mean to deploy machines that make decisions faster than we think, especially when it comes to the use of lethal weapons? In which areas of society could AI be used meaningfully and where should we prevent its use? How can we retain and regain control over digital infrastructures? How can we build them to serve all users, and determine where we neither need nor want them? All this really, then, begs a further question: can any of these questions be answered within capitalism?

NOTES

1   Paul Mason, *Postcapitalism: A Guide to Our Future*, London: Allan Lane, 2015.
2   UNIDO, *Accelerating Clean Energy Through Industry 4.0. Manufacturing the Next Revolution*, Vienna: UN Industrial Development Organization 2017; UNDEP, *Making Innovation and Technology Work for Development*, Opening remarks at UNGA side-event, 27 September 2018. Even from the perspective of the UNDP, it is advisable for developing countries to accept purely technical solutions for long standing – and increasing – social problems. No wonder that the initiative 'IBM Digital – Nation Africa', launched during Africa's Official Ministerial Summit on Innovation in 2017 in Maputo, Mozambique, was warmly welcomed by representatives from African countries. During this meeting, IBM announced the intent to invest $70 million for a cloud-based learning platform designed to provide free skills development programs for up to 25 million African youth over the next five years, thereby claiming to enable digital competence and support for a 21st century workforce in Africa. The meeting is documented here: www.invovation-africa.com.
3   Hildah Nduati, 'Cyber Security in Emerging Financial Markets', *CGAP Background Documents*, 2018, available at: www.findvgateway.org.
4   International Telecommunication Union, 'ITU releases 2017 global information and communication technology facts and figures', *ITU News*, 31 July 2017, available at: www.news.itu.int.
5   Philipp Staab and Florian Butello, Florian, 'Digitaler Kapitalismus – wie China das Silicon Valley herausfordert', *WISO direkt*, 3, Bonn: Friedlich Ebert Stiftung 2028, 2018, pp.1-4, available at: www.library.fes.de.
6   Randy Bryce, 'What happened to Foxconn's plan to build a $10bn factory in Wisconsin?', *The Guardian*, 31 January 2019.
7   Carl Benedikt Frey and Michael Osborne, *The Future of Employment: How Susceptible are Jobs to Computerisation?* Oxford: Oxford University Press, 2013.
8   International Federation of Robotics, *World Robotics*, 2018 edition, available at: www.ifr.org.
9   Victor Figueroa, 'New technology, labour and digital sovereignty', *Global Labour Column*, 315, November 2018, available at: column.global-labour-university.org.
10   Jeremy Bowles, *The Computerization of European Jobs*, Brussels European and Global Economic Laboratory (Bruegel), 24 July 2014, available at: bruegel.org.
11   See Ljubica Nedelkoska and Glenda Quintini, *Automation, Skills Use and Training*, Paris: OECD, Social, Employment and Migration Working Paper, N. 202, 2018; Melanie Arntz, Gregory Terry, and Ulrich Zierahn, *The Risk of Automation for Jobs in OECD Countries: A Comparative Analysis*, Paris: OECD, Social, Employment and Migration Working Papers, N. 189, 2016.
12   Ing DiBa, 'Die Roboter kommen (doch nicht)' *Economics & Financial Analysis*, 11 June 2018.
13   World Bank Group, *World Development Report: Digital Dividends*, Washington: World Bank, 2016; Mary Hallward-Driemeier and Gaurav Nayyar, *Trouble in the Making? The Future of Manufacturing-Led Development*, Washington: World Bank, 2017.
14   McKinsey Global Institute, *A Future That Works: Automation, Employment, And Productivity*, January 2017, available at: www.mckinsey.com; PriceWaterhouse Cooper, *Digital Factories 2020*, 2018, available at: www.pwc.de.
15   Jae-Hee Chang, Gary Rynhart, and Phu Huynh, *ASEAN in Transformation: How*

Technology Is Changing Jobs and Enterprises, Geneva: ILO, ILO Working Paper N. 10, 2016. In its 2017 report, the McKinsey Global Institute foresees a similar process for Africa, estimating jobs at risk of being automated ranging from about 40 to over 50 per cent. See also Karishma Banga and Dirk Willem de Velde, *Digitalization and the Future of Manufacturing in Africa*, London: Oversea Development Institute, 2018, available at: www.odi.org.

16   Verisk Maplecroft, *Human Rights Outlook 2018*, available at: www.maplecroft.com.

17   Valerio De Stefano, 'The Rise of the 'Just-in-Time Workforce': On-Demand, Crowd Work and Labour Protection in the 'Gig' Economy', *Comparative Labour Law and Policy Journal*, 37(3), 2016, pp. 471-503.

18   Antonio Caselli, 'Workers are the Heart of the Algorithm', *The Bullet*, 26 December 2017, available at: www.socialistproject.ca.

19   ver.di (Vereinigte Dienstleistungsgewerkschaft), *Digitalisierung und Arbeitsqualität. Eine Sonderauswertung auf Basis des DGB-Index Gute Arbeit 2016 für den Dienstleistungssektor*, available at: innovation–gute–arbeit.verdi.de.

20   In January 2019 Netherlands courts ruled in two decisions that the elimination of employment contracts by the food delivery company Deliveroo, and the legal transformation of couriers to self-employed status the year before, had not altered the fundamental relationships of authority and dependence. Thus, the couriers remain in an employment relationship as defined by Dutch law and Deliveroo's activities fell within the scope of the national collective agreement for the goods transport sector.

21   Such a UBI would weaken trade unions and the existing social rights of employees; it would allow a reduction of public services even further and make basic services more expensive.

22   See Elmar Altvater and Birgit Mahnkopf, 'The Capitalocene: Permanent Capitalist Counter-Revolution', in Leo Panitch and Greg Albo, eds., *Socialist Register 2019: A World Turned Upside Down?*, London: Merlin Press, 2018, pp. 79-99.

23   In June 2019, the Group of 20 finance ministers at least agreed to compile common rules to close loopholes used by global tech giants to reduce their corporate tax. This is encouraging, although it's only a first step to reach a global agreement. The new legislation enacted in 2018 by the EU to protect its citizen's personal data is also a step in the right direction (see: gdpr-info.eu).

24   As an example, the *Comprehensive and Progressive Trans Pacific Partnership* (CPTPP) agreement between, on the one hand, economically strong signature states such as Australia, Japan, Canada, but also Singapore, Brunei, and New Zeeland, and their weaker contractual partners in Mexico, Peru, Chile, Malaysia, and Vietnam, on the other, concluded in 2018. It mandates the unlimited and free movement of data flows across borders, and thus deprives governments of an important instrument to regulate the digital economy and, in the longer term, to develop their own digital infrastructures.

25   New estimations suggest that the carbon footprint of training just one large neural network is as much as 284 tons of carbon dioxide equivalent. This is five times the CO_2 emissions produced during the lifetime of an average car. See: Donna Lu, 'Creating an AI can be five times worse for the planet than a car', *New Scientist*, 6 June 2019, available at: www.newscientist.com.

26   As revealed by the most detailed study to date on the energy requirements of Bitcoins: Christian Stoll, Lena Klaaßen, and Ulrich Gallersdörfer, 'The Carbon Footprint of Bitcoin', MIT CEEPR Working Paper, 2018-018, available at: ceepr.mit.edu/files/papers/2018-018-Brief.pdf.

A NEW WORLD OF WORKERS: CONFRONTING THE GIG ECONOMY

MICHELLE CHEN

The twenty-first century workplace is no longer a single place, or even a physical place at all. And in many ways it's getting harder even to define what we actually do for a living. Technological advancement in machine learning, digital communication, and data processing is changing the way both labour and capital work – for some of us, beyond recognition. There are these days many conversations about the 'future of work,' ranging in tone from existential paranoia about our robot overlords, to techno-evangelical neoliberal euphoria. On the surface, the 'future of work' seems rather perilous for today's workers; fears of extinction and professional existential crisis abound. But it's more complicated than just robots robbing humans of their livelihoods. According to an analysis by the World Economic Forum, within the short window from 2018 to 2022, about 75 million jobs will be eliminated, while 133 million new jobs will be created, through the development of automation, artificial intelligence, digital platforms, and other innovations. Other projections have focused on the disproportionate impacts faced by specific groups. The World Economic Forum predicts, for example, that impending waves of automation will engender both job losses and new opportunities, but with the disturbing side effect of growing polarization between wealthy and poor.[1]

This essay will explore impending changes in the way globalization and technological innovation will shape how we work, live, and play, and more importantly, how we will identify as workers and as citizens. Mobile communications, automation, and artificial intelligence are opening up new realms of creativity, collaboration, and cultural interaction, while also widening economic and social rifts. The proliferation of new technologies and communications platforms provide corporations with new methods for extracting labour, information and time from labourers and consumers. Yet for all this daunting disruption, the way power operates between workers and their bosses remains largely the same – it's just mediated through the fluid mechanics of a fast-changing digital infrastructure. Nonetheless, the world of work – not just the goods and services produced but also how production is regulated or deregulated, the pace of the workday, and workers' needs for fair pay and just treatment – is evolving at an unprecedented rate. And the world of workers – how we see ourselves as a global labour force – is dramatically expanding and shrinking at once, distorting but also clarifying how much we all have in common, and revealing the distance between us.

We need not be alarmist when it comes to bleak predictions of the techno-dystopia of mass unemployment: the 15-hour workweek that Keynes predicted would be the norm by the turn of the millennium seems laughable in retrospect. We are witnessing a wholesale restructuring of industries, and inevitably, new opportunities to recast the economic landscape – hopefully with workers in the foreground.[2] At the same time, the projections of millions of jobs generated through technological change are meaningless from a labour perspective. Still to be determined are the quality of the jobs, who will work them, for whom, and on whose terms. After all, technology is the tool by which corporations consolidate their control over workers and profit streams, and workers can likewise wield technology to increase their own power and autonomy; the future of that rivalry remains unscripted. Concerns about automation as the new frontier range wildly from 'AI will kill development' to 'our robot overlords will rescue us from the drudgery of wage capitalism'. We're already living with the expanding influence of artificial intelligence (AI) – broadly defined as the ability of machines to make complex decisions in uncertain environments – perhaps as consumers who shop online in a sea of predictive marketing algorithms, or as workers who have seen their jobs get easier as a result of increased computing power, or rendered redundant by automation on the assembly line. As with globalization in general, there will be 'winners' and 'losers' in the new economy: an ergonomic lift at a skilled nursing facility could reduce a nurse's risk of injury on the job, but it could also reduce the staff and leave her assistant aide jobless. A 3D printer could replace a graphic designer, or alternately, become that designer's most indispensable tool of the trade.

It is impossible to estimate exactly how many, or whose, jobs will be 'lost' to technology, or which vocations will be 'replaced'. A World Economic Forum report anticipates that overall, across twelve major industries, the share of work tasks to be performed by machine and algorithm, rather than by a human, will rise dramatically in the coming years, from a 71-29 per cent human-machine ratio currently to 58-42 per cent – edging into the majority of work hours for some sectors, like data processing. So the pattern of displacement is clear. But how we will fare as individuals, socially or economically, will depend on how we co-evolve with our machines. Most projections suggest overall that the main job losses will be concentrated in lower-ranked service and processing jobs: clerical workers, secretaries, service jobs. Often jobs that are disproportionately performed by women, which require basic education and command basic wages, will likely face larger-scale replacement. Workers, who have for generations been advised to invest in education to enter their future careers, may see their ladder to the middle class start to fray, and further economic polarization and diminished social mobility could follow.[3]

Globally, technological development could also lead to further geographic stratification. By World Bank estimates, while fewer than half of US jobs can be expected to be eventually replaced through automation, the losses will be deeper in poorer, less resilient economies. Moreover, although economic growth driven by AI is expected to approach $16 trillion for the period from 2016 to 2030, just 30 per cent of that AI dividend is expected to accrue to the Global South, due to slower uptake of AI technology into local production systems in Africa and Latin America. Thus the lion's share of the benefits of innovation will be absorbed by the US and China. In other words, the winners of globalization 2.0 might well be a repeat of the first wave of neoliberal prosperity. Poorer countries, which have historically used their 'cheap labour' to spur export-driven growth, would continue to lag further behind in global trade, losing out on capital investment and transnational ties that could help upgrade their economies toward a more sustainable, or at least stable, industrial model.[4]

These countries are also where technological disruption could disproportionately affect the rising generation of workers, who most need to master the technological tools needed for long-term development. Young workers in poor and 'emerging' economies may be well educated, tech savvy, and well positioned to take advantage of online work platforms as a rare source of 'first world' income. Ideally, the digital divide between wealthier and poorer economies might shrink, through deep state investments in educational and technological infrastructure. However, youth also have more to lose in the global race to upgrade.[5]

A parallel, often overlapping and reinforcing, trend in the workforces of affluent countries is fragmentation and destabilization of labour, as jobs shift toward short-term, freelance, and 'non-standard' work arrangements. These may be contingent or casual jobs, project-based work, temporary contracts, or outsourced jobs that a parent company uses to shed the legal obligations of regular employment. Altogether these precarious (or more euphemistically, 'independent') workers, broadly lumped together as 'gig economy' workers, make up as much as 35 per cent of the US workforce (over 56 million) according to a 2017 study by the Freelancers Union and the platform job site Upwork, and the majority of workers will be freelancing in some form by 2027. But so far just a sliver of these jobs are currently completely performed through online platforms – reaching an estimated cumulative participation rate of 4.2 per cent of the workforce from 2012 to 2015. Yet technology is no doubt radically changing the structure of the economy and the dynamics of both on- and off-line labour.[6]

In rich and poor nations alike, technological innovation will disrupt the roles of the state and the power of the labour movement as much as it will disrupt the machinations of capital. Welfare systems must be overhauled to cope with a new landscape of human need, where we're no longer dealing with the material deficits of income loss, but the social deficits of a loss of lifestyle, community, and for many workers, identity. Strong welfare, workforce and educational policies could mitigate the costs of any structural change in the labour force – yet these are ultimately produced through political struggle, not technological teleology. The solution will be analogue: to retool democracy and social welfare, in real life.

No, we won't all be 'replaced' by machines, but we will likely cede some ownership of our communities, privacy, public space, and economic and political clout. And while there will be jobs to do even in our digitally-dominated future, if workers fail to seize the means of producing that future, they risk becoming reduced to its by-product. To avoid this will require redrawing the frontlines of labour struggle and forging new pathways of social advancement.[7] Although, as an official occupational category, gig work per se currently constitutes a relatively small slice of the workforce even in the most developed economies, there is no doubt that it is growing exponentially. And while this surge is inevitable, labour must expand on what so many are already demanding of the 'on-demand' economy – fair work, equity, and human rights, on and off the platform. Ultimately, the most effective way to tackle the labour abuses endemic in the gig economy may be organizing workers for sustained militant action, be it in the form of a global crowdworkers' guild, or an app-based collective-bargaining agreement. But gig economy jobs have abstracted the traditional role of the employer and employee into a triangular transaction among user, client, and platform. So how do you mobilize workers to fight the man, when the man is an algorithm?[8]

For labour, the constant risk of disruption brings the constant potential for transformation – as well as for degradation. The question that will determine the nature and role of work in the digital age is whether technology can help democratize globalization and expand the digital commons, or if it will simply enable capital to consolidate its power over the emergent global social infrastructure and capture more of our public sphere.

WORKING IN THE GLOBAL GIG ECONOMY

Change in the digital economy is perhaps most visible in two labour arrangements that are often, but not always, interlinked: the realm of casual, precarious, or temporary and project-based jobs, and the expanding sphere of the online employment platform. The platform-based labour market – exemplified by mobile-based services like the ride-hailing app Uber – channels the hiring process into a kind of digital hiring hall in the form of a mobile app. (The 'platform economy' is often examined in the same context as the gig economy. However, in contrast to the gig economy – a catch-all for various forms of precarious and contingent jobs – the platform is distinguished by the fact that its operations are anchored in an online communications sphere, typically revolving around labour that is negotiated, and often performed, through a digital interface.) Sometimes the work itself is performed remotely online, such as writing code or copyediting. After the task is completed, workers are rated, and quality control is enforced through subjective consumer assessments designed to provide 'accountability' in a freewheeling, scarcely regulated labour market. And who controls the quality of the job itself? The traditional determinants of job quality – wages, benefits, fair treatment – are largely detached from formal labour laws and standards, because legally speaking workers are typically deemed not employees of the company, but just users of the app; on paper, they are sole proprietors with 'clients'. Their virtual workspace triangulates authority between the consumer, the service provider, and the disembodied oversight of the platform. The app seems designed to 'serve' both sides of the transaction, but may end up controlling the worker as a de facto supervisor, human resources office, or when a conflict occurs, labour arbitration service.[9]

Complicating the regulatory landscape is the diversity of tech-driven work. The somewhat amorphous field of 'platform-based', 'on demand', or 'gig' work encompasses many trades old and new. There are service jobs negotiated through an online platform (rideshare drivers); miscellaneous odd jobs brokered over a web-based work portal and conducted on or offline; 'crowdwork' platforms that knit together a crowd-sourced workforce of independent collaborators (like participants in an online academic survey study). For all these occupations, the digital platform both facilitates the hiring process and provides workers, presumably, with a wider marketplace of gigs and work requesters or clients. Additionally, a digital platform could dramatically expand the potential labour pool for many tasks performed online, by tapping into distant and international applicant pools. A company's ability to assess, surveil, and rank workers will also extend as blockchain and predictive technology boost the employer or contractor's power to judge, manage, and watch workers in real time. The increasingly widespread and sophisticated use of on-demand, freelance or temp labour also make the pace and variety of work more volatile, which may have the impact of destabilizing employment and eroding wages, in both on- and offline work. Since they are exempt from many labour regulations due to their 'non-employer' status, firms take full advantage of this legal no man's land by operating with extreme opacity and creating a complex web of labour relationships that serve as a subterfuge for exploitation and wage theft, while further fissuring a marginalized labour force.[10]

Obviously, non-standard, irregular, and informal or contingent labour has always existed, just as the 'gig economy' existed for day labourers and buskers before the Internet Age. Though it's not Brave New World, today's digital side hustle has dramatically blurred the lines between formal and casualized employment. In the US and Europe, labour advocates have warned against attempts by on-demand service companies to seek special carve-outs from labour standards and regulations, or to develop alternative legal frameworks that exempt firms from having to provide standard benefits like social security, paid leave, unemployment insurance, or healthcare.[11]

But the underlying motives and drivers of capital have not changed: the current wave of technological advancement caps a decades-old, worldwide trend of global capital deskilling jobs, peeling away labour protections, and eroding unions. Platforms are an accelerant of neoliberal structural change, but they are built on the ravages of decades of deteriorating labour rights. Now, technology reshapes the experience of work in similarly disturbing ways. Studies of various platform and gig arrangements reveal the high risk of social isolation, income volatility, and economic insecurity, and exposure to a range of hazards at work: harassment from clients (like cyber-bullying from a contractor), unfair firing (or 'deactivation' in the digital parlance), and poor health and safety conditions (bike and traffic accidents without workers' compensation). An even more acute common experience is relentless social and economic stress, as people scramble to stack their $3 per hour micro-tasks to add up to something resembling a living wage, submitting to constant economic instability in exchange for the false freedom of 'being your own boss'.[12]

The digital architecture of the workforce is evolving not linearly but concentrically. The growing interconnectivity of corporations in networks of trade and communication parallels a growing density in the networks available for organizing, consciousness-raising, and solidarity across an expanding global proletariat. Yet gig workers, like the gig economy itself, have still not developed a concrete identity. One problem is an ideological one: the commercial buzz around platforms lionizes the digital *ubermensch* – the on-demand serf who straddles multiple gigs and touts a 'portfolio' of skills to be mixed and matched for the next company. The culture of microwork is reflected in the advent of 'Get my Peon', the on-demand errand app in India that has spun an ancient trade, the old-school jobber, into a twenty-first century professional freelancer, on call via mobile 24/7.[13] The rise of on-demand platform work might be viewed as a net positive for workers who benefit from greater flexibility in employment, which can foster autonomy, or perhaps more efficient, innovative, or stimulating ways of working. The flipside of 'flexibility', however, is marginalization and casualization – especially on platforms that orchestrate a client-worker relationship that provides the 'freelancer' virtually no leverage to resist mistreatment or exploitation.[14]

Indeed, the 'Uberization' of the economy is the combination of monopoly expansion and workforce fragmentation through a single, ubiquitous platform. Unlike the microwork hubs that offer an array of small projects, the Uber model delivers basically one service: private transportation. The company simultaneously captures local markets through relentless price competition, and monopsonizes the driver workforce through its market control. As a global brand, the dismantling of local regulatory regimes for incumbent cab services has boosted the explosion of the company (thanks in large part to Uber's multi-billion dollar lobbying team).[15] Not surprisingly, Uber has faced obstacles in expanding into the global market, often due to hostile government regulators or backlash from traditional cab drivers – often taking the form of militant protests. But the scorched-earth business model they pioneered is mushrooming in platform service industries worldwide.[16] In the Global South, Uberization can be an even riskier game. On the streets once clogged with moped taxis and careening tuk-tuks, ridesharing apps are emerging as a free-market solution to inadequate transit infrastructures, like an ad-hoc fleet of digital rickshaws. Despite the attractiveness of a high-tech fix, platform transport jobs are actually not all that distinct from other casual work. According to research by the Just Jobs Network, while the rideshare sector has exploded as a cheap and accessible local transportation system, casual workers have had to take on the risk of self-employment without the social protections that accompany conventional employment. A survey of drivers in Indonesia for the local ride-hailing service 'ojek' found that while the wages were a step up from their previous jobs, most still earned less than the minimum wage.[17]

But what about the more glamorous digital gigs for white-collar professionals? Platform work can enable many professionals to ply their trade for foreign firms as online freelancers, without leaving home. A platform interface might encourage corporations to offshore jobs to countries with lower labour costs, while facilitating upstream 'talent flows' from poor countries to rich ones. But greater access to an expanded job market does not mean equal opportunity. Studies of transnational online labour hiring patterns, based on contractors using a Spanish-speaking platform for professionals, show that in general, firms in relatively affluent Spain still employ local workers, rather than their Spanish-speaking peers in Latin America, suggesting that latent national biases persist on the part of employers, despite the virtually unlimited pool of 'cheaper' white-collar foreign labour.[18]

As for the workers, their collective identity as platform workers may prove more salient than the specific jobs themselves. Research surveys reveal that many young professionals in emerging economies feel empowered by gig work, as it opens fresh opportunities that they believe were previously economically or logistically unfeasible. Through the platform, they enter an online transnational community, distinguished by education and cosmopolitanism; they often reflect on themselves not in terms of labour consciousness, but rather the idiom of entrepreneurship, as self-starters and aspirant independent professionals. Perhaps a business student in Kenya can have her pick of copy editing gigs for dozens of firms all over the world. Yet these new connections raise ethical questions about labour arbitrage in a transnational job market. When a large California firm can outsource a major data-analysis project to crowdworkers in a much poorer country, this has the potential to degrade the relative value of the labour-power of their US workers. Or it can lead to a deskilling of a talented white-collar workforce in Kenya by compelling youth to leave their studies for a lucrative gig, and perhaps earn a better salary by doing data entry for an overseas law firm, than by actually working as a local attorney.[19]

Beyond the realm of freelance platforms, the expansion of digital labour might lead to massive changes in the offshoring practices of conventional multinational firms as well. Corporations have, of course, long relied on call centres to handle basic frontline service labour, such as tech support or customer service. But now many forms of IT labour are becoming increasingly fluid across global communications networks, potentially intensifying offshoring trends for knowledge workers. One stark illustration of these emerging labour dynamics is the use of China-based IT service contractors by Japanese firms. Although the Special Economic Zone of Dalian had long been a marketplace for call centre vendors, some Japanese firms are now dispatching Japanese staff to Dalian call centres, essentially using local workers overseas in order to take advantage of a 'cheaper' labour market, while still benefiting from language ability and skills of their 'native' staff. The staff are also able to train local Chinese workers to undertake the same labour, thus creating dual forms of transnational exploitation: migration of labour, in terms of the Japanese employees contracted out to China-based branches, and migration of capital within a firm that straddles two national markets. A new dynamic in labour migration emerges: Japanese workers volunteer to take offshored positions because the conditions in an up-and-coming Chinese metropolis seem relatively favourable, as the Japanese economy has, under decades of neoliberal policy, suffered long-term stagnation with eroding labour standards. Seeking an alternative, workers may seek casualized, 'low skill' frontline technical tasks in a 'de-territorialized' environment abroad, though they may ironically be training their future replacements. The offshoring of Japanese workers to a minimally regulated Chinese outpost presents a case study in how digital platform work has the ability both to enhance and curtail mobility for different groups, but always tends to move labour in a direction that disempowers labour and expands the power of employers. Ultimately, workers of either nationality are increasingly relegated to a deregulated arena of labour arbitrage.[20]

FROM REGULATING GIG WORK
TO ORGANIZING DIGITALLY

The very qualities that make the gig economy attractive are also those that make it oppressive: the freedom and flexibility of an autonomous job structure, the global diversity of work, and the entrepreneurial climate are inseparable from the social stress of an erratic, volatile schedule, fluctuating income, and the anxiety of constantly juggling multiple freelance gigs to try to cobble together a liveable income.[21] As the European Trade Union Confederation explained in a recent study, crowdwork and various other forms of platform labour are based on flexibility and protean markets for services and for labour. Yet 'the fragmentation of work' forms a barrier to unions fostering the organic collective solidarity needed to galvanize self-styled 'micro-entrepreneurs' – who currently have all the responsibilities of a boss and none of the power.

Gone are the regular shifts before and after which groups of workers would congregate to voice their grievances, the geographic proximity of workers with shared interests, and the sense of being a united workforce. Individual workers are left to fend for themselves: click workers are without guidance in selecting tasks online, and ride-sharing drivers are forced to hide out in increasingly rare open parking lots, often struggling to find a place to rest or even go to the toilet.[22]

With each worker operating as a 'sole proprietor' on the digital frontier, the International Labour Organization (ILO) writes, a constant state of dislocation breeds constant instability: 'Moving in and out of different "gigs" in a variety of sectors and often without the intention of long-term participation in the gig economy, inevitably negatively impacts workers' abilities to establish community and identify their shared interests.'[23] For workers who are alienated from each other and from society as a whole, forming a new labour community, with its own set of standards and protections, is both doubly difficult and doubly necessary.

The European Union recently passed the first legislation to protect 'non-standard' workers' rights – covering at least three million workers across all member states – establishing a general wage floor and baseline array of benefits for on-demand and platform workers, as well as others working in non-standard, precarious jobs. For example, workers with volatile schedules would be entitled to work cancellation compensation, as well as clear terms outlining standard hours. The law would also cap probationary periods for workers at a maximum of the first six months. Recently introduced legislation in the United Kingdom would similarly provide gig workers with concrete rights and benefits, like paid leave, but stopped short of mandating regular schedules. While no comprehensive legislation to protect gig workers exists in the US, some jurisdictions have introduced or enacted legislation to solidify the rights of rideshare drivers and freelancers.[24]

Despite these advancements, however, regulators are constantly playing catch-up with labour platforms as they proliferate new schemes to circumvent labour codes. The tech lobby has campaigned for sweeping regulatory rollbacks, premised on minimizing labour costs by classifying workers as 'independent contractors'. High-power lobby firms representing venture capital and Silicon Valley are peddling model legislation aiming to officially exempt corporations from liability for misclassifying their workers as contractors. Formalizing this loophole would allow Uber-type firms to effectively disown their workforces, while still exerting tight control over their 'non-employee' workers through an app that tracks and manages their every movement.[25] Meanwhile, the law also constrains labour's power to resist 'Uberization'. Antitrust laws thwart workers' organizing efforts in many cases when gig workers organize, because they are considered freelancers or self-employed, their collective labour action, including collective bargaining or striking, is vulnerable to legal sanction, under laws historically used to combat cartel ventures. Paradoxically, rideshare oligopolies that dominate city streets around the world somehow manage to evade antitrust regulators.[26]

Labour advocates in Europe and the US have gotten mixed results when seeking to reaffirm platform workers' rights through litigation. Uber has, for example, recently wriggled out of a major class-action lawsuit over misclassification with a $20 million settlement deal that provided some marginal commitments for transparency and consultation with drivers on corporate policies. But other legal claims brought by workers have led to more labour-friendly rulings: in New York, Uber drivers and taxi worker advocates waged a successful legal battle that forced the state's labour board to recognize Uber drivers' entitlement to unemployment benefits. In other claims litigated in the UK, Colombia and the European Court of Justice, Uber drivers have been legally recognized as employees. Still, the victories have been mostly piecemeal. And even if the industry's desired regulatory exemptions are not codified into law, on-demand labour services can keep slipping through loopholes in state and federal regulations – a rickety legal scaffolding held over from the early twentieth century. Given the sheer ubiquity of platform apps now, without clear global standards on who counts as a 'real' worker in a digital global economy, Uber's algorithm will keep ramming new rules into places where official law has yet to catch up.[27]

While the law may or may not gravitate toward workers in future court challenges, there's still something to be said for good old-fashioned street agitation. Globally, the onslaught of ridesharing has provoked enough outrage among traditional drivers to actually throttle Uber expansionism through brute force. As incumbent taxi industries have witnessed their street burgeoning with rideshare cars, demonstrations, riots, and street brawls have erupted, from Paris to Johannesburg to Nanjing, along with the grim spectacle of driver suicides – reportedly the result of debt and despair at the dregs of gigdom.[28]

The key to organizing in the digital economy is to reclaim the platform as a political arena and organizing asset. And it's not as hard as it looks: the architecture of digital labour is already being revamped to adapt elements of traditional unionism to a platformed world, with future-proofed institutions for worker representation.

The chief obstacle to systemic organizing is a self-perpetuating cycle of precarity, legal constraints, and atomization, which limits individual workers' ability to even interact with each other, let alone unify around a labour agenda. The sheer distance between workers – social and physical – is an acute impediment. Platforms are structured to keep the workforce centrally controlled but fragmented across a wide area, or across borders, leaving them exposed to extreme isolation and loneliness.

According to a recent study of Uber drivers in Washington, DC by Georgetown University researchers, drivers often sink into claustrophobic alienation as they trawl through traffic on endless shifts. Three in four of those surveyed 'said that they had never had a drink or meal with anyone else who had ever driven for Uber. The lack of physical spaces where workers meet or congregate creates a material barrier to collective identities, which shapes the geography of labour and narrows possibilities for collective bargaining in the platform workplace.'[29] But although their dependency on the app can be alienating, Uber drivers have also managed to create vibrant online communities, which serve as a safe space for digital shoptalk and social support. In the intimate anonymity of the driver forum, they can vent frustration with the job's singular hazards: getting shorted on a fare, or penalized for a bogus customer complaint. Although Uber has launched its own management-controlled union-type worker organization and advisory 'driver's council', the driver-led forums provide an autonomous space for organic socializing, where workers develop a subcultural identity that can seed a nascent class consciousness, even among drivers who may never meet in person.[30]

One curious side effect of the shift to platform work is the migration of the labour interface from worker–employer to worker–platform. Workers' sense of being tethered to the app, subjected to alienating and degraded work in a climate of isolation and anxiety, can become the germ for a unique type of class consciousness which Alex Wood and Vili Lehdonvirta call 'platform antagonism'. The angst of algorithmic oppression spurs workers to, quite literally, rage against the machine. One way to develop points of connectivity and leverage in such a fissured workforce, Wood and Lehdonvirta assert, is cultivating their own self-governed communications networks. Here, rideshare drivers and crowdworkers can forge intimate bonds outside the rigid constraints of the platform – defiantly forming the kind of community that their industry is designed to deny them. In the absence of concrete legal status as workers, or a physical shared workplace, a grassroots culture of camaraderie can blossom in an online community space – an alternative platform where workers think critically about their work and collective power. The community of 'structured antagonism' fosters a culture of quiet resistance, positioned against not a single employer but a common platform.[31]

The concept that workers are not merely interchangeable chips or data packets, but autonomous individuals – who are critical to production yet not beholden to it – forms a cornerstone of digital labour consciousness. Yet the work experience can also transcend traditional conventions of labour relations. Mark Graham and Jamie Woodcock point to a case study of a worker forum with both practical and political use for the crowdworkers employed in Amazon's 'Mechanical Turk' (MTurk) crowdsourcing marketplace that makes it easier for individuals and businesses to outsource their processes and jobs to a distributed workforce who can perform these tasks virtually. This forum, called Turkopticon, allowed technology-based workers to invert the surveillance framework that gave the platform its omnipotent collective eye. This involved:

> developing a browser plugin to allow workers to review the work tasks, attempting to reverse the Panopticon-like surveillance of the platform (hence the name). In addition to this, there is a forum for workers to communicate. This intervention provides one way to overcome the barriers between workers created by the platform organisation, while also foregrounding the activity of the workers involved.[32]

Similar spaces for MTurk workers have sprung up on other sites such as Reddit, where a number of groups now operate as information clearinghouses for the company's taskers, providing advice on connecting with clients or managing finances for MTurk revenues. More importantly, these parallel worker-led platforms provide a trusted space, independent of the platform itself.[33]

Like many contemporary protest movements, worker-led organizing initiatives have also fused social media and street action. Several mass uprisings and even wildcat strikes have been catalyzed through social media platforms. When workers develop their own networks of resistance, they can expand their digital diaspora across the platform workforce and well beyond – across sectors, cultures and borders.[34] Workers of the food-delivery app Deliveroo launched a series of spontaneous 'boycotts' in 2017 – shutting off the app and thus effectively staging a work stoppage – in response to reports that the immigration authorities were carrying out raids at a local fast food chain that was also one of Deliveroo's major clients. As Woodcock and Facility Waters observed, the call to boycott 'was spread through WhatsApp, social media, and moved, through the drivers, into different parts of the city.

These combined to create a climate in which there was greater cohesion and solidarity.' According to the data mapping projects later undertaken by researchers, the mass logouts – led by delivery workers with the food platforms Foodora, Deliveroo, and UberEats – resulted in forty-one direct actions across seven countries, affecting nearly 1,500 workers. Their collective action was reportedly met with collective consequences, triggering a steep drop in workers' hourly earnings. But the seemingly retaliatory move only spurred further protests, coupled with raucous street protests. In the end, the previously fissured workforce assembled a festive scene that, despite the isolated nature of their work, publicly, viscerally reaffirmed their identity and solidarity as coworkers.[35]

The flurry of boycotts that began in London did not shut down the service altogether, but similar actions unfolded throughout the second half of 2017 across Europe, in Belgium, France, Germany, Italy, the Netherlands, and Spain. Though organized informally, the strikes were backed by local unions, which could help lay the groundwork for future organizing. Gig worker organizing has been percolating across Europe and the UK, spearheaded grassroots initiatives like the Independent Workers Union of Great Britain, representing rideshare drivers, couriers and even foster-care workers, and Game Workers Unite, a network of code-smiths in the burgeoning and under-regulated games industry.[36] If such campaigns became a common resistance strategy for gig workers worldwide, freelance workers everywhere could turn around the asymmetry of the fragmented workforce, and transform what had been a structural weakness into a source of mass power.[37]

In New York City, the New York Taxi Workers Alliance (NYTWA), an affiliate of the AFL–CIO, organizes cabbies, but would not legally qualify as a union because many of its members are technically 'independent contractors'. Nonetheless, it has developed an innovative sector-wide organizing model that recruits members from the ranks of both traditional cabbies and rideshare workers. The group recently waged a successful campaign to raise rideshare drivers' base pay through a new system of calculating fares that takes into account Uber's dynamic pricing system, in order to stabilize net revenue for drivers and align roughly with New York City's minimum wage of $15 per hour. The Alliance has also pushed the boundaries of industrial action against exploitative businesses: they staged a brief strike and anti-Uber campaign at John F. Kennedy Airport to protest Trump's anti-Muslim travel ban in early 2017. In branding themselves as a group representing all for-hire drivers, NYTWA resists the 'divide and conquer' strategy that gives Uber its marketing edge.[38]

The group's latest action disrupted traffic around the world. The NYTWA collaborated with other driver groups to stage an international app strike in cities across the US and several countries on 8 May 2019. The event, which saw rolling strikes and street rallies in Los Angeles, New York, San Francisco, and other cities, mobilized drivers for Uber, Lyft, and other rideshare services to coordinate a work stoppage by shutting down the apps for a set period of time (a twenty-four hour boycott in Los Angeles, two hours during the morning in New York City). Though the action reportedly had no discernible impact on Uber's overall business, the drivers sent a powerful symbolic message: by coordinating across their networks, they could mobilize each other just as fast as they could take orders for pick-ups, and they weren't afraid to shut down their apps for a few hours, because they had created an alternative platform for socializing the risks.[39] As one Lyft driver and NYTWA member, Kevin Raghu, told me on the eve of the strike,

> There's no protection from Uber for us, as drivers for them. There's no security, there's no benefits, nothing. All this money that they're making – they're worth $90 billion now, all that money. Ask them if they profit share, and they won't … All they care about is to get more, more, more out of us. And that's why we want to [have this protest], because without the drivers, they don't exist.

Perhaps the most promising aspect of platform work is the horizon of opportunity to experiment with creative new forms of workplace structure and labour organization. The Bay Area start-up Loconomics, which provides personal and household services through an app-based listing system, has answered the question of organizing digitally by simply making workers the owners of the platform – as a cooperative. According to coop member Joshua Danielson, cooperative enterprises work to balance performance with self-sufficiency and shared labour equity, 'to ensure that our product, the services from the workers, isn't sacrificed for profits of external shareholders'. But in a more traditional corporate model, by contrast, 'it's important to remember that workers are the product, not the platform, and they hold an immense amount of power if they can organize'.[40]

NEW PLATFORMS, NEW RULES, NEW STRUGGLES

For platform workers, effective regulation must be both nimble enough to evolve alongside new technology, and firm enough to give workers a material stake in collective action, particularly if they risk being punished simply for speaking up to demand better labour conditions. Some nascent collective bargaining models, many of which do not take the form of formal unions, are already emerging for platform workers. In Seattle, the local government has sought to establish a voluntary tripartite collective-bargaining system for both cabbies and all ride-hailing platform drivers, which engages government, drivers, and representatives of the car-service industry.[41] Denmark has gone further by establishing a collective bargaining framework for advancing labour rights, which ensures that workers for the platform cleaning company Hilfr, primarily those who have logged above 100 work hours, will qualify for a nineteen-euro hourly minimum wage and various standard labour protections – an upgraded contract arrangement that helps formalize on-demand service platforms. Germany's Crowdsourcing Code of Conduct is a generic, open-ended, voluntary code, developed by the software firm Testbirds, which has expanded to cover a number of crowdwork platforms. It provides a sort of platform workers' Bill of Rights, including, among other things, fair payment rules, flexibility in scheduling and choice of work, and transparency rules for the assessment of work projects.[42]

Linking the workers to a wider regulatory regime can help combat tax avoidance on the part of freelance-based platform services.[43] The proliferation of platform work has also spurred the innovation of model policy frameworks that firms can adopt voluntarily. The Fairwork Foundation, an international coalition of private- and public-sector stakeholders, has created a framework of principles for platform work based on labour and human rights, recalibrating these principles to 'set and measure decent work standards in the platform economy'. In partnership with academic institutions and the ILO, a parallel mission is to 'conduct rigorous research to evaluate platforms against those thresholds, and publish our results in a transparent manner'. Collaborations with both platform corporations and universities in the UK and South Africa have yielded five core principles, including fair pay and conditions, occupational health and safety, and fair management protocols that include grievance procedures and processes for challenging disciplinary decisions. The program operates as a worker-driven ratings system, rather than a binding regulatory code: firms are awarded a Fairwork certification depending on the number of 'points' awarded for different criteria. As of mid-2019, the scheme had been piloted for several platforms in South Africa and Banglalore, India.[44]

Platforms are a new frontier for mainstream organized labour as well. Today, unions representing low-wage service workers are trying to get ahead of automation and machine learning in established sectors like hotel housekeeping (in which room-cleaning routines are increasingly micro-managed by software) and cashiers (who face obsolescence as self-checkout aisles proliferate). In the immediate term, unions are negotiating job protections designed to buffer against impending technological disruption, embedding them into contracts that normally deal with bread-and-butter issues of wages and benefits. Thinking existentially about technology's future influence is an insurance plan for workers and the labour movement itself. Seismic shifts in the organization and structure of the supply chain will compel unions to adapt either by directly organizing or by partnering with new gig-economy workers, continuing labour's longstanding struggle to organize excluded and marginal sectors. Those on the margins today are slowly subsuming the mainstream, as the musculature of labour climbs from the shop floor into the digital ether.[45] The emerging initiatives to organize and protect the most liminal facets of the tech-driven workforce should not only be models for traditional unions to explore, but also a crash course in organizing any workplace where the old rules no longer apply.

Yet even if new regulatory regimes could be developed to check future abuses driven by technological disruption, regulatory change alone would not resolve a fundamental asymmetry of power – hinging on control of the underlying technology itself. If machine learning and digital communications power our economy, the public and the broad mass of working people must not only have access to these innovations, but also the authority to determine how they are designed, by whom, for whom, and where. So any introduction of social modernization in the form of technology should also involve the wholesale transfer of technology and the indigenization of the skills, knowledge, and infrastructure that will foster future transformation.[46] This alone can ensure that in the future, the knowledge economy will not be about commodifying technology and pitting workers against machines, but about the distributed generation of people power. A socialized digital commons would belong to no one, be shared by everyone, and be stewarded by the workers who have always powered the soul of the machine.

NOTES

1   Centre for the New Economy and Society, World Economic Forum, 'The Future of Jobs Report 2018', World Economic Forum, 2018, available at: www3.weforum.org/docs/WEF_Future_of_Jobs_2018.pdf; OECD, 'Going Digital: The Future of Work for Women', OECD, 2017, available at: www.oecd.org/employment/Going-Digital-the-Future-of-Work-for-Women.pdf; International Labour Organization, 'Future of Work Research Papers', 2018, available at: www.ilo.org.

2   PwC, 'AI to drive GDP gains of $15.7 trillion with productivity, personalisation improvements', 2017, available at: press.pwc.com; World Bank, 'World Development Report 2016: Digital Dividends', Washington, DC: World Bank, 2016.

3   'The Future of Jobs Report 2018'.

4   Ian Goldin, 'Will AI Kill Development?', *BBC*, 7 April 2019; Matthew Smith, 'Excitement, concern, and hope for AI in the Global South', International Development Research Centre, 18 February 2019, available at: www.idrc.ca; United Nations Conference on Trade and Development, 'New digital era must ensure prosperity for all', 2 October 2017, unctad.org; PwC, 'AI to drive GDP gains of $15.7 trillion'. World Bank Development Report 2016: 'Digital Dividends'.

5   UNCTAD, see: 'New digital era must ensure prosperity for all'; International Labour Organization, 'World Employment and Social Outlook 2016: Trends for Youth', Geneva: ILO, 2016, available at: www.ilo.org; Ekkehard Ernst, Rossana Merola, Daniel Samaan, 'The Economics of Artificial Intelligence: Implications for the Future of Work', International Labour Office, Geneva: ILO, 2018.

6   Upwork and Freelancers Union, 'Freelancing in America, 2017', October 2017, available at: www.upwork.com; Ruth Berins Collier, V.B. Dubal, Christopher Carter, 'Labor Platforms and Gig Work: The Failure to Regulate', IRLE Working Paper No. 106-17, Institute for Research on Labor and Employment, 2017, available at: irle. berkeley.edu.

7   ILO, 'Future of Work Research Papers'.

8   Alexia Fernández Campbell, 'New York City passes nation's first minimum pay rate for Uber and Lyft drivers', *Vox*, 5 Dec 2018; Thomas Breen, 'Uber Bill Gets A Lyft', *New Haven Independent*, 20 March 2019, Sarah Holder, 'Why L.A.'s Ride-Hail Drivers Went on Strike', *CityLab*, 26 March 2019, available at: www.citylab.com.

9   For further definition of platform work and the platform economy, see: 'Platform Economy Repository: Typology,' *Eurofound*, 6 September 2018, available at: www. eurofound.europa.eu.

10   Susan Caminiti, '4 gig economy trends that are radically transforming the US job market', CNBC, 29 October 2018; Thor Benson, 'From Whole Foods to Amazon, Invasive Technology Controlling Workers Is More Dystopian Than You Think', *InTheseTimes*, 21 February 2018; Jeremias Prassl, 'Collective Voice in the Platform Economy: Challenges, Opportunities, Solutions', ETUC, 2018, available at: www. etuc.org. David Weil, 'The Fissured Workplace', available at: www.fissuredworkplace. net.

11   'Chapter 4: Changes in the Nature of Work and Its Organization', in National Academies of Sciences, Engineering, and Medicine, *Information Technology and the U.S. Workforce: Where Are We and Where Do We Go from Here?*, Washington, DC: The National Academies Press, 2017; Rebecca Smith and Sarah Leberstein, 'Rights on Demand: Ensuring Workplace Standards and Worker Security In the On-Demand Economy', NELP, September 2015; Victoria Fanggidae, Muto P. Sagala, Dwi Rahayu Ningrum, Perkumpulan Prakarsa, 'On-Demand Transport Workers in Indonesia: Toward Understanding the Sharing Economy in Emerging Markets', JustJobs Network, 2016, available at: www.justjobsnetwork.org; Sangeet Paul Choudary, 'The Architecture of Digital Labour Platforms: Policy Recommendations on Platform Design for Worker Well-Being,' ILO, 15 May 2018, available at: www.ilo.org.

12   Platform Economy Repository: Dossiers', Eurofound, 6 September 2018, available at: eurofound.europa.eu; Julia Ticona, Alexandra Mateescu, Alex Rosenblat, 'Beyond Disruption: How Tech Shapes Labor Across Domestic Work & Ridehailing', *Data & Society*, 26 June 2018, available at: datasociety.net.

13   Vaishnavi Kanekal, 'GetMyPeon.Com, A First Personal Concierge Service Of It's Kind!', Trak.in, 3 Jan 2017, available at: trak.in.

14   'Chapter 4: Changes in the Nature of Work and Its Organization', Choudary, 'The Architecture of Digital Labour Platforms'; Jon Messenger, 'Working Time and the Future of Work', ILO, International Labour Office, Geneva: ILO, 2018, available at: www.ilo.org.

15   Marshall Steinbaum, 'How Widespread Is Labor Monopsony? Some New Results Suggest It's Pervasive', Roosevelt Institute, 18 December 2017, available at: rooseveltinstitute.org; Glenn Fleishman, 'Uber and the appropriation of public space', *BoingBoing*, 30 June 2014, available at: boingboing.net; Ignacio Herrera Anchustegui, Julian Nowag, 'Buyer Power In The Big Data And Algorithm Driven World: The Uber & Lyft Example', *Competition Policy International*, 15 September 2017, available at: www.competitionpolicyinternational.com.

16   Owain James, 'Uber and Lyft are lobbying states to prohibit local regulation', Mobility Lab, 24 July 2018, available at: mobilitylab.org; Biz Carson, 'Where Uber Is Winning The World, And Where It Has Lost', *Forbes*, 19 September 2018.

17   Sabina Dewan, 'Wired for Work: Exploring the Nexus of Technology & Jobs', JustJobs Network, in *Growth and Reducing Inequality Working Paper Series*, G-24 and Friedrich-Ebert-Stiftung, New York, 15 December 2018, available at: www.g24.org.

18   Dewan, 'Wired for Work'.

19   A. J. Wood, V. Lehdonvirta, and M. Graham, 'Workers of the Internet unite? Online Freelancer Organisation Among Remote Gig Economy Workers in Six Asian and African Countries', *New Technology, Work and Employment*, 33(95-112), 2018; Ernst, Merola, Samaan, 'The Economics of Artificial Intelligence'.

20   Kumiko Kawashima, 'Service Outsourcing and Labour Mobility in a Digital Age: Transnational Linkages Between Japan and Dalian, China', *Global Networks*, 17 January 2017.

21   'Chapter 4: Changes in the Nature of Work and Its Organization', Choudary, 'The architecture of Digital Labour Platforms'; Messenger, 'Working Time and the Future of Work'.

22   Jeremias, 'Collective Voice in the Platform Economy'.

23   ILO, 'Future of Work Research Papers', available at: www.ilo.org.

24   'EU law fixes minimum rights for "gig economy" workers', *BBC*, 16 April 2019; 'Workplace reforms "will protect gig economy workers"', *BBC*, 17 December 2018; Campbell, 'New York City passes nation's first minimum pay rate for Uber and Lyft drivers'; Breen, 'Uber Bill Gets A Lyft'; 'Freelance Isn't Free Act', New York City Department of Consumer Affairs, available at: www1.nyc.gov/site/dca/about/freelance-isnt-free-act.page.

25   Maya Pinto, Rebecca Smith, Irene Tung, 'Rights at Risk: Gig Companies' Campaign to Upend Employment as We Know It', National Employment Law Project, 25 March 2019, available at: www.nelp.org.

26   Conversation with ILO researcher Hannah Johnston, April 2019; Garden, Charlotte, 'Antitrust/Pro-Worker', Take Care (blog), 31 December 2018, available at: takecareblog.com.

27   Pinto et. al., 'Rights at Risk'; 'Uber Must Make Unemployment Insurance Contributions for New York Drivers Following Company's Withdrawal of Appeal', Legal Services NYC, 4 March 2019, available at: www.legalservicesnyc.org; Nancy Cremins, 'Insight: The Evolving Gig Economy – On-Demand Workers and Arbitration Clauses in the U.S. and Abroad', Bloomberg Law, 26 March 2019, available at: news.bloomberglaw.com; Nancy Cremins, 'There is No One-Size-Fits-All Approach to Global Worker Classification', Globalization Partners (blog), July 2018, available at: www.globalization-partners.com; Kate Conger, 'Uber Settles Drivers' Lawsuit for $20 Million', New York Times, 12 March 2019.

28   'China's Ruling on Taxi Apps Could Spark Social Tensions', Radio Free Asia, 1 August 2016, available at: www.rfa.org; Jason Burke, 'Violence erupts between taxi and Uber drivers in Johannesburg', The Guardian, 8 September 2017; NYTWA, 'NY Uber Drivers Are Employees with Right to Unemployment Insurance', 19 July 2018, available at: www.nytwa.org.

29   Katie J. Wells, Kafui Attoh, and Declan Cullen, 'The Uber Workplace in Washington, D.C.', Kalmanovitz Initiative for Labor and the Working Poor at Georgetown University, 2018, available at: lwp.georgetown.edu.

30   Alex Rosenblat, 'The Network Uber Drivers Built', Fast Company, 9 January 2018, available at: www.fastcompany.com.

31   A.J. Wood, V. Lehdonvirta, 'Platform Labour and Structured Antagonism: Understanding the Origins of Protest in the Gig Economy', Paper presented at the Oxford Internet Institute Platform Economy Seminar Series, 5 March 2019; 'Platform Economy Repository: Initiatives', Eurofound, 6 September 2018, available at: eurofound.europa.eu.

32   M Graham, and J. Woodcock, 'Towards a Fairer Platform Economy: Introducing the Fairwork Foundation', Alternate Routes, 29, 2018, pp. 242-53.

33   TurkerNation reddit channel, available at: www.reddit.com/r/TurkerNation; Rochelle LaPlante, M. Six Silberman, 'Weaving Relations of Trust in Crowd Work: Transparency and Reputation Across Platforms', presented at workshop co-located with WebSci '16, Hannover, Germany, 22-25 May 2016, available at: trustincrowdwork.west.uni-koblenz.de/sites/trustincrowdwork.west.uni-koblenz.de/files/laplante_trust.pdf.

34   'Platform Economy Repository: Initiatives', available at: www.eurofound.europa.eu.

35   Jamie Woodcock, Facility Waters, 'Far From Seamless: a Workers' Inquiry at Deliveroo', Viewpoint Magazine, 20 September 2017; Callum Cant, 'The wave of worker resistance in European food platforms, 2016-17', Notes From Below, 1, available at: notesfrombelow.org; Weil, 'The Fissured Workplace'.

36   'About Us', Game Workers Unite, available at: gameworkersunite.org/about-us; 'About Us', Independent Workers' Union of Great Britain, available at: iwgb.org.uk/page/about/about; Jamie Woodcock, Marx at the Arcade: Consoles, Controllers, and Class Struggle, Chicago: Haymarket Books, 2019.

37   Cant, 'The wave of worker resistance in European food platforms, 2016-17'; Joe Hayns, 'A Sharing Economy Strike', Jacobin, 16 August 2016; Waters Woodcock, 'Far From Seamless'; Lehdonvirta et. al., 'Workers of the Internet unite?'.

38   NYTWA, 'NYTWA Statement on the Muslim Ban'; 'China's Ruling on Taxi Apps Could Spark Social Tensions', Radio Free Asia, 1 August 2016, available at: www.rfa. org; Jason Burke, 'Violence erupts between taxi and Uber drivers in Johannesburg'; Mike Isaac, 'Uber Adds E-Hail Taxi Fee for New York City Riders', *New York Times,* 24 December 2014.

39   Dalvin Brown, 'Here's why the Uber, Lyft protests might not even work', *USA Today,* 8 May 2019; Laurel Wamsley, Vanessa Romo, 'Uber And Lyft Drivers Are Striking – And Call On Passengers To Boycott', *NPR,* 8 May 2019; 'Protesting "Poverty Wages" and Exploitation, Uber and Lyft Drivers Go on Strike Across the Globe', CommonDreams, 8 May 2019, available at: www.commondreams.org.

40   Michelle Chen, 'Can Worker Co-ops Make the Tech Sector More Equitable?', *The Nation,* 21 December 2017; Loconomics Cooperative, loconomics.com.

41   'For-Hire Driver Collective Bargaining', Seattle Business Regulations, available at: seattle.gov.

42   'Code of Conduct: Paid Crowdsourcing for the Better', available at: crowdsourcing-code.com.

43   'Historic agreement: Digital platform concludes collective agreement', Hilfr.dk (blog), available at: blog.hilfr.dk; 'Historic agreement: Digital platform concludes collective agreement', 3H, Fagbevægelsens Hovedorganisation, available at: fho.dk/blog.

44   'Ratings,' Rankings Guide, Fairwork, available at: fair.work.

45   Wade Rathke, 'The Challenges of Organizing "Gig" Workers,' Working-class Perspectives (blog), 29 April 2019, available at: workingclassstudies.wordpress.com; Jonathan Vanian, 'How Unions Are Pushing Back Against the Rise of Workplace Technology', *Fortune,* 30 April 2019; Hannah Johnston and Chris Land-Kazlauskas, 'Organizing On-Demand: Representation, Voice, and Collective Bargaining in the Gig Economy', International Labour Organization, 29 March 2018, available at: www. ilo.org; Hannah Johnston and Chris Land-Kazlauskas, 'On-demand…and organized!', Work in Progress (blog), ILO, 16 April 2018, available at: iloblog.org.

46   Michael Smith, 'Excitement, concern, and hope for AI in the Global South', S.M. West, M. Whittaker, and K. Crawford, 'Discriminating Systems: Gender, Race and Power in AI', AI Now Institute, 2019, available at: ainowinstitute.org.

ALL WORKERS ARE PRECARIOUS: THE 'DANGEROUS CLASS' IN CHINA'S LABOUR REGIME

YU CHUNSEN

The intensive nature of Chinese labour regimes has been integral to the high speed of socioeconomic development in China. The formation of authority in these labour regimes derives not only from the factories in which they are deployed but also from the competitive strategies of the foreign-owned firms and the local Chinese authorities. Under conditions of increasing global integration and neoliberalism, the development of export-oriented industries – long the preferred macroeconomic policy of the Chinese state at both the central and local levels – has relied on the low salaries of workers. Their restricted workplace rights under state laws and enforcement practices have been a key element in attracting both domestic and international capital investment to the high-tech manufacturing industry, and also to its very rapid growth in profits.[1] In order to obtain maximum profits, leading transnational brands such as Apple (as well as other operators of complex supply chains) most often place Chinese high-tech manufacturing factories, with their cheap labour, at the low end of the value chain.

Many labour experts have discussed the 'dormitory labour regime' in China's manufacturing industry, addressing especially how the dormitory housing offered to workers nearby their workplaces comes with paternalist managerial practices facilitating control over the labourers and maximizing exploitation.[2] As dormitories have been less frequently deployed within manufacturing factories, others have contended based on data collected between 2010 and 2014 from seven garment factories in the Pearl River Delta, that a new labour regime of 'conciliatory despotism' has been forming.[3] As we shall see in this essay, however, there is clear evidence of what deserves to be called a new 'precarious labour regime' emerging within the high-tech manufacturing sector in both processing and assembly factories. This regime operates directly in the production process through three specific mechanisms of labour control, to be elucidated below, which are applied to formal workers. Through a phenomenon known as the 'cascade effect',[4] the firms at the top of global supply chains place pressure on all firms in the chain, which with their tight profit margins in turn pass the pressure on to their employees, thereby exploiting the labourers who are notably rural migrant workers. In the labour regime of these high-tech factories, transnational capital, local state authorities, and factory management combine to treat rural migrants as cheap disposable labour without proper employment security, regardless of the signing of labour contracts. Capitalists increase profits and maximally decrease labour costs through this new labour regime. Due to the high frequency of involuntary employment turnovers this new labour regime entails, formal workers are 'precarious' even within large and formal high-tech factories. These precarious migrant factory workers are at the core of the making of a new Chinese working class. Since the members of the class are increasing in number dramatically, identify themselves as a group of '*gongyou*' (workmates) with common interests, and are willing to take collective actions for the improvement of their employment and social security for themselves and families, this new class is dangerous for both capitalists and central and local governments.

TYPES OF CONTROL IN THE NEW LABOUR REGIME

Chongqing and Shenzhen are two important Chinese cities that have extensively developed high-tech industry in their local areas. The fieldwork I report on below investigates the new precarious labour regime, and is based on six high-tech processing and assembly manufacturing factories (four Taiwanese-owned – Pegatron, Wistron, Compal, and Foxconn; and two Chinese owned – Huawei and Lenovo). It involved interviews with over 160 rural migrant factory workers, as well as with governmental officials, factory managers, and staff from the factories' human resource departments, from various labour agencies, and from labour-friendly NGOs.[5]

According to my fieldwork, formal workers are forced to change their jobs frequently due to: variations in seasons of production; '*zhiyuan*' or the loaning of workers to other departments or factories and even companies; '*fenliu*' which includes changing the job specifications and labour relationships of workers; and an abusive labour regime that involves the use of 'constructive dismissal'. Despite the signing of formal labour contracts, the employee turnover rate is still high within high-tech manufacturing in both Chongqing and Shenzhen. In both cities, formal workers can leave factories freely – if they are content to forego their final salaries from their employers. Rural migrants in Chongqing and Shenzhen have experienced forced dismissal and have had to leave the factories, which contributes to the high turnover. However, Chongqing has an even higher turnover rate than Shenzhen, as many existing mature rural migrants leave and many new young workers enter factories every day.

Theoretically, the signing of labour contracts helps protect the legal rights and responsibilities of employers and employees; however, in practice, the contracts do little to limit either side, which increases workers' precariousness. Nevertheless, while rural migrants, and especially the formal workers among them, welcomed being able to move to other jobs, either upwards or (more likely) horizontally to other low-paid jobs, they also face other types of precarious employment. The labour regime, characterized by *zhiyuan*, *fenliu*, and 'constructive dismissal' forms of control, creates a precarious employment relationship between formal workers and factories. Most rural migrants, including the formal workers, are not particularly familiar with the contents of the labour contracts they have signed; in fact, they tend not to read through and understand all the conditions, rights, responsibilities, and benefits before or after signing. For their part, employers find many ways to 'get around' the restrictive roles of labour contracts.

Labour control by zhiyuan

Employers frequently require assembly line workers to change working positions and job types to different work sites and departments, sometimes even in different factories or other cities, which are not based on the job descriptions agreed in the labour contracts. This phenomenon is called *zhiyuan*, which means 'supporting' departments and sites that lack workers.

From my fieldwork in Chongqing, it became apparent that the *zhiyuan* scheme was commonly used at both Wistron and Compal, as they each have two sets of assembly lines at two different production workshops. This is the first form of *zhiyuan*, in which labourers from one factory are sent to the other factory within the same city to do similar assembly line work. Pegatron exercised a second, more extreme form of *zhiyuan*, by recruiting workers in Chongqing and then reallocating them to eastern areas of China such as Shanghai, where factories are often lacking enough workers. In addition to these two forms used in Chongqing, in Shenzhen there is a third, even more extreme form of *zhiyuan*, especially in factories operated by Foxconn, whereby labourers from one high-tech enterprise are reassigned to support a different company's factory in another city. According to a formal worker and a member of Human Resources staff from Foxconn in Shenzhen, Foxconn has used this approach since 2015, when it signed labour sharing agreements with Quanta factories in Shanghai and Suzhou to supply and send Foxconn labourers to these plants. In doing so, Foxconn acts like a labour agency, taking a share of the profits from supplying labourers for the other firm in a kind of 'profit chain' from inter-enterprise cooperation in labour control and the exploitation of workers.

These factories routinely violate labour contracts to change the work, content, and locations agreed to with the formal workers, effectively 'selling' labourers from the original factories to other factories or firms. This issue not only breaches rural migrants' legitimate rights according to their signed labour contracts but also breaks labour laws by changing the terms of working conditions without notice. These three types of *zhiyuan* are organized arbitrarily in high-tech factories, although Foxconn restricts the *zhiyuan* scheme to once a year for formal workers. But the scheme still means that formal workers' positions and employment are always precarious due to the capacity of the firms to shift workers to new locations.

All three types of *zhiyuan* are deployed according to the 'peak' or 'off-peak' seasons of each factory's production schedule, which principally determine the demand for labour. According to twenty-four formal workers interviewed from Foxconn, although the factory specifies that *zhiyuan* is voluntary, if they refuse to participate in the scheme they are not assigned to assembly lines that have more overtime. This is actually a penalty for formal workers who are reluctant to change their jobs and worksites through *zhiyuan*. When it becomes difficult for workers to bear the condition of the low overtime salaries, they are forced to leave the factories. In other words, managerial controls exercised by factories force the enrolment of formal workers in the *zhiyuan* scheme.

The relocation of workers to factories in other cities is also important. Different provinces in China have different standards of salary payment and other social benefits. Formal workers in the *zhiyuan* scheme may, therefore, receive a different salary in their reassigned area, despite their employers' agreement to pay workers the amount stated in the minimum wage standards of the original areas. In Chongqing, factories cheat workers by advertising higher salaries when recruiting, which are in fact only available through participation in *zhiyuan* and moving to other cities (although even then the advertised higher pay may not be forthcoming). By contrast, a large number of formal workers in Shenzhen, especially at Foxconn, are misled that the Shenzhen salary standards will continue to be paid when taking part in *zhiyuan* at other factories located elsewhere with lower salary standards; however, in reality, workers face a gap in salary payment when they are moved to the new area.

Formal workers in both Chongqing and Shenzhen stated that they actually receive no positive benefits from the *zhiyuan* scheme. Formal workers who have been re-assigned to two or more different cities, and promised the same salaries as in the original areas, fall into two situations. One is that formal workers actually only receive salaries based on the local basic salary standards of the original areas where they worked, rather than the increased standards of the new areas. For example, this circumstance happens in Shenzhen for formal workers who are dispatched to Shanghai, which has a higher basic salary standard. Many formal workers who had taken part in *zhiyuan* to support Shanghai factories thus complained about the gap between expectation and reality. The rest of their salary became a 'bonus' paid for formal workers, rather than overtime salaries. These bonuses were calculated as one-and-one-half to three times the basic salary of the original areas. Formal workers complained that 'bonuses' were lower than overtime salaries, normally two to three times local basic standards of salaries. If all overtime salaries are paid in the form of 'bonuses', factories can change the total amount paid according to their own standards rather than government-regulated standards in local areas. In other words, the overtime salaries calculated according to the basic standards of new areas can actually be higher than the bonus payments, especially for formal workers dispatched to areas with high basic salary standards.

Workers who participate in the *zhiyuan* scheme in areas such as Zhengzhou and Chengdu, which have lower basic salaries than Shenzhen, are also treated badly by the factory. They are paid the basic salary standards of the new areas rather than according to Shenzhen's basic salary standards as the factory promises, and 'bonuses' are also used to pay a part of their overtime salaries. A 26-year-old male formal worker, from rural Nanning in Guangxi Province, working at Foxconn Shenzhen for four years, had signed up to a *zhiyuan* scheme to support Chengdu Foxconn. He complained that he was sent to Chengdu city in Sichuan Province to support Foxconn's factories in 2014. Before he went there, the Foxconn Shenzhen factory promised he would receive the same salary standards as in Shenzhen. However, once he had worked for a month in Chengdu, he received only Chengdu's total salary based on local basic standards of 1,800RMB, which was lower than the 2,300RMB he received in Shenzhen. This part of the salary was paid as bonuses, which are lower than if calculated by the overtime standards of salaries.

By contrast, formal workers who are dispatched from original areas with low basic salary standards to new areas with higher basic salary standards also do not receive the salaries they expect. This particularly happens in Chongqing, which has a lower basic salary standard than in Shanghai. To illustrate, a 23-year-old female formal worker, from rural Chongqing, working at Pegatron, took part in *zhiyuan* to support Pegatron Shanghai factories and complained that she did not receive better pay. She pointed out that a member of Human Resources staff from the factory persuaded her to sign up to *zhiyuan* to support the factory in Shanghai, as her salary would be paid by Shanghai local basic salary standards. Nonetheless, when she had worked there for two months, she received only the total salary calculated by Chongqing's local basic standards. The factory claimed that it would pay extra salaries to her by other means, i.e. 'bonuses of performance'. Nevertheless, when she finally received her salary, she felt this was lower than calculated by the overtime rates of salaries based on Shanghai's standards. After the six-month *zhiyuan*, the factory did not pay extra salaries, such as subsidies for food and accommodation, which were promised to her to replace overtime salaries.

A large number of formal workers interviewed who had participated in *zhiyuan* in both Chongqing and Shenzhen also complained that they had received overall monthly salaries (including overtime) that were lower than they deserved. Again, the employer did this by using 'bonuses' and 'subsidies' in place of the agreed overtime pay. High-tech factories thus avoid paying high overtime salaries for formal workers based on the local basic standards within the receiving or original sending areas, in order to achieve maximum profits and minimum labour costs.

Labour control by fenliu

Performing the same function, *fenliu* involves factories forcing formal workers to move *across* different factories, as with *zhiyuan*, but rather change their labour relationships *within* different assembly lines and departments within a factory without their consent. A typical view of *fenliu* came from a female formal worker, 22 years old, from rural Guang'an in Sichuan Province, working at Foxconn in Shenzhen. She complained that she and her colleagues had no choice but to agree to *fenliu*, or involuntarily leaving the factory without notice. When they were forced to divert to other departments, the feeling was as though they were entering the factory for the first time. This was because they needed to sign labour contracts again with new manufacturing departments. Once they had been diverted to other departments and had signed new labour contracts, they could not return to the original department. Factories thus find ways to 'get around' laws and evade responsibilities, as with hiding illegal behaviours under the innocuous-sounding terms of *zhiyuan* and *fenliu*, to make the frequent changing of labourers' jobs appear legal.

Fenliu, used particularly by Foxconn Shenzhen, is in some ways even harder on workers than *zhiyuan*, since formal workers are forced to change their current labour relationships and even to sign new labour contracts when they are moved from one assembly line or department to another without their consent. The purpose of *fenliu* is the same as *zhiyuan*, which is to divert idle labourers from one assembly line or department that has few assignments to busy assembly lines or departments that lack labourers.

A minority of rural migrants would like to divert to other assembly lines or departments in order to earn higher monthly salaries due to more overtime. Nevertheless, the majority of workers still feel the *fenliu* is unreasonable, because of its methods of enforcement. A male formal worker, 24 years old, from rural Xiangtan in Hunan Province, working at Foxconn in Shenzhen, had a typical experience of *fenliu*. He suggested that due to the *fenliu*, many of his colleagues were forced to leave the factory. Because of decreasing orders in 2014, Foxconn forced them to leave current assembly lines that were soon to be closed, and diverted them to other assembly lines within departments by forcing them to sign new labour contracts without their consent. If they refused to do this, the employer threatened them with decreasing their overtime. He and many of his colleagues who did not leave the factory tried to seek help from the trade union; however, the official trade union assisted the factory in persuading them to accept the *fenliu*. They were not assigned jobs during that period. Other colleagues who were extremely unsatisfied by the factory's behaviour were forced to leave the factory immediately and did not receive compensation for dismissal.

Team leaders of the assembly lines were also diverted with the assembly workers. Their roles in the new assembly line were to carry out assembly work, as assembly-line formal workers. A 26-year-old male team leader, from rural Changsha in Hunan, working at Foxconn in Shenzhen, complained that he was a team leader who also needed to obey Foxconn's regulation of *fenliu*. He thought he also would be a team leader on the new assembly line in the new department; however, he was in the same position as other formal workers who also relocated to carry out assembly line work. He was very dissatisfied with the *fenliu* since he was moved from a 'good' working position to a basic-level position. Foxconn formally gave the workers a chance to choose whether to agree to the *fenliu* or not. However, whatever they chose, Foxconn made its own decision to divert them to other departments without consideration of their choices. This meant that the workers had no choice but to accept the *fenliu*.

The core difference between *zhiyuan* and *fenliu* is whether formal workers have been forced to change their labour relationships across different workplaces or rather between different types of jobs in the same workplace. But *zhiyuan* and *fenliu* also overlap for formal workers when assembly lines within different departments of production are restructured, contributing to the involuntary turnover of formal workers in high-tech factories. Large-scale and formal high-tech factories find these two managerial strategies useful in getting around national labour-related laws and evading responsibilities or regulations, thus hiding informality and precarity in employment. These processes are not based on the legal process to dismiss formal workers or change their work roles and locations, and companies do not pay any compensation for dismissing formal workers. A typical case was described by a 25-year-old female formal worker from rural Guang'an in Sichuan Province, working at Foxconn producing high-tech products for Apple, Huawei, Xiaomi, and other brands. She recalled that she was engaged in the production department for Apple. From the beginning of 2015, the Human Resources staff and supervisors of production began to persuade formal workers on their assembly lines to relocate to other production departments for Huawei and Xiaomi. They were told that the department in which they had been working would be 'sold' to other departments and they were required to sign new labour contracts with those departments. Some workers who rejected the *fenliu* were forced to *zhiyuan* to other assembly lines temporarily, while the rest of the workers were forced to sign new labour contracts with other production departments. For those who were reluctant to *fenliu*, Foxconn undertook other actions: from February 2015, their salaries and social insurance began to be paid by new production departments. Even the hospitals for the workers' healthcare were changed without their consent.

A male 26-year-old male formal worker from rural Changsha in Hunan province, working in the same factory, also experienced forced *fenliu* and *zhiyuan* in 2015, and tried to take action against it with the support of some of his workmates. He told me that they were very dissatisfied with *fenliu* and *zhiyuan*, which forcibly changed labour relationships without signing new labour contracts. They complained about this to the trade union; however, the trade union supported the factory's right to take these actions, and argued that the workers should obey the factory's arrangements. The trade union did not let them know about compensation for forced changes in labour relationships. Although after this collective action the new production departments agreed to send back workers who rejected *fenliu*, they were forced to agree that they would not complain about the new production departments that did not sign new labour contracts, nor that they should have been paid double salaries for these illegal actions.

Labour control by 'constructive dismissal'

Aside from *zhiyuan* and *fenliu*, the additional mechanism creating precarity in the employment of formal workers in both Chongqing and Shenzhen is the use of 'constructive dismissal'. This tactic involves strategic abuse, including verbal and physical abuse and harassment in terms of work assignments and conditions, from team leaders of assembly lines, which is specifically designed as one of the disciplinary practices of the labour process to force employees to quit. According to all formal workers I interviewed in both Chongqing and Shenzhen, if they left without notice, they would not receive a salary. The factories, therefore, oblige team leaders to conduct abuses to force employees to leave factories immediately. This strategy of evading the responsibilities set out in the contracts makes it appear that workers chose to leave the factory voluntarily, and thus hides the true degree of precarity in these workers' employment.

A study of China's automobile industry conducted by Lu Zhang in Changchun, Yantai, Qingdao, Wuhu, Shanghai, and Guangzhou, suggests that work groups and team leaders can work together to manage assembly line workers and to reduce direct labour-management conflicts.[6] I found that in both Chongqing and Shenzhen the intermediary role of team leaders in implementing managerial policies and evading regulations through the use of constructive dismissal does decrease direct labour-management conflict. But it does so only by increasing indirect labour-management conflicts at the shop floor level. As in Nelson Lichtenstein's conception of the 'foreman' as 'the man in the middle' within US automobile factories,[7] the team leaders interviewed during my fieldwork also faced a large amount of psychological and organizational pressure in balancing the demands and interests of management and workers. However, unlike the US foreman who has an official managerial position, the team leaders in Chongqing and Shenzhen high-tech manufacturing factories had been selected from assembly-line formal workers. They are 'grassroots managers', who have a direct relationship with assembly line workers.

According to a middle-level manager from a workshop in Lenovo in Shenzhen, team leaders face a high level of pressure every day. If they do not lead assembly line workers to finish their daily production assignments, they receive criticism from group leaders and section managers. In addition to allocating assembly tasks to their groups and supervising formal workers on the assembly lines (conducting performance appraisals, awarding bonuses, and reporting attendance), team leaders in both Chongqing and Shenzhen are required to discipline formal workers on assembly lines by using 'constructive dismissal'. These young team leaders are selected from assembly lines and lack experience; they often directly copy the abusive methods of management from their supervisors. According to one middle-level manager, team leaders will abuse assembly line workers without reason after being criticized by their supervisors. If direct conflicts between employees and employers are decreasing, conflicts between team leaders and assembly line formal workers are increasing due to the abusive approach of constructive dismissal.

The system of 'management by stress', designed for assembly and manufacturing production in the US,[8] certainly operates in China's high-tech manufacturing factories, and puts incredible pressure on team leaders and workers on assembly lines. Team leaders have to take on administrative and managerial responsibility. Because of these managerial approaches to work intensification, assembly line workers complain that they face significant pressures due to a very high daily target. The team leaders are, moreover, very rigid in exercising labour controls, and frequently abuse workers whose productions on the assembly lines do not meet their targets. Many other circumstances, including being late, disobeying minor factory regulations, and making mistakes on assembly lines also contribute to abuse from team leaders. A female formal worker, 23 years old, from rural Changsha in Hunan, working at Foxconn in Shenzhen, complained that she was abused by her team leader because she was late. The team leader pointed at her and shouted that if she was late again, he would mark her 'lateness' for work as an absence, which would affect her salary, promotion, and year-end bonus. Two male formal workers I interviewed from Jiangxi and Henan provinces, also at Foxconn, also received abuse, because one used a mobile phone and the other took a pack of cigarettes into the factory. The former was abused by his team leader, and the latter was punished by being made to write a paper of self-criticism.

Team leaders are directed by their managers to exercise individual discipline over workers and even to carry out these abuses, all of which contribute to the practice of 'constructive dismissal'. Assembly line workers find it difficult to get 'proof of leave' from their team leaders during peak seasons of production; employees are thus forced to wait to receive their salaries before they can leave the factories. However, especially in the off-peak seasons, both abuse from team leaders and 'leave without notice' increase for employees, because the factories do not need as many labourers and they want to dismiss assembly line workers without paying severance fees. The high-tech manufacturing factories deliberately use abuse from team leaders as a normal managerial practice to dismiss redundant labourers.

Typical forms of abuse include shouting, negative nickname calling, foul language, and physical penalties. A 20-year-old female formal worker, from rural Chongqing, working at Pegatron, provided a typical perspective on the phenomenon of abuse from team leaders. As she described, 'I still remember the moment that our team leader shouted at us. If we do not perform very well on the assembly lines, just leave, actually by using a very bad and rude word, "*gun* (fuck off)"'. Workers in Shenzhen also reported similar abuse from team leaders, which was particularly common at Foxconn. A male formal worker from rural Zhengzhou in Henan, working at Foxconn, complained that Foxconn had very bad management and often verbally abusive team leaders on the assembly lines. Abuse can also take physical form. A young woman migrant, 21 years old, from rural Chongqing, working at Pegatron, experienced both types of abuse from her team leader. She complained that when she made a small mistake for production on her assembly line, her team leader not only criticized her with bad language but also punished her by making her stand all day. Both verbal and physical abuse towards workers is used on assembly lines from team leaders, at the direction of management, to create the workplace conditions for constructive dismissal.

A staff member of Pegatron's Human Resources Department in Chongqing attempted to explain the reason why such abuse is a typical occurrence on assembly lines as a difference between new and older generation rural migrants. She suggested that the current generation of assembly line workers has more individuality and is more difficult to manage than older generations. Many years ago, the older generations were obedient and carefully worked on assembly lines. By contrast, currently, the new generation of rural migrants disobey regulations freely and frequently. A typical example, she suggested, is that assembly line workers will respond in turn with abuse if they feel team leaders have mistreated them. This explanation from management, however, did not fit my findings based on interviews with the migrant workers. The majority of formal workers on the assembly lines could not bear the abuse from team leaders and felt forced to leave their original factories to find jobs elsewhere.

A 22-year-old woman migrant from rural Chongqing, working at Pegatron, complained that once workers did something wrong on the assembly lines, team leaders pointed at their heads and abused them, both male and female workers. As a result, her colleagues who could not bear the team leaders' abuses left the factory voluntarily. An interview with a female team leader from Foxconn Shenzhen, herself a migrant from rural Anyang in Henan Province, confirmed that, at the instruction of factory managers, she deliberately created intolerable working conditions in order to encourage assembly line workers to quit. She pointed out that, in responding to a request to decrease the number of labourers from Foxconn, those who were the least compliant with management controls would be the first targeted for dismissal. Together with the practice of abuse, she would decrease their normal working hours and overtime, so that assembly line workers would have weekdays and weekends without any assignments. Without proper normal salaries plus overtime salaries, many workers would automatically leave the factory without notice.

As is clear from this statement, the main purpose of the factories' use of constructive dismissal is to control the number of workers employed, especially during off-peak seasons of production, and team leaders assist in implementing this policy in how they manage on the assembly line. Many formal workers, therefore, are forced to leave factories due to the abuse from team leaders. In effect, this makes their employment precarious, even though they have signed labour contracts with factories. The contracts do not protect them from being put in intolerable working conditions and forced to leave without notice or final pay. These high-tech firms quite deliberately employ managerial strategies that allow them to evade their responsibilities as well as to conceal the extensive informality and precarity that pervades their supposed 'full-time' employment.[9] For example, it might slow its normal recruitment for a period, and wait for 'voluntary' turnover by slashing working time. More extreme measures might include targeted abuse: if the company wants to fire a specific employee, but cannot find a proper excuse to take such an action, it will assign the worker to unpopular shifts, or arrange for the worker to be placed in awkward work settings.

It can be seen that, in order to pursue maximum profits and minimum labour costs, labour control methods like constructive dismissal can successfully force a large number of employees to take 'pseudo-voluntary' resignations, so that even formally regulated large companies are able to reduce the size of their labour force without paying the extra costs triggered by the involuntary redundancy of workers.

MAKING CHINA'S NEW DANGEROUS CLASS

In summary, I have argued that a new precarious labour regime, consisting of the disciplinary practices of '*zhiyuan, fenliu*, and constructive dismissal', has been developed in high-tech manufacturing factories in both Chongqing and Shenzhen. Even though rural migrant factory workers have signed formal labour contracts, employers are able to evade the responsibilities enshrined in the contract without fear of repercussions through the use of these managerial methods that maximize profits and minimize labour costs. These extensive informal practices are concealed within the formal employment relations of large high-tech manufacturing factories. It is a challenge for central and local policymakers to implement relevant employment policies to protect rural migrant factory workers' employment security, since the new labour regime makes even formal workers' employment security precarious. Indeed, local government policy-makers are most often in support of the precarious labour regime.

Yet what we can potentially see with these precarious migrant factory workers in the high-tech processing and assembly manufacturing industry is the making of China's new working class. This is because, as I have argued elsewhere,[10] these precarious migrant factory workers, who spontaneously have called themselves and their workmates '*gongyou*', are seeking to unite to struggle for their labour rights and work-relevant benefits. The new 'bottom-up' formation of *gongyou* class identity, which crosses all boundaries of gender, industries, and geographic areas in China, is, in essence, the catalyst today for establishing a common class-consciousness.

One important way of doing this is through their own worker-initiated collective actions, sometime with the support of local NGOs, rather than through the official trade union. The All-China Federation of Trade Unions (ACFTU) is the official government-affiliated trade union organization in China, without the organizational independence typical of unions in other countries. All its sub-branches, including those established in Taiwanese-owned manufacturing factories and other different types of enterprises, are controlled and managed by the ACFTU. The particular purpose of establishing sub-branches of the ACFTU for rural migrant workers within Taiwanese manufacturing factories is, first, to support the marginalized workforce and, second, to avert further social conflicts between migrant workers and the capitalist employers. However, the ACFTU officially and directly represents the Chinese central and local governments rather than migrant workers, and its task is to maintain social stability. As an official government-affiliated organization, in most circumstances, it stands by the side of factories in order to mediate conflicts between employers and employees and defuse collective actions and strikes conducted by migrant workers in China.[11]

Thus, in China, the trade union typically plays an intermediate role in defusing labour issues and disputes between the state and workers as well as between employers and workers. According to rural migrants interviewed in both Chongqing and Shenzhen, the trade union plays only a very limited role in representing rural migrants' interests. And since the trade union does not represent workers' interests in China, many new-generation rural migrants are engaging in spontaneous collective actions by themselves, forming membership-based collective identity. In fact, the new generation of rural migrants interviewed who were engaged in high-tech manufacturing within both Chongqing and Shenzhen expressed a great sense of pursuing their interests for themselves in order to struggle for their wages, their job security, and, where relevant, their social security.

The inability of the official Chinese trade union to support workers' rights against employers, instead playing a mediating role to defuse workers' collective actions, has led to the emergence of a class identity through collective actions organized by groups of workers themselves, sometimes with the support of labour NGOs (in the case of Shenzhen). The China Labour Bulletin has recently documented a significant rise in the number of strikes since 2011 in Chinese manufacturing industry, amounting to no less than 3,220 strikes until May 2019.[12] Of these, 1,047 were conducted in Guangdong alone (there were 48 in Chongqing), involving some form of collective action to claim back unpaid salaries, increase salary standards, improve employee benefits, and other work-relevant appeals. While rural migrants in Shenzhen get very limited assistance from the trade union, and more effective assistance from a range of labour NGOs, those in Chongqing cannot gain helpful protections at all, as Chongqing has fewer labour NGOs than Shenzhen based on my fieldwork. Nevertheless, rural migrants in both sites have, to differing extents, begun to strike to negotiate better employment conditions. Rural migrants in the Pearl River Delta have also engaged in many spontaneous strikes over the last few years, rather than pursuing legal protection from governmental organizations. Famous examples have included the Nanhai Honda strike in Foshan (2010), the Yue Yuen (a shoe factory) strike in Dongguan (2014), a number of strikes in the sanitary industry in Guangzhou (2007–2014), and the Jasic (a metal fabrication company) mobilization in Shenzhen (2018).[13]

Based on my fieldwork, many new-generation rural migrants in Shenzhen spontaneously express their collective class-consciousness by organizing the members of the *gongyou* together to protect their legitimate labour rights and social protections, a sign of the collective class-consciousness and class struggles in the making in high-tech manufacturing in China. The Nanhai Honda strike in Foshan as mentioned above is an important example of a successful class struggle between rural migrants, as the members of the *gongyou*, and factory owners, which was a turning point for rural migrants pursuing their own labour protections and increasing their basic salaries in Guangdong province.[14] The strike deeply influenced other rural migrants' strikes for labour protections across different factories, industries, and regions in 2010.[15] Migrants broke down social barriers, including the limited roles of the trade union in organizing collective actions, to form a common class identity. Additionally, the Jasic strike saw factory workers spontaneously take collective actions to form their own trade union, demonstrating an important progression – 'Chinese (migrant factory) workers have already transformed from purely economic subjects into political subjects with class consciousness'.[16]

Although my interview data between 2014 and 2016 suggests that a minority of new generation rural migrants still do not want to make problems bigger and more complicated, because they feel that laws and policies largely protect advantaged people while they still stand at the lowest level of Chinese society, many are now bravely willing to engage in collective actions up to and including strikes, most recently in Shenzhen. All this suggests that workers are well into a long process of class formation through undertaking collective actions that go beyond the individual worker struggling for his or her interests. These activities are part of a process of formation of collective class consciousness for rural migrants within high-tech manufacturing, and thus class formation. The absence of a trade union that can support migrant actions makes it difficult for migrant workers to organize, but when rural migrants do represent themselves in taking collective actions to pursue better livelihoods, employment security, or social security in high-tech manufacturing, this is likely to have an even greater impact in terms of the bottom–up emergence of class consciousness. Guy Standing's claim that members of the 'precariat' increasingly lose 'representation security' from relevant unions at work[17] is of little relevance in the Chinese case, since workers have not lost trade union representation as they never had it at all.

As William Hurst suggests, since they are 'unable to provide institutionalization and genuine political incorporation to workers left socially dislocated by the advance of the market, the CCP (Chinese Communist Party) and the Chinese state are forced to contend with workers' ongoing mobilization and increasingly radical activism'.[18] Hurst also points out that without proper independent organizations, Chinese workers may be in a precarious but potentially powerful position. Through their own disunited activism, migrants are expected to at least ferment current circumstances and perhaps even advance some new employment security and social welfare provisions.

The new precarious working class of the *gongyou* in China is dangerous for capitalists and central and local governments since the members of the new class are willing to take collective actions and pursue more employment security and better social security for themselves and families. Because of the formation of the common and collective class consciousness, those precarious rural migrant factory workers who comprise the members of the *gongyou* could come together as a kind of spontaneous 'class for itself'. The *gongyou* class may thus increasingly threaten both local Chinese states and capitalists, because its members are growing in number significantly, and are more willing to take spontaneous collective actions including strike actions (the number of which is increasing dramatically) against global neoliberalism and the growing precarity of their employment, in order to seek more stable employment security and proper social security for themselves and families in China.

The new precarious working class of the *gongyou* is thus an important and emerging group with common interests. It is likely to play a significant role in shaping the future developmental direction of Chinese society. As E. P. Thompson famously put it: 'Class happens when some men, as a result of common experiences (inherited or shared), feel and articulate the identity of their interests as between themselves, and as against other men whose interests are different from (and usually opposite to) theirs.'[19]

NOTES

1   Chien-Hsun Chen and Hui-Tzu Shih, *High-Tech Industries in China*, Cheltenham: Edward Elgar Publishing, 2005.

2   See especially Chris Smith, 'Living at Work: Management Control and The Dormitory Labour System in China', *Asia Pacific Journal of Management*, 20(3), 2003, pp. 333–58. See also Ngai Pun and Chris Smith, 'Putting Transnational Labour Process in Its Place: The Dormitory Labour Regime in Post-Socialist China', *Work, Employment and Society*, 21(1), 2007, pp. 27–45; Chris Smith and Jenny Chan, 'Working for Two Bosses: Student Interns as Constrained Labour in China', *Human Relations*, 68(2), 2015, pp. 305–26.

3   Kaxton Siu, 'Labour and Domination: Worker Control in A Chinese Factory', *Politics & Society*, 45(4), 2017, pp. 533–57.

4   Peter Nolan, Jin Zhang, and Chunhang Liu, 'The Global Business Revolution, the Cascade Effect, and the Challenge for Firms from Developing Countries', *Cambridge Journal of Economics*, 32(1), 2008, pp. 29–47.

5   The fieldwork was conducted between 2014 and 2016 in both cities. Semi-structured interviews were used to collect primary data from 164 rural migrant factory workers (including fifty-nine formal workers) to understand the labourers' side of the impact of labour control on the production process. As well, twenty people were interviewed from governmental officials, Human Resources staff from factories, staff from labour agencies, factory managers, and staff from labour NGOs to understand the factory managerial side of labour control during the production process. It is difficult to get accurate data at the factory-official level since researching labour-relevant issues is sensitive in China. Rather than audio recordings, I took notes during the interview process, as it was easier for me to establish trust with the interviewees and create a relaxed talking environment. All the references to individual discussions of labour control in the essay are drawn from these interviews in this time period.

6   Lu Zhang, *Inside China's Automobile Factories: The Politics of Labour and Worker Resistance*, Cambridge: Cambridge University Press, 2014.

7   Nelson Lichtenstein, 'The Man in the Middle: A Social History of Automobile Industry Foremen', in Joyce Shaw Peterson, Nelson Lichtenstein, and Stephen Meyer, eds., *On the Line: Essays in the History of Auto Work*, Urbana: University of Illinois Press, 1989, pp. 153–89.

8   Mike Parker and Jane Slaughter, 'Unions and Management by Stress', in Steve Babson, ed., *Lean Work: Empowerment and Exploitation in the Global Auto Industry*, Michigan: Wayne State University Press, 1995, pp. 41–53.

9   The use of constructive dismissal as a way of reducing the workforce is hardly unique to the high-tech industry cases of Chongqing and Shenzhen discussed here. A similar world of precarious employment security for labourers is generated in other sectors in other parts of the world. Workers at Wal-Mart in the US, studied by Nelson Lichtenstein, face quite similar practices of dismissal. When Wal-Mart wants to reduce the size of its labour force, it deploys parallel labour control practices to avoid formal redundancy procedures and the accompanying compensation for unemployment. See: Nelson Lichtenstein, 'In the Age of Wal-Mart: Precarious Work and Authoritarian Management in the Global Supply Chain,' in Carole Thornley, Steve Jefferys, and Beatrice Appay, eds., *Globalization and Precarious Forms of Production and Employment: Challenges for Workers and Unions*, Cheltenham: Edward Elgar, 2010, pp. 10–22.

10   Chunsen Yu, '*Gongyou*: The New Dangerous Class in China?' *Made in China: A Quarterly on Chinese Labour, Civil Society, and Rights*, 2, 2018, pp. 36–9.

11   Feng Chen, 'Trade Unions and The Quadripartite Interactions in Strike Settlement in China', *The China Quarterly*, 201, 2010, pp. 104–24; Tim Pringle, *Trade Unions in China: The Challenge of Labour Unrest*, New York: Routledge, 2011; Ying Zhu, Malcolm Warner, and Tongqing Feng, 'Employment Relations "With Chinese Characteristics": The Role of Trade Unions in China', *International Labour Review*, 150(1–2), 2011, pp. 127–43.

12   China Labour Bulletin, 'CLB Strike Map' [Online], *CLB*, 2019, available at: maps.clb.org.hk/strikes/en.

13   Ngai Pun and Huilin Lu, 'Unfinished Proletarianization: Self, Anger, and Class Action Among the Second Generation of Peasant-Workers in Present-Day China', *Modern China*, 36(5), 2010, pp. 493–519; Chris King-Chi Chan and Elaine Sio-Ieng Hui, 'The Development of Collective Bargaining in China: From "Collective Bargaining by Riot" to "Party State-Led Wage Bargaining"', *The China Quarterly*, 217, 2014, pp. 221–42; Pringle Tim, 'Strikes and Labour Relations in China', *Workers of the World*, 1(8), 2016, pp. 122–42; Stefan Schmalz, Brandon Sommer, and Hui Xu, 'The Yue Yuen Strike: Industrial Transformation and Labour Unrest in the Pearl River Delta', *Globalizations*, 14(2), 2017, pp. 285–97; Yueran Zhang, 'The Jasic Strike and the Future of the Chinese Labour Movement', *Made in China: A Quarterly on Chinese Labour, Civil Society, and Rights*, 3, 2018, pp. 12–7.

14   Eli Friedman, 'China in Revolt', *Jacobin*, 1 August 2012, available at: www.jacobinmag.com.

15   Mimi Lau and Chi Yuk Choi, 'Hundreds Clash as Labour Strife Widens: Worker Unrest Spreads to Yangtze River Delta', *South China Morning Post*, LXVI(158), 2010, B1&A5.

16   Ngai Pun, 'guandian: Shenzhen jia shi gongren weiquan de liang da yiyi [Opinion: The Two Significant Aspects of Jiashi Workers' Rights Protection]' [Online], *BBC zhongwen*, 17 August 2018, available at: www.bbc.com.

17   Guy Standing, *The Precariat: The New Dangerous Class*, London: Bloomsbury Academic, 2011, p. 17.

18   William Hurst, 'The Chinese Working Class: Made, Unmade, in Itself, for Itself, or None of the Above?', *Made in China: A Quarterly on Chinese Labour, Civil Society, and Rights*, 3, 2016, pp. 11–14.

19   E. P. Thompson, *The Making of The English Working Class*, New York: Vintage Books, 1966, p. 9.

SOCIAL REPRODUCTION IN TWENTY-FIRST CENTURY CAPITALISM

URSULA HUWS

It is a truism of socialist feminism that the reproduction of capitalism depends crucially on the unpaid labour that takes place within the home. This labour nurtures the next generation of workers, provides them with physical care and nutrition, and schools them in the social and cultural skills that they need for survival in the labour market. Once they have joined this labour market, however tenuously, it maintains their bodies, launders their clothing, prepares their food, and keeps their homes in working order. If they are too disabled or sick or old to do paid work, it still provides care for them. This labour of personal maintenance and social reproduction is carried out by people for themselves and for others and is embedded in broader divisions of labour that have a gendered character, but are also shaped by class and ethnicity.[1] It is supported, to varying degrees in different national contexts, by other forms of labour provided by extended family and broader communities, by various state institutions, and by formally or informally paid labour.

There is abundant evidence that women do a disproportionally high share of this unpaid labour. For example the most recent international compilation of statistics on unpaid care work shows very large disparities between countries, as expected, but no sign that the average gap has disappeared anywhere.[2] The ratio of men's to women's hours of housework stands at 10:25 in Pakistan and 6:22 in Turkey, but remains at 1.49 even in egalitarian Sweden, 1.61 in the US and 1.85 in Great Britain. Even in the best cases, therefore, women are still doing significantly more such work than men. Gershuny amalgamates care work with cleaning, cooking, and administration into a larger category of 'committed time' which, in his analysis, shows, despite variations, an 'overall trend of gender convergence, with the ratio regularly falling' but with the rate of change slowing.[3] An exhaustive analysis of trends over the past fifty years by Altintas and Sullivan also showed that, despite wide differences between countries, there has been a general move towards increasing gender equality in the household division of labour, although this appears to be slowing down in more gender-equal countries.[4] In the US, for example, the gender gap in minutes of housework per week shrank from 195 minutes in 1965 to 65 minutes in 2010. However this was not so much because men were doing more (the male mean increased by only 24 minutes during this period) but because women were doing less, with a mean drop of 105 minutes. It is sometimes pointed out that if you add up the number of paid and unpaid hours of work done by men and by women the totals are not so very different, but, as Gershuny points out, 'This is not equality, since men do substantially more paid work, and women do substantially more unpaid. And this inequality has, in turn, important consequences for inequality in earnings'.[5]

Because of this fundamental asymmetry, it has long been argued by feminists that the emancipation of women depends crucially on the emancipation of both men and women from responsibility for unpaid reproductive labour. However opinion has been sharply split about how this should be addressed.

Several first wave feminists argued that capitalism had done away with the kinds of production previously carried out in the home by transferring it to the factory and that housework now consisted only of unproductive work that created no value for the economy.[6] Communism, Marxist feminists claimed, would be able to liberate women from the exhausting burden of carrying out this work by collectivising it, in the form of state-provided restaurants, laundries, 'clothes-mending centres', and childcare facilities. Other first-wave feminists put their faith in new technologies to automate away the need for domestic labour and thereby bring about equality between the sexes, as imagined by H.G. Wells in his 1905 *A Modern Utopia*.

There were also intensive debates about domestic labour among second-wave feminists, writing in the 1970s. Some socialist feminists held that the socialisation of housework was a necessary pre-condition for liberation, arguing for public laundries, childcare facilities, and the like.[7] In recognition of the role played by public services in providing these, this underpinned a wave of feminist political activism in support of expanding public services, and, later, defending them against cuts in welfare spending. A variant position – interested in establishing prototypes in the here-and-now – experimented with forms of communal living in which housework could be shared equally among men and women.[8] Counterposed to the socialist feminist position was a radical feminist one, notably advocated by Dalla Costa and James and Federici, which proposed that the labour of housework should be paid, in a position that has now evolved into an argument for a basic citizen's income.[9] There were also discussions during this period about the potential of automation to dispense with the need for housework.[10]

All of these positions suffered to some extent from class-blindness, colour-blindness, and Western-centredness, tending to presume a normative household based on a nuclear family, with a male head of household and a female housewife, rendering invisible not only the unpaid labour that was carried out within the extended family and the broader community but also the paid labour carried out by domestic servants within households. They also, by and large, signally failed to anticipate the capacity of capitalism to expand to incorporate housework within its scope.

It is this expansion of capitalism based on a commodification and marketization of domestic labour that forms the focus of this essay. I argue here that a critical investigation of the changing dynamics of domestic labour is an essential precondition for understanding the current restructuring of capitalism – and hence of labour – in the context of globalisation and digitalisation, and that, furthermore, such an analysis is useful not just for understanding the social and economic upheavals currently taking place in the labour market, but also for developing strategies around social reproduction that simultaneously open up new choices for men and women in the organisation of their personal lives, and create the potential for building new kinds of public services based on decent employment standards.

THE CONCEPTUAL FRAMEWORK: DRAWING ON MARX

I have drawn on Marx to develop a conceptual framework for this analysis.[11] The household is not a topic that is addressed specifically or separately in Marx's writing. Nevertheless its implicit presence permeates his thinking and it is addressed indirectly in a variety of contexts, relating to different aspects of capitalism. I argue here that bringing these together in order to construct a rounded picture of the household is useful not just for understanding the dynamics of change in capitalism as it has evolved since Marx's time, and not just for pinpointing some of the contradictions that were left unexplored by Marx and Engels, and questions that remained to be answered in the future, but also for understanding what is going on in the global economy at the end of the second decade of the twenty-first century in order to inform socialist and feminist responses.

In Marx's understanding of capitalism the household plays a number of crucial roles simultaneously. First, it is a site of *primitive accumulation* (where activities can be found whose use values can become the basis for exchange values when they become the basis of new commodities). It is also (in some cases) a site of *production* of commodities for the market. Simultaneously it is both a site of *consumption* and of *social reproduction* and, more specifically the place where the *reproduction of labour power* takes place.

The household has its own internal social relations, with some members exercising power over the labour of others, labour which might be paid or unpaid. The social, sexual, and emotional complexity of these internal household relations can be illustrated by Marx's own cash-strapped household, in which the reproductive labour of his wife and daughters was supplemented by the paid labour of a servant, Helene Demuth, who was also the mother of his – formally unrecognised – son as well as a political comrade.

Whether or not one wishes to probe deeply into the contradictions of such intra-household social relations, the very fact that most households include more than one person poses challenges to what is perhaps *Capital's* most celebrated cornerstone: the labour theory of value, a crucial component of which is the concept of the cost of the worker's subsistence (which has to be subtracted from the total value produced by the worker in order to calculate the surplus value that accrues to the capitalist). While workers enter the labour market (and create value for their employers) as individuals, they consume, produce children, and reproduce their own labour power in shared households. Whose subsistence, then, should be included in the worker's subsistence cost? And how is this distributed if more than one member of the household engages in productive work?

Marx and Engels were not unaware of this contradiction. In *The German Ideology,* it is argued that the other household members are, in effect, slaves of the male head of the household (the 'husband'), constituting his personal property:

> The division of labour … is based on the natural division of labour in the family and the separation of society into individual families opposed to one another, is given simultaneously the distribution, and indeed the unequal distribution, both quantitative and qualitative, of labour and its products, hence property: the nucleus, the first form, of which lies in the family, where wife and children are the slaves of the husband. This latent slavery in the family, though still very crude, is the first property, but even at this early stage it corresponds perfectly to the definition of modern economists who call it the power of disposing of the labour-power of others.[12]

From this premise, it was possible to conclude that, when machinery was introduced, lowering the requirement for physical muscle-power, and women and children were set to work for capitalists, they did so as slaves of this head of household. Engels wrote in 1877:

[there is an] immediate increase in the number of wage-labourers through the enrolling of members of the family who had not previously worked for wages. Thus, the value of the man's labour-power is spread over the labour-power of the whole family – i.e., depreciated. Now, four persons instead of one must perform not only labour, but also surplus-labour for capital that one family may live. Thus, the degree of exploitation is increased together with the material exploitation ... Formerly, the sale and purchase of labour-power was a relation between free persons; now, minors or children are bought; the worker now sells wife and child – he becomes a slave-dealer.[13]

The valid argument is that the participation of women and children in the labour market lowers the cost of subsistence of an individual worker (whose wages, it is implied, previously covered the cost of subsistence of the entire family), but the status of these women and children as independent workers is left ambiguous, to say the least.

Their position also, of course, opens up larger questions about how Marx and Engels viewed gender relations. However it is not the purpose of this essay to explore such questions, important though they are. Rather, my aim is to focus on the household as a socio-economic space in which changes in capitalism can be examined in a rounded way that makes it possible to see not just how new kinds of commodity emerge, but how these commodification processes change the composition of the working class, drawing more and more workers into the conflictual labour relations that constitute the essence of capitalism and, associated with this, transform the nature of the labour of social reproduction. Examining these changes in detail sheds light on the continuing relevance of a number of the key concepts that can be found explicitly proposed or more implicitly suggested in *Capital*: the relationship between technological change and the falling rate of return on capital; the role of the reserve army of labour in exerting downward pressure on wages; the cheapening of the price of consumer goods as a means of drawing workers away from subsistence production and turning them into enforced consumers of mass-produced commodities; the substitution of goods for services.

A key feature of this analysis is the distinction between what Marx called 'productive' and 'unproductive' labour which forms a cornerstone of the labour theory of value. I use this distinction (rechristening 'unproductive labour' as 'reproductive labour')[14] and analyse changes in the distribution of these types of labour, in particular looking at the complex and shifting changes between 'unproductive/reproductive' and 'productive' forms of labour as well as between paid and unpaid labour.

TYPES OF LABOUR

It is in households that just about all labour power is produced and reproduced, and most final consumption takes place. It is thus necessary to plot what takes place in the household against *all* forms of labour under capitalism, whether these are productive or reproductive, paid or unpaid, in order to understand changes in the character of labour.

I therefore begin by classifying all labour into six broad categories.[15] In the following section I will look at the dynamics of change within and between these categories, as labour is transformed by the continuous and destructive restructuring of capitalism that takes place over time. These categories are, of necessity, broad and schematic but I hope serve as a framework that makes visible the unstable and shifting relationships between them.

Unpaid labour in the home and community – subsistence labour for social reproduction

The first of these categories refers to the kind of unpaid labour that takes place outside the scope of the money economy, producing only use values. Some of this labour, such as that carried out by hunter-gatherers or in subsistence agriculture, predates capitalism by many centuries. But many forms have persisted in the capitalist era. These do not just involve activities related to physical reproduction and family maintenance (bodily care of the self and others, preparing food, cleaning, etc.) but also social and cultural production and reproduction (teaching children to speak, singing, passing on stories, adornment, etc.). The fact that this labour is unpaid does not, of course, necessarily imply that it is entirely voluntary. It may be carried out unwillingly, within coercive social relationships, and with strong sanctions for those who transgress social and cultural norms. But of course it may equally be a source of joy. To the extent that it includes the possibility of applying one's mind to solving new problems creatively, as opposed to mechanically repeating a known activity, this kind of labour is perhaps the closest that many people get to the experience of what Marx in the *Grundrisse* described as 'free labour' in the following terms:

> this overcoming of obstacles is in itself a liberating activity – and [that,] further, the external aims become stripped of the semblance of merely external natural urgencies, and become posited as aims which the

individual himself posits – hence as self-realization, objectification of the subject, hence real freedom, whose action is, precisely, labour.[16]

In other words, this kind of labour may be regarded as unalienated. It sits firmly outside capitalist relations.

Paid private service work in homes or farms – servant labour

The second type of labour, which also predates capitalism, is work carried out by paid servants, like Marx's sometime employee, Helene Demuth. Marx was emphatic that this form of labour was not 'productive' in the sense of producing surplus value.

> Certain labours of menial servants may therefore equally well take the form of (potential) commodities and even of the same use-values considered as material objects. But they are not productive labour, because in fact they produce not 'commodities' but immediate 'use-values'.[17]

Whether or not labour is 'productive' in his view does not depend on its material characteristics but derives from the social relations of production in which it is produced:

> An actor, for example, or even a clown, according to this definition, is a productive labourer if he works in the service of a capitalist (an entrepreneur) to whom he returns more labour than he receives from him in the form of wages; while a jobbing tailor who comes to the capitalist's house and patches his trousers for him, producing a mere use-value for him, is an unproductive labourer. The former's labour is exchanged with capital, the latter's with revenue. The former's labour produces a surplus-value; in the latter's, revenue is consumed.[18]

From this we can deduce that the provision of services is only transformed into productive labour if it is supplied by a capitalist intermediary who takes a profit from this service provision rather than being supplied directly to the end user.

Paid private service work for companies – capitalist service work

My third category of labour consists of service work that has made this transition and is supplied to customers by workers employed by service companies, for example shops, restaurants, hotels, transport companies, security companies, cleaning companies or private schools.

Paid public service work

My fourth type of labour, like the first two, is labour that is dedicated to the provision of public services, a category that grew dramatically in the twentieth century. To the extent that it involves the provision of use values directly to the population or to state bodies, it is not 'productive' for capital. This is not to say, of course, that it does not indirectly benefit capitalism, for example by providing infrastructure, policing the population, or contributing to the reproduction of labour power. It is therefore, like the first two categories, what Marx would have termed 'unproductive' and what I would prefer to call 'reproductive' labour.

Paid labour for companies in production industries – capitalist production work

My fifth category is the one to which Marx paid most attention: labour involved in the production of commodities for the market. This category – which he expected to continue growing under capitalism – places workers into a directly conflictual relationship with capital (a relationship which also applies in the case of capitalist service work), with capitalists seeking to appropriate as large as possible a share of the value of workers' labour as surplus value. In this process, capitalists use every means available to them for cheapening the value of labour and/or increasing its productivity, including deploying members of the reserve army of labour to substitute for organised workers, and introducing machinery that simplifies tasks and deskills workers.

Unpaid labour in the home and community – consumption work

My final category is one that has received rather little attention in Marxist theory but, I argue, plays an important role in facilitating both the transformation of 'reproductive' labour into 'productive' labour, and in intensifying the exploitation of 'productive' workers. This is the unpaid labour carried out by consumers associated with the purchase, operation, maintenance and transportation of commodities purchased in the market. Many of the tasks involved in this consumption labour involve activities that were previously carried out by paid 'productive' workers that have been transformed into unpaid labour in a process of externalisation, often assisted by technology. These might include such things as self-service in supermarkets, the purchase of tickets online or the use of ATM machines to withdraw cash from a bank.[19] Consumption labour does not produce surplus value directly, but is implicated in the externalisation of tasks formerly carried out by paid workers and could thus be regarded as contributing indirectly to the exploitation of the labour of productive workers by capitalists.

These six categories therefore break down into two types of 'productive' labour (capitalist service work and capitalist production work) and four types of 'reproductive' labour, two of which are paid (either as servant labour supplied directly to households or as service work) and two unpaid (subsistence labour and consumption work).

The history of capitalism can be regarded synoptically as the history of the dynamic transformation of each of these types of labour into another, with (as Marx predicted) the overall effect of driving a higher and higher proportion of human labour into the 'productive' category where it is disciplined by, and produces value for, capitalists. Since most of these transformations take place within the household, or rely on the household for their reproduction, the household provides the ideal observatory for analysing these transformations. The next part of this essay offers an overview of these changes. Limitations of space, of course, mean that this overview is schematic and over-simplified.

THE DYNAMICS OF LABOUR CHANGE

Primitive accumulation – the generation of new commodities

Most commodities have a use value (in addition to an exchange value), and therefore provide the satisfaction of human needs that existed before capitalism supplied them via the market. So it could be said that the majority of commodities are replacements for goods or services produced in the household or its surroundings by unpaid labour in previous periods. Thus the clothing industry can trace its origins back to home-based spinning, weaving, knitting, and sewing, and the same can be said for the manufacture of tools, soap, pottery, furniture, and a multitude of other products. Of course these industries did not appear overnight but came about as a result of complex changes in social and economic relations, such as the roles of traders and their monopolisation of certain routes and markets and of rentiers, including the owners of the first factories who provided space for independent hand-loom weavers to work in rather than directly employing them.[20]

However long and tortuous the transition from an unpaid domestic or community-based activity to full market production under the control of a capitalist, the unpaid activities carried out in the household still represent a reservoir of activities which can be commercialised to become the basis of new goods or service industries: from cosmetics to psychotherapy; from washing machines to powdered baby milk; from ready meals to Netflix. This process of generating new commodities should not be viewed as something which only took place in the past but as part of an ongoing process which, if anything, is gathering momentum in the twenty-first century, when new commodities are generated *inter alia* from human biology, affect, and sociality as well as art and culture.[21]

Social inequalities and the dynamics of change in paid service labour

The introduction of paid labour into households and the larger communities in which households are embedded also predates the development of capitalism, and has complex origins. The power to dispose of others' labour has not, historically, rested on purely market relations but is linked to other social hierarchies – of gender, caste, status etc. – and has not always involved the exchange of money. Nevertheless, the master- (or mistress-) servant relationship has persisted, and evolved, over the centuries and continues to do so.

Although, in most developed economies, there are fewer bourgeois households or family farms employing live-in staff, there are large numbers of households making use, on an occasional or regular basis, of the paid services of cleaners, carers, babysitters, window cleaners, handymen, gardeners and so on. When these workers are hired directly, they fall into the category of 'unproductive' or 'reproductive' servant labour, paid for from surplus household income.

If the work is for a single household, a degree of social inequality is implicit in many of these relationships – the income of the master or mistress must be presumed to be considerably higher than that of the servant, in order for there to be enough surplus to pay their wages. The large-scale entry of middle-class women into the labour market in most developed economies in the latter part of the twentieth century was enabled in no small part by the much cheaper labour of other women, many of them migrants, who cleaned their homes and cared for their children.[22]

However there are other kinds of service work provided to households on an occasional basis where the premise of social inequality does not necessarily hold true. This includes a range of specialist services such as cleaning windows, clipping hedges, hairdressing, installing appliances, or putting up shelves; services which may well be supplied to households with a lower income than those of the workers. Where the providers of these services operate as independent tradespeople, or do the work for cash payment in the informal economy, they are not producing surplus value and should therefore be classed as servant labour.

The size of this population of paid reproductive service workers expands and contracts in response to other developments in the economy. Demand increases in response to urbanisation, with migrant households deprived of the services supplied outside the market by extended family and neighbours that were available in rural communities. It also increases in response to a high demand for women's labour outside the home – requiring some replacement for the unpaid reproductive work they would otherwise supply. Social polarisation adds to demand, by producing wealthy households with a desire to employ servants to support a luxury lifestyle.

Demand for this kind of labour decreases if there is a provision of public services that contribute to social reproduction. It also decreases when capitalist firms intervene to provide such services in the market, extracting surplus value from the workers they employ to provide them. These processes are described below.

Recommodification of public services

Perhaps one of the most striking features of capitalism in the twentieth century was the particular accommodation that was reached between capital and labour after the Second World War that resulted in many developed Western economies in the creation of welfare states in which public resources were used to provide social reproductive services to citizens, most notably in health, education, and social care. This development, often viewed as a 'decommodification' of the capitalist provision of services in the previous period, can also be seen as a response by the capitalist class to the real fear that the working classes of Europe (and perhaps even of North America) would turn to communism.[23]

Since the fall of the Berlin Wall in 1989 and the collapse of the Soviet Union in 1991 heralding the opening up of most of the world to capitalist markets and the triumph of neoliberalism, this fear has lost its sting. Public services have become a new arena of capitalist accumulation; the simple production of use values under the control of the state have been transformed through privatisation or outsourcing into services that can be exploited for profit by capitalists.[24] In the process, large numbers of workers have thereby been transformed from being 'reproductive' public service workers to 'productive' workers producing surplus value for capitalists.

Expansion of 'productive' private services

The growth in the number of workers working for capitalists providing private services comes in part from an inflow of public sector workers, as described above. However it also results from a much older trend whereby the supply of private services to households, previously provided by directly employed servants or tradespeople, now comes from for-profit companies, ranging from laundries to purveyors of ready-cooked meals. The growth of these service industries is driven by a complex interaction between supply and demand which cannot be decoupled from other changes in the structure of social relations in the household and the divisions of labour related to this.

On the demand side, as in the case of the 'reproductive' services described above, migration to cities (where housing is poor and land lacking), combined with a lack of time because of the need for all household members to seek paid work, makes it difficult or impossible for these services to be provided by the labour of these household members themselves. Newly arrived migrants may also lack the social networks that allow them to find suppliers of such services informally and employ them directly. On the supply side, service supply companies are able to recruit vulnerable workers easily and work them hard, cheapening the cost of the services and thus making them affordable for larger numbers of people. This puts competitive pressure on the costs of services that are *not* provided through companies, thus accelerating the shift from 'reproductive' to 'productive' service labour. The demeaning character of the servant role may also play a role in reinforcing this trend in some cases, especially where the labour is racialized, with some workers preferring to dispose freely of their labour power on the market, however exploitative the employer, rather than cope with the daily humiliations of working for a tyrannical master, with its associations with bondage. Those who have in the past worked independently, on the other hand, may experience the change negatively, with enforced employment under capitalist conditions depriving them of the autonomy they previously enjoyed as independent traders.

In the second decade of the twenty-first century, it is becoming evident that both of these processes have been taking place on an enormous scale. On the one hand, the outsourcing of public services has created an exponentially growing global workforce of capitalist service workers, some providing physical services (for example care workers or prison guards) and some information-based services that can be provided from a distance online (such as IT maintenance or dealing with queries from welfare claimants). Even if they retain the ethical values of public servants, such welfare workers are now firmly part of the productive workforce, often working for giant corporations that supply the same outsourced services to both public and private sector clients.

On the other hand, privately-provided services are being dragged within the scope of another new breed of multinational company: online platforms. Expanding exponentially since the 2008 financial crisis, online platforms now account for a significant proportion of the supply of domestic services such as cleaning (e.g Taskrabbit, Helpling, Housekeep), household maintenance services (e.g Trustatrader, Mybuilder, Local Heroes), cooking (e.g. Feastly, Chefxchange), food delivery (e.g Foodora, Deliveroo, Uber Eats), taxi services (e.g. Uber, Lyft), as well as a range of other services including babysitting (e.g. Findababysitter, Childcare.co.uk), dog walking (e.g. PetSitter, Fetch!), providing private tuition for schoolchildren (e.g Tutorhub, Mytutor), and so on.[25] At present most of these platforms do not regard themselves as employers, and use business models that entail taking some sort of rent (a flat fee, or a percentage cut from the employer, the worker, or both). However they exert considerable control over the working conditions and earnings of workers, and where legal test cases have been taken the workers have generally been deemed to be subordinate workers, rather than the 'independent contractors' the platforms consider them to be. The rent-seeking behaviour of these platforms is not unlike that adopted by the earliest factory owners at the beginning of the industrial revolution. It seems likely to be a transitional business model that will be replaced, as these platforms reach maturity, by the more conventional employment models of other service companies (such as shops, cafes, warehouses, etc.) which, in the twenty-first century, also increasingly practice 'just-in-time' forms of work organisation management (such as the use of zero hours contracts) that are digitally mediated.[26]

In short, the pool of workers now working for private companies supplying reproductive services to households is growing fast, fed by these two different, and increasingly convergent, sources.

Substitution of goods for services

This huge influx of labour into private service provision, under the control of capitalists is not, of course, the whole story. In fact, viewed through a long historical lens it is a mere staging post in a larger trend: the substitution of goods for services. There is a limit to how much the productivity of an individual service worker can be increased, however hard that worker is forced to work. A cleaner with a mop can only cover so much square footage of floor in a given time; a nurse can tend physically to only so many patients; a courier's muscles can cycle only so many miles.

Once a business model has been established, and competitors have entered the field following the same model, perhaps with lower start-up costs and cheaper labour, the law of dwindling returns on investment sets in. Capitalism's relentless need for expansion requires something more radical than just more of the same, especially during periods of restructuring after its recurrent crises. This is where science and technology come in.

One of the most striking features of the history of capitalism – indeed, some would argue, its main characteristic – has been the pattern whereby waves of innovation have generated new commodities to satisfy needs that were previously met through the labour of service workers, whether paid or unpaid, productive or reproductive. In the early days of capitalism, inventions such as the power loom, the printing press, and the steam train displaced earlier forms of manual labour (some if not all of which had previously been carried out in the household) and increased the productivity of the remaining workers by orders of magnitude. They made possible the production on a very large scale of standardised commodities that previously had to be laboriously made by hand. But these new means of production had themselves to be manufactured too. Thus there had to be factories to make looms as well as factories to make cloth; factories to make vats as well as factories to make soap; bringing into being the proletariat Marx wrote about so eloquently.

The impacts of automated means of production on earlier forms of labour are not always easy to plot. For example the sewing machine was used by unpaid workers in the home who had previously made and mended their families' clothes by hand, and by paid seamstresses employed privately, as well as by workers employed to work in clothing factories, or as outworkers supplying their owners. Nevertheless, broad patterns can be discerned whereby, for example, the use of washing machines displaced laundry workers, the use of automobiles displaced stable hands, and the radio and recorded music industries displaced itinerant musicians. The typical historical shift is from unpaid reproductive work to paid reproductive service work to paid productive service work to paid productive manufacturing work.

The twentieth century provided innumerable illustrations of this trend – and so does the twenty-first century already. Each crisis of capitalism has triggered a wave of restructuring, and each restructuring has launched the development of new industries manufacturing commodities, many of which arise from or substitute for what were previously service industries, often introducing 'labour saving' commodities that affect both paid and unpaid reproductive labour, from vacuum cleaners to Amazon's Alexa. As the total amount of manufacturing grows around the world, so too does the number of workers involved in the directly exploitative form of labour that goes into producing these commodities – not just in factories but all along the value chain from design to distribution.

Externalisation of labour and the growth of unpaid consumption work

The promise of labour-saving commodities is that they will reduce the amount of unpaid reproductive labour that household members must perform, and one of the main incentives to purchase them is the time that will be saved – time that is, of course, at a premium precisely because of the intensification of capitalist pressure on workers to produce more in their 'productive' employment. However, the consumption of these commodities creates new kinds of unpaid labour as companies externalise to customers as many tasks as possible in order to increase the productivity of paid service workers, or lower the cost of production: from keying in orders to collecting packages; from checking out groceries to assembling flat-pack furniture.

The announcement in 2017 by Ikea (which built its global business on the basis of customers assembling their own furniture) that it had purchased the online platform Taskrabbit (one of whose most popular offerings is the assembly of flat-pack furniture) gave graphic evidence that consumption work is indeed experienced as real labour. Taskrabbit (along with other platforms, such as Lineangel and Placer) also offers busy or lazy consumers the opportunity to pay a 'tasker' to wait in a queue on their behalf, or stay in their house to await a delivery.

The tightening of the knot

It can be concluded from this brief analysis that the characteristics of capitalism described by Marx are still with us. It continues to expand exponentially, penetrating ever more areas of life and dragging them into the market where living labour can be used for the production of surplus value. The numbers of workers drawn into this relationship continue to grow.

The workplace (or, to be more specific, the labour relationship between worker and capitalist) remains the site of antagonism where the struggle is waged over what proportion of the worker's time is exchanged for how much money (or, put another way, how much surplus value can be extracted from the worker's labour). However, many of the parameters of this exchange are set in the household, which can also be seen as the cauldron in which changes in the scope and structure of capitalism are brewed, as well as the site in which its contradictions are played out.

The household represents, simultaneously, a reservoir both of supply and of demand: for labour power and for new commodities. It is where that basic raw material of capital – human labour time – is produced and fought over in a multidimensional struggle. Some labour time is supplied, more or less willingly, or at least by agreement, by workers to their employers during their formal working hours. Other time is snatched more covertly from the household by capital: the time that was spent in the past on their education and upbringing and in the present on their bodily maintenance. Yet more time is snatched by the creeping extension of the working day: for example the time spent preparing for and travelling to work; or the time spent working outside formal working hours dealing with communications from the employer. To this must be added the time that is contributed to other capitalists by consumption work: time, for example, spent in a telephone queue waiting to talk to a call centre worker in order to maximise that worker's productivity; or going to the supermarket. The more time-poor the household, the greater the conflicts between household members over the domestic division of labour and the greater the pressure to purchase more commodities in the market in the hope that they will save time. Which of course leads to increased pressure to earn more money in order to pay for these commodities. Which then leads to an even greater squeeze on household time. Thus does the knot of capitalism tighten. And thus does capitalism grow. As the twenty-first century approaches its third decade, Marx's analysis could not be more relevant.

POLITICAL IMPLICATIONS

So what are the political implications of these developments? It is clear that the current wave of capitalist restructuring is bringing about a marketization and commodification of social reproduction on a vast scale.

On the one hand, as the real value of wages falls and the neoliberal welfare regimes that consolidated their grip after the 2008 crisis triumph, it is now the expectation in most economies, developed or developing, that both women and men should carry out paid work in the labour market in order to keep their households afloat, leaving less and less time available for subsistence labour. This situation is exacerbated by reductions in publicly provided welfare services. In the resulting time squeeze, people are turning more and more to the market to provide them with basic social reproductive services. The labour that is employed by the capitalists who provide these services is, meanwhile, increasingly precarious and low paid. In their capacities as consumers, people have an interest in these services being as cheap and easily available as possible; but in their capacities as workers they want security, decent wages and predictable hours.

It must be emphasised that the users and consumers of these market services are often *the same people*. My research has shown that the users of online platforms for household services are not higher earners (though they are more likely to be working full time) than the average. Indeed, 84 per cent of those who work supplying household services are also customers for them, while 91 per cent of those who work as drivers or delivery workers for online platforms are also customers for these services.[27] So the relationship between these workers and their customers cannot be characterised as that of a new servant class serving the bourgeoisie. On the contrary, the new market in social reproduction services has to be seen as something going on *within* the working class: a working class in which the labour of social reproduction shifts unstably between the categories outlined above, sometimes paid, sometimes unpaid, sometimes delivered within the household by family members, sometimes provided externally, sometimes purchased as a service, sometimes as a product. But this is a working class that is increasingly atomised, with its members not necessarily recognisable to each other as such.

The manner in which the supply and demand for household services is mediated by online platforms mitigates the development of solidarities within the working class among people in their capacities as workers and as consumers. Just as customers may shop in Wal-Mart, even though they may be aware that the cheapness of the goods is based on the exploitation of production labour in China and retail labour closer to home, because they feel that they have little choice but to seek the lowest prices, so online platforms are sought out as global brands that can offer cheap prices, regardless of how their workers are treated. Furthermore, drawn as they are from the most expendable and vulnerable sections of the labour market, those who work for these platforms may well be immigrants, lacking the language skills to communicate effectively with their customers and not recognisable as neighbours or kin. Potentially dehumanising perceptions of these workers as 'other' are exacerbated by practices such as requirements to rate their performance using telephone apps. More sophisticated users may even consciously exploit this facility in the knowledge that if they give a negative rating to the worker they may be able to persuade the platform to give them a discount on the price (perhaps unaware that this may result in the worker not being paid, or being dropped from the platform). The erosion of solidarities within an atomised working class is certainly not unique to the platform economy; it is, however, accentuated by digital management practices.

A reliance on platform-mediated services to substitute for unpaid household labour also exacerbates social differences. While it is possible to see this market simply as an exchange of services among the time-poor and the money-poor, this picture must also take into account different degrees of poverty on both fronts. Those with the lowest earnings are also likely to be working the longest hours (my research found that platform work is most usually carried out on top of another main job by those who are financially desperate), so those who arguably have the greatest need for these services are also those least able to afford them, ratcheting up a continuing spiral of financial pressure, time pressure and stress.[28]

This shifting market in reproductive services is not, of course, unprecedented. The history of the working class has always involved such a dynamic mix of labour. Readers of Henry Mayhew's (1851) accounts of metropolitan street life in *London Labour and the London Poor* will recall the vivid picture he conjured up of jostling costermongers on the pavements offering everything from baked potatoes to chimney sweeping services.[29] The interactions between the suppliers and purchasers of these goods and services was probably not very different in kind from those between the itinerant care workers, rushing, mobile phone in hand, from one fifteen-minute appointment with an elderly client to the next, and the Deliveroo and Uber Eats riders and their customers on the streets of London in the twenty-first century.

We can however state with some certainty that this new wave of marketization and commodification of housework, and social reproduction in general, is a development that few feminists and socialists predicted. It points to the inadequacy of traditional strategies considered alone, whether these consist of demands for the socialisation of housework, payment for housework, or technological solutions to the 'housework problem'.

First, it becomes clear that the demand for socialising domestic labour and creating good jobs in the public sector to deliver household services is vulnerable on two fronts. On one hand, the trend for substituting goods for services may provide a way for these services to be bypassed, consigning to the market functions that the original plans hoped to decommodify. On the other, as recent history has shown, public services are very vulnerable to privatisation and outsourcing – another form of recommodification. Campaigns for further decommodification run the risk of becoming merely rear-guard actions to minimise cuts and reverse the incursion of the market, unable to advance radical programmes for improvement.

Second, the demand for payment for housework emerges as problematic if treated in isolation, even if this is reformulated as a demand for basic income for all, regardless of gender or family circumstances. If this demand is made in isolation from efforts to protect the provision of collectively provided universal public services it can be seen simply as a means to allow citizens to purchase more and more household services and goods in the market. And, as we have seen, market forces left unchecked do not necessarily free us from the burden of housework. While some tasks are rendered easier, new ones are imposed, with the resulting time squeeze creating a vicious circle in the political economy of social reproduction whereby the cost of the goods and services required to compensate for the shortfall in time results in a further loss of time. Depending on how any basic income is paid for, its introduction could be redistributive towards the lower paid, and towards households with children and, like the demand for better public services, could be progressive. However it could not, on its own, address the contradictions of commodification and the capitalist market. In other words, the problem cannot be solved just by throwing money at it.

Finally, it is apparent that there is no simple technological fix for the problem of housework. While technologies are controlled by corporations and serve the interests of creating profit, they cannot fulfil their promise of eliminating the need for drudgery. The dynamics of capitalist restructuring create low-paid jobs for workers even while they create cheap commodities, with the earnings of the former never quite catching up with the cost of the latter, in a ratcheting spiral of exploitation.

Nevertheless, it is possible that the digital technologies used by online platforms to match supply and demand for household services could, if allied with demands for public provision of these services, create the basis for a new kind of welfare state: one in which reproductive services such as childcare, cleaning services, meals for the housebound, and nursing care for the chronically ill are supplied on demand, in response to social need, by workers who are well-paid public sector workers, employed by democratically accountable bodies.

Housework, it turns out, is at the epicentre of capitalism. And the labour of social reproduction, which underpins it, also represents its future potential for expansion. Socialist and feminist strategies for addressing it will therefore have to take on capitalism itself if they are to bring about the liberation of women and, in formulating these strategies, it will be necessary to combine demands for public services, demands for basic income, *and* demands for bottom-up design of technologies that serve the needs of households and communities rather than those of big business.

NOTES

1   For a discussion of the role of migration in the social reproduction of the working class at a global level, see: S. Ferguson and D. McNally, 'Precarious Migrants: Gender, Race and the Social Reproduction of a Global Working Class', in L. Panitch and G. Albo, eds., *Socialist Register 2015: Transforming Classes,* London: Merlin Press, 2014.

2   OECD, *Gender, Institutions and Development Database*, Paris: Organisation for Economic Co-operation and Development, 2014, available at: stats.oecd.org.

3   J. Gershuny, *Gender Symmetry, Gender Convergence and Historical Work-Time Invariance in 24 Countries*, Oxford: Centre for Time Use Research, University of Oxford, 2018.

4   E. Altinas and O. Sullivan, 'Fifty years of change updated: Cross-national gender convergence in housework', *Demographic Research*, 35, (16), 2016, pp. 455-70.

5   Ibid, p. 12.

6   See for example A. Kollontai, 'The Social Basis of the Woman Question', in *Selected Writings of Alexandra Kollontai*, Translated by A. Holt, London: Allison & Busby, 1977

[1909]; C. Zetkin, *Social-Democracy and Women's Suffrage*, Translated by J. Bonhomme, London, 1906, available at www.marxists.org; A. Clark, *Working Life of Women in the Seventeenth Century*, London: Routledge and Kegan Paul, 1982 [1919].

7   See for example J. Gardiner, 'Women's Domestic Labour', *New Left Review*, I/89(January-February), 1975, pp. 47-58; S. Himmelewit and M. Mackintosh 'Women's Domestic Labour', *Bulletin of the Conference of Socialist Economists*, 4(2), 1975; W. Seccombe, 'The Housewife and Her Labour Under Capitalism', *New Left Review*, I/ 83(January-February), 1974, pp. 59-71.

8   Chronicled, *inter alia*, in L. Segal, *Making Trouble: Life and Politics,* London: Serpents Tail, 2007.

9   M. Dalla Costa and S. James, *The Power of Women and the Subversion of the Community*, Bristol: Falling Wall Press, 1973; S. Federici, *Wages Against Housework*, Bristol: Power of Women Collective and Falling Wall Press, 1975.

10   See for instance: J. Zimmerman, ed., *The Technological Woman: Interfacing with Tomorrow*, New York: Praeger. 1983; J. Terry and M. Calvert, eds., *Processed Lives: Gender and Technology in Everyday Life,* New York: Routledge, 1997.

11   This conceptual framework is discussed more fully in U. Huws, *Labour in Contemporary Capitalism: What Next?* London: Palgrave Macmillan, 2019.

12   F. Engels and K. Marx, 'Division of Labour and Forms of Property – Tribal, Ancient, Feudal', in *The German Ideology*, Part 1 A, 1845.

13   F. Engels, *On Marx's Capital*, Moscow: Progress Publishers, 1956 [1877], p. 89.

14   This reconceptualization of unproductive labour as reproductive labour is explained in U. Huws, 'The Underpinnings of Class in the Digital Age: Living, Labour and Value', in L. Panitch and G. Albo, eds., *Socialist Register 2014: Registering Class,* London: Merlin Press, 2013.

15   This typology is described in greater detail in: Huws, *Labour in Contemporary Capitalism*.

16   K. Marx, *Grundrisse,* Chapter 12, London: Penguin, 1973.

17   K. Marx, *Theories of Surplus Value,* Chapter IV, Moscow: Progress Publishers, 1863.

18   Ibid.

19   This is discussed more fully in Chapter 11: 'Who's Waiting? The Contestation of Time', in U. Huws, *The Making of a Cybertariat: Virtual Work in a Real World*, New York: Monthly Review Press, 2003.

20   See: E.P. Thompson, *The Making of the English Working Class,* 1963. See also E.M. Wood, *The Origin of Capitalism,* 1999; and F. Braudel's magisterial three-volume *Civilization and Capitalism: 15th-18th Century,* 1967-1979.

21   I discuss this in greater depth in U. Huws, *Labor in the Global Digital Economy: The Cybertariat Comes of Age*, New York: Monthly Review Press, 2014.

22   See for example B. Ehrenreich and A. R. Hochschild, *Global Woman: Nannies, Maids and Sex Workers in the New Economy,* New York: Henry Holt, 2004.

23   See for example G. Esping-Andersen's *Three Worlds of Welfare Capitalism,* 1990.

24   I have discussed this more fully in U. Huws,'Crisis as Capitalist Opportunity: New Accumulation Through Public Service Commodification', in L. Panitch, G. Albo, and V. Chibber, eds., *Socialist Register 2012: The Crisis and the Left,* London: Merlin Press, 2011.

25   I have written more about this in U. Huws, 'Where Did Online Platforms Come From? The Virtualization of Work Organization and the New Policy Challenges it Raises',

in P. Meil and V. Kirov, eds., *The Policy Implications of Virtual Work,* Basingstoke, UK: Palgrave Macmillan, 2017, pp. 29-48.

26   For a fuller discussion of these trends see: U. Huws, 'Logged Labour: A New Paradigm of Work Organisation?', *Work Organisation, Labour and Globalisation,* 10(1), 2016, pp. 7-26.

27   U. Huws, Spencer, D. Coats, and C. Holts, *The Platformisation of Work in Europe,* Brussels: Foundation for European Progressive Studies, 2019.

28   Ibid.

29   H. Mayhew, *London Labour and the London Poor: a Cyclopædia of the Condition and Earnings of Those That Will Work, Those That Cannot Work, and Those That Will Not Work,* London: G. Woodfall and Son, 1851.

WAYS OF MAKING A LIVING: REVALUING THE WORK OF SOCIAL AND ECOLOGICAL REPRODUCTON

ALYSSA BATTISTONI

In San Jose, California, teachers can't afford to live in the communities where they work; in San Francisco, even highly paid tech workers are living in dormitories.[1] Across the US, people are raising money for urgent health procedures on online platforms like GoFundMe; in elder care facilities, robots put the elderly to bed.[2] Elementary school students go hungry when they cannot afford lunch or incur 'school lunch debt' and an estimated 45 per cent of college students are food insecure.[3] The mortality rate of white Americans is rising for the first time in decades, driven in large part by the opiates crisis; drug overdose is the leading cause of death in Americans under fifty, and is particularly concentrated in long-neglected areas like West Virginia. Between 2008 and 2016, the suicide rate increased 16 per cent; and the overdose rate by 66 per cent.[4] The US has among the highest rates of infant mortality in the developed world, driven largely by the disproportionate deaths of black babies; black mothers are 3.5 times more likely to die in pregnancy and childbirth than white ones.[5]

These crises of daily life under American capitalism are punctuated by news of existential ones. In fall 2018, the Intergovernmental Panel on Climate Change announced that climate change is happening more rapidly, with worse effects, than was previously understood. The world is on track, the IPCC reported, for more heat-related deaths, smaller crop yields, more extreme weather events, and hundreds of millions more people in poverty.[6] Insect populations are declining rapidly as the result of industrial mono-cropping and overuse of pesticides, threatening ecosystem function the world over. A recent report by the Intergovernmental Science-Policy Platform on Biodiversity and Ecosystem Services (IPBES) warns that biodiversity is declining rapidly, 'significantly reducing nature's capacity to contribute to people's well-being'.[7]

What these reports make clear is that life is under threat in a number of ways. We have long known that capitalism is exhausting. Marx famously observed that capital 'usurps the time for growth, development, and healthy maintenance of the body. It steals the time required for fresh air and sunlight … it reduces the sound sleep needed for the restoration, reproduction, and refreshment of the bodily powers to just so many hours of torpor as an organism, absolutely exhausted, renders essential.'[8] Today it is increasingly clear that capitalism is exhausting not only human workers but also the many other organisms that make up our living world – so much so that Ajay Singh Chaudhary proposes that the anti-capitalist subject of our present moment might be thought of as 'the exhausted'.[9] William Clare Roberts similarly argues that Marx's focus on *overwork* rather than the extraction of 'real' value is critical to Marx's theory of capitalism: capital, Roberts argues, pushes both man and nature to exhaustion.[10] The most crucial question of the twenty-first century is how this drive toward exhaustion can be stopped.

Yet the crises of social and environmental exhaustion have typically been treated as separate problems. The crisis of care is to be addressed by Medicare for All; the crisis of the environment, by the Green New Deal (GND). Calls to 'green the economy' via the latter typically propose a simple replacement of energy sources and infrastructure while leaving other aspects of production and consumption intact.

This energy-focused framework has been prominent in the discourse around the GND even on the left. Robert Pollin's argument for a Green New Deal in the *New Left Review*, for example, understands the GND as primarily a program for replacing fossil fuels with clean energy: 'the core feature of the Green New Deal,' Pollin argues, 'needs to be a worldwide program to invest between 1.5 and 2 per cent of global GDP every year to raise energy-efficiency standards and expand clean renewable-energy supplies.'[11]

Transitioning away from fossil fuels is, of course, imperative. But a truly 'green' or 'sustainable' political economy entails a much more significant transformation, towards properly valuing the work of social and ecological reproduction, and around diminishing work in general. This will ultimately require a break from capitalism. For the immediate future, however, the GND presents an important opportunity for the socialist left to intervene in the shaping of the political economy that will structure our lives and possibilities for decades to come. In particular, the vision articulated in the resolution introduced by Alexandria Ocasio-Cortez and Ed Markey in February 2019 represents a major shift in political understandings of the relationship of climate change and other ecological problems to 'social issues', from inequality to deindustrialization to the prevalence of insecure work. Indeed, it is remarkable how little the language of stimulating growth or reviving American economic dominance enters into it: it is focused instead on meeting human needs for healthcare, housing, and access to nature.

In considering the possibilities before us, I pose three major questions regarding how we think about work specifically: first, what kinds of work we value; second, how we distribute that work; and third, how much work we do. I conclude with thoughts on the political challenges that socialists must face and address in our efforts to remake work.

WHAT IS A GREEN JOB?

'Green jobs' have typically been framed as replacements for environmentally harmful work in extractive and related industries, intended to appeal to the fossil fuel industry workers – from the dwindling numbers of lifelong coal miners to construction workers hired onto temporary gigs building oil pipelines – who will be out of work if fossil fuel companies and related industries shut down. These are imagined to substitute one kind of blue-collar job (e.g. building solar panels and wind turbines) for another (e.g. the extraction of oil and coal). More generally, environmentalism is understood as an issue supported by the middle class, people with the luxury of caring about clean air and water; 'green jobs' are thus the mechanism for building support among working-class people.

Political anxiety about such workers has only intensified in the wake of Donald Trump's election. As one representative analysis stated, 'right-wing nationalist-cum-populist forces have been able to capitalize on the profound distress and disaffection of working people far more effectively than has the radical left … by bringing behind them various native working-class constituencies that once constituted the main social base of the center-left parties but have long been ignored by them – notably factory workers and miners hard hit by economic stagnation, technological advance, and globalization.'[12] It is these industrialized workers that most green jobs programs have in mind. And it is these workers that invocations of the 'working class' more broadly tend to conjure. Yet as Gabriel Winant argues, 'to imagine that we should look for "class" and see hard-hats mistakes a particular historical manifestation – the industrial working class – for a general category whose ranks are always changing.'[13] Today, Winant points out, the working class is increasingly doing kinds of work that do not require hard hats.

A just transition away from fossil fuels does require that workers whose livelihoods are in extractive industries and other carbon-intensive sectors have other options. But truly remaking the economy will also require thinking more broadly about the purpose of economic activity – a project that will entail recognizing and revaluing other forms of labour. A green economy must value work that improves the quality of people's life in non-resource-intensive ways; work that meets people's needs rather than chasing profits; work that provides use values for people, not surplus value for capital. Low-carbon work includes work teaching and nursing, growing sustainable food and preparing it, caring for those who need it, making culture and art. Ways of living in the twenty-first century, that is, must center the low-carbon work of care for people and ecosystems while also seeking to diminish work overall.

The social reproduction tradition offers critical insights into the role that unwaged labour plays in capitalism, and into the relationship between 'the social' and 'the economic.' Johanna Brenner and Barbara Laslett define social reproduction as 'the activities and attitudes, behaviours and emotions, and responsibilities and relationships directly involved in maintaining life, on a daily basis and intergenerationally.'[14] More recently, Nancy Fraser, Tithi Bhattacharya, and Cinzia Arruzza have described social reproduction as the work of 'people-making', consisting of the 'activities that sustain human beings as *embodied social beings* who must not only eat and sleep but also raise their children, care for their families, and maintain their communities, all while pursuing their hopes for the future.' Although the work of 'people-making' is necessary for the work of 'profit-making', they observe, it is largely unwaged and treated as distinct from capitalist production. Thus, the authors argue, 'the division between profit-making and people-making points to a deep-seated tension at the heart of capitalist society'.[15] Yet social reproduction theory is resolutely focused on the making of human beings and human labourers; it has little to say about the ecological crisis in which we find ourselves. I argue that we must connect this work to what I call the work of ecological regeneration: the work done by the so-called 'life support systems' of planet Earth – the carbon cycle, water purification, soil fertility and many other things often referred to as 'ecosystem services', as well as to the work done by humans to sustain those functions. Like the work of social reproduction, these activities have been undervalued and treated as background conditions against which the formal economy can function. But they are crucial to maintaining a habitable, and liveable, future on earth. Capitalism, that is, 'free rides' not only on people-making activities, but also on planet-making ones.

Our understanding of the crisis of care, then, must encompass the multispecies relationships necessary for sustaining life on earth. This definition of care is closer to that offered by the political theorist Joan Tronto, who describes 'care' as 'a species activity that includes everything that we do to maintain, continue, and repair our "world" so that we can live in it as well as possible.' That world, Tronto argues, 'includes our bodies, our selves, and our environment, all of which we seek to interweave into a complex, life-sustaining web.'[16] Today the web of life is breaking down: it needs care, repair, and maintenance. We must think about how to support and expand forms of work oriented towards caring for the ecosystems that keep the earth habitable.

In the US, Stephanie Kelton, a major advocate for a federal job guarantee program, has argued that this should focus on 'delivering public goods, aimed broadly at three areas: caring for people, caring for the planet, and caring for communities'.[17] Pavlina Tcherneva has similarly called for a jobs guarantee program to be designed as a 'National Care Act', again foregrounding care for the environment, people, and communities.[18] Canada's Leap Manifesto, written by a coalition of labour Indigenous, environmental, and social justice organizers in 2015, calls for an economy centered around 'caring for the earth and one other'. The Manifesto's vision of 'an economy in balance with the earth's limits' argues for a transition going beyond a simple replacement of energy sources:

> We could live in a country powered entirely by renewable energy, woven together by accessible public transit, in which the jobs and opportunities of this transition are designed to systematically eliminate racial and gender inequality. Caring for one another and caring for the planet could be the economy's fastest growing sectors. Many more people could have higher wage jobs with fewer work hours, leaving us ample time to enjoy our loved ones and flourish in our communities.[19]

Such timely proposals raise new questions around the distribution and valuation of care work and its limits – as well as about how this new world is to be won.

WHO DOES WHAT WORK?

The division of labour is central to capitalism's productivity, and different kinds of labour are intensely gendered and racialized. That is, different kinds of people tend to do different kinds of work – and the way certain kinds of work are valued is intimately related to who does them. To understand the multiracial working class today requires understanding not only the new kinds of work that people today do, but understanding the way that these kinds of work are shaped by interpersonal difference. Matching workers with green jobs is already a challenge. To take a stylized example, a person, probably a man, who loses a job as a coal miner in West Virginia might not be able to get a job building or maintaining wind turbines in Texas or California – not only is the new job located in a different place, but it requires a different set of skills. Many green jobs programs have focused on the question of skill, offering job-training programs that train people in clean energy work but leave it up to them to get a private-sector job. When, as I have argued above, the task is to revalue different kinds of work, this challenge becomes even more substantial. The challenge is linked to issue of the kinds of people who do certain kinds of work. As Kathi Weeks argues, 'gender identities are coordinated with work identities in ways that can sometimes alienate workers from their job and at other times bind them more tightly to it'.[20]

Care work is an intensely gendered form of work, often descried as 'pink collar labour', or 'feminized labour'. Much of the work of 'people-making' falls into this category. Women perform a great deal of care work unpaid, and far more perform paid care work than do men. Generally, the lower-status the job, the more likely women are to do it. Jobs also tend to be paid less when women start doing them and work becomes 'feminized', as has happened in teaching and nursing. Similar dynamics are apparent with race: the less well paid the job, the more likely it is that a person of color is doing it. Many of the worst paid jobs – like those of home health aides, who are little protected under current labour law – are done by women of color. Waged domestic and care work in the Global North are deeply reliant on immigrant labour: this division of labour allocates low-cost domestic work to immigrant women, freeing middle- and upper-class parents to work out of the home for higher wages while creating a 'chain of care' stretching across the globe.[21]

Women go into care work jobs because they've already been trained to do them. Women are seen as naturally nurturing and caring; they are considered 'suited' to these jobs – and, crucially, men are seen as *not* suited to them. It is for this reason that denaturalizing labour was always a crucial part of the Wages for Housework project. Federici argues that 'housework was transformed into a natural attribute, rather than being recognized as work, because it was destined to be unwaged' – though its naturalness was belied by the fact that it in fact took years of training, in the form of gender socialization, to teach women to perform the work at hand. The wage, then, was not only about the money, but about denaturalizing the relationship between women and the kinds of work they did: it was, Federici argued, 'the demand by which our nature ends and our struggle begins because just to want wages for housework means to refuse that work as the expression of our nature, and therefore to refuse precisely the female role that capital has invented for us'.[22]

Care work represents a rapidly growing sector of the economy, and there are likely to be many more jobs in this sector in coming years as the American population ages. The projected growth in home health aide jobs from 2016 to 2026 is estimated to be 86 times the growth in wind turbine service technicians – though the turbine technicians are paid, on average, twice the salaries of the home health aides. But these jobs may not be ones that men want to do. As always, this work is stratified by race as well as gender: black men are three times more likely to take lower-rung health jobs than white men; other men of color are also significantly more likely to take health care jobs in the lower levels, as nurses or aides rather than doctors.

In the United States today, the jobs traditionally associated with the just transition – whether in the extractive industry or the green industries towards which we are to transition – are jobs dominated by men. Men make up about 87.5 per cent of extractive industry workers, 95 per cent of 'installation, maintenance, and repair workers, including wind turbine technicians' and 98 per cent of electricians and pipe-layers, and hold over 70 per cent of manufacturing jobs. On the other hand, the economy oriented around care that I have argued for is currently dominated by women: women make up nearly 75 per cent of education workers, 66 per cent of 'community & social workers', and 75 per cent of healthcare workers – a number which goes up to 90 per cent if restricted only to nurses.[23] So if the aim is not only to move people out of extractive industry jobs but towards an economy built around 'caring for each other and the planet', more men will likely need to do kinds of work that they may not 'identify with', at least under the current regime of gendered labour. Transitioning to an economy centered around care, that is, will therefore require a reckoning with the ways that different kinds of work have been shaped by gender and race, and valued accordingly.

Perhaps the most famous example of environmental work was the New Deal's Civilian Conservation Corps, which took on a wide array of nature-oriented work: forest and soil conservation, the construction of hiking trails and recreational facilities, flood control, disaster relief. The CCC was all male, and the work itself – mostly hard labour – was seen as ruggedly masculine, intended to turn sickly poor boys into strapping specimens of American manhood. Its militaristic inspiration was reflected in the description of the program as a 'corps' and those who participated as 'soil soldiers'; workers lived in barracks and obeyed military discipline. (Not for nothing did the socialist leader Norman Thomas argue that the CCC's 'work camps fit into the psychology of a fascist, not a Socialist state.')[24] Meanwhile a short-lived women's CCC – known as the She-She-She – met with resistance from those who thought women should not work outdoors, and was ultimately deemed too expensive. Today, explicitly conservationist work reflects the lineage of the environmental movement, which has been dominated by the white middle class; that image is reflected in the demographics of who does explicitly conservationist work. The permanent staff of the National Parks Service, for example, is older and whiter than the American population. Other conservation work is done on the cheap, either by young people on service years, as in the California Conservation Corps (motto: 'hard work, low pay, miserable conditions, and more!'), or by incarcerated people, who make up one-third of California's firefighting force.

The agriculturalist Wendell Berry has since the 1970s advanced a model of labour oriented around caring for the earth, which he describes 'husbandry' – defined as 'all the practices that sustain life by connecting us conservingly to our places and our world; it is the art of keeping tied all the strands in the living network that sustains us'.[25] Berry argues that traditional, labour-intensive farming models are better for the earth than models premised on fossil-fuelled technology and chemical fertilizers, and can be a source of employment. Contemporary American agriculture, however, does not incorporate much care for the earth, nor for those who work it, in sharp contrast to Indigenous communities whose relationships to land are premised on reciprocity rather than exploitation – a relationship of mutual use and dependence.[26] Farmworkers today are nearly all Latino, and largely male: the National Agricultural Workers Survey, conducted by the Department of Labor, suggests that over 80 per cent of farmworkers are Hispanic, and nearly 75 per cent are immigrants; an estimated 49 per cent of farmworkers are undocumented.[27] Farmworkers are among the most exploited workers in the country, working brutally long hours for low pay, and are still excluded from many forms of labour protections. Integrating care for the earth into the American agricultural system will require reckoning with the exploitation of these workers, and of undocumented labourers more generally.

MORE CARE, LESS WORK?

Calls for a caring economy often present care itself as an unambiguous good. Socialists should be more critical: care fulfills crucial human needs, but providing it is still work – often taxing and difficult work. We must take care that in our efforts to make visible and payable the unwaged work on which capitalism relies, we resist the tendency to overly valorize or even romanticize that work and what it reproduces. One of the major challenges for an economy oriented around social and ecological care, then, is how care can be appropriately valued without being overly venerated, and how an emphasis on necessary care can also make space for leisure. Visions of ecologically caring labour are perhaps particularly susceptible to romantic tendencies. Berry, for example, argued that 'labour-saving' technology was only necessary because industrialized production had so degraded labour. He articulates a classic dignity-of-labour narrative: work done in and for communities confers independence, skill, and respect.[28]

Yet even if we recognize that labour-intensive forms of production may be more ecologically beneficial, we can respond pragmatically to those demonstrated needs without embracing labour as a moral good in its own right.[29] Here we can think of Federici's response to calls for ecologically motivated returns to labour-intensive production in the 1970s: 'is this idyllic picture of a life built entirely around reproducing oneself and others not the same life that women have always had? Are we not hearing again the same glorification of housework, which has traditionally served to justify its unpaid status, by contrasting this "meaningful, useful, and more importantly unselfish activity", with the presumably greedy aspirations of those who demand to be paid for their work?'[30] Visions of the good life in an ecologically sustainable future often center activities like cooking, gardening, preserving – that is, forms of work that had traditionally been assigned to women, now reconceived as leisure. When held up as answers to ecological catastrophe, that work becomes harder to refuse and limit. The obvious social value of care, education, and other people-making activities has often licensed overwork and exploitation on the grounds that it constitutes a calling or a 'labour of love'. Like other forms of work, care work, housework, and other forms of reproductive labour can be physically difficult, mentally challenging, and simply boring. Simone de Beauvoir argued that 'few tasks are more like the torture of Sisyphus than housework, with its endless repetition'.[31] Angela Davis similarly thought that no one should do housework if it could be helped: 'no one should waste precious hours of their lives on work that is neither stimulating, creative, nor productive.' Davis argued that domestic work should be minimized, industrialized, and socialized.[32]

Reducing ecologically destructive forms of consumption need not entail austerity, but rather an abundance of time and leisure. Yet we should also remember that these forms of abundance do not mean the end of work altogether. Calls for a shorter work week and the replacement of work with low carbon leisure, both necessary components of an ecologically sustainable way of life, should take socialist feminist warnings into account: Maria Mies argues that 'the vision of a society *in which almost all time is leisure time* and labour time is reduced to a minimum is for women in many respects a vision of horror' – schemes for the reduction of work have rarely extended to the work done by women and indeed might intensify the burden on those so often tasked with 'life-making' activities.[33] In the household, meanwhile, the introduction of ostensibly 'work-saving' technologies substituting nonhuman energy sources for human labour did not, in fact, lessen housewives' workload: instead, as Ruth Schwartz Cowan shows, the standards for domestic work rose, such that houses were expected to be cleaner, children better dressed, meals more elaborate, and so on.[34]

Valuing these forms of work will therefore also require reorganizing them. Here, the socialization of domestic and care work has long been a socialist feminist demand. In one of the first analyses of domestic work, Margaret Benston advocated converting domestic labour from private work to industrialized, socialized, public forms. In a socialist society, she argued, 'the forces of production would operate for human welfare, not private profit, and the result should be liberation, not dehumanization'. There was no reason why, if housekeeping were socialized, via communal laundries, kitchens, nurseries, and so on, it 'should not result in better production, i.e. better food, more comfortable surroundings, more intelligent and loving child-care, etc. than in the present nuclear family'.[35] Benston held that women could be understood structurally 'as that group of people who are responsible for the production of simple use values in those activities associated with home and family', yet argued that women 'are not merely discriminated against, we are exploited. At present, our unpaid labour in the home is necessary if the whole system is to function.'[36]

Wages for Housework thinkers took up the question of value more directly, rejecting the argument that domestic work was the source of 'mere use values'. Mariarosa Dalla Costa insisted that 'domestic work not only produces use value but is essential to the production of surplus value'; Federici similarly argued that domestic work was 'essential to the production of surplus value'.[37] Without domestic work, they argued, the production of commodities could not continue. Critics argued that while domestic work was indeed necessary for capitalism to function, it did not really produce surplus value. Wally Seccombe, for example, agreed that housework was necessary, comparing it to the work behind the scenes of a play – 'although these workers are out of sight and therefore out of mind, they are nonetheless indispensable to the entire production' – but arguing that this 'did not make the case for it being a productive labour in the specific context of capitalist production'.[38] Margaret Coulson, Branca Magaš, and Hilary Wainwright put it more bluntly, arguing that although housework was undoubtedly useful, 'it nevertheless does not create value at all, because its immediate products are use values and not commodities'.[39] But the domestic labour debates ultimately died in the weeds of Marxist value theory. Regardless of the kind of value produced, most agreed that the prospect of paying for unwaged work would represent a major economic shift. 'To pay women for their work', Benston argued, 'even at minimum wage scales, would imply a massive redistribution of wealth.'[40] Andre Gorz, though approaching the Wages for Housework movement as a critic, made the similar argument that 'if housework were remunerated at the marginal price of an hour's work ... the cost of domestic payments would be so high as to exceed the capacities of even the most opulent society'.[41]

Increasingly domestic labour *was* waged as the service sector grew, which effectively commodified many forms of household labour, from cooking to cleaning. The term 'social reproduction' has come to refer not only to unpaid labour but to a wide range of activities that (re)produce people physically and socially, paid or unpaid, creating use values or exchange. The work of preparing food to sustain a waged worker could be done 'by a family member as unwaged work in the household, by a servant as waged work in the household, or by a short-order cook in a fast-food restaurant as waged work that generates profit' – and all now tend to fall under the banner of 'social reproduction'.[42] Today, as care and domestic work are increasingly done for wages, and indeed represent the fastest-growing sectors of the economy, it is clear that social reproduction can be commodified and made profitable. (Despite warnings about the commodification of 'ecosystem services', meanwhile, efforts to commodify the work of nature have thus far been largely unsuccessful.)[43] Even where public provision of goods and services had previously been won through feminist and working-class struggles, capital has refused its tax and regulatory burden and moved to privatize previously public services – often while still relying on public funds – and offload ecological and social costs onto the public. The result is differentiated access to care and other services: those who can afford to pay for privatized social reproduction do; some unionized workers are able to bargain for these services in the form of benefits; those who can do neither simply absorb the labour and costs within family and kin structures. Yet the tension between the rising demand for care, still seen by many as a basic right, and the rising costs of 'people-making' makes care in particular a key site of struggle over the question of who will pay for social reproduction.[44] The impacts of climate change, representing environmental costs externalized by capital, are another.

It would seem that both advocates and critics have been proven right regarding the bill for social reproductive activities: as services once provided within the household for free have become commodified and waged, their costs have skyrocketed. After all, there are only so many productivity gains to be had in the 'stagnant' service sectors, as William Baumol argued; the provision of, say, twenty-four-hour care cannot be reduced. Baumol thought this phenomenon could be managed through redistributive policy amounting to a gradual socialization of parts of the economy.[45] In the United States, instead, the rising costs are falling largely on individuals and families, and on the workers burdened with providing care to more patients. As Melinda Cooper shows, as neoliberalism has diminished state provision of goods and services, the family has played a crucial role in absorbing the rising costs of healthcare and education, providing a privatized safety net in place of the welfare state.[46]

If, as I have been arguing, capitalism free rides on the un- and under-paid work of provisioning and caregiving, any effort to expand publicly provided, well-paid care work will impose costs that capital is unlikely to be willing to pay. As Cedric Johnson points out, what was 'exceptional' about the New Deal is that 'capital was forced to take responsibility for the costs of social reproduction of labour'.[47] But today, after decades of neoliberal decimation of the welfare state, even its relatively mild goals seem radical. Even the moderate welfare state of social democracy instituted by the New Deal, after all, was ultimately deemed 'unaffordable'.[48] The decline of living standards in the past few decades is the direct result of increased global competition that has forced corporations to drive down prices and in tandem, wages. The combination of stagnant wages and the rising cost of living are pinching working people from both sides. Under these circumstances, forcing capital to pay for the reproduction even of its own workers will be challenging enough; forcing capital to pay for ways of living that do not serve capital directly – that is, for the likes of universal public services – will be even more difficult. Capitalism's golden age was an aberration, a short-lived illusion. Allusions to it aside, the Green New Deal will not bring it back. Socialists must engage in the question of what will come next.

POLITICAL STRUGGLES

As I have suggested in this essay, we should see workers performing the work of social and ecological reproduction, whether for wages or not, as workers who can form part of the political force for left climate programs. Yet the disjuncture between the sites of militant labour struggle and the sites of capital accumulation that I have just described is likely to produce new contradictions as the former build power. Where, in such an economic arrangement, will the leverage to command such major concessions from capital come from?

Here, it is worth again returning to early socialist-feminist debates. Wages for Housework theorists were deeply influenced by the Italian autonomist concept of the social factory, according to which it was necessary to look beyond the relationship between worker and capitalist to see that all of society functioned according to capitalist logics. It suggested the necessity of fighting capitalism not only in the factory, but also in the whole of society. Following from this analysis, Dalla Costa observed that the capitalist organization of labour was mirrored by the separation of labour organizing and community organizing. To treat women and the community outside the industrial workplace as 'appendages' or 'auxiliaries' to male-dominated unions, she argued, was to accept a division within the working class that ultimately benefited only capital: 'at every stage of the struggle, those most peripheral to the productive cycle can be used against those at the center', she argued, 'so long as the latter ignore the former.'[49] Dalla Costa and others therefore called on unions to organize household workers but also to look to sites of class struggle beyond the workplace – in schools and homes, neighbourhoods and nurseries. They also called for action specific to housework, calling on housewives to 'abandon the home' en masse – to go on strike by refusing domestic labour. As Dalla Costa argued, '*No strike has ever been a general strike.* When half the working population is at home in the kitchens while the others are on strike, *it's not a general strike.*'[50] Seccombe was more sceptical: 'this is surely the stuff of revolutionary fantasy – a general strike of housewives, crippling the economy.'[51] Davis likewise expressed doubt that women isolated in private homes could be effectively organized. Seccombe did, however, see potential in other forms of struggle around social reproduction, such as boycotts, rent strikes, and campaigns for welfare services.

Such forms of organizing have turned out to be an important part of contemporary struggles. As Asad Haider and Salar Mohandesi write, 'lines of political contestation are thus being drawn squarely through the terrain of social reproduction – soaring rents, crumbling buildings, underfunded schools, high food prices, crippling debt, police violence, and insufficient access to basic social services like water, transportation, and health care.'[52] Nancy Fraser similarly sees in movements around healthcare, housing, immigration rights, and public services 'the demand for a massive reorganization of the relation between production and reproduction: for social arrangements that could enable people of every class, gender, sexuality and colour to combine social-reproductive activities with safe, interesting and well-remunerated work.'[53]

With the rise of paid care and service work have also come more serious efforts to organize workers engaged in the work of social reproduction, broadly defined; indeed, these workers have been among the most militant in recent years. The US Bureau of Labor Statistics reports twenty work stoppages involving 485,000 workers, with education, health care, and 'social assistance' industries accounting for over 90 per cent of workers on strike. The BLS also reports that 'between 2009 and 2018 the educational services and health care and social assistance industries accounted for nearly one half of all major work stoppages'.[54] Many of these strikes have also taken on a distinctive form. Using a framework known as 'Bargaining for the Common Good', teachers have intentionally rejected the division between workplace and community, organizing with and alongside students, parents, and community members to win victories around both community and teacher demands. Teachers' strikes in Los Angeles and Arizona were not general strikes, but nevertheless brought thousands of community members into the streets to support teachers' action in the workplace. The diffuse nature of the shop floor, meanwhile, has typically lead domestic workers to organize around legislative protections and demands for other forms of state action.[55]

Indeed, from the *indignados* to Occupy, Nuit Debout to the London riots, Black Lives Matter to Red for Ed, today's most significant struggles combine critiques of wealth inequality, renewed labour militancy, and attention to the spaces of daily life; struggles over clean water in Flint and at Standing Rock meanwhile suggest that daily life extends to the conditions for ecological reproduction. These struggles represent resistance to capitalism both in and out of the workplace.

NOTES

1   Dana Goldstein, 'The Fight to Keep Teachers in Tech Hubs from Being Priced Out', *New York Times*, 1 January 2019; Nellie Bowles, 'Dorm Living for Professionals Comes to San Francisco', *New York Times,* 4 March 2018.

2   Constance Gustke, 'Managing Health Care Costs with Crowdfunding', *New York Times*, 31 January 2015.

3   Jessica Fu, 'As school lunch debt skyrockets, little is known about its real cost', The New Food Economy, 8 January 2015, available at: www.newfoodeconomy.org; Sara Goldrick-Rab, Christine Baker-Smith, Vanessa Coca, Elizabeth Looker, and Tiffani Williams, 'College and University Basic Needs Insecurity: A National #RealCollege Survey Report', The Hope Center, Temple University, April 2019.

4   Cynthia Koons and John Tozzi, 'As Suicides Rise, Insurers Find Ways to Deny Mental

Health Coverage', *Bloomberg Businessweek,* 16 May 2019.

5   Linda Villarosa, 'Why America's Black Mothers and Babies Are in a Life-or-Death Crisis', *New York Times,* 11 April 2018.

6   IPCC, 'Global warming of 1.5°C. An IPCC Special Report on the impacts of global warming of 1.5°C above pre-industrial levels and related global greenhouse gas emission pathways, in the context of strengthening the global response to the threat of climate change, sustainable development, and efforts to eradicate poverty,' 2018, available at: www.ipcc.ch.

7   Intergovernmental Science-Policy Platform on Biodiversity and Ecosystem Services, 'Summary for policymakers of the global assessment report on biodiversity and ecosystem services of the Intergovernmental Science-Policy Platform on Biodiversity and Ecosystem Services', 6 May 2019, available at: www.ipbes.net.

8   Karl Marx, *Capital* Volume 1, London: Penguin Classics, 1992.

9   Ajay Singh Chaudhary, 'Subjectivity, Affect, and Exhaustion: The Political Theology of the Anthropocene', *Political Theology,* 25 February 2019.

10   William Clare Roberts, *Marx's Inferno: The Political Theory of Capital,* Princeton: Princeton University Press, 2016.

11   Robert Pollin, 'De-Growth versus a Green New Deal', *New Left Review,* 112(July-August), 2018.

12   The Editors, 'Introducing Catalyst', *Catalyst,* Issue 1, Spring 2017.

13   Gabriel Winant, 'The New Working Class', *Dissent,* 27 June 2017.

14   Barbara Laslett and Johanna Brenner, 'Gender and Social Reproduction: Historical Perspectives,' *Annual Review of Sociology,* Vol. 15 (1989), pp. 381-404.

15   Cinzia Arruzza, Tithi Bhattacharya, and Nancy Fraser, *Feminism for the 99%: A Manifesto,* New York: Verso, 2019.

16   Bernice Fisher and Joan C. Tronto, 'Toward a Feminist Theory of Care', in *Circles of Care: Work and Identity in Women's Lives,* Emily K. Abel and Margaret K. Nelson, eds, Albany: State University of New York Press, 1990.

17   Kate Aronoff, 'A Guaranteed "Jobs for All" Program is Gaining Traction Among Democratic Hopefuls', *The Intercept,* 1 April 2018.

18   Pavlina R. Tcherneva, 'Job Guarantee: Design, Jobs, and Implementation', *Working Paper 902,* Levy Economics Institute, Annandale-on-Hudson, NY: 2018.

19   'The Leap Manifesto: A Call for Canada Based on Caring for the Earth and One Another', 2015, available at: www.leapmanifesto.org.

20   Kathi Weeks, *The Problem with Work: Marxism, Feminism, and Postwork Imaginaries,* Durham: Duke University Press, 2011, p. 10.

21   Barbara Ehrenreich and Arlie Russell Hochschild, eds, *Global Woman: Nannies, Maids, and Sex Workers in the New Economy,* New York: Henry Holt & Company, 2003.

22   Silvia Federici, 'Wages Against Housework', *Revolution at Point Zero: Housework, Reproduction, and Feminist Struggle,* Oakland: PM Press, 2012, p. 18.

23   Bureau of Labor Statistics, 'Labor Force Statistics from the Current Population Survey', 18 January 2019, available at: www.bls.gov.

24   Lacie Alexander, *The Soil Soldiers: The Civilian Conservation Corps in the Great Depression,* Chilton Book Company, 1976.

25   Wendell Berry, *The Unsettling of America: Culture and Agriculture,* San Francisco: Sierra Club Books, 1977.

26   Glenn Coulthard, *Red Skin, White Masks: Rejecting the Colonial Politics of Recognition,* Minneapolis: University of Minnesota Press, 2014.

27   Trish Hernandez and Susan Gabbard, 'Findings from the National Agricultural Workers Survey (NAWS) 2015-2016', A Demographic and Employment Profile of United States Farmworkers.

28   Wendell Berry, *Home Economics: Fourteen Essays,* New York: North Point Press, 1987.

29   Robert Pollin, for example, also argues that 'building a green economy entails more labour-intensive activities than maintaining the world's current fossil fuel-based energy infrastructure', but does not connect this point to a moral agenda. 'Degrowth vs. the Green New Deal', *New Left Review,* 112(July-August), 2018, pp. 10-11.

30   Silvia Federici, 'The Restructuring of Housework and Reproduction', p. 53. See also Helen Hester, 'After Work: What's Left and Who Cares?' Lecture, Goldsmiths, University of London, 22 April 2016.

31   Simone de Beauvoir, *The Second Sex,* translated H.M. Parshley, New York: Vintage Books, 1989 [1949], p. 451.

32   Angela Davis, *Women, Race, and Class,* New York: Vintage, 1981, p. 223.

33   Maria Mies, *Patriarchy and Accumulation on a World Scale: Women in the International Division of Labor,* New York: Zed Books, 1986, p. 217.

34   Ruth Schwartz Cowan, *More Work for Mother: The Ironies of Household Technology from the Open Hearth to the Microwave,* New York: Basic Books, 1983.

35   Margaret Benston, 'The Political Economy of Women's Liberation', *Monthly Review,* 21(4), 1969.

36   Benston, 'The Political Economy of Women's Liberation'.

37   Mariarosa Dalla Costa, 'Women and the Subversion of the Community', in *Women and the Subversion of the Community: The Mariarosa Dalla Costa Reader,* Oakland: PM Press, 2019, p. 28; Silvia Federici, 'Wages Against Housework', in *Revolution at Point Zero: Housework, Reproduction, and Feminist Struggle,* Oakland: PM Press, 2012.

38   Wally Seccombe, 'The Housewife and Her Labour Under Capitalism', *New Left Review,* I/83(January-February), 1974.

39   Margaret Coulson, Branka Magaš, and Hilary Wainwright, 'The Housewife and Her Labour Under Capitalism: A Critique', *New Left Review,* I/89(January-February), 1975.

40   Benston, 'The Political Economy of Women's Liberation'.

41   Andre Gorz, *Farewell to the Working Class: An Essay on Postindustrial Socialism,* London: Pluto Press, 1982, p. 83.

42   Evelyn Nakano Glenn, 'From Servitude to Service Work: Historical Continuities in the Racial Division of Paid Reproductive Labor', *Signs,* 19(1-43), 1992.

43   Patrick Bigger and Jessica Dempsey, 'The Ins and Outs of Neoliberal Natures', *Environment and Planning E: Nature and Space,* 1(1–2), 2018, pp. 25-43.

44   Gabriel Winant, *Crucible of Care: The Fall of Steel, the Rise of Health Care, and the Making of a New Working Class,* Cambridge: Harvard University Press, forthcoming.

45   William J. Baumol, 'Macroeconomics of Unbalanced Growth: The Anatomy of Urban Crisis', *American Economic Review,* 57(3), 1967, pp. 415-426; Winant, *Crucible of Care.*

46   Melinda Cooper, *Family Values: Between Neoliberalism and the New Social Conservatism,* Cambridge: MIT Press, 2017.

47   Cedric Johnson, 'Coming to Terms with Actual Black Life', *New Politics,* 9 April 2019.

48   The Editors, 'Introducing Catalyst'.

49   Dalla Costa, 'Women and the Subversion of the Community', p. 39.

50   Mariarosa Dalla Costa, 'On the General Strike', in *Women and the Subversion of the Community*, p. 54.

51   Seccombe, 'The Housewife and Her Domestic Labour'.

52   Asad Haider and Salar Mohandesi, 'Making a Living', *Viewpoint*, 5, October 2015.

53   Nancy Fraser, 'Contradictions of Capital and Care', *New Left Review,* I/100(July-August), 2016, p. 110.

54   Bureau of Labor Statistics, 'Work Stoppages Summary', 8 February 2019.

55   Eileen Boris and Jennifer Klein, 'Frontline Caregivers: Still Struggling', *Dissent* Winter 2012.

FOR A SUSTAINABLE FUTURE: THE CENTRALITY OF PUBLIC GOODS

NANCY HOLMSTROM

The most recent report of the UN's Intergovernmental Panel on Climate Change (IPCC) makes it absolutely clear that ways of living in the twenty-first century must be premised on the existential threat to our survival posed by multiple ecological crises. Indeed it could all be over before the end of the century. If we do not radically suppress global CO_2 emissions, global warming will rise to the point where it cannot be stopped. While not long ago the word 'catastrophe' seemed hyperbolic to many, today few could deny it is fitting. Melting glaciers, rising sea level, drought, fires, and flooding all over the world and the resulting migration are catastrophes for those who suffer them – and give us a taste of far worse catastrophes to come. Already the World Health Organization (WHO) estimates that there are 150,000 excess deaths per year due to climate change, likely to double by 2030.

After the 9-11 attack on the World Trade Center we heard the word 'security' incessantly, almost always invoked as *intentional* threats to our safety and well-being, which of course means they are threats by people, whether they be individuals, groups, or nations. Global warming, on the other hand, is a threat from nature that is an *unintended* result of human action – not what is usually intended by a 'security' threat, and it does not grip our imagination and fears in any way proportional to its severity. But it is not only intentional acts that can threaten our safety and well-being. Once threats to our security are conceived more broadly, consider the greater dangers from unclean air and water and contagious diseases, whatever the mix of intentional and unintentional acts that created the problem.

The narrow conception of security may be beginning to change as the threat from climate change becomes more apparent to more people. Bernie Sanders said in the announcement for his 2020 campaign for President that the greatest security threat we face is global warming. Even while the US spends over three billion dollars on the military[1] (as Desmond Tutu once said, 'you don't get true security from the barrel of a gun'), a broader understanding of the meaning of security has become more common. Since the economic crisis of 2008, amidst ongoing austerity and inequality, there have been more references in the mainstream US press to the number of Americans who are 'food insecure'. Indeed, even the 2019 Worldwide Threat Assessment, issued by the Director of National Intelligence, brings the two ideas of (in) security together in their warning that 'climate-driven food shortages could increase the risk of social unrest, migration and interstate tension.'[2]

While the Pentagon has said repeatedly that climate change is a national security threat, what they have in mind is that climate change is likely to destabilize some countries, threatening US military installations and leading to mass migration, intra-state conflicts, and terrorism, thus threatening 'national security'. So the concept of security is still understood in these warnings simply as protection against intentional threats by other people. While we used to worry about intentional threats only from criminals, now more and more people have to carry, even to wear, ID cards, big concrete blocks line the sidewalks of many of our streets, and our access to countless public buildings is tightly controlled by phalanxes of security guards and video monitors. But most people pay little attention; the possibility of terrorist attacks has been normalized.

The left's most urgent ideological task in the face of this, as well as the environmental crisis itself, is to make people see the world and themselves in broader and more inclusive terms. As Dr Robert Bullard, often called the father of environmental justice, once put it: 'There's no Hispanic air, no African American air, or white air, there's just air. ... if you're concerned about the quality of that air, I would consider you an environmentalist ... you just might not know it.'[3]

RETHINKING PROPERTY AND RATIONALITY: FROM THE INDIVIDUAL TO THE COLLECTIVE

The concepts of property and rationality are foundational to the way we think about society and about ourselves. The predominant ways these are commonly understood serve to support capitalism. If we are to have a sustainable future, making an appreciation of public goods and a new understanding of 'the commons' central to a transformed 'common sense' understanding of security, we need to start by transforming the meanings of property and rationality.

Unlike the technical definition of mainstream economists, by public goods I am referring to goods that all can share because they are not privately owned; they are not commodities. My enjoyment of them does not preclude your enjoying them as well. Some goods are public because of their intrinsic nature, like air, others are public because their nature makes it too inconvenient to make them private (a lighthouse), and still other goods like education or health care are public – if they are – only because people have struggled to take them out of the private for-profit sector and make them available to all.

Public goods satisfy universal needs, though the importance of their being public varies. Even for the intrinsically public goods, whose importance is universal, there are still class variations. If water is unclean, some people can buy it, but most cannot. Air has not yet been commodified, but if air is not clean, the rich can buy gas masks or move; hence the thousands of middle-class Chinese fleeing the country. But this is obviously a very poor substitute. Though society as a whole benefits from good systems of public education and medical care, their importance to individuals varies greatly by class. They provide far better education and medical care than most everyone can achieve on their own, but the rich do not need them. Public parks provide what only the very wealthy can provide for themselves. Moreover, public goods are interconnected; people without one tend to be deprived of others.

Property

When can we say of something that 'it's mine?' – that it belongs to me, that it's my property? Leaving aside our bodies and body parts, which are inseparable from us,[4] there is one kind of property everyone has. It might be as little as the clothes on one's back, or a bicycle, some furniture, and a modest pension plan, or for the more fortunate among us, several houses filled with furniture and clothing along with cars in the garage and a great deal of money set aside for retirement. Whether a bare minimum or a great deal, if this property is all just for one's personal use, then it should be called *personal* property. On the other hand, if the cars were part of a taxi business, or the houses part of a real estate development, then they are not for personal use but function as capital because they are used to make more money. In this case, they are not personal property but *private* property. This is the kind of property Marx defined as depending on the non-existence of property in the hands of the majority – and which thereby allows the capitalist to subjugate the labour of others – while pointing to the abolition of private property as required to overcome this.

Note: *first*, that property is a right not a thing and *second*, that the key to having both personal and private property is the right not only to use the property, but also to exclude others' use of it, and to sell or otherwise dispose of the property. They are essentially rights of exclusive use on the part of the property owner and exclusion of all others. In contrast, common or collective property (whether called public goods, or the commons), such as a public park, is by definition open to all. Every individual has a right to use the park. Thus – a *third* essential point – common property involves an individual right to property just as much as private property does. This fact is usually overlooked, because of the equation of an individual right of property with private property.[5] The difference between these kinds of individual rights to property is simply that common property does not entail a right of exclusion. Historically, in England, 'the commons' referred to land on which commoners had the right to graze their animals, forage for wild food, and collect firewood, rights they lost in the enclosure movement at the beginning of capitalism. Not surprisingly, the commoners saw the enclosures as theft of their land; each one lost his/her right to use the land. Similar processes occurred around the world then – and continue today – as people lose access to lands that had been held communally for centuries. This happens wherever capitalism extends its reach into non-capitalist regions, whether in a geographical sense or into new sectors of society.[6] Laws are then changed or reinterpreted to lend legitimacy to the theft.

Today the term 'commons' is used more broadly than it once was, not only for land and other natural resources, but for the cultural/intellectual sphere as well – radio waves, the Internet, scientific knowledge, etc. All are part of our common human heritage, created by countless people around the globe, throughout human history, building one upon the other. Hence they are all collective human products, whatever particular individuals have contributed most recently. When something that was or could be accessible to all is made private, whether it is water or seeds, medicine or music, or education, this privatization can be conceived as an enclosure too. The fundamental question is who should have the right to use and control these goods? Why should some have the right to exclude everyone else?

Across the political spectrum in capitalist society the default is private property. *Our task as socialists is to turn that capitalist assumption on its head and make public goods/the commons the default.* The pragmatic reason for this is that this is the only way common goods can be protected from profit-driven development.[7] Logical, moral, and political reasons also argue for making common property the default. Hence it is privatization, taking away the right of use, that should have to be justified.[8] Furthermore since all human beings are equal from a moral point of view, the basic assumption should be in favour of equal access to the Earth's resources and to collective products of humankind – and also equal right to decide how they are used. So again the burden of justification should be on those who would exclude, i.e. on claims to private property. This prioritization of common property provides a philosophical justification of civil disobedience in defense of the environment.[9]

In the case of natural resources, speaking in terms of property *of any kind* is problematic. Marx suggested that one day the idea of ownership of the Earth would seem as morally repugnant as the idea of owning another human being. Better, he suggested, to see humans as caretakers of the Earth for future generations;[10] as Native Americans believe, 'for the seventh generation'. Stewardship rather than ownership as the proper relationship between humans and the natural world is a common tenet of most of the world's religions, showing the potential for the broadest of coalitions to fight for taking our natural resources out of the hands of capital and putting it under popular democratic control.

Rationality

According to the individualist model of rationality that is dominant in the social sciences and philosophy, as well as being the modus operandi of capitalism, fully rational behaviour can lead to the destruction of the species. How could such a bizarre conclusion follow?[11]

Given the importance of public goods – even sometimes life and death importance as in the case of clean air and water – it would seem the most rational thing in the world to work together to achieve them. But according to the dominant model, known as Individual Utility Maximization (IUM), which is supposed to apply to persons, organizations, including corporations, or countries, it is not. When an individual's behaviour is rational, she aims to maximize her own utility, *whatever* that might be. Offered as both a descriptive and a normative theory, IUM is inadequate on both counts. Allowing no judgment as to the ends themselves, it reduces them all to the one quantifiable end of utility and assumes we want to maximize them all. Not only does this fail to do justice to the diversity of our goods; it is particularly dangerous because it lends ideological support to capitalism's endless growth machine. Certainly many times human beings do act as the theory describes, especially in our society, but the fact is that people do not always choose what is individually best rather than what is best overall, even in laboratory situations, and it begs the question to say that their behaviour is therefore irrational. Human choices and preferences are far more complex than IUM allows, as has been shown a long time ago.[12]

In the real social world IUM generates puzzles as to how collective action, e.g. working in an environmental group, ever takes place and how it could be rational. Since, according to IUM, groups are only collections of individuals, it is only rational to do something if it is rational for the majority of individual members. But since each individual could get the benefits of a clean environment without contributing, it would be irrational for them to do so, a conclusion known as the free rider problem. Though they might do so out of moral conviction, emotion, or coercion, this would not be rational. However, if many act rationally they will not get what would benefit them all, even their own self-preservation. Certainly, building the solidarity necessary to override the free rider problem is a challenge, but it happens and it is not therefore irrational. Nor must rational behaviour be devoid of moral conviction or emotion, as Hume and Aristotle recognized.

The most fundamental problem with IUM is that it starts from the assumption that rationality is primarily ascribed to the individual and only derivatively to the group or a society. This implies that the individual can be understood independent of society, a highly dubious assumption since the very notion of an isolated individual only arose in the context of a very particular kind of social organization. Instead, rationality should be looked at first from within a social context, and if there is a conflict, the social point of view should take priority.

Because individuals can identify with others and have irreducibly social goals as well as egoistic ones (a fact omitted by IUM), sometimes the distinction between behaviour that is individually and collectively rational is not clear. But when the distinction is clear, e.g. if I want to dispose of my company's waste into a stream because it is most convenient and cheaper, and because I can get away with it, IUM would say that is the rational choice (even if it is immoral) and it would be irrational not to do so. On the other hand, from a social model of rationality, which involves taking a long-term perspective, it is very irrational. Note that if one were to say that there are simply two perspectives on what is rational (a relativist position), this suffices to refute the IUM claim that cooperative behaviour is irrational (or could be rational only under special conditions e.g. with material incentives to cooperate). However, I suggest that the relativist position is too weak; rather than being neutral we can say that taking the long term social point of view is simply more rational, as well as the right thing to do from a moral or political point of view. After all, 'short-sighted' is practically synonymous with 'foolish', 'far-sighted' with 'rational'. Thus if our polluter were to switch from the individualist to the social perspective, it is not just a *different* outlook but also an *advance* in consciousness. A society that disallowed production of designed-obsolescent products would be more rational than one that encourages throwaway products because they are more profitable.

For consider the function of rationality. Clearly it is the chief evolutionary advantage humans have, giving us control over the world, including ourselves, which we would otherwise lack. Our ability to think, discuss, plan and cooperate with others for long and short-term ends extends this advantage. After all, not all our goals can be accomplished individually no matter how rational we are. When people cooperate to achieve some common goal, e.g. to shut down a nuclear plant, or when they join together in a union or a political group, their individual capabilities become collective capabilities, allowing them to achieve what they could not otherwise. Since prioritizing long-term interests gives people greater control over their world – the way rational behaviour is supposed to do – it is reasonable to consider this *an expansion of rationality*.

That thoroughly rational behaviour would lead to the destruction of the species is the *reductio ad absurdum* of the IUM perspective. It remains dominant only because it fits so well with capitalism. It is long past time to replace the individualist utility maximization model with a social model of rationality that will facilitate the creation of a sustainable future.

FROM COMMON SENSE TO COMMON PRACTICE: STRUGGLES AROUND PUBLIC GOODS

'When Did The Common Good Become A Bad Thing?' stood out among the many wonderful creative signs from the Occupy Wall Street protests. The central focus of socialist strategy in the twenty-first century should be protecting and radically expanding public goods/the commons. We should use every means we can to raise peoples' understanding that public goods/the commons, especially natural resources 1) are the only basis of real security; 2) should be accessible by all as a right, and hence no one should be excluded by the alleged rights of private property; and 3) are foundational to the most rational way to organize society. Making those re-conceived collectivized concepts of security, property, and rationality central to our organizing is a way to resist capitalism and can help to inspire more radical visions and strategies. I will discuss examples based in the US that fit this approach, though clearly the principles must be taken to the international level.

Since auto-related emissions are the lion's share of emissions in the US, let us compare the radical liberal environmentalist position with that of the eco-socialist. Most proposals for a massive switch to electric cars, away from fossil fuels, are advanced without calling for cutbacks on growth. This is completely insufficient. First of all, most of the pollution from producing *any* car comes before it gets on the road. Second, producing electric cars is even more polluting than producing gasoline-powered cars. Thirdly, much as we would like to have it all, we can't; growth simply must be curtailed. So what is to be done? Eco-socialists reject market solutions like carbon taxes which leading oil companies actually support because they just add a cost to their business (which can be passed along to consumers) and do not put any limits on growth. Moreover, they have not worked, since they were always too low to make a difference.

While the scientific facts and the daily news reports of 'extreme weather incidents' have been most crucial in creating a new sense of urgency, socialists have an important role to play combatting ideological resistance to governmental action and helping people to see that it is their right to decide what to do regarding this existential threat. We must always stress the necessity of democratic control. There are risks to almost everything we humans do and we often have competing goals. This means that complex decisions and often trade-offs have to be made, and no one is in a better position to make these decisions than the people who are most directly affected. Bhopal and Chernobyl remind us of the dangers of undemocratic control, whether private or public.

However, to translate these ideas into social power the support of the labour movement is crucial. They should be allies and leaders in this struggle since, as the slogan goes, there are no jobs on a dead planet. But that is the long run. Meanwhile, most unions see their principal task as defending the immediate interests of their members; thus, the AFL-CIO Energy Committee, dominated by the building trades and utility company unions, followed their short-term interests and rejected the Green New Deal. However, some more far sighted unions like the National Nurses Union and the American Transport Union have signed on, and some locals have supported it, like the Los Angeles United Steelworkers local − whose resolution was endorsed by the LA Central Labor Council, the second largest in the country. Clearly this will be a critical struggle; to take the position that is in their members' *long-term* interest, the major labour unions in the United States will have to be convinced that their members will be protected in the transition while being pushed from below and outside to be sure that this happens.

The recent battles in the US for public education are very significant and inspiring for the broad solidaristic politics they have manifested, and could be a model for a revived labour movement. Words are important. Not only were their demands broad and inclusive, but they also said explicitly that they were striking for the common good. Over time, that kind of solidarity is the best way to overcome distrust and change minds. Public employees combining with those they serve is a huge step forward and hopefully can be emulated in other sectors.[13] Too often workers and consumers are pitted against one another – and workers with some benefits and protections are pitted against those who lack them. Public employees are especially vulnerable to this kind of divisive anti-working class ideology in the United States because it is taxpayers who pay their salaries, and fewer and fewer workers in the private sector have union protections.

Meanwhile, faced with closures of several auto plants in the US and Canada, and the loss of 14,000 jobs in Michigan alone, some movement along eco-socialist lines has sprung up among autoworkers. Instead of struggling vainly to keep the plants open making ever more cars, a number of radical autoworkers have campaigned to convert the plants to producing wind turbines, electric buses, trains, and any elements of the infrastructure that needs to be rebuilt. Back in 2008 when the US government bailed out General Motors, a group calling itself the Autoworkers Caravan went to Washington, calling for the nationalization and conversion of the US auto industry. It got little attention – but today a bit more so, as Congresswoman Rashida Tlaib and the Detroit branch of the Democratic Socialists of America (DSA) now back it. Such a conversion is definitely doable from a technical point of view; it was only months after Pearl Harbor that auto plants were making planes, tanks, guns, and ammunition. As a Swedish autoworker and union leader stressed, autoworkers have the tacit knowledge of both mass production and the potential for change: '... the auto industry is not a coalmine. It's a flexible machine that society can use to make almost anything on a large scale. Send us the blueprints for socially useful stuff, and we'll make it.'[14]

The importance of models should never be underestimated; they build experience, capacities, and serve as examples for other initiatives. The Plan developed by rank-and-file workers at Lucas Aerospace in 1976 for the conversion of their largely military production to socially useful production was hugely influential in the '70s and '80s, even being nominated for the Nobel Peace Prize. Workers came up with 150 doable ideas, relying on their tacit knowledge of the production process. Such a model of worker-controlled production for social good rather than profit is frightening not only to the capitalists, but also to mainstream trade union leaders and the Labour Party – as seen by their tepid support. Unfortunately this potential was killed by the rise of Thatcherism, but the Lucas Aerospace Plan still inspires activists.[15] In times and places with greater acceptance of government involvement in the economy, and with some supporters in the government – and yet more climate disasters – such ideas might have a better chance, starting perhaps at a local level. Since this is a broad issue affecting not only workers, they could try to organize councils including the community and the anti-war and environmental movements.

Cooperation Jackson (Mississippi) provides another kind of exciting model that is compatible with this.[16] A local community network connected to the Our Power Campaign of the Climate Justice Alliance, influenced by the radical black nationalist tradition, along with Marxism and anarcho-syndicalism, Cooperation Jackson is explicitly anti-capitalist and eco-socialist, carrying forward the vision of Mayor Chokwe Lumumba, after his untimely death in 2013, to establish a network of living/working self-sustaining cooperatives along with decision-making Peoples' Assemblies. By reducing reliance on fossil fuels, producing renewables, and reducing consumption, they aim to create an ecological city resting on economic democracy and black self-empowerment. However, being a small and very poor city, they desperately need capital and have not yet been able to build a sufficient number of cooperatives to equal 10 per cent of the city's GDP, which was their goal at this stage. Cooperation Jackson thus shows the strengths and weaknesses of a local community-based approach. They are well aware that their success will depend on larger political forces. The US does not have a radical party that could give them the kind of support they need, but should the Green New Deal come into existence they could benefit.

But cooperatives can end up just competing with one another. To avoid this tendency, they need to encourage broader goals, connect with other small-scale efforts and make connections with eco-socialists and labour groups. A network of radical municipal initiatives around the world, such as the exciting experiment of a new kind of bottom-up party in Barcelona,[17] would be an important goal. As Hilary Wainwright has argued: 'In many diverse locations, grassroots trade union and community alliances have been a driving force in the defence and improvement of public services or utilities in the face of privatization.'[18] Since Americans in particular are facing what can be definitely be called a crisis of social reproduction, perhaps that conceptualization, popular among socialist feminists today, will prove to be a useful way of bringing together diverse struggles. But socialist feminism has always stressed that the lives of working women do not begin and end at the workplace and so it is necessary to bring together issues affecting their families and their communities. Beyond education and health care, there is no issue more important for communities today than the ecological one. The rational transformation of our global economy of the magnitude and scale that is necessary for genuine security may seem impossible. But the visionary yet practical examples now coming forward, such as from Canadian postal workers' campaign 'Delivering Community Power' point to what an eco-socialist future could look like.[19]

The Labor Network for Sustainability (LNS) and Trade Unions for Energy Democracy (TUED) are trying to make this happen. LNS, whose mission 'is to engage workers and communities in building a transition to a society that is ecologically sustainable and economically just', has recently issued a report called 'Clean Energy Future' that offers an optimistic approach to the jobs vs. environment conundrum, contending that there are jobs in protecting the environment.[20] Sean Sweeney of TUED has argued that because renewable energy is not sufficiently profitable at this stage for private enterprise to make the conversion, it requires public ownership or government loans along the lines of Roosevelt's Rural Electrification Administration.[21] Although this does not address all the other industries heavily dependent on energy, it's an important point that could be repeated for other industries. The LNS report is along the lines of the Green New Deal, and Jeremy Brecher, the LNS's Research and Policy Director, has drawn up a detailed prescription of how a Green New Deal could be enacted.[22] Yet while stressing the importance of labour activism and community and environmental groups – not least in terms of strengthening the left of the Democratic Party – there is no mention of capitalism.

Alexandria Ocasio-Cortez's Green New Deal proposal has definitely opened the conversation about climate change, and pushed it away from sole reliance on market-oriented solutions. But it contains no explicit call to stop the endless growth of the economy, does not explicitly call for shutdowns of any industries, and does not propose nationalization. However, all of these would seem to be entailed by the call for 'de-carbonization'. How else could this be accomplished? While also starting from the example of FDR's command and control economy, in which he ordered auto makers to produce tanks, planes, etc. instead of private cars, Richard Smith has gone further in proposing 'a strategy of rationally planned, democratically managed transition to renewable energy that avoids economic collapse and guarantees re-employment for the affected workers'. Smith's specific proposal is based on four points:

1. Declare a State of Emergency to suppress fossil fuel use: ban all new extraction, ration gasoline, ban production of new fossil-fuel vehicles. Nationalize the fossil fuel industry to phase it out. We propose to do this by means of a government buyout at fair value (fair to both owners and society). Nationalize downstream fossil fuel industrial consumers … whose business is irreversibly based on fossil fuels and which without a

government buyout would be bankrupted.

2. Institute a new federal Public Works Administration-style jobs program to re-employ every worker in the fossil fuel-related industries at equivalent pay and benefits in other useful but low-emission work.

3. Launch an emergency state-directed program to phase-in renewable electric generation, replace fossil-fuel powered transportation with electric propulsion, discourage individually-owned vehicles, and encourage public transit, shared vehicles, bicycles and other non-fossil fuel modes of transportation.

4. Develop emergency plans to phase out wasteful, destructive and polluting industries from arms production to needless toxics, designed-to-be-obsolesced iPhones, cars etc. Develop emergency plans to shift from fossil-fuel dependent factory farms to fully-organic agriculture.[23]

Smith calls de-carbonization a 'self-radicalizing transitional demand'. The immensity of the full political, economic and social transformation required need not lead to fatalism; on the contrary facing head-on what is needed to avoid catastrophe can be highly motivating. As 16-year-old Greta Thunberg said to world leaders at Davos: 'I don't want your hope. ... I want you to panic. I want you to feel the fear I feel every day.' The activism by millions of children on this issue is the brightest spot on the horizon. Perhaps some modest victories, even if inadequate, combined with the continuing ecological crises, will help to build a movement that can push beyond to the kind of vision eco-socialists put forward. We also cannot ignore the historical lesson which tells us that, in conjunction with policy proposals, more radical disruptive direct action tactics along the lines of the Sunrise Movement and the Extinction Rebellion will be necessary.

In response to an Intergovernmental Panel on Climate Change (IPCC) report, UN Secretary-General Antonio Guterres warned world leaders to 'Do what the science demands before it's too late'.[24] Yet the impossibility of doing this within a capitalist system, where profit maximization through economic growth must be systematically prioritized, has become ever clearer with each passing decade of unimpeded global warming.[25] Humans have always taken things from nature and transformed them for sustenance, but capitalism's relentless transformation of nature as part of its accumulation strategy (Marx refers to fish as a productive force in the fishing industry) has led to depletion of what's needed for human sustenance. This same imperative for growth explains the attack on the public sector. Capitalism needs to search out ever new areas of profitability, both geographically and in non-capitalist areas of society, by commodifying what had been free, whether parts of nature like air and water, labour (care work for example), or public services. Capitalist globalization has meant deregulation and privatization of public goods all over the world. The effect has been, predictably, disastrous for the majority of the world's populations, especially the poorest. As Elmar Altvater succinctly puts it: 'Social, economic and political security depend on public goods being readily available.'[26]

Deregulation and privatization are exactly the opposite of what we need. Instead we need to move to a radically different system with more ecologically sustainable production and consumption patterns and lifestyles. This requires planning. At what level should the planning be? Local knowledge tends to be more reliable, as Ostrom's work shows, but many things cannot be accomplished at a local or even a countrywide level. The whole planet shares the air. The issue is not primarily whether planning is local, regional, national, or even international, but *what kinds of institutions enable rational democratic control from below and effectively address our environmental crisis.* Whatever markets there are should be embedded in the larger social economy. But the very word 'planning' brings massive opposition from all quarters, because planning is equated with the centralized command planning of the Soviet system that did not work. Elmar Altvater and others explain this failure by the absence of democratic feedback needed for corrections, innovation, and dynamism, as well as the inertia and paralysis at the center, and the alienation of working people.[27] Their unutilized capacities and tacit knowledge, however, would be liberated in a genuinely democratic system.[28]

Marx's vision of socialism, as rational democratic planning, shows that planning and democracy are not counterposed. In *Capital* Volume III, he says that while after capitalism, in a new 'higher form of society,' i.e. socialism, there will always be material production:

> Freedom in this field can only consist of ... the associated producers, rationally regulating their interchange with Nature, bringing it under their common control ...; and achieving this with the least expenditure of energy and under conditions most favourable to, and worthy of their human nature. But it nonetheless still remains a realm of necessity. Beyond it begins that development of human energy which is an end in itself, the true realm of freedom, which, however, can blossom forth only with the realm of necessity as its basis. The shortening of the workday is its basic prerequisite.[29]

If we add 'consumers' to the 'associated producers,' we have a vision of a radically democratic society where we can choose if, where, and how we want to grow. Whereas in capitalism, every technological advance in production leads to more production (the Jevons paradox), in socialism we could take advantage of technological progress to produce less and work less. Unlike capitalist democracies, the most crucial decisions affecting us all: what to produce (gas-guzzling and driverless private cars versus buses and trains), how to produce (fossil fuels or renewables), and the all-important question of *how much* to produce would be decided democratically, most likely by councils of producers and consumers. Expertise is only required to lay out the implications of different options and then to figure out how best to implement their decisions.[30] This of course does not entail that producers and consumers will always make the right decisions, but without the built-in pulls in other directions (as in capitalism), and because of the fact that it is they who will bear the consequences, mistakes are less likely and would be corrected. This illustrates the point that different modes of production will have different measures of efficiency and different rationalities.[31]

That we cannot have socialism in one country is even more apparent when we are talking of eco-socialism. Based on a global commitment to public goods/commons as the default and a social rationality we can aim for the *'buen vivir'* for all. To achieve that we need to contract in the over-producing/consuming countries of the North and expand (sustainably) in the South, thus leading to a contraction and convergence. An important step in that direction would be something like the Green New Deal on a global scale, including a commitment to regenerative agriculture.[32] This all would require more institutions of international governance, that is, planning and regulation, such as a United Nations of socialist societies, as well as local, regional, and national institutions. This now seems impossible, but if civilization is to survive the twenty-first century, we have to do our best to make it begin to seem inevitable.[33]

NOTES

1   For an analysis of where US tax dollars go, see the famous pie chart from the War Resisters League, available at: www.warresisters.org/resources/pie-chart-flyers. The latest figures, for 2020, show 1.7 trillion dollars going to the military, a figure obscured in US government calculations.

2   Coral Davenport, 'Climate Panel Could Question Scope of Threat,' *New York Times*, 21 February 2019. Oftentimes these warnings focus on population growth as the principal cause, which then are used to justify strict population control measures focused on women in the Global South. For a critique see Jael Silliman and Ynestra King, eds., *Dangerous Intersections: Feminist Perspectives on Population, Environment and Development*, Cambridge, MA: South End Press, 1999.

3   Quoted in Kali Akuno and Ajamu Nangwa, eds., *Jackson Rising*, Quebec: Daraja Press 2017, p. 217.

4   Whether individuals can in some sense own themselves has been much debated among political philosophers. For arguments that this idea of self-ownership functions as a defense of capitalism and that it is not a helpful way for the left or for feminists to claim individual rights, see Nancy Holmstrom and Ann Cudd, *Capitalism For and Against: A Feminist Debate*, Cambridge, UK: Cambridge University Press, 2011, pp.167-73.

5   Cf. C.B. Macpherson's magisterial *The Political Theory of Possessive Individualism*, Oxford: Oxford University Press, 1962.

6   Capitalism has also expanded into post-capitalist societies. See Nancy Holmstrom and Richard Smith, 'The Necessity of Gangster Capitalism: Primitive Accumulation in Russia and China,' *Monthly Review*, 51(9), February 2000; He Qinglian, 'The Land-Enclosure Movement of the 1990s,' *The Chinese Economy*, 33(3), May-June 2000. David Harvey's influential concept of 'accumulation by dispossession' includes capital's geographic expansion to commodification of things and services that had formerly been free to large capital's taking over small capital. See for instance: 'The "New" Imperialism: Accumulation by Dispossession,' in Leo Panitch and Colin Leys eds., *Socialist Register 2004: The New Imperial Challenge*, London: Merlin Press, 2003, and other works.

7   Contrary to the 'tragedy of the commons argument', long exposed as a fallacy, there are countless cases of resources held in common that have been managed in sustainable ways, sometimes for centuries. Nobel Prize winner Elinor Ostrom's work on 'common pool resources' shows that groups as well as individuals can cooperate and plan, and negotiate and abide by rules that they devise. See: *Governing the Commons,* Cambridge, UK: Cambridge University Press, 1990, and other works.

8   Cf. Anatole Anton, 'Public Goods as Commonstock,' in Anton, Fisk and Holmstrom eds., *Not For Sale: In Defense of Public Goods,* Boulder: Westview Press, 2000.

9   Recent court cases in the US appealing to the public trust doctrine (which says that the government is responsible for protecting natural resources) have presented protestors as law-*enforcers* rather than law-*breakers*. Several cases on behalf of children against the US government for promoting fossil fuels and thereby de-stabilizing their future environment have been allowed to proceed in the courts despite vigorous opposition from both business and government. See: *Juliana v United States of America*, and others on the state level, including *Aji P v State of Washington*.

10   Karl Marx, *Capital* Volume 3, New York: International Publishers, 1967, p. 776.

11   The following rests on earlier work: 'Rationality and Revolution,' *Canadian Journal of Philosophy*, XIII(3), September 1983; as well as 'Rationality, Solidarity and Public Goods,' in Anton, Fisk and Holmstrom, *Not For Sale*. I cannot do justice in this paper to the very technical literature on rational choice theory (including by some writers sympathetic to Marxism).

12   See Amartya Sen's classic 'Rational Fools: A Critique of the Behavioral Foundations of Economic Theory,' *Philosophy and Public Affairs*, 6(4), Summer 1977, pp. 317-44; and Robert Kuttner, *Everything for Sale,* New York: Knopf, 1997.

13   For example, transit workers' unions could reach out to riders about common interests, like better staffing. For a more radical strike tactic, bus drivers could not collect fares. Hilary Wainwright, *Reclaim the State*, London & New York: Verso, 2003, has several examples like this. Too often public employees' unions, including teachers, have had a narrow trade union orientation that alienated them from the public they serve.

14   Lars Henriksson, 'Can Autoworkers Save the Planet?', *The Bullet*, 13 October 2015. For how a conversion could happen under public ownership see Sam Gindin, 'GM Oshawa: Making Hope Possible,' *The Bullet*, 13 Dec 2018. The Autoworkers' Caravan is part of the Detroit Green New Deal Coalition, along with DSA and community groups. They propose a Great Lakes Authority modeled after FDR's Tennessee Valley

Authority to 'make the Rust Belt Green.' See *Democratic Left*, Spring 2019, on the Green New Deal.

15   Adrian Smith, 'The Lucas Plan: What can it tell us about democratizing technology today?' *The Guardian*, 22 Jan 2014.

16   Akuno and Nangwaya, *Jackson Rising*.

17   Greig Charnock and Ramon Ribera-Fumaz, 'Barcelona en Comu: Urgan Democracy and the "Common Good",' in Leo Panitch and Greg Albo, eds., *Socialist Register 2018: Rethinking Democracy*, London: Merlin Press, 2017.

18   Hilary Wainwright, 'Radicalizing the Party-Movement Relation: From Ralph Miliband to Jeremy Corbyn and Beyond,' in Leo Panitch and Greg Albo, eds., *Socialist Register 2017: Rethinking Revolution*, London: Merlin Press, 2016, p. 94.

19   See Canadian Union of Postal Workers, "Delivering Community Power," at www.deliveringcommunitypower.ca.

20   Jeremy Brecher, 'The Clean Energy Future: Protecting the Climate, Creating Jobs and Saving Money,' Labor Network for Sustainability, 2019, available at www.labor4sustainability.org.

21   Sean Sweeney, 'When "Green" Doesn't Grow: Facing Up to the Failures of Profit-Driven Climate Policy,' *Monthly Review Online*, 3 Jan 2019.

22   Jeremy Brecher, *18 Strategies for the Green New Deal: How to Make the Climate Mobilization Work*, Labor Network for Sustainability, 2019, available at: http://www.labor4sustainability.org/wp-content/uploads/2019/02/18Strategies.pdf.   See   also Jeremy Brecher, Ron Blackwell and Joe Uehlein, 'If Not Now, When? A Labor Movement Plan to Address Climate Change,' *New Labor Forum*, 1(7), 2014.

23   Richard Smith, 'An Ecosocialist Path to Limiting Global Temperature Rise to 1.5°C', *Real World Economics Review*, 87, 2019. See also, Richard Smith, *Green Capitalism: The God That Failed*, London, UK: World Economics Association Books, 2016. Others who have argued for nationalization to phase-out fossil fuels include Carla Skandier, 'Nationalize the Fossil Fuel Industry,' *In These Times*, 17 November 2017; and 'Quantitative Easing for the Planet,' *The Next System Project*, 30 August 2018; Peter Gowan, 'A Plan to Nationalize Fossil Fuel Companies,' *Jacobin*, March 2018.

24   Somini Sengupta, 'Projection on Climate is Ominous. Now What?', *New York Times*, 10 October 2018.

25   See the website for System Change not Climate Change, www.SCNCC.org. The eco-socialist position has been developed by many writers, including Elmar Altvater, Ian Angus, John Bellamy Foster, Joel Kovel, Michael Lowy, Fred Magdoff, Richard Smith, Daniel Tanuro, Brian Tokar, Chris Williams and others. Not all critics of growth agree that a socialist alternative is desirable or necessary. Herman Daly in the United States and the decroissance school in Europe seem to believe that growth can be a choice. If it should turn out that capitalism could be reformed so as to become sustainable, it would be such a radically transformed system that it is not clear it should be called capitalism.

26   Elmar Altvater, 'What Happens When Public Goods are Privatised,' *Studies in Political Economy*, 74(1), Autumn 2004, p. 1. Elmar Altvater, 'Obsession With Growth', in Leo Panitch and Colin Leys, eds., *Socialist Register 2002: A World of Contradictions*, London: Merlin Press, 2002, shows that growth has also failed to solve the problems of unemployment, inequality and economic instability that mainstream economists claimed for it.

27   Elmar Altvater, *The Future of the Market*, Translated by Patrick Camiller, New York: Verso, 1993.

28   Hilary Wainwright, 'Forging a "Social Knowledge Economy"', in Paul Christopher Gray, ed., *From the Streets to the State*, Albany: State University of New York Press, 2018, p. 183.

29   Karl Marx, *Capital* Volume III, New York: International Publishers, 1967, p. 820.

30   After the near-meltdown at Three Mile Island one woman said that if they had just explained the possible consequences of relying on nuclear reactors to get cheap energy, she would have preferred to hang her clothes out to dry. If the community's values had been in place, they would not have come to near-catastrophe. Raymond L. Goldsteen and John K. Schorr, *Demanding Democracy After Three Mile Island,* Gainesville, Fl: University of Florida Press, 1991.

31   Nancy Holmstrom and Richard Smith, 'Their Rationality and Ours,' in Anatole Anton and Richard Schmitt, eds., *Toward a New Socialism*, Lanham, MD: Lexington Books, 2007.

32   Curt Ries, 'A Green New Deal Must Prioritize Regenerative Agriculture,' *Truthout,* 9 May 2019.

33   This vision of a democratic planning in an eco-socialist future is elaborated in Michael Lowy 'Ecosocialism and Democratic Planning,' in Leo Panitch and Colin Leys, eds., *Socialist Register 2007: Coming to Terms with Nature,* London: Merlin Press, 2006; and Richard Smith, 'Six Theses on Saving the Planet,' available at: www.thenextsystem.org/six-theses-on-saving-the-planet. Also see Fred Magdoff and Chris Williams, *Creating an Ecological Society,* New York: Monthly Review Press, 2017, pp. 283-304.

THE AFFORDABLE HOUSING CRISIS: ITS CAPITALIST ROOTS AND THE SOCIALIST ALTERNATIVE

KARL BEITEL

Since the 1980s, many major cities have been undergoing a process of investment redevelopment marked by major inflows of capital and residents into formerly disinvested urban spaces and places of residence. One of the most striking features of the post-1980 urban environment has been the rapid rise in property values and rents at rates far in excess of the growth of average income levels. The paradigmatic instance of this process is the United States, where years of disinvestment associated with white flight and suburbanization have been reversed by large-scale flows of investment into property development in major urban centres, and the deepening imbrication of urban real estate within globalized circuits of finance and banking. This has coincided with the emergence of new industrial sectors and the massive expansion of financial and business service activity that have concentrated large numbers of highly paid skilled workers and capitalist owners able to pay very high rents and housing prices.

The effect for many working-class populations – cultural workers, those employed in the moderate- to lower-paid segments of the social and human services and retail sectors – has been a rise in the percentage of incomes these households must devote to housing payments. The effect is seen in the resulting rise in the percentage of 'rent burdened' households in many US cities. Many residents, particularly immigrants, may find themselves forced into crowded housing situations, and may be required to make offsetting economic sacrifices to secure their housing requirements.[1] Households unable to afford rising market rents are displaced into the urban periphery, leading to longer and more costly daily work-related commutes. Global cities have accordingly become battlegrounds defined by struggles over who shall have the right to inhabit these sought-after urban spaces, and under what terms. Urban politics is increasingly defined by conflicts pitting capitalist developers and financiers, often aligned with the municipal executive, against tenant groups, community housing organizations, neighbourhood associations, and political activists seeking to resist the rapid transformation of existing urban neighbourhoods, and to defend the rights of working-class communities to continue to reside in established neighbourhoods.

This struggle to define the nature of the city – who will live in existing urban spaces, and whose interests and needs will shape the future course of urban development – is a contest that is also being played out in the realm of ideas. Orthodox economists have consistently asserted that the roots of the crisis lie in excessive regulatory enactments that inhibit the efficient operation of urban property markets: limited land-use densities, inclusionary housing requirements, rent control, and various fiscal exactions that, these economists assert, exceed the actual costs of the 'externalities' associated with new development. This is one of the core functions of neoclassical economics, namely providing pseudo-scientific justification for policies that serve to further capitalist interests by creating a bounded, well-policed political space that determines the parameters of acceptable political and policy discourse.

Any housing initiative – for instance, to increase the percentage of affordable units that must be included in new development – is thus vetted according to whether the initiative would constitute an undue imposition of regulatory restrictions that impair the optimal functioning of the market. What is striking to any observer of debates over the need to allow the market to freely increase supply to meet increased demand is that developers know that 'the market' will never supply housing affordable to the majority of the city's current residents. As a long-term observer and participant in these struggles, I have heard developers state in public forums that the only way to provide housing affordable to moderate-income, much less lower-income residents, is through public subsidies. I have also had debates with developers in which they have freely admitted as much.

Hence, mounting a coherent challenge that demonstrates the fallacies of neoclassical arguments is a matter of direct political import, as these arguments are mobilized to legitimate a form of development predicated upon ongoing displacement of existing working-class residents from areas designated as prime sites for luxury housing development. In what follows, using categories deployed by Marx in his analysis of production and circulation processes I will show why, in already densely developed, highly built-out cities that are prime investment sites, 'the market' will never produce housing affordable to moderate- to lower-income working-class residents. This analysis, which is simple in its essentials, albeit complex in details, provides the basis for a complete refutation of the core tenets of the neoclassical arguments. It also clearly demonstrates the fact that reconciling the goal of reducing CO_2 emissions through promoting dense in-fill development with the goal of creating genuine equality in the housing market will require a fundamental transformation of the way housing is produced and distributed, a transformation that cannot be realized under current social arrangements. I will then sketch out the broad contours of how housing provisioning could be transformed in the transitional period of a socialist project.

In this essay, I will primarily discuss the economics of new construction in already densely developed urban environments. Paradigmatic cases of the type of development dynamics that this essay will discuss are found in cities such as New York, San Francisco, London, and Paris. This might seem an inappropriate limitation, given that the vast majority of both owner-occupied and rental housing is acquired on the secondary market – e.g. the market in which existing properties are bought and sold. In part, this limitation is due to space considerations: the interactions between various sub-sectors and sub-markets that compose the total environment in which housing is supplied and procured are complex, and are properly the subject of a longer work. There is another reason, however, that compels the focus on newly constructed units. Despite the fact that most housing is procured on the secondary market, new construction is central to the debate over how cities must act to accommodate increased demand due to population growth and the shifting spatial patterns of employment. In addition, new development has the ability to rapidly transform existing patterns of land use and the physical and sociocultural composition of the built environment. For these reasons, new production is critical to current struggles over whose interests shall be served by this development, and who has the rights to enjoy access to the existing – and newly created – urban environments. It also forces us to confront the question of how socialist urbanism will foster diverse urban spaces that can accommodate different requirements and preferences, and that ensure equitable allocation of resources to meet the needs of all urban residents.

The essay proceeds as follows: I begin with a short summary of the argument advanced by neoclassical economists that assert that the root of the affordability crisis is excessive regulatory interference on the part of governments. This is followed by a section presenting an alternative approach that draws heavily on Marx's own work on the circuit of capital to explain the factors underlying the long-term inflation of building costs and housing prices. I briefly discuss the impacts of the long-term decline in interest rates and 'financialization' on housing prices in major capitalist cities. I conclude with a section that outlines how socialists can envision the transformation of the provisioning of housing during the transitional phase of creating a post-capitalist, socialist economy.

NEOCLASSICAL FALLACIES

Neoclassical economic theory asserts that any excessive rise in housing prices is due to government land use and building controls that inhibit the efficient operation of the basic demand and supply dynamic. In the basic neoclassical model, producers are assumed to increase supply up to the point at which marginal revenue, or the price received from the sale of the final unit of output produced, is equal to marginal cost, or the cost of producing this unit of output. Consumers maximize utility, so that bid prices express the marginal utility private agents expect to receive from an additional unit of housing purchased. If an 'exogenous shock' occurs that increases demand, prices will undergo an initial rise. In the absence of politically imposed supply constraints, producers will increase output to the point at which marginal revenue again is equal to marginal cost. Increased supply reduces prices up to the point where all surplus profit is eliminated. However, if governments institute policies that inhibit the supply response – limits on building density, conditional use reviews, overly complex permitting processes, and mandated affordability requirements – this inhibits the ability to expand production in response to rising prices. The result is that the market clears at higher prices than would obtain in the absence of government interference.

The policy conclusions are obvious. To lower housing costs, local governments need to remove zoning restrictions that impose 'artificial' barriers on supply – for instance, easements to allow for higher-density zoning, policies that streamline and expedite the building approvals process, and codes that limit options for local residents to file blocking appeals and other measures that can delay breaking ground on new developments. The salutary result is that higher demand would be matched by the appropriate level of new supply, easing pressures on prices.[2]

I will not here engage in a critique of neoclassical economics, but will confine these comments to discussing recent work by Glaeser and Gyourko, who are currently the leading protagonists in the ideological attack on local regulation in the United States.[3] These authors completely mis-measure the relation between costs and prices that they claim establishes a strong empirical correlation between excessive regulation and over-inflated housing prices. In their most recent work, the authors estimate the cost of new construction for a single-family economy detached dwelling, drawing on the main database (RSMeans) used by construction industry professionals themselves.[4] These per-unit cost estimates are then adjusted to account for the assumption, based on statements received from an ad hoc survey of home building, that in a 'well functioning' market, land accounts for 20 per cent of total costs. These adjusted costs are then multiplied by 1.17 to incorporate developer profit into the final estimation of the new supply price in a properly regulated market. The authors then compare this calculation to the data on actual prices for comparable units across various cities, using self-reported information given by homeowners in the American Housing Survey.[5] Cities are sorted into categories based on how much homeowners' reported estimate of home value deviates from the estimate of the price that would obtain in a well-functioning market. This is then compared to the score this city has received on the Wharton Residential Land Use Regulatory Index.[6] The authors find that certain very expensive housing markets – San Francisco–Silicon Valley and New York, for instance – have actual prices far in excess of the authors' estimates of prices that would obtain in 'efficient' markets, and that these cities score high on the Wharton Regulatory Index. The authors conclude that excessive regulation is what drives the rise in housing prices through its effect of inhibiting timely and sufficient adjustment of supply to accommodate the influx of higher-income residents.

While the authors do admit that it is difficult, indeed impossible, to establish clear lines of causality – since regulations could be imposed in an attempt to mitigate the displacement effects induced by rising housing prices – they conclude that the major 'distortion' is excessive regulation that inhibits efficient processes of price-based, market-led adjustment. The political implications are self-evident, namely to ease restrictions on new construction and expedite the permitting process to open up all existing spaces to the maximal level of development.

This methodology completely misrepresents the actual costs of new construction in dense, highly built-out urban environments. Below, I present data on affordable housing costs in San Francisco and New York that fully invalidate the authors' basic argument. What is notable about their paper, and other works of Glaeser and Gyourko, is that they recognize that higher-density development has higher per-square-foot costs, yet they use a type of housing unit – the single-family, economy unit – that is rarely built in cities such as San Francisco, New York, Portland, or Washington, D.C. This is due to both limited land availability for siting such development, and policy decisions to promote dense in-fill development with ample access to public transit. Hence, we do not need to engage in an extensive critique of the underlying methodology and assumptions of neoclassical urban economics (although it is certainly possible to do so). Rather, our line of attack can move directly to the outline of an alternative approach, and to showing how this accounts for the actual cost structure we observe in markets that Glaeser and Gyourko claim suffer from inflated prices due to overzealous and misguided regulatory enactments that impose distortions on the allocative efficiencies of markets.

In fact, the type of housing development that currently characterizes many major US – and global – cities has an inherent inflationary bias that results in housing prices increasing at rates that far exceed the rate of growth of worker incomes.[7] Contra the claims of the neoclassical economists, the fundamental factors driving housing prices have little to do with overly restrictive regulatory enactments. Rather, in this section I discuss how the long-term inflation of housing prices observed in cities such as San Francisco and New York reflect the combination of inherent features of vertically intensive construction processes, and the nature of urban land markets. In subsequent sections, I discuss other impacts of rising income disparities, the deepening integration of urban property markets within international circuits of banking and finance, and the long-term decline in real interest rates. While the shift toward higher-density in-fill development should be one component of any future socialist urban project, the pursuit of this form of development within the current capitalist context will not reduce prices to levels affordable to the majority of current urban residents. Achieving an egalitarian city will necessitate a phased-in and complete removal of new housing production from the private market, together with a transitional program that will provide larger-scale subsidies to ensure affordability. I return to these themes in the final section of this essay.

A MARXIAN ALTERNATIVE EXPLANATION

To establish context, I begin with an account of some core propositions of an alternative theory of housing prices that is based on Marxian capital theory.[8] My starting point is Marx's formula for the rate of profit, which can be used to identify certain key features that help to account for the observed pattern of rising prices and ground rent inflation that is a ubiquitous feature of the twenty-first-century global city.

Factors underlying rising housing costs

As presented in volumes two and three of *Capital,* the rate of profit is calculated as the ratio of the flow of surplus value to the sum of money advanced as variable and constant capital that remains 'tied up' over one complete production and circulation cycle. In his discussion of the effect of the turnover time of capital on the rate of profit, Marx uses the weekly working period as his basic unit of time measure. The sum of money capital that must be advanced is therefore a function of two variables. The first is the total weekly outlay of variable and constant (fixed and circulating) capital. Dividing this figure by some measure of the output produced by productively employed labour allows us to derive the cost per unit of newly produced use value – housing units, in the case of the construction sector. The second is the total turnover time, measured in weeks, required for the money initially advanced over the course of the weekly production period to be valorized within production and subsequently recovered (realized) at the time of final sale. The turnover time required to achieve the full metamorphosis that defines the circuit of capital as a whole (M–C–P–C´–M´) is a function of: (a) the production period, or the number of weeks required to produce new use value (housing, in our following examples); (b) the circulation period, or time required to convert the newly produced commodity capital back into money-value, which occurs at the time of final sale; and (c) the financial period, or the time between sale and the conversion of the quantum of money that recovers the initial outlay on variable and constant capital plus the increment of surplus value back into renewed elements of productive capital.

To illustrate the basic principle, let us assume that a quantum of money equal to $100m is advanced within the construction sector to secure the production and circulation (sale) of a given quantity of newly produced commodity capital – housing units, in the present example. The weekly advance consists of $40m outlays on wages (variable capital), $40m advanced as constant capital (the purchase of means of production and materials), and $20m for the purchase of land. The production period is ten weeks. Hence, the sum of money value advanced and tied up in production is $1,000m. The time required to convert the newly produced use value (commodity capital) back into money - the circulation time – is also ten weeks. At any given time, capitalists will therefore have a stock of unsold inventory priced at $1,000m. The total sum of money capital advanced is therefore $2,000m – i.e., the weekly advance on money capital multiplied by the time required to complete one production and circulation cycle. If we set the annual general rate of profit - the rate of profit calculated on the social capital as a whole – at 20 per cent, the required weekly flow of realized profit that ensures the representative capital invested in construction is rewarded at the prevailing general rate of profit is $7.69m, or the total annual profit of $400m divided by 52, or number of weeks in one year. The total weekly flow of sales revenue is thus equal to $107.69m, of which $80m represents the recovery and replacement of the initial advance of money on wages and material at the beginning of the production period, $20m replaces the portion of the global surplus value captured by land owners, and $7.69m is the required increment of weekly profit.

This basic schema can be used to analyze both supply-side and demand-side factors that function to introduce inflationary pressures into land and housing prices. Given our (provisional) assumption that the average construction capital is rewarded at the prevailing general rate of profit, any increase in per unit production costs will induce an inflationary bias into housing prices, as capitalist developers will seek to pass on higher costs by increasing the per unit mark-up they assess on prime costs. Any lengthening of the total turnover period will also function to introduce an inflationary bias in the urban real estate markets. As can be immediately extrapolated from the simple example above, any lengthening of the turnover period means a greater quantum of money-value is tied up in the construction circuit over any given weekly period. Assuming the weekly flow of output is constant – e.g. that a constant weekly advance of money to production continues to employ the same number of workers who produce the same quantity of weekly output – higher prices will be required to insure the greater quantum of money tied up in the construction circuit continues to return the general rate of profit.

It can also be shown that any rise in rents and prices due to increased demand emanating from the entry of very high-income renters and buyers into a market sub-sector has the effect of increasing land prices at a proportionally greater rate than the rate of increase in prices. This reflects the general principle that the initial appearance of surplus profits created by the demand-induced rise in prices will be eliminated by capital inflows that bid up land prices. The surplus profits are capitalized into higher land prices, which rise until the return on the total money capital invested is once again equal to the social average. Higher land prices in turn establish a higher overall level of average production costs. Moreover, because land is not itself produced by means of application of labour and capital in a 'land production' process, the demand-induced increase in land prices cannot be offset by increased supply or cheapening of per unit production costs. If capitalist households and the most well-paid sectors of the urban salariat are receiving a rising share of total income, this is an additional factor that causes prices and rents to rise at rates far in excess of the growth of average money wages. Finally, if the full operation of the typical mechanisms used to boost returns through reducing per unit costs is inhibited – i.e. technological substitutions that reduce labour costs, improving supply chain and inventory management, and shortening of the circulation period – the combined operation of these factors means land and housing prices will show a pronounced inflationary bias. Demonstrating these claims is relatively straightforward, although it requires a bit of mathematics. Interested readers are referred to the Appendix.

All these factors are at work in the case of the type of vertically intensive in-fill development that characterizes most new housing development in densely developed urban markets. For one, higher-density development typically requires more extensive up-front outlays on building design, architectural commissions, and engineering services. More vertically intensive in-fill development may incur major costs related to land clearance and site remediation, and has far more complex foundation and structural frame requirements, using more expensive materials to comply with various building and safety codes. In addition, complex construction processes typically require a higher share of skilled craft workers able to command higher wages. Holding labour productivity constant, it follows that costs associated with producing the same number of total square feet in the weekly working period will rise as production is shifted into higher-density in-fill development. This is a major factor underlying the inflation of prices and rents observed in many major US and global cities over recent decades.

Second, the shift towards more vertically intensive in-fill development will result in longer turnover times. The extent of the increase in the production period can be very significant relative to the production of a 'standard' economy housing unit on vacant land that does not require extensive site remediation or privately financed 'horizontal' infrastructural investments. This factor is particularly pronounced if new in-fill urban development occurs on former industrial and commercial sites that may require extensive remediation to be made suitable for residential development. Production periods increase due to the greater complexity of the production process – the time taken to demolish existing structures, conduct environmental clean-up, and construct a multi-story building complex will typically exceed the time required to produce a standard, detached single-family housing unit on a 'greenfield' site. The circulation period – the time taken to rent or sell the newly produced units (the realization process in Marx's theory of the circuit of capital) – will not show any particular difference according to type of unit or sub-market, but rather reflects overall demand prevailing in a given market segment at the time new units are brought to market. However, the financial lag – the time taken to convert money recovered from sales plus the increment of profit back into functioning elements of the production process – will typically be greater for production occurring within dense, built-out urban environments. This reflects the longer time period needed to identify new potential sites, acquire the necessary approvals and permits, raise financing from equity investors, and secure long-term loan commitments. This is the phase of the development process where more complex and restrictive building requirements, more stringent approvals processes, and the like can contribute to lengthening the total turnover time of capital invested in the property circuit. As I show below, however, these factors do not account for, or explain, the current scale of the affordability crisis observed in major urban regions throughout the US and Europe.

Longer turnover time means that a greater quantum of capital value is advanced and tied up at any given time in the circuits of construction capital. As noted, this lowers the rate of profit unless offset by higher per-unit output prices. This factor can be very significant in densely developed urban regions, where it is not unusual for a major development to require up to five years to complete from the time of commencement.[9] Maintaining a rate of return sufficient to justify additional investment requires that capital be shifted toward production for higher-income households able to pay higher rents and prices. This is a major factor underlying high construction costs and rising prices on new development observed in cities such as London, San Francisco, and New York.

Third, the peculiar nature of land also contributes to the observed rise in housing prices and the emergence of 'rent gaps'.[10] Land is a non-produced condition of production. Supply is fixed in an absolute sense, and cannot be increased in response to higher demand. Any increase in demand in densely developed urban regions, where most land is already under some type of dedicated usage, requires either a shift toward more high-density usage, and/ or conversion of sites from industrial and commercial to residential uses. As sites are redeveloped with higher densities and for wealthier residents, this increases the total volume of rental payments per square foot of land usage. As land prices move toward a new, higher overall level within a given sub-market sector, this increases the overall cost structure confronting developers. Hence, higher prices are required to ensure that additional investment returns at least the average rate of profit.

Rising land prices formed in the luxury sector in turn create 'spill-over' effects into adjacent lower-cost, lower-income areas.[11] 'Shadow prices' – the prices of land that would be paid to acquire and redevelop these sites for higher-income residents – begin to exceed the residual land prices implied if existing structures were rebuilt at current replacement prices. Land prices in urban sub-sectors undergoing vertically intensive redevelopment, and adjacent locations, will thus tend to increase at rates in excess of incomes of existing residents as these sites are redeveloped and sold to higher-income occupants. The effect is to inhibit any possibility of using 'market incentives' to increase the supply of housing affordable to the area's existing working-class, often lower-income, tenants. None of this is caused by 'distortions' due to excessively restrictive regulatory controls, as is maintained by the neoclassical economists. Rather, it is inherent in the normal functioning of the capitalist land market. Gentrification and displacement are endogenous features of the contemporary capitalist development process – so long as developers find a sufficient number of wealthier buyers able to afford the higher prices.

Finally, certain features that characterize the construction process inhibit the ability to offset the rise in per-unit production costs by introducing more capital-intensive production methods to boost output per working hour and lower per-unit labour cost. Property development is characterized by a lower average ratio of fixed capital relative to money outlay on wages than is observed in the economy as a whole, and manufacturing in particular. Construction capital is also characterized by a high ratio of money advanced as circulating constant capital (for building materials in particular) relative to outlays on fixed capital. Hence, the 'traditional' mechanisms through which capitalist employers counter rising wages (cost of labour) – substituting capital technologies for living labour to reduce costs, weakening worker bargaining power, and increasing real output per working hour – have limited efficacy in the construction sector. Rising costs can be offset by practices such as standardization of inputs through prefabrication, and more effective 'just-in-time' inventory management. But effects are limited, so that the massive reductions in socially necessary labour observed in sectors such as agriculture and manufacturing have not been replicated in construction. This is a structural factor that underlies the relative (and absolute) rise in the price of housing.

In summary, as construction is shifted toward more high-density in-fill development, capitalists must advance an ever-greater quantity of total money capital to produce and acquire any given level of new output. Both per-unit and total costs will tend to rise, unless offset by increased output per hour of labour input. This may be difficult to achieve, given the limited degree of substitution of capital for labour that characterizes the construction sector. Rising prices and rents are endemic to the current form of development that predominates in many of the world's major capitalist cities. This is why supply-side approaches to the current affordability crisis will not, as a general rule, lead the market to lower rents and prices. In fact, during the expansionary phases of the building cycle, higher production volumes can lead the market toward a higher overall average price level. The current affordability crisis is therefore endemic to the structural characteristics of the type of urban development found in major US and global cities, and there is no basis to claims that deregulation will result in prices that are affordable to the majority of current working-class residents.

The impact of Airbnb, financialization, and capitalist luxury consumption

There are several factors contributing to the rising price of rental housing that I will not address in detail in the paper, but which should be briefly mentioned in order to indicate the full spectrum of forces that explain the systemic underproduction of affordable housing. One, the emergence of online rental platforms such as Airbnb has resulted in the conversion of rental housing units into short-term tourist accommodations. The effect is to reduce the total rental housing stock available for long-term residence. However, it is not clear that this is a major driver of rising rental costs, which are related to more fundamental forces such as interest rates, income distribution, and factors underpinning construction costs.

Second, the long-term tendential decline in interest rates observed since the mid-1980s has introduced a prolonged inflationary dynamic in urban real estate markets – albeit one punctuated by periods of crisis and widespread devaluation of the market prices of property assets. Low interest rates allow buyers to carry and service higher debt loads and hence to pay higher acquisition prices. Falling interest rates will similarly lower the discount rate and increase the market prices of property assets, including the prices paid for newly constructed multi-unit rental property investments. Rising prices, in turn, create surplus profits within the construction circuits, which, as argued above, are subsequently capitalized into higher land prices and redistributed as increased profits and incomes throughout the sectors linked to property development.

Self-reinforcing interactions develop between credit-fuelled growth cycles that allow banks to transform the debts of workers, governments, and productive capitals into the incomes received by financial owners, and the need to re-convert the incomes of capitalist households back into yield-bearing financial titles. Direct equity investment into property capitals, lending to funds that buy and trade properties on the secondary re-sale markets, and the purchase of structured securities (CMOs, CDOs, CLOs) and equity instruments (REITs) created from underlying property portfolios and mortgage pools, have all become major conduits for transforming pools of surplus (potential) money capital into claims on future surplus values. The absorption of these liquid savings into property equity investments and property-linked financial titles introduces additional inflationary dynamics into real estate assets and land prices. Rising property and land values will in turn tend to lower the capitalization rate – i.e. the rate at which rental flows in excess of cost (net profits) – are capitalized into current market prices of existing and newly produced housing units. This further increases the nominal prices of real estate assets, which in turn attracts additional capital inflows. The result is the creation of self-reinforcing feedback effects that sustain prolonged cycles of rising prices and the formation of destabilizing property bubbles.[12]

Third, rising income inequality and the disposal of the extraordinarily high incomes realized by the upper tier of capitalist households has created high levels of demand for luxury real estate consumption. Formerly disinvested sites in major US cities are today populated with multi-million dollar condos. Many of these luxury units sit vacant much of the year, emblems of capitalists' conspicuous consumption and the obscene misdistribution of income and wealth that has emerged over the last four decades. This colonization of urban space by underutilized luxury high-rises is a primary factor that inflates land and property prices in adjacent locations, and effectively eliminates any possibility of using these sites for affordable housing development (see below for further discussion).

All of these factors are inherent in the 'normal' workings of the global financial and urban property markets under current social arrangements. The effect is witnessed in the systematic overproduction of luxury dwellings and underproduction of housing affordable to working-class residents. Rising housing prices cannot be treated as distortions introduced by overzealous regulatory controls or excessive investment restrictions imposed by local governments. On the contrary, these 'distortions' are due to the inherent logic of financial liberalization and the deepening imbrication of urban property markets within global financial and banking circuits.

THE CASES OF SAN FRANCISCO AND NEW YORK

There are no readily available comprehensive, detailed breakdowns of the cost and price structures of private developers engaged in building 'market rate' high-density multi-unit, multi-floor condominiums and luxury rental housing. However, it is possible to use data from local governments on the cost of developing new units of affordable housing to get some estimate of the costs associated with new production in densely developed, high-cost city-regions. In addition, data on the cost of development of new high-density private housing may be obtained from inclusionary housing feasibility studies. Given space limitations, I will not present an extended analysis of data on the economics of housing development in high-cost, high-rent cities. Rather, I limit myself to presentation of some data on San Francisco and New York, two cities that are often held up as preeminent examples of the negative consequences of 'excessive' regulatory restrictions. I devote particular attention to the case of San Francisco, given that it is often deemed the leading example of the types of market distortions that result from overly restrictive regulation. As I will show, even a cursory examination of actual data on multi-unit construction costs completely undermines the claims of the mainstream economists and provides strong 'first cut' validation of the alternative framework set out above.

Table 1 shows data on the cost of developing new units of affordable housing in San Francisco. These are typically developments of 50 to 150 units, with four or more floors, and without any of the features that distinguish 'luxury housing' developments. All figures are costs and estimated market prices per square foot. We see that for affordable – i.e., 'economy' – units currently under development, the sum of soft and hard costs was $666 per sq. ft as of May 2019. I here use Glaeser and Gyourko's assumption that land prices will comprise 20 per cent of total development cost in a 'well functioning' urban land market. I use this to estimate total development costs of an economy unit in the San Francisco market, while noting that actual land costs during housing booms may be much higher. I further assume, based on information from prior studies on the San Francisco market (as well as feasibility studies conducted on Los Angeles and New York), that developer capital will require a minimum rate of return of 20 per cent. This is broadly in line with Glaeser and Gyourko's assumption of a return of 17 per cent. Here also, I note that the actual rate of profit realized on capital invested in the built environment may be much higher during the expansionary phase of the construction cycle, during which time prices and rents may increase at rates in excess of the rise in land prices.

As noted above, Glaeser and Gyourko use data on the standard detached 1,900 sq. ft single-family economy home as the basic estimate of the costs of new development. For San Francisco, in 2013 this was reported as $283,000. This is the basis of the authors' claim that development costs per square foot, excluding land cost, were $149. In fact, construction cost without land for an affordable unit in 2018 is around $650 per square foot. The number utilized by these authors to justify the claim that excessive regulation is at the root of the astronomic rise in prices observed in the San Francisco market fundamentally misrepresents actual costs of producing new housing. This invalidates all the 'empirically based' claims supposedly justifying the need for radical market deregulation.

We find that, given these far more accurate estimates for cost of development of an 'affordable' housing unit in San Francisco, and with

Table 1: Costs per sq. ft for an 1100 sq. ft affordable unit, San Francisco, 2019

	Hard Costs	Soft Costs	Hard and Soft Costs	Land at 20%	Total Development Cost	Price at 20% ROP	Monthly Rent	Annual Income at 30%
Completed	$397.00	$80.00	$477.00	$95.40	$572.40	$755,568.00	$3,981.53	$159,261.33
Under Development	$479.00	$187.00	$666.00	$133.20	$799.20	$1,054,944.00	$5,228.93	$209,157.33
Pre-Development	$518.00	$151.00	$669.00	$133.80	$802.80	$1,059,696.00	$5,248.73	$209,949.33

With Soft costs at 10%	Hard Costs	Soft Costs	Hard and Soft Costs	Land at 20%	Total Development Cost	Price at 20% ROP	Monthly Rent	Annual Income at 30%
Under Development	$479.00	$53.22	$532.22	$106.44	$638.67	$843,040.00	$4,346.00	$173,840.00
Pre-Development	$518.00	$57.56	$575.56	$115.11	$690.67	$911,680.00	$4,632.00	$185,280.00

Source: Mayor's Office of Housing and Community Development. See note 14.

adjustments for land prices and the rate of return that would be demanded by private developers, the sale price of a 1,100 sq. ft unit – a modest 1-2 BR condo or apartment – is $1,054,944. Under the currently prevailing rate of return that is demanded by property capitalists as a condition for purchasing rental property in the San Francisco market, the reasonable assumption of $10,000 in per-unit annual maintenance costs, and assuming a low 5 per cent capitalization rate, we find that the monthly rent that would be required to sell a property developed as private 'market rate' rental units is $5,229. Assuming residents pay 30 per cent of *gross* income in monthly rent, newly developed housing is only affordable to a household earning $209,157 per year. The current area median income of the greater San Francisco market for a three-person household is $106,550. The vast majority of current Bay Area residents cannot affordable a standard, economy unit. I note, again, that these estimates, which are based on adjustments to actual construction costs, conform to what Glaeser and Gyourko define as a 'well functioning' market.

Table 2: Effects of shift towards higher-density development, cost per sq. ft

Building Height	50 feet	85 feet	85-240 feet	Over 240 feet
Costs per sq. ft				
Land	$217	$185	$159	$145
Hard costs	$397	$477	$556	$621
Soft costs	$130	$129	$130	$145
Total	$744	$790	$845	$911
Turnover time★	3.1	3.7	4.7	5.5

Source: San Francisco City Planning Department.

★ Turnover time is measured in years, and is the total time from initial site identification to final sale. This reflects, but does not precisely correspond to, turnover time as defined above.

To show the cost and price effects associated with the shift toward higher-density development, Table 2 reports data from a study commissioned by the San Francisco Planning Department in 2006.[13] The firm that conducted this study was able to receive estimates from private developers on the costs and the demanded rates of return for new investment in the San Francisco housing market. To calculate the monthly rent required to validate the property investment shown in Table 1 under the assumption of a 5 per cent capitalisation rate, I multiply the total supply price of a 1,100 sq. ft

Table 3: Reported costs of multi-story development in New York

	Average Unit	Total Cost sq. ft	Average Unit Cost	Total Cost sq. ft	Average Unit Cost	Price at 20% ROP	Monthly Rent	Annual Income at 30%
"Very Strong Market"	1,115	$489.79	$546,252.83	$558.36	$622,728.22	$747,273.87	$4,063.64	$162,545.64
"Strong Market"	1,093	$411.49	$449,821.15	$469.10	$512,796.11	$615,355.33	$3,513.98	$140,559.22

Source: *New York City Planning Department, BAE Urban Economics.* Minor discrepancies due to rounding.

unit (which is equal to the cost of production plus the 20 per cent profit) by the capitalisation rate, add annual operating and maintenance costs, and then divide by 12.[14] I then adjust the per-unit construction costs to derive 2018 equivalents using *Engineering News-Record* cost indexes. We see that, as expected, the shift toward more high-density development is associated with a rise in costs per square foot, lower per-unit land costs, and a lengthening of the time required to develop and sell new units.

Finally, I note that variances in the relative degree of housing price inflation observed across major urban regions reflect adjustments in overall average incomes, and the level of income inequality between the top 20 per cent of households and the median. We see that costs and prices in San Francisco are, in general, higher than those in Los Angeles or New York. This is not primarily due to a more restrictive regulatory environment. Rather, it reflects the fact that cost will be led by, and adjusts to, the incomes of the upper tier of households. This is due, in part, to factors I have already discussed that introduce a structural inflationary bias into building costs and output prices in densely developed urban environments. Our account is still incomplete, however, as there are additional factors we must consider to round out our account of the failures inherent in the capitalist market.

THE SEGREGATED HOUSING MARKET

To complete the basic framework, we must take into account the way supply decisions transpire within a segregated housing market composed of various sub-sectors differentiated by residents' class position and income. We accordingly need to reject the (naive) neoclassical assumption that the price-quantity demand function can takes the form of a smooth, continuously downward-sloping demand curve. Housing is not a homogeneous good, but is differentiated by quality and location within the existing (or emerging) socio-spatial hierarchy. In contemporary capitalist society, characterized by vast and widening income disparities, individuals and households have very different capacities to pay for housing. Given the underlying inflationary bias inherent in per-unit production costs and land prices in the densely developed urban environments discussed above, capital will flow almost exclusively into production for the upper tier – luxury – market. It can further be shown that under such conditions, an increase in supply, in response to rising demand emanating from the upper tiers of the class stratum, may not result in a reduction of prices in the luxury sector, but rather will lead the entire market toward a new, higher price level.

For expository purposes, I here divide the urban housing system into 'superior', 'ordinary', and 'inferior' segments. Let us suppose that a regional employment boom occurs rooted in high-wage sectors – computing, biotech, advanced producer services, and finance being paradigmatic examples. This will lead to increased demand for housing emanating from high-income households. This demand will fall upon the existing housing stock in 'superior' segments, and may also begin to spill over into adjacent 'ordinary' sectors. Within the 'superior' sector, rising prices will bring about surplus profits – i.e., prices rise to levels that allow developers to begin to realize rates of profit in excess of rates required to validate additional investment. Rising prices will lead to increased supply. However, the increase in supply will not necessarily lead to a reduction in output prices. In part, this is due to the dynamics I have discussed at length in the preceding sections – the inflationary bias in per-unit construction costs due to the shift into more vertically intensive, dense in-fill development. To these considerations I here add two others. For one, as demand for building sites increases, some portion of the surplus profits will be capitalized into higher land prices. If these factors are significant, prices per square foot of land and per square foot of space will both rise. As discussed above, lowering land cost per square foot of new units produced will require a shift toward ever more vertically intensive development. The effect is to induce a rise in per-unit costs that must be validated through even higher prices.

Second, rising construction volumes increase demand for the services of designers and architects, structural engineers, financial and legal advisers, private appraisers, etc. Firms that supply these specialized labour services can capture some portion of the surplus profits by increasing supply prices. This allows these firms to participate in the redistribution of the surplus profits generated within the circuits of property capital. Moreover, during periods of robust expansion, firms may need to offer employees higher wages in order to attract and retain adequately qualified labour power. In this manner, surplus profits are initially redistributed throughout the interlocking circuits of capital tied to the property sector, and are eventually eliminated through the combination of increased land prices, higher direct construction costs, and the higher prices charged for proprietary services.

In dense markets characterized by high per-unit production costs such as San Francisco, there is no evidence that private developers, left to their own devices, will supply *any* new housing for moderate- and lower-income residents seeking housing in the ordinary and inferior segments. For reasons that should now be evident, new production will be oriented almost exclusively to the superior sector. Systemic underproduction for the ordinary and inferior sectors is therefore inherent in the normal functioning of the capitalist market in these types of urban environments. Given the systemic undersupply for these markets, any increase in demand will translate into increased share of income consumed by rent payments. This explains the growing prevalence of 'rent burdened' households observed in most major US city-regions over recent decades.[17] Alternatively – and concurrently – working-class and moderate- to lower-income households will be forced to relocate ever further out to the 'urban periphery', leading to longer and more costly commutes. This process, and the subsequent acquisition and redevelopment of ordinary and inferior market segments for higher-income residents, underlies the widespread patterns of gentrification and displacement that are ubiquitous features of contemporary urban development.

Increased supply can therefore have the seemingly 'perverse' effect of leading the market toward higher prices. The longer-term trend is therefore for housing prices and rents to rise relative to the incomes of the majority of existing urban residents. This process has been underpinned by lower interest rates that have enabled a historically unprecedented financial expansion and prolonged asset inflation. Prices will therefore tend to rise unless offset by counteracting factors. These include stagnation in the growth of incomes of capitalist owners, major reductions in income inequality, higher interest rates, and higher labour productivity. We have already seen that achieving major increases in labour productivity is limited in the case of the construction industry. As I briefly discuss below, it is unlikely that major central banks would raise interest rates to levels that would induce a major decline in the market prices of fictitious capitals. Hence, within the current context, any significant reduction in prices of newly produced housing will require a major recession-induced crisis of overproduction. This would put limits on, and could even reverse, the rate of growth of the capitalist income share. Overproduction in the property sector, if sufficiently severe, would lead to rising vacancies. Rents would be reduced in order to fill vacant units in an effort to generate additional, albeit reduced, earnings on existing property investments. If rents continued to fall, this could trigger defaults on existing debt obligations. Repossession of underlying collateral by lenders and subsequent liquidations would further depress market prices of property shares, and overheated markets would enter into a protracted recession characterized by falling rents and asset prices. This would put caps on income growth in firms and industries tied to the development process, imposing a long-term depression in incomes and rents created by and extracted from capital invested in the built environment.

TRANSITION TO A SOCIALIST ECONOMY:
THE ROLE OF HOUSING

Housing and real property, and the debts attached to their production and purchase, make up one of the largest single asset classes in contemporary capitalist society. The home is also the central site of social reproduction of the individual and the family, and is embedded within, and part of, the larger urban socio-spatial residential hierarchy that is a fundamental determinant of the social allocation between classes. Housing policy will therefore be central to any socialist transition strategy to an egalitarian society. Moreover, in the case of the US and many other capitalist counties, housing-related mortgage debt and housing-related structured securities are the single largest asset class that underpins bank profits and financial market liquidity. Instituting a system of housing provision based on use value will require a phase of financial deflation and property devaluation as part of the 'de-financialization' of housing provision, and the reassertion of the primacy of use value over exchange value that is central to any process of decommodification. For these reasons, transformation of the production and distribution of housing will be inextricably tied to the transformation of the current organization of finance and banking.

In addition, creating an egalitarian socialist city will require attention to principles of urban design and architecture. Most fundamentally, this means that building urban environments, and places of domestic habitation, should be guided by a vision of the city as diverse and heterogeneous, characterized by variegated building types and architectural styles. Housing will be based on an ethos that places household reproduction at the centre of the system of needs and priorities that should guide all aspects of housing provision. This will necessitate accommodation of population increase, shifting patterns of household formation, and changes in demographics and age composition within a system of socialized planning and egalitarian distribution. Socialist urbanity must be centrally concerned with the constituent factors that enter into the production and reproduction of 'everyday life' – how to celebrate variety and difference, to preserve the variegated rhythms and non-homogenous nature of urban life. This is what Lefebvre has termed 'differential space', a world no longer dominated by the imperative to maximize production, but rather a city full of culture and sensuous activity (the body at play), an urban space predicated upon the celebration of non-identical polymorphous diversity.[18] And further, a city predicated on an underlying foundation of shared social solidarity, and an ethos of care and reciprocity. These must be the guiding principles of any twenty-first century eco-socialist society.

Toward a Phased-in Transitional Strategy

The core of a planned socialist transitional housing strategy will have to involve, first of all, massive funding allocated for a large-scale municipal acquisition program that will begin to buy up (where outright expropriation is not advisable or feasible) existing privately owned rental housing and converting its existing rental units into permanently affordable social rental housing. The objective, over time, is to convert the majority of private rental housing stock to social housing that is no longer organized on the basis of private property and governed by metrics of profitability. All units acquired in this manner will become the property of the entire community, and will be held under public or communal custodianship in perpetuity.

Second, this acquisition program will be complemented by large-scale production of new permanently affordable housing. The actual planning of new production, decisions regarding land use, and overall principles regulating building and street design will be undertaken by local deliberative bodies composed of urban planners and representatives of local neighbourhoods and regional councils, construction workers' associations, and other popular constituencies. New production will promote mixed ownership structures. Owner-occupied units will be developed as assets that will be held in perpetuity in various municipal and regional community land trusts, and other cooperative ownership structures such as limited-equity co-ops. Owners may undertake improvements, and are entitled to recoup these costs at the time of sale. At the time of sale the property is returned to the trust or land cooperative, and is then transferred to the new buyer. Prices paid by the buyer will therefore equal the replacement cost of the structure. This is an essential aspect of the decommodification of housing, as it reasserts the primacy of use value as the motive that would guide the acquisition of owner-occupied housing, as opposed to purchase on a basis of expected future monetary gain. The decision to buy a home or apartment will henceforth be conditioned on practical and aesthetic qualities, and by the desire to be rooted over time in a particular locale and community.[19]

In the case of social rental housing, where the units are the property of the entire municipal community, it will be necessary to create municipal bodies and tenant representative councils responsible for the management and ongoing maintenance of these properties. These bodies and councils will carry out both administrative and physical maintenance functions, and will be responsible for developing guidelines for building modifications. In addition, municipal governments may set up alternative management systems in which units will be placed into community land trusts overseen and operated by joint non-profit property management associations and resident councils.

All social rental housing will be subject to strict provisions that cap rental payments as a portion of household net income. Over time, rental payments can be set at levels that will allow households to acquire the non-housing consumption items necessary for full participation in the basic institutions of the emerging society. I note this is very different from the definition of 'poverty level' income that defines an absolute minimum subsistence income. A basic social income, as defined in the transitional period of the construction of a socialist society, is not only much higher than the minimum subsistence income, but will be continually adjusted to accommodate the growth of new social needs and requirements, based on the development of existing levels and forms of social production.

Third, during the initial phases of the transition, where a significant portion of rental housing will remain under private ownership, vacancy controls will be established in municipalities in which the average market price of private rental housing differentiated by size and number of bedrooms is above 25 per cent of net median household income. Specifically, controls will be based on comparison of the average price of various sizes of units (studio, 1 BR, 2 BR, and so on) and the median income of the type of household that would be expected to occupy the median-priced unit based on household size and number of children. No vacant unit could be rented at more than 10 per cent above the rent paid by the prior tenant. (This form of vacancy control is already in effect in some major capitalist cities, such as Berlin.) In the event that placement of a vacancy cap limits the property owners' ability to undertake necessary improvements to bring units up to acceptable standards, public subsidies will cover the difference between rental earning and the cost of necessary improvements.

Fourth, complementary policies will be phased in over time to impose limits on price inflation (price appreciation) of private owner-occupied housing. These measures include (a) phased-in elimination of tax incentives in the form of federal and state mortgage interest-rate tax deductions; and (b) imposition of strict limits on loan-to-value and loan-to-income ratios to limit debt-fuelled property appreciation. These policies are already broadly accepted, in principle, across the liberal span of the political spectrum as prudent responses to abuses and instability created by credit-fuelled price appreciation and speculation. Many technocrats, who understand the pernicious effects of credit-fuelled property appreciation – albeit within a context that is largely limited to strategies of more effective macroeconomic 'prudential' regulation – support them today. In the United States, the standard 'conforming' mortgage that has historically been the core of the securitization programs operated by FMLHC and FNMA generally requires a 20 per cent down payment – or a loan-to-value ratio of 80 per cent. This ratio could, over time be adjusted to an initial target of 70 per cent. Once secondary markets adjusted to a new, lower loan-to-value ratio, a further phased-in increase could be instituted to lower the ratio to 65 per cent or even 60 per cent of total home value. This would induce a process of property devaluation, and would place strict limits on future price appreciation.[20]

To institute such a program, equity considerations will require establishing mechanisms to compensate households that have purchased housing at higher loan-to-value ratios, and that have acquired homes at highly inflated prices during real estate booms driven by low interest rates and credit-fuelled appreciation. The basic principle would be to reduce debt payments to ensure that households continue to pay no more than 80 per cent of total home value in interest and principal. Price deflation would be offset by reductions of existing debt obligations, so no homeowners would find themselves 'under water' – i.e., owing more on debt than the property's current market value. Moreover, because caps on loan-to-value ratios would be instituted on a national level, this would lead to a generalized price deflation that would preserve the property's real housing-specific purchasing power. Hence, households would not experience a net loss of purchasing power in terms of the relative exchange value, as all homes and properties would be undergoing a similar loss of nominal market value.

Banks and lenders would experience balance sheet deflation. Losses would need to be written off due to restructuring of households' mortgage obligations. Losses imposed on major lending institutions would be compensated through publicly financed equity injections undertaken as part of a comprehensive socialization of the core components of the banking and financial system. While further discussion of this is outside the scope of the current paper, it is clear that transforming the financial system is central to any socialist transition based on the various initiatives outlined in this section.

Property devaluation, rental deflation, and reduction in land prices will begin to ease rental payment burdens for all sections of current 'rent-burdened' populations. In addition, devaluation and de-financialization will lower the cost of site acquisition and new construction. Over time, if large-scale property acquisition programs and social rental housing are designed and maintained to achieve high standards of quality, this will lead to a process of de facto decommodification, as demand will shift towards permanently affordable public and cooperative housing (land trusts). Moreover, by inducing a decrease in housing prices, and placing strict limits on loan-to-value ratios, this will limit any future price increases and undo the basis of real estate speculation, in which units are acquired under the expectation of future appreciation. Housing will be supplied that is of high quality, has a variety of styles and design features, and is purchased based on use value and attachment to place and the larger community, as opposed to a private wealth-formation strategy. It should be clear, therefore, that implementing an egalitarian socialist housing policy would involve a deep transformation of the motives and ethical frameworks that have become deeply embedded in the everyday conscious and 'common sense' of advanced (late) capitalist society.

A transitional tax plan to finance social housing

Implementing these strategies will need to be complemented by a transitional tax plan to finance acquisition and new construction, and to compensate homeowners for losses through major debt write-downs. I would like to suggest here that the guiding principles of a transitional tax program should be to impose very high tax rates on higher-income, high-net-worth households as one part of the phased-in expropriation and redistribution program. At the same time, a transitional tax plan should exempt the profits of firms from taxation if these funds are necessary to finance planned capital investment, or if retained (non-distributed) profits are placed into tax-exempt investment vehicles and financial conduits set up to channel surplus savings back into circuits of social investment. The major broad-brush components of a transitional tax program are as follows.

One, immediately reinstate a highly progressive tax system with a 90 per cent top marginal tax. This will be coupled with a strongly progressive gradation of tax rates. The basic blueprint for such a tax system is provided by fiscal and tax policies instituted under the aegis of Roosevelt Administration during the New Deal period. If implemented in the United States, this measure would raise trillions of dollars over the transitional period. These monies would be used to finance increased social expenditure and outlays on CO_2-reducing infrastructure. In addition, it will be a major source of funding for investments in social housing and bank nationalization as part of converting the core components of the banking system into a public utility. A corollary effect of this tax will be to introduce deflationary effects in the prices of financial assets – including investment properties – as surpluses that presently fuel the inflation of fictitious capitals are redirected back into circuits of social investment.

Two, at the firm level, all retained profits required to finance current, or actually planned, investment expenditures of the enterprise would be exempt from taxation. All non-distributed profits not needed for current investment purposes, and the untaxed portion of household savings, will be eligible to be invested in tax-exempt money market funds and longer-term investment vehicles that will be operated as worker-managed cooperative enterprises. In addition, surpluses not needed for immediate investment purposes could be held as tax-exempt time deposits at municipal and regional development banks. These vehicles and financial conduits will be designed as tax-exempt 'qualifying investments' to the extent that these loans supply funds to support new capital investment, as opposed to disposing of these surpluses through acquiring existing financial assets (equities and bonds) on the secondary markets, or through funding mergers and acquisitions that simply restructure – and centralize – existing ownership relationships. Surpluses directed into these qualified investments would be used to support new investment, including financing of investment in social housing. In addition, these vehicles could support restructuring of the existing debt obligations of homeowners, primarily in the form of equity injections into banks to absorb loan write-downs as part of a program of bank nationalization. Firms and households that place surpluses into nationalization funds would be eligible to receive tax-exempt dividends. In addition, these financial vehicles would be a source of short-term loans to meet firms' working capital requirements.[21]

Three, surpluses of firms and capitalist households held in 'non-qualifying' investment vehicles and conduits would be subjected to high rates of taxation on income received from investments (interest and dividend earnings), and capital gains would be taxed at the top marginal tax rate. The net effect of this form of financial restructuring, much of it directly linked to the 'de-financialization' and decommodification of housing, will be: to reduce financial speculation; to impose a needed, and controlled, debt deflation and devaluation of financial capitals; and to provide funding for major social investment programs, including sizable outlays for acquisition programs and large-scale investments in infrastructure and new housing construction.

Complex questions remain that are related to the relative mix of centralized and decentralized planning, and the role of markets – if any – in coordinating the system of resource allocation and distribution. As a general principle, I would advocate for the majority of allocation decisions to be instituted through a system of planning that would have both centralized and decentralized components depending on the nature and type of resources being allocated. Some degree of centralized planning must be brought to bear on investments in education, healthcare, medical research, schooling (including early childhood education), major infrastructure that has impacts on land use, urban spatial organization, and the distribution of economic activities between different regions – all closely integrated with the production and allocation of housing. All these sectors produce public goods having broad 'positive externalities' that impact the spatial organization of cities, and patterns of resource utilization, and are essential components of the society's cultural and scientific institutions that sustain new forms of knowledge production and cultural innovation. These are 'foundational goods', and must be provided in sufficient quantities to allow all individuals to participate fully and freely in social life and the society's various institutions. The issue is how to embed planning practices in a system that is accountable to the actual needs of the emergent society, and that is committed to a thoroughgoing eco-socialist transition strategy.

APPENDIX

The annual rate of profit on construction capital is a function of total units produced and sold in each weekly period, the total weekly outlays for wages and materials, and the turnover time of capital, or the time required for money advanced to purchase labour power and means of production to be realized and converted back into functioning elements of productive capital. The basic relation is given as:

Eq 1

$$annual\ rate\ of\ profit_j = \left(\frac{52}{no.\ of\ weeks\ in\ one\ turnover\ period_j}\right) \cdot \left(\frac{sales_j(per\ week) - money\ advanced_j(per\ week)}{money\ advanced_j(per\ week)}\right)$$

Or alternatively:

Eq 2

$$annual\ rate\ of\ profit_j = \left(\frac{52}{no.\ of\ weeks\ in\ one\ turnover\ period_j}\right) \cdot \left(\frac{sales_j(per\ week)_j}{money\ advanced_j(per\ week)} - 1\right)$$

where j refers to a specific market sub-sector differentiated by location and occupant income.

Following Marx, I set the working period equal to one week. Sales is the total money realized per working period by the representative capital invested in market segment j. 'Money advanced' is the weekly outlay on wages, materials, and land that is advanced at the beginning of the production period. Total turnover time is the sum of the production and circulation period plus the financial lag, or time taken to transform money that replaces the initial outlay plus the increment of profit back into fresh outlays on labour power and means of production.

Multiplying the weekly profit by 52, or the number of working periods per annum, gives the total annual profit. This is the numerator of Eq 1. The denominator is equal to the total money capital advanced per week multiplied by the total number of weeks in one turnover period. This is the total quantum of money that must be advanced at any given time in the construction circuit to secure the production of a given volume of weekly output, holding per unit production costs constant. This ratio is what Marx defines as the annual rate of profit. (I assume that the production and circulation process is a continuous flow transpiring over multiple turnover periods. This is not the case in fact, as activity in the construction industry is subject to discontinuities, ruptures, and breaks. The assumption is made here for illustrative and simplification purposes, and does not compromise the general results of the analysis.)

To simplify, I assume a constant flow of throughput is occurring during each weekly period. Let us also presume that the profit realized by the representative, or average, capital invested in sub-sector j will tend to gravitate towards the general rate of profit, and that over the short period, the general rate of profit can be treated as a constant.

By direct inspection of Eq 2, we can see that a rise in weekly production costs due to a shift towards more complex, vertically intensive, forms of infill development will require an equiproportional rise in output price in order to maintain a constant rate of profit. A lengthening of the total turnover period will similarly require output prices to rise. And vice versa – a reduction in the turnover time will introduce deflationary dynamics into output prices. I here note that the required rate of change in prices needed to equalize the rate of profit will rise (fall) at a proportionally lesser rate then the increase (decrease) in the turnover period.

Finally, a demand-induced rise in output price due to the entry of high-income buyers into the sub-sector, holding per unit outlays on wages and material and the turnover period constant, will induce a rise in land price per sq. ft. The increase in land price functions to absorb and eventually eliminate the surplus profit. Alternately, the demand-induced formation of surplus profits can be eliminated by a rise in per unit input costs, including a rise in the costs of proprietary design, architectural and engineering services. Surplus profits initially created through the demand-induced rise in prices are in this case redistributed in the form of higher hourly wages and salaries. This increases the costs and hence the mark-ups and money profits realised by the various capitals tied to the construction process. This process continues until the rate of profit is once again equalized, albeit at a new, higher overall level of production costs and output prices.

I have argued in the main text that denser, vertically intensive construction processes will tend to increase per unit production costs. I here note two other relevant dynamics that function to introduce inflationary pressures into rents and housing prices. One, an increase in sq. ft of building space per sq. ft of land base that exceeds any change in the weekly flow of output will lengthen the total production period:

Eq 3

$$production\ period_j = \frac{total\ sq.ft\ of\ average\ building\ in\ subsector\ j}{total\ sq.ft\ produced\ per\ week}$$

As shown above, longer turnover times introduce inflationary pressures into unit rents and sale prices.

Second, if we provisionally hold land cost per sq. ft constant, an increase in density will lower the total required money outlay for land purchase:

Eq 4

$$total\ money\ outlay\ on\ land_j = (land\ price\ per\ sq.ft_j) \cdot \left(\frac{constant\ plot\ size_j}{total\ sq.ft\ of\ avg.\ building\ in\ subsector\ j} \right)$$

Maintaining a constant rate of profit requires land prices per sq. ft to rise. Increased density will thus introduce an inflationary bias into per sq. ft land prices. These relationships, taken in sum, demonstrate why the current pattern of urban development has inherent inflationary biases that tend to lead the market to a higher general price level.

NOTES

1   Joint Center for Housing Studies of Harvard University, *The State of the Nation's Housing*, 2017.

2   For various versions of this argument, see: Edward Glaeser and Joseph Gyourko, 'The Economic Implications of Housing Supply', *Journal of Economic Perspectives*, 32(1), 2018, pp. 3-30; J. Quigley and S. Raphael, 'Regulation and the High Cost of Housing', *American Economic Review*, 95(2), 2005, pp. 323-8; Edward Glaeser and Joseph Gyourko, 'The Impact of Building Restriction on Housing Affordability' *Federal Reserve Bank of New York Economic Policy Review*, 9(2), 2003, pp. 21-39; Edward Glaeser, Joseph Gyourko, and Raven Saks, 'Why Have Housing Prices Gone Up?' *American Economic Review*, 95(2), 2005, pp. 329-33; Richard Green, Stephen Malpezzi, and Stephen Mayo. 'Metropolitan-specific Estimates of the Price-Elasticity Supply of Housing, and their Sources', American *Economic Review*, 95 (2), 2005, pp. 334-9; Stephen Malpezzi, 'Housing Prices, Externalities, and Regulation in U.S Metropolitan Areas', *Journal of Housing Research*, 7(2), 1996, pp. 209-14.

3   See Stephen Keen, *Debunking Economics*, London: Zed Books, 2011, for an accessible critique of the theoretical underpinnings of neoclassical economics. See also Joan Robinson, *Economic Philosophy*, New York: Routledge, 2017 [1962], pp. 47-72.

4   Edward Glaeser and Joseph Gyourko, 'The Economic Implications of Housing Supply', *Journal of Economic Perspectives*, 32(1), 2018, pp. 3-30.

5   US Census Bureau, *American Housing Survey*, available at www.census.gov. The version of the American Housing Survey used by Glaser and Gyourko has data covering the years 1985-2013, and is based on homeowners' self-reported estimates of the market prices of their homes.

6   For a description of this index, see Joseph Gyourko, Albert Saiz, and Anita Summers, 'The Wharton Residential Land Use Regulatory Index', *Urban Studies*, 45(3), 2008, pp. 693-721.

7   This section builds upon the author's prior work on this topic. See Karl Beitel, 'Circuits of Capital, Ground Rent, and the Production the Built Environment: A New Framework for Analysis', *Human Geography*, 9(3), 2016, pp. 27-42.

8   For Marx's own discussions of the relation of turnover time and the rate of return, see Karl Marx, *Capital*, Volume 2, London: Penguin, 1978, pp. 334-93; Karl Marx, *Capital*, Volume 3, London: Penguin, 1981, pp. 163-9. In addition, this section draws upon Duncan Foley, *Understanding Capital: Marx's Economic Theory*, Cambridge, MA: Harvard University Press, 1985, pp. 63-91; and Marco Passarella and Herve Baron, 'Capital's Humpback Bridge: Financialization and the Rate of Turnover in Marx's Economic Theory', *Cambridge Journal of Economics*, 39(5), 2015, pp. 1415-1441.

9   This refers to the time from initial identification of a potential building site and initial planning and design through actually hiring architects and designers, securing funding, application for building permit, compliance with any local or state regulatory reporting and other requirements, site clearance and remediation, actual construction, and rental or sale of newly built units.

10 For discussion of the Marxist theory of the rent gap, see Neil Smith, *The New Urban Frontier: Gentrification and the Revanchist City*, New York: Routledge, 1996, pp. 51-74; Eric Clark, 'The Rent Gap and Transformation of the Built Environment', *Geograpfiska Annaler*, 70(2), 1988, pp. 241-54; Eric Clark, 'The Rent Gap Re-examined', *Urban Studies*, 32(9), 1995, pp. 1489-1503; Johannes Jager, 'Urban Land Rent Theory: A Regulationist Perspective', *International Journal of Urban and Regional Research*, 27(2), 2003. pp. 233-49; and Karl Beitel, 'Circuits of Capital, Ground Rent, and the Production the Built Environment: A New Framework for Analysis', *Human Geography*, 9(3), 2016, pp. 27-42. A major contribution to Marxian analysis land use and ground rent theory is provided in Alain Lipietz, 'A Marxist Approach to Urban Ground Rent: The Case of France', in *Land Rent, Housing, and Urban Planning: A European Perspective*, Michael Ball, et al., eds., London: Croom Helm, 1985, pp. 129-55.

11 Beitel, 'Circuits of Capital, Ground Rent, and the Production the Built Environment'.

12 For analysis of the relation between finance and urban property markets see: David Harvey, *The Limits to Capital*, London: Verso, 2006, pp. 367-72; David Harvey, *The Urban Experience*, Baltimore: John Hopkins University Press, pp. 59-89; David Harvey, *Rebel Cities: From the Right to the City to the Urban Revolution*, London: Verso, pp. 27-66; Karl Beitel, 'Financial Cycles and Building Booms: A Supply-side Account', *Environment and Planning A*, 23(12), pp. 2113-2132; Karl Beitel, 'The Subprime Debacle', *Monthly Review*, 60(1), May 2008, pp. 27-44; Kevin Fox Graham, 'Creating

Liquidity Out of Spatial Fixity: The Secondary Circuit of Capital and the Restructuring of the US Housing Finance System', in *Subprime Cities: the Political Economy of Mortgage Markets*, Manual Aalbers, ed., Malden, MA: Blackwell, pp. 25-52; and Manual Aalbers, *The Financialization of Housing*, New York: Routledge, 2016.

13   'Summary Report, Inclusionary Housing Program Sensitivity Analysis', Keyser Martson Associates, prepared for San Francisco City Planning Department, July 2006.

14   The capitalization rate is the ratio of net operating income to supply price, or $c = NOI/price$. NOI equals annual rent minus annual operating and maintenance costs, or $NOI = 12 \cdot R - OC$, where R is per month rent, and OC is annual per unit operating cost. Required monthly rent is derived as $R = 1/12 (c \cdot price + OC)$. Annual required income is simply the annual rent divided by 0.3, or 30 per cent.

15   'Market and Financial Study NYC Mandatory Inclusionary Housing', BAE Urban Economics, Inc., prepared for New York City Housing Development Corporation, September 2015.

16   It should be noted that private developers in New York often charge rents well in excess of the figure reported here. My calculation will underestimate the actual extent of the rise in market rate rents.

17   Joint Center for Housing Studies of Harvard University, *The State of the Nation's Housing*, 2017.

18   Henri Lefebvre, *The Production of Space*, 1991 [1974], Malden, MA: Blackwell Publishing, pp. 52-67.

19   See David Madden and Peter Marcuse, *In Defense of Housing*, London: Verso, 2016, pp. 191-218.

20   Manual Aalbers, *The Financialization of Housing*, New York: Routledge, 2016, pp. 134-50.

21   Some merger activity would be desirable in a socialist economy, but should not be a primary means of disposing of surpluses if socially useful and necessary investments exist that require funding in excess of retained earnings or if new enterprises need initial funding to launch a new product or service.

COMMUNISM IN THE SUBURBS?

ROGER KEIL

Mike Davis's signature book, *City of Quartz*, the dystopian reading of 1980s Los Angeles, famously begins at the periphery of the Southern California metropolis. Viewed from the ruins of the 'alternative future' of Llano del Rio, an early twentieth-century socialist commune in the desert north of the city, late twentieth-century Los Angeles looks particularly monstrous.[1] As he visits the ruins of Llano del Rio, Davis notes the approach of suburbia, the preparation of suburban land – as we now realize, one of the staple crops of financialized real estate capitalism[2] – and the slithering snake of commuter traffic that makes its way from the Antelope Desert to the valleys of economic opportunity below. The utopians of Llano del Rio decamped in 1918 for greener pastures in Louisiana, but they left behind, besides the ruins on which Davis stood, a plan for a socialist garden city designed, in 'distinctly feminist and California' style, by a former Llano communard, the socialist architect Alice Constance Austin. Her innovative design, never fully realized, was based on non-patriarchal principles which involved, for example, houses without kitchens, collective food preparation, and other labour saving devices meant to improve women's (and everyone's) lives. Her plans for Llano del Rio included a circular plan for about 10,000 people that would distinguish the colony from the common developer-led suburbanisms of the day.[3]

Of course, utopian attempts like that of Llano del Rio have failed repeatedly. But they have continued to be revived again and again, in continuity, conversation, and conjunction with the larger forces that transform society over time. They are eruptions of that metaphoric beach under the cobblestones from which '*Mai 1968*' took its inspiration. And indeed, one of the most influential architects of mid-century progressive Los Angeles, Gregory Ain, himself a child of Llano del Rio, 'believed that modern architecture could and should deliver affordable housing (a dire need in postwar years) that amplified, rather than confined, its residents'.[4] Although his plans to 'refine and dignify the low-cost house' were never realized 'because banks were uncomfortable with the kind of collective ownership he was proposing', such plans were infused with the spirit of the impossible histories and geographies that were created by Los Angeles's social movements through the 1930s and 1940s, which the work of late socialist scholar Don Parson so richly uncovered in recent decades. While Davis's invocation of the utopia of Llano del Rio highlights the early twentieth century, the focus of Parson's research and the font of his optimism of a better urban future for all was the mid-century constellation of radical ideas and popular tendencies that propelled the public housing movement in Southern California in particular.

In fine-grained historical detail, Parson's work brought to life the hopeful monuments to a possibly socialist, multi-racial Los Angeles, especially in the field of housing:

> The progressives' work on housing reform in Los Angeles helped establish the direction for the local public housing program of the 1930s and beyond. A multiethnic and working-class Eastside and an African American ghetto to the south of downtown counterposed to a Westside Anglo suburbanization would define the geography of the city's public housing program. Issues that were delineated by progressive reformers – of race, class, architectural design of housing, women's work, and the paternalism of housing reformers – were to become central concerns of the public housing movement.[5]

In sharp contrast to the usual recycled old stereotypes about Los Angeles as 'The City That Never Quite Came Together',[6] with no progressive civic elites, Parson's work on the history of alternative futures points us in a different direction. Los Angeles (or any place) could never be saved by its elites, but its diverse and multifold masses provided a better shot at salvation – and they still do. Don Parson's work – exemplary for its 'recovering and retelling the histories of ordinary people and places' in the Los Angeles region[7] – powerfully made the case for a politics and governance from below, and from the periphery. The elites may have failed the centre and the region. But there is life in the neighbourhoods and projects of the people. Don Parson's detailed historical analyses provided nodes in the more granular understanding of historical events and geographical realities that is needed today to revive the utopian vision and practice, serving as a reminder that we cannot allow ourselves to be drawn into historical pessimism. It is a starkly lit signpost of how regular people, when they organize, and individuals, when they are courageous, can change things. This is well-expressed in a recent *People's Guide to Los Angeles*: 'We have thought to uncover and share places that might be overlooked as unremarkable, places where people have nevertheless confronted power and, in doing so, have been transformed by those struggles.'[8]

This is the core message also of this essay: focus on the small and hidden histories, the buried stories of the everyday, the extinguished but smoldering fires at the grass roots of urban society. History understood in these critical terms remains crucial to finding our way in these darker times: it is a history made by humans. It is made with the objective of improving an ever changing urban environment to create collective economic institutions not entirely reliant on the market, provide more and better – social and public – housing, to engender social relationships in solidarity, free from oppression based in class and race relations. The alternative is not an option: a history of dead signifiers, fixed capital, and enshrined privilege. We need to counteract the view of a history that is empty and rather present a view of history as made by people for people, by communities for their city. The Los Angeles that comes to life in Parson's work is the city in which its diverse communities can thrive and have a vibrant future rather than a past built in architectural symbolism. It is the city built by and for humanity.

Both the early twentieth-century commune and the progressive reforms of mid-century in Los Angeles were not untypical for what was happening around the world at those times by way of experiments in widespread reform, or even revolution. None of these led sustainably to what the dreamers, reformers, and revolutionaries had hoped for: a different society, a new world. Ultimately, experiment and reform in housing and urban life were perverted by the bureaucracies perpetuating the survival of capitalism, as well as by the bureaucrats constructing 'real existing socialism' in Eastern Europe.[9] Henri Lefebvre, addressing the state-built housing machines of the *banlieue* as the dreaded 'habitat' of the 'society of bureaucratic consumption', once powerfully exposed how France's urban policy has had quite the opposite effect of what both experiment and reform had intended: 'The population in the metropolis is regrouped into ghettos (suburbs, foreigners, factories, students), and the new cities are to some extent reminiscent of colonial cities.'[10] Yet in these histories we find sedimentations of possibilities that I will take up in this essay.

THE FABRIC OF 'EXTENDED URBANZATION'

Working my way through historical and present day Los Angeles, I will re-approach the topic of the commune as community, and the city as the site of communism. I will put forward the thesis that today we have to focus on the extended urbanization by which our planet is currently characterized. This means we need less focus on the historical centrality of cities and the agora at their core. This implies a shift from the centrality of the point of production to the sphere of reproduction.[11] Rohan Quinby has formulated this shift succinctly: 'Within the postmetropolis, a reconfiguration of the meaning of urbanism is taking place. Centrality is increasingly reserved for immaterial networks of power and the physical assets that support them, while bodily existence within the postmetropolis is increasingly moved to the periphery.'[12] In addition to moving our attention to the periphery of the urban region, we also need to diverge from how the city was treated in the classics of historical materialism. Henri Lefebvre once noted that for Marx, '[t]he city, as such, is part of those historical conditions, which are involved in the growth of capitalism'.[13] The assumed agglomeration effects of big industry, centralized urbanity and modern society were at the heart of strategic thinking of the left since the end of the nineteenth century. For Marxists, big cities and big industry were the launching pads for revolutionary strategy; the commune was mostly imagined from the experience in the streets of arguably the most developed and most exciting city in the world in 1871. Today, instead, the growth of capitalism is tied directly to extended urbanization as a global phenomenon and most of that happens in the rapidly urbanizing regions outside of North America and Europe.[14]

The notion of 'extended urbanization' refers back to Lefebvre's much-cited idea that urbanization occurs through 'the tremendous concentration … of urban reality and the immense explosion, the projection of numerous, disjunct fragments … into space'.[15] The 'immense explosion' of the people, activities, wealth, goods, objects, instruments, that has constituted 'urban reality' into a new 'urban fabric' of peripheries, suburbs, vacation homes, satellite towns makes the conventional concept of the city obsolete. It forces us to think more generally of urban society as a universal phenomenon. Metropolitanization as well now needs to be understood as a process that produces not just one centrality and one periphery (as the history of the twentieth century seems to have suggested) but a complex mesh of centralities and peripheries that make up the urban fabric.

Today, the search for a post-capitalist world needs to recalibrate its thinking about space, geography, and urbanization: 'On the worldwide scale, space is not only discovered and occupied, it is transformed, to the extent that its "raw material", "nature", is threatened by this *domination*, which is not *appropriation*. Generalized *urbanization* is an aspect of this colossal extension.'[16] While in previous periods of modern urbanization, diversity, complexity, and social segmentation were attributes mostly of dense inner cities, those tendencies can now be found predominantly in the urban periphery while many urban cores are gentrified and normalized through corporate landscapes.[17] In addition, the massive urban peripheries that already exist from vast suburbanization processes over the past few decades experience contradictory and generative processes of post-suburbanization with mixed densities, diverse populations and economies.[18] From all of this springs a new politics of the periphery. Los Angeles, an urban region at the cusp of many new developments in capitalist urbanization over the past century and a half, is a good place to find those contradictions.[19]

LEARNING FROM LOS ANGELES

In his satirical novel *The Sellout,* set in a fictional Los Angeles, Paul Beatty has his main character involved in the following conversation:

'Isn't there something else that would make you happy?'
'Bring back Dickens.'
'You know that is impossible. When cities disappear, they don't come back.'[20]

This may be true. But the notion that cities as built forms are congealed societal process is equally valid. As I have argued elsewhere at greater length, we can start from the assumption, 'that "planetary urbanization" or the "completely urbanized" world society in the Lefebvrian sense will indeed create the minimum conditions, as it were, to begin thinking about humans making their own history and geography, and stripping conditions of their natural character and creating a basis for human unity and self-production'.[21] Effectively, this entails the idea that, philosophically, communism is 'the real movement which abolishes the present state of things'.[22] Urban society hence is a precondition for what Marx in his early work called '*die Verkehrsform selbst*', a non-metaphysical human self-production in the course of history (and one might add geography).[23] In practical terms, this means understanding and mobilizing the previous conditions and contradictions of the 'urban commonwealth',[24] based on popular forces that coalesced to make a better world.

The example of mid-twentieth century Los Angeles and the decades it took to dismantle its possibilities serves as the inspiration for new possibilities today. The possibilities that were opened up in Los Angeles then were real outcomes of activism and social struggle and were built in brick and mortar, institutions and community memory. But memory itself has been erased and other memories recreated often in a city that has excelled in 'forgetting'.[25]

Yet, perhaps more than ever, the memory of that other Los Angeles is in need of conjuring up in our collective contemporary imagination, and it can perhaps guide us beyond the idiosyncrasies of the southern California metropolis. So, despite the dry humour in the quip from Paul Beatty's novel, the city of the past may be kept alive as a spectre that orients us today.

Don Parson's *Making a Better World: Public Housing, the Red Scare, and the Direction of Modern Los Angeles* (2005), as well as his more recently published work in *Public Los Angeles,* are exemplary in this respect. They reveal the complicated history of how public housing, once celebrated as a positive force in the struggle for better and more housing for the masses, was turned into a threat to American society as its Cold War opponents redbaited anyone and anything that had an association with the idea and the projects. Parson contrasted 'the community modernism of public housing advocates and the corporate modernism of urban renewal advocates'. Emphasizing 'the agency of housing directors and residents who used tenant organizations and the physical space of public housing itself as important platforms for labor and civil rights struggles', Parson treated housing as a real process through which 'urban society' emerges through the purposeful action of 'colorful revolutionists'.[26]

The great urbanist Jane Jacobs, who was no friend of Los Angeles (both as a concept and a city), bemoaned the lack of urbanity in Southern California. Her observation directly fed off the idea that 'Los Angeles is an extreme example of a metropolis with little public life, depending mainly instead on contacts of a more private social nature'.[27] Yet the interplay of the private and the public has in fact been a perennial concern in Los Angeles. And it has real lessons for what is happening everywhere today in a neoliberal capitalism feeding on rapacious property development. The fight over the use and meaning of public space and collective property is central to challenging capitalist hegemony in Los Angeles and elsewhere. In Ed Soja's words, '[a]lthough seeking spatial justice should not be confined only to struggles over public space, such struggles are vital and can be extended in many different directions in the search for justice and the right to the city'. This is why, he argues, we should 'use a critical spatial perspective to open up a fresh look at the subject of public versus private space and to explore the possibilities for developing new strategies to achieve greater socio-spatial justice'.[28]

What, then, does Los Angeles have to offer in approaching the core concern of this essay: the restoration of a conversation on experiment, revolution in line with an emerging planetary sub/urban society? Los Angeles is a 'real and imagined' place[29] at the far end of the American 'manifest destiny', the city from where the United States turned back east and looked at itself as a space contained, after all, by geography. Born disparate, dispersed and suburban, Los Angeles grew into one of the densest carpets of urbanized humanity anywhere in the world, tied together by a federally financed and globally fuelled infrastructure of the military, media, and mobility. The Southern California metropolis was at once the largest industrial city in the West and anyone's post-industrial dream, sweatshop nightmare, and postmodern phantasmagoria all in one. The Southland had megacity ambitions as it outpaced most economies in the United States and elsewhere.

Los Angeles inspired 'new geographies of theory'[30] in urban studies, especially, at first, by visitors from afar. Between Anton Wagner's 1935 landmark study *Los Angeles: City of Two Million in Southern California*[31] and Reyner Banham's *Los Angeles: The Architecture of Four Ecologies* just over three decades later, observers swerved from disdain to curiosity and explanation.[32] Mike Davis took up the cues from both Wagner and Banham but viewed the place from the inside. His *City of Quartz* painted a much more prohibitive and dystopian picture of Los Angeles.[33]

The most far-reaching rewrite of the conceptual geography of Los Angeles was provided by the so-called Los Angeles School towards the end of the twentieth century.[34] The LA School writers made three important advances that contextualize our contemporary view of Los Angeles: they discussed the (new) urban form of Los Angeles as paradigmatic for urbanism more generally; they changed the channel on centrality: instead of seeing either a place of desolation or a place of eviction, they pointed to the post-Fordist economic districts that enliven the core; this led to celebrating the alternative political possibilities resting in the cosmopolitan, globalized immigrant city after Fordism.

It has been noted that LA's extended form of urbanization is now everywhere. Beyond mere form, the Los Angeles urban model has given rise to claims about (post)modern urban society generally, where traditional scales and hierarchies of urban living are suspended in a topologically organized grid of flows that renders centres unimportant or sees them as organized from the periphery.[35] Postsuburbia's 'composite' character – with its global manifestations, divergences, and mixing of discordant land uses, less predictable geographic forms, new politics, new work-residence relations – describes well the complexity of form, structure, and politics we find in Southern California.[36] It is the inverted city. Peripheral urbanization provided the main narrative of (post)metropolitanization in the Southland. The growth of self-governing cities in Southern Californian suburbia represented a form of peripheral urbanization, which included the concentration of jobs, factories, offices, and commercial areas in addition to residential expansion. It also structured the region's landscape of racial and class segregation.[37] Los Angeles has been one of the chief urban areas in which the fusion of neoliberalization and urbanization has created a peculiar form of privatized vulgarity that has characterized the early years of twenty-first century American suburbanization.[38] As Dear and Dahman have noted, 'the altered geographies of postmodern urbanism are redefining the meaning and practice of urban politics' that potentially leads to 'the subordination of the local state to plutocratic privatism'.[39] Yet, there are new political possibilities, not least generated in the increasingly vocal immigrant workforce, which simultaneously enables certain autonomies, creative local economies and innovative labour, ecological and community politics.[40]

THE URBAN LABORATORY OF LOS ANGELES TODAY

It was in the Southern California suburbs where many of the region's foreclosures took place during the 2008 crisis. In the smouldering ruins of the 'Great Recession', in places as far out as Rialto, the push of the 'desert frontier' came temporarily to a halt and the inner reworkings of the suburbs began.[41] Incidentally, it is in the rapidly changing Los Angeles suburbs that social service needs have become greatest.[42] Of course, Los Angeles has been showing features of peripheral poverty and diversity for a very long while, as even well before the 1970s 'segregation of minorities had been built into the structure of the city'.[43] And by the 1990s, almost one-third of all new immigrants coming to the region had settled directly in the suburbs.[44] The LA area also produced North America's first 'ethno-burbs' where (typically non-European) immigrants live in a new type of middle-class suburb – the new 'arrival city' – that is tied into both local ethnic economies and cultures and into world-market based networks.[45] At the same time, LA's downtown has been the site of an aggressive gentrification process often celebrated in the media. One observer wrote even that 'downtown Los Angeles has, on the whole, made the most impressive recovery of any American central city in the 21st century'.[46] The 'inversion' that was thrown into stark relief elsewhere more recently, among other things, by the crisis in Ferguson, Missouri,[47] has been a defining fact of the Southern California landscape for decades. Driven by, and itself co-producing, dynamic processes of globalization, neoliberalization, immigration, and regionalization, the Southern California metropolis remains today a city of multiple contradictions.[48]

Whereas to many Los Angeles is a powerful symbol of capitalist accomplishment, a land of opportunity under sunny skies, it has also served as the prototype of a dystopian strand of urbanism which sees the place as the paradigmatic city of disaster and mayhem and a site of struggle over environmental and social justice.[49] The spread of either image throughout the global channels of hype, the 'sunshine and the noir' to paraphrase Mike Davis, is invariably tied into the power grids of LA's most trademark industry that put LA on the mental and visual map of the globe. In Hollywood, Los Angeles has had its one strong base for globalized self-production. The other process through which LA propels itself to global significance is through the shameless boosterism of its elites. But, as I have been suggesting here, not all politics in LA is elite. In fact, the city has given the world some of the most pervasive images of popular politics and violent uprising, peaceful protest, and mass democracy: Watts 1965, the Chicano moratorium 1970, Rodney King and the LA uprising of 1992, the Bus Riders Union's Consent Degree, and the social unionism of its immigrant labour organizations as well as recent struggles around housing and homelessness. It is from these contestations that LA has rejuvenated itself periodically.

Today, Los Angeles is one of the densest urban areas in North America. Perpetually growing economically and demographically although not at the clipped speed of previous decades, it remains international and culturally diverse in population. The region has also become a site of significant transit development based on an ultimately extensive rail network and environmental innovation, as the once smoggy air is cleaned up and its namesake river begins to be a green spine rather than a concreted flood control channel. Los Angeles remains the place where the world's dreams are produced and televised in motion pictures, while it continues to provide opportunity for millions of its inhabitants as well as newcomers to help define the notion of living the urban revolution.

The suburban landscape of Los Angeles was envisioned – and has been much analyzed – as an expression of individualism, class difference, and segregation. In its post-suburban phase, it has become something quite different: the terrain for social change. As the downtown makes its transition from redeveloped corporate citadel surrounded by skid row poverty and sweatshop industrial district to a gentrified urban playground, the diverse suburban expanses of the region gain significance as sites of everyday life and innovative civic politics.

The Los Angeles of the mid-twentieth century cemented an industrial suburbanization dominated by large builders of small homes. As Greg Morrow reminds us, only one third of Angelenos actually live currently in owner-occupied single-family houses.[50] While the large infrastructure projects – the LA River, the freeways, the ports, sports stadia and so much more – were never far away, the appearance of the bourgeois utopia of the subdivisions have crowded out all other representations of Los Angeles. The landscape that was built during the postwar decades also concretized the powerlines of race, class and gender in the Southland on a register of white privilege and white supremacy. As Laura Pulido once put it: 'In the case of Los Angeles … [b]ecause industrial land use is highly correlated with pollution concentrations and people of color, the crucial question becomes, how did whites distance themselves from both industrial pollution and nonwhites?'[51] The horizontal suburbanity of Los Angeles has continuously reproduced – and hidden – tremendous socio-economic and environmental inequities. A suburb in Los Angeles can be a privileged gated community or a polluted industrial district.[52]

Today, a different Los Angeles emerges but very similar questions continue to be asked. Once again Los Angeles has become a focus of progressive options in a general context of retrograde politics in a nation that shuts down against all things foreign and different. Among other things, a region often vilified as a bastion of white supremacy has become a leader in a growing municipal sanctuary movement that defends the rights of immigrants and refugees against sanctions by the federal government under the Trump administration.[53] A strong grassroots housing movement has recently challenged both the traditional preference for ground related home ownership in the Southland and the (tech industry supported) so-called YIMBY-movement (Yes In My Back Yard). YIMBY has been criticized for championing free market solutions that may lead to pressure on communities of colour and enable land grabs in poor neighbourhoods.[54] The progressive movement and civic culture in Los Angeles has been in the making for a generation, perhaps since the anti-plant closing struggles of the 1970s that ultimately spawned organizations such as the Labor/Community Strategy Center and the Bus Riders Union. Much of this organizing and many of these struggles have been linked to the particular extended urban form of Los Angeles. Activists have appropriately rephrased the slogan of the Right to the City into the Right to the Suburb.[55] And since the uprising of 1992 there has been a persistent shaping of an organizational infrastructure and an everyday politics that propelled labour, social justice, transit justice, and environmental organizations to the fore while neoliberalization and entrepreneurialism became the determining factors in Los Angeles's development.[56]

As Ananya Roy reminds us in a powerful commentary in which she channels the intellectual authority of W.E.B. Du Bois, we live in an era of reactionary (racial capitalist) reconstruction not unlike the reconstruction of capitalist power during the early years of the Cold War, after the impressive popular front openings that were created at the tail end of the Depression before the Second World War.[57] Like in the period from the late 1930s to the 1950s, we are now facing a backlash against institutions and movements of collective power. Housing stood out then and stands out now in the development of political alternatives. And the relationships of race and class are once again rearticulated in Los Angeles and elsewhere in the era of Trump.

There is no concluding verdict on what the public possibilities are in this private city. Dark ages are not made to last. Things can be turned around. For that to happen we need to learn from mistakes without abandoning the project of building a better society. The lessons we learn from Parson's mid-century Los Angeles and from the projects that carried its utopias forward need to be drawn honestly and in a productive fashion. Erik Swyngedouw has reflected on this dark age that, in his words, is also a post-political age, an age with apparently little space for emancipatory politics. The 'specter of a once existing but failed communism' of the twentieth century, which Swyngedouw describes,[58] and the formidable counter-revolutionary forces that helped defeat it are present in the histories of mid-century Los Angeles. Perhaps, then, there is also hope that a revived 'communist hypothesis' might be the right recipe for finding a new politics of emancipation: 'Communism as an idea manifests itself concretely each time people come together in-common, not only to demand equality, to demand their place within the edifice of state and society, but also to stage their capacity for self-organization and self-management, and to enact the democratic promise, thereby changing the frame of what is considered possible and revolutionizing the very parameters of state and government, while putting tentatively and experimentally new organizational forms in their place.'[59]

Los Angeles is a harbinger of the world in which we will live. The suburban planet on which we now reside, work, and play challenges us to rethink once again the terrain and the theatre, the scene and the off-scene from which we construct different futures. For mid-twentieth century Italian Marxist Amadeo Bordiga, 'Capitalism [was] verticality. Communism will be "horizontality"'.[60] As we are hurtling into a completely urbanized future – which I have been positing is an extended urban future – we need to come to terms with the past, present, and emergent suburbanity of our lives. The Lefebvrian projection of planetary urbanization has immediate consequences for the possibility of humans to exit their prehistory. It is, for starters, the precondition for the abolition of the contradiction of city and countryside. This means accordingly, following Bordiga, that complete urbanization is ultimately the conceptual opposite of the megaurbanization engendered by global capitalism: Post-capitalist possibilities must lie beyond the city as centrality: 'The revolutionary fight for the destruction of the dreadful tentacular urban agglomerations can be so defined: communist oxygen versus capitalist cesspool. Space versus cement ... What causes the race toward density is the requirements of the mode of capitalist production that inexorably pushes always farther its prospecting of labour within the masses.'[61]

If we imagine the emerging horizontal landscape of today's suburban planet as the terrain of the political, as the launching pad for a post-capitalist future, we need to revolutionize our perspective. This envisioned revolution in our patterns of settlement and daily life rocks the landscape of the sub/ urban planet to its foundation. It gets us back to the notion of contradiction as evoked at the start of this essay. Lefebvre displayed a healthy ambiguity vis-à-vis the urban revolution. He realized that what globalizing capitalism has left us is a landscape of deep contradiction. Under capitalism we already see the dissolution of the contradiction of the city and the countryside. Here is Lefebvre, once more reading Marx and Engels on the history of urbanization:

> Suburban areas, half-town, half-country (that is, neither town nor country), arise from this pressure. The owner of a plot of land imagines himself to be a rural landowner, the owner of a fragment of nature. But he is neither peasant nor citizen. Urbanization extends to the countryside but is degraded and degrading. Rather than the city absorbing and reducing the countryside, we have a kind of reciprocal degradation: the city explodes into outlying areas and the village deteriorates; an uncertain urban fabric proliferates throughout the entire country. A shapeless magma is the result: slums and metastasized cities.[62]

It is a landscape rife with difficulty yet also with the possibility of a planetary society and politics. In yet another context, AbdouMaliq Simone has spoken about a 'new era of geographies' of emerging urban worlds outside of the West.[63] As our suburban planet gets more populated, our perspectives need swift readjustments. And, of course, the building of cities and suburbs as projects of revolution or reform, whether escapist in small intentional communities, or in the perverted forms of modernist massive housing in the twentieth century, have in reality often been part of the same colonial and settler narrative.[64] This needs correction.

So, can there be communism in the suburbs? Perhaps we need to be more modest. As Amanda Kolson Hurley has reminded us in an important new book on *Radical Suburbs*, in which she reviews alternative suburban projects in the eastern United States during the twentieth century:

> Utopia is, by definition, not achievable. But all of these experiments succeeded to a degree that may come as a surprise. They represent real, viable challenges to what can still seem like immovable pillars of suburban life: the traditional single-family home, the self-sufficient nuclear family, racial and economic segregation, and the stark separation of residential from nonresidential spaces.[65]

So, maybe not communism, just bits and pieces of collectivism, communalism, cooperatives, and commonwealth, perhaps a bit of the 'urban commons' that are on a lot of people's mind these days.[66] Focusing on the problematique of pervasive suburbanization may also be our best chance to deal with a warming planet.[67] Kolson Hurley concludes her study with the insight that 'many suburbs are palimpsests of successive communities that have been forgotten – especially if they were informal and/or non-white communities. A lot of suburban history no doubt remains to be written.'[68] This essay, then, is at its minimum an appeal to not forget the progress we made and the possibilities that remain. The communist hypothesis remains alive in this sense.

On this note, we finally return to the desert outside of Los Angeles which is still full of utopian potential. Noah Purifoy, African American assemblage artist and first director of the iconic Watts Towers Arts Center in South Central Los Angeles, moved to Yucca Valley in the high desert in 1989 and produced, until he died in 2004, a remarkable body of work that is now exhibited in the Noah Purifoy Outdoor Art Museum of Assemblage Art. Strolling through the grounds on a sunny April afternoon in 2019, admiring the transgressive humanity of Purifoy's pieces, surrounded by hipster millennials returning from the simultaneous Coachella music festival, we channel the ghost of Llano del Rio and the spirit of Don Parson, whose vision of a Public Los Angeles and a better world coincide in the desert dust.

NOTES

This essay is based on the prefatory material I wrote for a book I co-edited with Judy Branfman, *Don Parson: Public Los Angeles: A Private City's Activist Futures*, Athens: University of Georgia Press, 2019. I also draw on recent articles: 'The empty shell of the planetary: re-rooting the urban in the experience of the urbanites', *Urban Geography*, 10(39), 2018, pp. 1589-1602; 'Extended urbanization, "disjunct fragments" and global suburbanisms', *Environment and Planning D: Society and Space*, 36(3), 2018, pp. 494–511.

1   Mike Davis, *City of Quartz: Excavating the Future in Los Angeles*, London: Verso, 1990.
2   Richard Harris and Ute Lehrer, eds., *The Suburban Land Question: A Global Survey*, Toronto: University of Toronto Press, 2018.
3   See: Dolores Hayden and Alice Constance Austin, *Pioneering Women of American Architecture*, available at pioneeringwomen.bwaf.org; Don Parson, 'Housing is a Labor Process', in Keil and Branfman, eds., *Don Parson: Public Los Angeles: A Private City's Activist Futures*, Athens: University of Georgia Press, Chapter 5.
4   Greg Goldin, 'Ben Margolis and Gregory Ain: A Meeting of Radical Minds,' in Keil and Branfman, eds., *Don Parson: Public Los Angeles*, Chapter 9..
5   Don Parson, 'A Mecca for the Unfortunate', in Keil and Branfman, eds., *Don Parson: Public Los Angeles*, p. 48.
6   See for instance: Tim Arango and Adam Nagaourney, 'A Paper Tears Apart in a City That Never Quite Came Together', *New York Times,* 30 January 2018; An excellent embedded summary of reactions can be found in the weblinks of Christopher Hawthorne, 'Los Angeles, Houston and the Appeal of the Hard to Read City', *Los Angeles Times*, 8 February 2018.
7   Laura Pulido, Laura Barraclough, and Wendy Cheng, *A People's Guide to Los Angeles*, Berkeley: University of California Press, 2012.
8   Ibid., p. 13.
9   Steven Logan, 'Learning from the Socialist Suburb', in K. Murat Güney, Roger Keil, and Murat Üçoğlu, eds., *Massive Suburbanization: (Re)Building the Global Periphery*, Toronto: University of Toronto Press, 2019, pp. 94–110; Douglas Young, 'Decline and Renewal in Toronto's High-Rise Suburbs: The Tragedy of Progressive Neoliberalism,' in Güney, Keil, and Üçoğlu, eds., *Massive Suburbanization*, pp. 111-25.
10 Henri Lefebvre, cited in Tom McDonough, 'Invisible Cities: Henri Lefebvre's *The Explosion*', *Artforum*, May 2008; Stefan Kipfer, '(De)Constructing Housing Estates: How Much More than a Housing Question?', in Güney, Keil, and Üçoğlu, eds., *Massive Suburbanization*, pp. 142-64.
11 Kacper Pobłocki, 'Suburbanization of the Self: Religious Revival and Socio-Spatial Fragmentation in Contemporary Poland,' *International Journal of Urban and Regional Research*, forthcoming.
12 Rohan Quinby, *Time and the Suburbs: The Politics of Built Environments and the Future of Dissent*, Winnipeg: Arbeiter Ring Publishing, 2011.
13 Henri Lefebvre, *Marxist Thought and the City*, Minneapolis: University of Minnesota Press, 2016, p. 117.
14 Güney, Keil, and Üçoğlu, eds., *Massive Suburbanization*.
15 Henri Lefebvre, *The Urban Revolution*, Minneapolis: University of Minnesota Press, 2003, p. 14.
16 Lefebvre, *Marxist Thought*, p. 148.
17 Roger Keil, *Suburban Planet: Making the World Urban From the Outside In*, Cambridge: Polity, 2018.
18 Güney, Keil, and Üçoğlu, *Massive Suburbanization*.
19 Roger Keil, *Los Angeles: Globalization, Urbanization and Social Struggles*. Chichester: Wiley, 1998.
20 Paul Beatty, *The Sellout*, New York: Picador, 2015, p. 78.
21 Roger Keil, 'The Empty Shell of the Planetary: Re-Rooting the Urban in the Experience of the Urbanites', Urban Geography, 39(10), 2018, pp. 2-3.

22   Karl Marx and Friedrich Engels, 'Excerpts from the German Ideology', in Lewis S. Feuer, ed., *Marx & Engels: Basic Writings on Politics and Philosophy*, New York: Anchor Books, 1959, p. 257.

23   Karl Marx, *The German Ideology*, 1845, available at: www.marxists.org.

24   Margaret Kohn, *The Death and Life of the Urban Commonwealth*, Oxford: Oxford University Press, 2016.

25   Norman M. Klein, *The History of Forgetting: Los Angeles and the Erasure of Memory*, London: Verso, 1997.

26   Michael Nevin Willard, 'Nuestra Los Angeles,' *American Quarterly*, 56(3)(September 2004), p. 814.

27   Jane Jacobs, *The Death and Life of Great American Cities*, New York: Modern Library, 1993, p. 95.

28   Edward W. Soja, *Seeking Spatial Justice*, Minneapolis: University of Minnesota Press, 2010, pp. 44-6.

29   Edward W. Soja, *Thirdspace: Journeys to Los Angeles and Other Real-and-Imagined Places*, Oxford: Blackwell, 1996.

30   Ananya Roy, 'The 21st-Century Metropolis: New Geographies of Theory', *Regional Studies*, 43(6), 2009, pp. 819–30.

31   Anton Wagner, *Los Angeles: Werden, Leben und Gestalt der Zweimillionenstadt in Südkalifornien*, Leipzig: Bibliographisches Institut, 1935.

32   Reyner Banham, *Los Angeles: The Architecture of Four Ecologies*, Harmondsworth: Pelican, 1971.

33   Davis, *City of Quartz*.

34   Michael Dear and Nicholas Dahman, 'Urban Politics and the Los Angeles School of Urbanism', in Dennis Judd and Dick Simpson, eds., *The City Revisited: Urban Theory from Chicago, Los Angeles, New York*, Minneapolis: University of Minnesota Press, 2011, p. 74.

35   Martin Murray, *The Urbanism of Exception: The Dynamics of Global City Building in the Twenty-First Century*, Cambridge: Cambridge University Press, 2017.

36   Renaud Le Goix, *Sur le front de la métropole: Une géographie suburbaine de Los Angeles*, Paris: Publications de la Sorbonne, 2016.

37   Charles Hoch, 'Municipal Contracting in California: Privatizing With Class', *UAQ*, 20, 1985, pp. 303-323; Edward Soja, 'Los Angeles, 1965-1992,' in Edward Soja and Allen Scott, *The City: Los Angeles and Urban Theory at the End of the Twentieth Century*, Berkeley: University of California Press, 1996, pp. 426-62.

38   Jamie Peck, 'Chicago-School Suburbanism,' in Pierre Hamel and Roger Keil, eds., *Suburban Governance: A Global View*, Toronto: University of Toronto Press, 2015; Paul L. Knox, *Metroburbia, USA*, New Jersey: Rutgers University Press, 2008.

39   Dear and Dahman, 'Urban Politics'.

40   Derek Brunelle and Roger Keil, 'Changing the Suburban Terrain: Narrative and material struggles in the Los Angeles region,' in Jan Nijman, ed., *The Life of North American Suburbs*, Toronto: University of Toronto Press, forthcoming; Genevieve Carpio, Clara Irazabal, Laura Pulido, 'Right to the Suburb? Rethinking Lefebvre and Immigrant Activism', *Journal of Urban Affairs* 33(2), 2011, pp. 185-208; Eric Mann, *Taking on General Motors: A Case Study of the UAW Campaign to Keep GM Van Nuys Open*, Los Angeles: Center for Labor Research and Education, Institute of Industrial Relations, UCLA, 1987.

41   Reinhold Martin, Leah Meisterlin, and Anna Kenoff, *The Buell Hypothesis: Rehousing the American Dream*, New York: The Temple Hoyne Buell Center for the Study of American Architecture, 2011.

42   Scott Allard and Benjamin Roth, 'Strained Suburbs: The Social Service Challenges of Rising Suburban Poverty', Brookings Institute, 2010, available at: www.brookings.edu.

43   Robert Fishman, 'Foreword', in Robert Fogelson, *The Fragmented Metropolis* Cambridge: Harvard University Press, [1967] 1993, p. xviii.

44   Enrico A. Marcelli, 'From the Barrio to the 'Burbs: Immigration and the Dynamics of Suburbanization', in Jennifer Wolch, Manuel Pastor, Jr, and Peter Dreier, eds., *Up Against the Sprawl: Public Policy and the Making of Southern California*, Minneapolis: University of Minnesota Press, 2004, p. 142.

45   Wei Li, 'Anatomy of a New Ethnic Settlement: The Chinese Ethnoburb in Los Angeles', *Urban Studies* 35(3), 1998, pp. 479-501; Doug Saunders, *Arrival City: The Final Migration and Our Next World*, Toronto: Alfred A. Knopf, 2010.

46   Colin Marshall, 'The Gentrification of Skid Row – A Story That Will Decide the Future of Los Angeles', *The Guardian*, 5 March 2015.

47   Elizabeth Kneebone, 'Ferguson, Mo.: Emblematic of Growing Suburban Poverty', *The Avenue*, 15 August 2014, available at www.brookings.edu.

48   Keil, *Los Angeles: Globalization, Urbanization and Social Struggles*.

49   Mike Davis, *Ecologies of Fear*, London: Verso, 1998; Gene Desfor and Roger Keil, *Nature and the City: Making Urban Environmental Policy in Toronto and Los Angeles*, Tuscon: University of Arizona Press, 2004.

50   Greg D. Morrow, 'How to Make Los Angeles More Affordable and More Livable', *Los Angeles Times*, 24 July 2015.

51   Laura Pulido, 'Rethinking Environmental Racism: White Privilege and Urban Development in Southern California', *Annals of the Association of American Geographers*, 90(1), 2000, p. 14; Laura Pulido, 'Geographies of Race and Ethnicity 1: White supremacy vs White Privilege in Environmental Racism Research', *Progress in Human Geography*, 39(6), 2015, pp. 809-17.

52   Christopher G Boone and Ali Modarres, 'Creating a Toxic Neighborhood in Los Angeles County: A Historical Examination of Environmental Inequity', *Urban Affairs Review* 35(2), November 1999, pp. 163-87.

53   Ruben Vives, 'California "Sanctuary Cities" Vow to Stand Firm Despite Trump Threats of Funding Cutoff', *Los Angeles Times*, 25 January 2017.

54   LA Tenants Union, 'Dropping the Hammer on YIMBYism', *Medium*, 19 March 2019; for California more generally, see: Toshio Meronek, 'YIMBYs Exposed: the Techies Hawking Free Market "Solutions" to the Nation's Housing Crisis', *In These Times*, 21 May 2018.

55   Carpio et al., op.cit.

56   Julie-Anne Boudreau, *Global Urban Politics*, Cambridge: Polity Press, 2017; Laura Pulido, *Black, Brown, Yellow, and Left: Radical Activism in Los Angeles Berkeley and Los Angeles*, Berkeley: University of California Press, 2006.

57   Ananya Roy, 'Divesting from Whiteness: The University in the Age of Trumpism', *Society + Space*, 2016, available at: societyandspace.org; W.E.B. Du Bois, *Black Reconstruction in America: An Essay Toward a History of the Part Which Black Folk Played in the Attempt to Reconstruct Democracy in America, 1860-1880*, Oxford: Oxford University Press, 1935 [2007].

58   Erik Swyngedouw, *Promises of the Political: Insurgent Cities in a Post-Political Environment*, Cambridge: MIT Press, 2018, p. 167.
59   Ibid., p. 168.
60   Amadeo Bordiga, 'Space versus Cement', in *Espèce humaine et croûte terrestre*, Translated by Nathan Schaffer, Paris: Payot, 1978.
61   Ibid.
62   Lefebvre, *Marxist Thought and the City,* p. 140.
63   AbdouMaliq Simone, *For the City Yet to Come: Changing African Life in Four Cities*, Durham: Duke University Press, 2004.
64   Roger Keil, 'Canadian Suburbia: From the Periphery of Empire to the Frontier of the Sub/Urban Century', *Zeitschrift für Kanada-Studien*, 38, 2018, pp. 47-64
65   Amanda Kolson Hurley, *Radical Suburbs: Experimental Living on the Fringes of the American City*, Cleveland: Belt Publishing, 2019, p. 22.
66   Mary Dellenbaugh, Markus Kip, Majken Bieniok, Agnes Katharina Müller, and Martin Schwegmann, eds., *Urban Commons: Moving Beyond State and Market*. Basel: Birkhäuser, 2015.
67   Samuel Alexander and Brendan Gleeson, *Degrowth in the Suburbs: A Radical Urban Imaginary*, Singapore: Palgrave Macmillan, 2019; Roger Keil, 'Paved Paradise: the Suburb as Chief Artefact of the Anthropocene and Terrain of New Political Performativities', in Henrik Ernstson and Erik Swyngedouw, eds., *Urban Political Ecology in the Anthropo-obscene: Interruptions and Possibilities*, London: Routledge, 2018, pp. 165-83.
68   Kolson Hurley, *Radical Suburbs*, p. 159.

THE RETROACTIVE UTOPIA
OF THE SOCIALIST CITY

OWEN HATHERLEY

In the centre of contemporary Manchester, you can find two artefacts of the Soviet Union's attempt to fuse art, architecture and everyday life. One of them is now fairly well known. Standing in the newly created Tony Wilson Square, a developer-owned 'Private Public Space' standing in front of the arts centre 'Home', facing various new luxury office and residential units, is a statue of Friedrich Engels. It was brought to Manchester, the city which Engels worked in for many decades and which provided the model for his and Marx's analysis of advanced industrial capitalism, by the artist Phil Collins – but it originally stood in Mala Pereshchipina, a village outside of the central Ukrainian city of Poltava. It wasn't the first time that Manchester tried to acquire a Soviet statue of Engels. In the early 1990s, the city council, which was running an exhibition of Soviet art at the time, asked its twin town of St Petersburg, then starting to denude itself of Communist statuary, for one, but was told that unfortunately there were no statues of Engels in Soviet Leningrad. So Collins, for an exhibition inaugurating the new gallery at Home, decided to salvage one of the many casualties of Ukraine's state-directed 'Decommunisation' campaign.[1] When the statue was installed in Manchester, a rally was organised by Collins, and Gruff Rhys performed a song entitled 'Communism's Coming Home'. Watching this on YouTube, it is hard not to be a little moved – the bright-eyed, mainly young audience, gleeful at seeing this monument to international socialism placed in this deeply capitalistic city. But there's no getting the taste out of your mouth – this is the result of the total destruction of the left in the places where the Great October Proletarian Socialist Revolution actually happened, and here, it's a bauble, albeit a potentially subversive one, atop yet another space of corporate consumption, speculation, and leisure in England's second city.

And the statue? Well, it appears to be standard-issue stuff of the long Brezhnev era, from which so many Soviet statues date, though it is interesting how little of the commentary on its moving to Manchester has to say about who designed it or when – somehow it just 'happened'. So it is clear and figurative, as most Soviet sculpture was from the late 1920s onwards when 'Socialist Realism' became the government-sanctioned style, but it also partakes of the post-Khrushchev 'severe style'. From the fifties on, sculptors started to engage again with the (by then quite established) avant-garde, borrowing the abstracted approach to the human body found in the work of Parisian exiles from the Russian Empire, like Jacques Lipchitz or Osip Zadkine. So the plinth, the beard, the facial features, and the frock coat are all chopped from the granite into sharp angles. Vladimir Tatlin's 'Monument to the Third International' was intended when proposed as an alternative to figurative statues of great socialists. Instead, it was the abstract personification of international socialism: an open, tilting, cylindrical steel tower with dialectical rotating offices for the Comintern. Vladimir Mayakovsky called it 'the first monument without a beard'. The USSR would erect very many monuments with beards, and they stood in most urban squares, glowering over the populace.

To see a monument without a beard, you need walk fifteen minutes up Deansgate and turn off into the People's History Museum. This riverside building, hemmed in by speculative offices and an enormous plate glass and steel Civil Justice Centre, contains the archives of the Labour Party, the Communist Party of Great Britain, and numerous trade unions. A regularly renewed permanent exhibition shows these to the public. The rooms on the post-war, pre-Thatcher decades contain a particularly unusual trade union banner. There are many of these on show, and for all their colour and visual richness, they stay, right up until the 1990s, in a realistic, ornate Arts and Crafts style that could be called Socialist Realism were it not for the fact that the term conjures up more aggressive and angular artworks, such as Mala Pereshchipina's Engels statue. Then you'll chance upon a banner from the famous Grunwick Strike of 1976-78, when the mainly Asian and female workforce of a photo-processing plant in west London walked out over their particularly poor pay and conditions. Seen as a test case for industrial power by both the Conservative Party's far-right outliers, such as the National Association For Freedom, and by flying pickets reinforcing it from the far-left, led by Arthur Scargill, and unique for the time as a major strike led by Asian women, it is one of the pivotal moments in British working-class history – and one which would be hard to represent in the Victorian idiom of the average union banner. The Grunwick banner is credited to 'Jayandi, painted with Vipin Magdani', who are described as 'workers at the Grunwick factory'.[2] The acronyms 'APEX' (the union the Grunwick workers were part of) and 'TGWU' appear on a red sphere, surrounded with swirling red, grey, black abstract shapes on a white background; these charge forward, with a white polygon that features the words 'GRUNWICK STRIKE COMMITTEE', into a black wedge, with the slogan 'DEFEND THE RIGHT TO STRIKE' below, on a black empty space.

Anyone who knows a bit of twentieth-century art history will recognise the source for the banner – the 'Suprematist' strain in early Soviet avant-garde art. Driven by the almost cult-leader-like figure of Kasimir Malevich, with major contributions coming from the architect El Lissitzky, Suprematists imagined a Cosmic Communist future that could be prefigured in the free-floating, surging abstract space of their canvases. Eager to contribute to the revolutionary effort, they would design everything from posters and clothes to plates and cups, and, eventually, buildings. The most famous of their images in left-wing politics is El Lissitzky's Bolshevik civil war poster 'Beat the Whites with the Red Wedge' (1920), and the People's History Museum credits this as inspiration, although it looks to my eyes more like a creative response to that poster than one of the very many copies. But the most important thing is this: British Asian women involved in one of the pivotal strikes in British history turned to the revolutionary Russian avant-garde in order to represent and propagandise their struggle. Here, although little more de facto than an exhibit in a museum, is all the truly world-transformative potential of that moment in one image, used nearly sixty years later, in a totally different context, but for the same essential aims. In both of these artefacts, the ghosts of Soviet socialism linger in a contemporary capitalist city. But these are only two examples of the extremely widespread proliferation and penetration of Soviet ideas on art, architecture, and the city that have spread across such urban environments over the last fifty years. The (re)discovery of the Soviet avant-garde – which eventually meant that a striking worker in Dollis Hill in 1976 could know who El Lissitzky was, and create an image based around his – is a complex story of misunderstandings and appropriations. This essay will try and trace how these fed into British life in particular, mainly through art history – and will follow the spread of these ideas to the point where they've become sources for everything from the Anti-Nazi League to the arts buildings of the United Arab Emirates. Finally, we will ask whether these are just floating signifiers that can be used by pretty much anybody – or if there is still something inherently revolutionary in the ideas of the socialist city.

WHAT WAS THE SOCIALIST CITY?

The story of Soviet architecture and urbanism is convoluted, but can be told in its essentials in a few paragraphs. In the first decade after the revolution, relatively little was built, but academic debate was fervent from Tatlin's 'Monument to the Third International' onwards. There was particular contention between the Constructivists and the Rationalists – both committed to Soviet socialism and to a version of Taylorism and Fordism, but with greater emphasis on functionalism and links with trends in the west such as the Bauhaus in the former, and upon form in the latter, who also had a keen interest in gestalt psychology. In terms of what was actually built, the NEP-era Soviet state preferred to give town planning and engineering commissions to proven pre-revolutionary professionals like Alexei Shchusev in Moscow or Alexander Tamanyan in Yerevan, both of which oversaw essentially nineteenth-century plans in the 1920s. But in fact, many workers' clubs, houses of culture, small housing schemes, garages, and in some places, like then-Ukrainian capital Kharkiv, entire government complexes were awarded to the avant-garde, who were then taking the dynamic abstractions previously only on canvas and adapting them to the needs of modern, functional public buildings. This moved to another level with the announcement of the first Five Year Plan, which called for building dozens of new towns, new factories, new suburbs, and new public buildings.

Initially, this saw a huge rise in commissions for Soviet modernist architects, as they were expected to plan these new settlements. But it also led to a decisive splintering, as various extravagant utopian plans – from the high-rise super-communes in the 'Urbanism' of Leonid Sabsovich, to the American-style 'Disurbanism' of single-family or even single-person houses and mass-car ownership advocated by the one-time left oppositionist Mikhail Okhitovich, and the ultra-Taylorist Linear City devised by Nikolai Milyutin, the head of the People's Commissariat of Finance – were supplemented even before 1933 by more pragmatic but still strongly modernist master plans by émigrés from increasingly far-right Germany, such as Ernst May, planner of Frankfurt, Bruno Taut, architect of Berlin's social housing estates, and the former Bauhaus director Hannes Meyer. The tension between Soviet architects rose into bitter polemics, with a new 'Proletarian' group (whose architecture was basically modernism plus monumental sculpture) attacking the Rationalists, the Constructivists, and the Classicists, and relying heavily on implicit and explicit state backing. This ended in 1932, when the various associations were wound up into a single Union of Soviet Architects, and a neoclassical skyscraper with a giant Lenin on top won an international competition for a Palace of the Soviets.

Then, a 'Socialist Realist' architecture was mandated. Although often compared with the work of architects under German or Italian Fascism – with some justification, due to its domineering scale and obvious intent to represent and enforce absolute power – there are significant differences. One is sheer quantity, as this period – at least twenty years, from 1934 to 1956 – happened to coincide with the industrialisation and urbanisation of the USSR, and with the bulk of reconstruction after the almost unquantifiable destruction of the Great Patriotic War. This architecture, much of which was designed by former adherents of the avant-garde, would shift in its emphases as time went on. Post-war projects are particularly opulent, decorative, and stupefyingly vast, but they tend to combine a certain avant-garde sense of revolutionary surging and striving with a nineteenth-century approach to the city – all grand boulevards, pompous monuments, heavy materials, and obligatory heroic sculpture. This in turn was sharply and suddenly rejected under Khrushchev, leading to a re-engagement with what was now seen as a 'western' modern architecture, which had in fact drawn extensively on the Soviet design of the twenties. Glass skyscrapers, mass-produced concrete housing and so forth emerged at a rapid rate, and from the mid-seventies onwards was supplemented by a more nationalistic and monumental version of these trends – a sort of fusion of modern and 'Socialist Realist' ideas. The Gorbachev years were defined by scattered experiments in Postmodernism and by dystopian, fantastical 'paper architecture'. On the collapse, very few people had much that was complimentary to say about this massive experiment in building cities without landlords or property owners.

It is also worth noting that in English-speaking countries, very little of this was widely publicised and discussed at the time it was actually happening (though there was much more extensive engagement in Germany, the Netherlands, and Eastern Europe before the war, and in France and Italy after it). The genre of books where intellectuals and professionals toured 'the great experiment' frequently involved a stop at a Constructivist workers club, factory kitchen, or house of culture, something which became prevalent enough for Orwell to specifically mention the doubtful propaganda value in Britain of the widely circulated images of the Dnieper Dam in Zaporizhia, Ukraine, a co-production between American engineers and the Constructivist architects, the Vesnin brothers. A special issue of *Architectural Review* involved a survey of Soviet architecture and planning by Party loyalist émigré Berthold Lubetkin, written in strikingly Marxist language for its time and place. Of course, Communist Party publications showcased the Moscow Metro and similarly grandiose projects, but it's a fact that – despite the rather McCarthyite language with which they were still denounced in Reyner Banham's 1966 book *The New Brutalism* – the many Communist architects and planners in post-war Britain modelled their work on Stockholm and Copenhagen, not Moscow and Kyiv. Meanwhile, aside from some scattered translations in the US – such as the collaborative utopian project *The Ideal Communist City*, a late product of the Khrushchev Thaw[3] – there was extremely little interest in the west at the shift back towards modernism in Soviet architecture. This means that the engagement with the Soviet socialist city has mostly been retroactive, and so has almost always been, from quite early on, a matter of recording and lamenting a great idea destroyed, many decades before its actual demise in 1991. This would gradually become something more conscious – a retroactive utopia.

RESUSCITATING THE GREAT EXPERIMENT

Uncovering this retroactive utopia involved, first of all, finding out that it existed in the first place. Many of the most widely read books on modernism published in English, for instance, simply ignored the Russian and Soviet contribution altogether. It is almost wholly absent from Nikolaus Pevsner's *Pioneers of Modern Design* (1936) and Herbert Read's *Art Now* in the same year, which likely reflects both a desire to detoxify what was widely regarded by the right as 'cultural Bolshevism' and a rejection of modernism within the Stalinist USSR itself. But the publication in 1962 of the British art historian Camilla Gray's *The Great Experiment: Russian Art 1863-1922*, and her exhibitions on El Lissitzky and Kasimir Malevich, reintroduced these largely forgotten artists (who were being rediscovered within the USSR at the same time). And in 1971, the Hayward Gallery exhibition *Art and Revolution*, which Gray had largely organised, was the most complete picture of what actually happened in art and architecture between 1917 and 1932 that had been staged anywhere up to that point. It also involved the first reconstruction of Vladimir Tatlin's 'Monument to the Third International', the first of several which would be built around the world in retrospective exhibitions, as satire, and as part of a quixotic project to actually build the thing, piece by piece. Of nearly equal importance to Gray were the voluminous publications of the designer David King. A member of the Workers Revolutionary Party in the UK, his edited books on Soviet art, photography and crafts, a huge documentary monograph on Trotsky, research on the purges, and commissioned cover designs for books by everyone from Solzhenitsyn to Trotsky, all decisively brought the ideas and motifs of Lissitzky, Malevich, Rodchenko, Stepanova, et al. into circulation on the British left, particularly through his Rodchenkoesque designs for the posters and publications of the Anti-Nazi League in the late 1970s.[4]

Much of the reception of this work came specifically through a filter of Communist politics, albeit of a fairly unorthodox sort. In France, this was seen particularly through the Marxist Anatole Kopp's detailed, thoroughly researched *Town and Revolution*, published in 1967 and translated into English three years later. But the engagement with this moment in British architectural culture was convoluted, beginning with partial, barely understood recognition that something important happened here – without knowing exactly what it was – and then shifting into utopian speculation. The earliest attempt to write the Soviets back into architectural history came in Reyner Banham's 1960 *Theory and Design in the First Machine Age*. His primary interest was to restore the position of Italian Futurism in the history of modern architecture and the modern city. Accordingly, he brings in the 'Wesnin Brothers (sic) and El Lissitzky' as 'sophisticated descendants of Sant'Elia's town planning ideas',[5] and credits Lissitsky as 'one of the great "ideas-men" of the Modern Movement', a 'species of ambassador at large of a new Soviet culture that appeared to many at that time almost as Futurism made fact'.[6] His references to these figures come almost entirely from German or Dutch magazines such as *G* or *De Stijl*, with a glancing reference at the El Lissitzky and Ilya Ehrenberg-edited bilingual Soviet-French-German journal *Veshch-Gegenstand-Objet,* but overlook the Soviet avant-garde's own publications, such as *Art of the Commune, Lef* or *SA*; he incorrectly claims that Lissitzky's neologism *Proun* (a mock Bolshevik portmanteau, condensing 'project for the affirmation of the new') is merely a Russian word for object. He also gives some prominence to the Gosprom building in Kharkiv, the extremely dramatic avant-garde headquarters of the Ukrainian Soviet Socialist Republic, but he calls it the 'State Industry Building', and credits it as one of only two 'extreme' buildings 'to rival, or exceed, the scale of the Bauhaus buildings'.[7] That noted, Banham's rediscovery of the buildings of the time, paralleled by the researches of Alison and Peter Smithson in the magazine *Architectural Design*, would see motifs borrowed from the Soviets recur in much Brutalist architecture. One of the iconic buildings of this trend, James Gowan and James Stirling's Engineering Building at the University of Leicester, has two features directly taken from Soviet buildings of the 1920s: a cylindrical glass stairwell projecting from the main facade, taken from the 1929 Moscow Planetarium by Mikhail Barshch, and an angular cantilevered lecture theatre, similarly clearly borrowed from Konstantin Melnikov's Rusakov Workers Club of 1927.

Some, if not all, of this would be corrected by later histories that had the benefit of reading Camilla Gray and Anatole Kopp's much better researched work. The Marxian architect and historian Kenneth Frampton's 1980 *Modern*

Architecture: A Critical History was the first widely read survey of twentieth-century architecture and urbanism to treat it in serious depth. There is a cogent account of its failures, as well. Frampton argues that 'the historical circumstances were such that the people were largely incapable of adopting the way of life posited by the socialist intelligentsia. Furthermore, the failure of the architectural avant-garde to match their visionary proposals with adequate levels of technical performance led to their loss of credibility with the authorities.' As an analysis of how the avant-garde fell out of favour, this has the benefit of avoiding heroism or demonology, though he ends with the more questionable claim that the avant-garde's:

> appeal to an international socialist culture was clearly antithetical to Soviet policy after 1925, when Stalin announced the decision to 'build socialism in one country'. That Stalin had no use whatsoever for elitist internationalism was officially confirmed by Anatole Lunacharsky's nationalist and populist cultural slogan of 1932, his famous 'pillars for the people', which effectively committed Soviet architecture to a regressive form of historicism from which it has yet to emerge.[8]

There are two curious things happening here. One is that the analysis of what went wrong in the Soviet city owes much a great deal to Berthold Lubetkin's reminisces, published in the early fifties in the *Architectural Association Journal* despite the fact that Lubetkin had not been involved in Soviet architecture for decades. And it makes the extraordinary claim that Soviet architecture had not emerged from historicism in 1980, when in fact it had shifted back to modern architecture at least two decades previously, and had rehoused a huge proportion of the population in far from historicist mass-produced modern housing.

After Frampton, the engagement with the Soviet avant-garde in architecture and architectural history goes in two distinct paths. One is driven by a particular kind of left-wing melancholia, where the 'Great Experiment' that was quashed by Stalin is an example of the inevitable tragedy of the avant-garde and its inherent inability to realise its utopia in a non-utopian context. In this category we could put the work of the Italian Communist and architectural historian Manfredo Tafuri. His work was widely translated and read in the more intellectual circles of Anglo-American architecture in the 1970s and 1980s, and his longest engagement with the Soviet legacy comes in his two-volume *Modern Architecture* (1976), written with his more Eurocommunist colleague Francesco Dal Co. In terms of research, this goes way beyond the second-hand ideas in most British and American accounts. Tafuri and Dal Co visited and documented Soviet buildings, and read where possible the original publications and manifestos. Because of this, they give for the first time a serious account of what was actually *built* before Stalinism, giving full credit to real completed buildings in how Ilya Golosov and Konstantin Melnikov's workers clubs, the Gosprom complex in Kharkiv or the Pravda headquarters in Moscow, in the Moscow Planetarium, 'Soviet architecture created works of admirable quality'[9] – that is, they moved beyond the paper architecture with which they were usually credited. Moreover, Tafuri and Dal Co pointed out that the modernists seduced the eclectics into their orbit, for a time, with the traditional and classical architects designing in a Constructivist manner in the late 1920s and early 1930s. However, this is all in the service of an essentially tragic tale, where first, 'by appropriating the city to themselves, making it the object of collective celebration, the avant-garde was able to purge itself of its own anguish',[10] but they were inevitably crushed by the very forces they celebrated. And yet, reflecting their political commitments as (unorthodox) Italian Communists, they were quite dialectical on Stalinist planning. It is seen as a realistic, practicable response to the pipe dreams of the avant-garde, as successful propaganda where 'in the new monumental centers the working class must be led to admire the symbols of its own power',[11] and as a response to the multinational nature of the USSR, where the ornamental 'kitsch' was frequently an attempt to represent 'every ethnic group' in the Soviet Union through references to their local stylistic and building traditions.

The strangest and most creative reinterpretation of the utopian Soviet city came in the work of the London-based Dutch architect and teacher at the UK's venerable Architectural Association School of Architecture (AA), Rem Koolhaas. Among the tall tales in his semi-historical book *Delirious New York* (1978) is a parable entitled 'The Story of the Pool'. This uses an imaginary building project as a way of telling the story of the Soviet influence on modern architecture, its disappearance, and its return.

> MOSCOW, 1923: One day, a student designed a floating swimming pool. Nobody remembered who it was. The idea had been in the air. Others were designing flying cities, spherical theatres, whole artificial planets. Someone *had* to invent the floating swimming pool.[12]

The idea is a parody of Tatlin's 'Monument to the Third International', with a hint of another extravagant 1920s project, the Flying City of the architect Georgy Kriutikov – dialectical objects, free-floating in cosmic Communist space. 'The prototype became the most popular structure in the history of Modern Architecture', Koolhaas says, much as images of the 'Monument to the Third International' circulated the world over in the 1920s. Yet here, this process of circulation becomes one of outward movement. The architects/builders, who served as its lifeguards, found that if they swam together in the same direction, they could move the pool. This became useful during the shift to Stalinism, when 'an idea such as the pool, its shiftiness, its almost invisible physical presence, the iceberg-like quality of its submerged social activity, all these became suddenly subversive. In a secret meeting, the architects/lifeguards decided to use the pool as a vehicle for their escape to freedom'.[13] First they arrive at Wall Street and swim away, assuming from the uniform suits of the bankers that Stalinism has arrived there too; a few years later they return, and this time, the architectural historians know who they are – 'some quite famous, others long thought to have been exiled to Siberia – if not executed'. However, this is the late 1970s, during Postmodernism, with its sharp reaction to technocratic utopia of the Constructivists: 'The New Yorkers did not hesitate to criticise the design of the pool. They were all against Modernism now … they complained that the pool was so bland, so rectilinear, so boring: there were no historical allusions; there was no decoration.'[14]

Of course, this parable is an elaborate architectural joke, but it is serious in a sense. When considered with the rest of *Delirious New York*, with its prospective designs for Manhattan borrowed from the work of Constructivists like Ivan Leonidov, and with its semi-factual account of the influence upon Rockefeller's Radio City Music Hall of the kinetic, overwhelming architecture of Konstantin Melnikov, it forms part of what Koolhaas calls a 'Retroactive Manifesto' where Constructivism is severed from its complex and ambiguous engagement with Marxism-Leninism, its political compromises, its rooting in specifically Soviet history, and its ability to create actual useful buildings, and turned into a free-floating utopia of surrealist spectacle. This is what Koolhaas, and colleagues at the Architectural Association such as Zaha Hadid and Bernard Tschumi, would now proceed to build, primarily through the Rotterdam-based but internationally prestigious architectural firm, OMA (the Office for Metropolitan Architecture).

CONSTRUCTIVIST OLIGARCHITECTURE

In 1988, American architect and one-time fascist activist Philip Johnson organised an exhibition at the Museum of Modern Art in New York called *Deconstructivist Architecture*. This coinage came partly from Derrida, but also from the ever-increasing interest in Constructivism – increasingly becoming a catch-all term for any and all Soviet avant-garde architecture.

One irony of this is that Johnson was a pioneer in writing the USSR, and socialism more generally, out of the history of modern architecture. Many of the buildings that were sources for the exhibition came not from by now familiar sources such as Camilla Gray and Anatole Kopp, but from the two most important historians of Soviet architecture up to this point: the Soviet writer Selim Khan-Magomedov, and his colleague, the British critic, translator, and historian Catherine Cooke.[15] In the pages mainly of the London-based journal *Architectural Design*, these two had revealed not only the extent of actually constructed avant-garde architecture, but also a much larger quantity than hitherto realised of paper architecture, particularly in the form of the abstract spheres and pyramids and eerie utopian gridded disurbanist city plans of Ivan Leonidov – whose influence on Koolhaas we have already noted – and through the series of riotously colourful, whimsical, and exciting 'Fantasies' of the industrial architect Yakov Chernikhov. Many of these were placed in Johnson's exhibition, intended to stand as antecedents to the work of Koolhaas, Zaha Hadid, Frank Gehry, Coop Himmelb(l)au, Peter Eisenman, Daniel Libeskind and others. Cooke was scornful, pointing in 1989 through a guest-edited issue *Architectural Design* to the facile way in which the architects and curators approached the Soviet work, and how at the time 'a Russian connection was a sine qua non of fashionability in the USA', leading to a 'shape-spotting worthy of six-year olds'.[16]

But paradoxically, greater knowledge of the actual politics, theory, and working conditions of Soviet avant-garde architecture, with Cooke regularly publishing articles and translations throughout the 1980s, went alongside an all-consuming interest in its aesthetics. In the mid-1980s, an architect from an older generation than the AA 'Deconstructivists', Richard Rogers, pointed to Chernikhov as an influence on the new office block he had designed for Lloyds of London. But the Deconstructivists would mostly be paper architects themselves in the 1980s and 1990s, their work still far too dissonant and unsentimental to appeal to many clients in the Postmodernist period, with its longing for elaborate architectural jokes about the nineteenth century. It has only really been in the twenty-first century that these structures have been built in any great number. The work of Zaha Hadid began with a straightforward application of the ideas of Kasimir Malevich to a site in central London, at Hungerford Bridge, and continued to flit between painting and three-dimensional architectural planning throughout the 1980s and 1990s, in a visually hugely impressive digital and acrylic extension of the work of El Lissitzky into the computer age – while dropping all of the social ideas, without exception. When this generation began to build at large, the possibilities of the digital had taken over the analogue dialogue with the Soviets, but there are instances of explicit tribute. Hadid's Museum of Contemporary Art in Cincinnati and MAXXI in Rome are both unimaginable without the precedents of Malevich and Melnikov, respectively.[17] Bernard Tschumi's Parc la Vilette was an application of early Soviet paper architecture to the 'follies' of a canal side post-industrial reclamation scheme (and unlike most of its ilk, a public project). A lesser Dutch member of this cohort, Erick van Egeraat, even proposed a series of towers in Moscow called 'Avant-Garde', that would pay tribute in skyscraping form to four avant-garde painters, Kandinsky, Popova, Rodchenko, and Exter;[18] versions of these were built in drastically reduced form as part of the Moscow City central business district.

Many of these architects have deliberately avoided theorising what it is they are doing: as Cooke pointed out in 1989, they like the shapes, and the sophistication of their dialogue with their Soviet precursors does not go far beyond this. Koolhaas and others in his firm, the Office for Metropolitan Architecture (OMA), found in the 1970s a strain of extravagant, futuristic, kinetic, overwhelming spectacle in Soviet work of the 1920s, which he has consciously attempted to revive in the work of OMA. One can easily trace this concern with 'spectacle' into the 'iconic' architecture that most Deconstructivists found themselves building in the twenty-first century, where the jarring and exciting visual presence of huge and strange architectural objects is paramount for the success of the project. But there is more going on than this. In large-scale projects in China, such as the Shenzhen Stock Exchange or the CCTV building in Beijing, it's not hard to point to the specific *visual* sources of the buildings in early Soviet example. The extremely abstracted composition methods of Ivan Leonidov, and the combination of monumentality and weightlessness in El Lissitzky's 'Horizontal Skyscraper' proposals for 1920s Moscow are two obvious examples. But along with this is a specific theoretical and ethical inheritance of one of the main ideas of the Constructivist architects: the 'social condenser', where a refusal of 'zoning' between different functions (and by implication different classes) would be abolished in favour of dense spaces where disparate public functions – a cinema, a communal house, a gym, a library, an office, a radio station – would be brought together in the same structure through generous public circulation spaces.[19] This, applied at an urban scale, has been a watchword for OMA, something they have adapted into the *intensification* of congestion and visual conflict, rather than its amelioration or reduction. In theoretical work, such as the *Harvard Project on the City: Great Leap Forward* volume in 2001, this has been used as a way of explaining the urbanisation of contemporary China, particularly in the Pearl River Delta. In these buildings, the architects have found it in themselves to enjoy and revel in the sublimity, complexity, and surreal juxtapositions thrown up by the Dengist project of managed neoliberalism.

OMA, out of a combination of loyalty to their roots and an eye to a growth market, have retained a strong interest in the newly capitalist former USSR. Koolhaas was instrumental in setting up the Strelka School of Architecture in Moscow, which revived interest in the avant-garde and has acted as an increasingly official urbanism consultancy for the Moscow Mayoralty. Meanwhile, the personal project of the oligarch Dasha Zhukova, Roman Abramovich's one-time partner, to create a sort of Tate-style modern art foundation – named Garage after its one-time home in a bus garage in the north of Moscow designed by Konstantin Melnikov – commissioned OMA to design their main gallery/museum space as part of the redesign that Garage and Strelka were then executing in Gorky Park. The building used was a 1960s cafe, a modest modernist building with an attractive mural in the 'severe style'. Where most architects would have demolished, OMA treated the building as a sort of Palace of Knossos, a historical fake built around a real object of archaeology, restored to a sheen that it could never possibly have had at the time, while leaving the ravages of time in select places, so that the artifice is clear. At the same time, as a sort of sideline, it seems some members of OMA have lamented the effects of neoliberal capitalism and the obliteration of the welfare state, particularly in the writings of its partner Reinier de Graaf.[20] How seriously this should be taken is unclear, but if nothing else it does make clear the apparent inability of architects *not* to become complicit in neoliberalism.[21]

Yet one of the most telling examples of the curious penetration of avant-garde architecture came in the form of a 2010 exhibition curated by Hadid's partner Patrik Schumacher for Svarovski, at the Galerie Gmurzynska in Zurich. Like the Deconstructivist Architecture show in 1988, it juxtaposed the Soviet avant-garde with works by Zaha Hadid, as a visual means of pointing out the affinities between their work. A text by Patrik Schumacher called 'A Glimpse Back into the Future' explained this as follows: 'Ninety years ago … the October Revolution ignited the most exuberant surge of creative energy that has ever erupted on planet earth. This amazing firework of creative exuberance took off under the most severe material circumstances – fuelled by the idealistic enthusiasm for the project of a new society. This would define the art and architecture of the twentieth century'. He continues: 'The pace, quantity and quality of the creative work in art, science and design was truly astounding, anticipating in one intense flash what then took another 50 years to unfold elsewhere in the world.'[22]

No tragic irony there. If Koolhaas and De Graaf have tried to have their cake and eat it – to adapt the ideas of the Communist avant-garde to a neoliberal context while retaining a (largely nebulous) 'criticality' – Schumacher is more realistic. In recent years, since taking over management of Zaha Hadid's architectural firm after her death, he has engaged in deliberately inflammatory, hard neoliberal public statements proposing the abolition of all social housing and building upon London's parks. And there is an iron logic to this. For Schumacher, a repentant former Trotskyist, the zeitgeist is with neoliberalism – the force that is revolutionising society, destroying all the pre-existing social links, creating a ruthlessly modernising, unsentimental built environment, where all that is solid melts into air. Once the vehicle for this was the Bolshevik Party – now it is the Chinese Communist Party, along with the royal families of Qatar and the United Arab Emirates, and those 'global entrepreneurs' who, even if they stop in a city like London 'for a few weeks, they throw some key parties and these are amazing multiplying events'.[23]

STILL SOCIALIST?

While the Soviet avant-garde appears to have become just another part of art and architectural history, there has been, in the last decade or so, a flurry of interest in the side of architecture that, according to Kenneth Frampton's *Critical History*, never happened in the first place: the post-Stalin modernism that essentially became the official style between 1956 and 1991, the most ignored period of all. The story of the avant-garde was familiar enough, as was its replacement with the disturbing world of Stalinist architecture, but the years after the despot's death were a huge and untapped resource. In English-language publishing, the pace was set by a series of coffee table photo books, in the form of surprise bestsellers such as Frederic Chaubin's *CCCP: Cosmic Communist Constructions Photographed* (2011), Rebecca Litchfield's *Soviet Ghosts* (2013), and Christopher Herwig's *Soviet Bus Stops* (two volumes – 2015 and 2018), among others. These depicted a previously unknown, 'undiscovered' world, where familiar modernist motifs – the concrete walkway, the daringly engineered dome, the cantilever – were taken to extremes, with most of the buildings depicted (aside, of course, from the bus stops) on a massive and cyclopean scale. Few if any of these books made even the slightest attempt to consult historians within the cities they were describing, something which has rather unsurprisingly led to their being attacked as a form of orientalism.[24]

Perhaps the main positive effect of this has been the publication in English of research on this newly fashionable subject by post-Soviet historians. This includes several specialised books on specific figures, such as one on the architect Felix Novikov, edited by Philipp Meuser at the German-based Dom Publishers, and volumes on certain regions. For instance, Meuser or Boris Chukhovich's work on Tashkent, Ruben Arevshatyan's on Armenia, or Marija Dremaite's on the Baltic states chart the distinct architectural and planning cultures in the non-Russian republics of the union, and the tension between 'westernisation', Russification, and the apparently anti-colonial nature of Leninist nationality policies. Dimitrij Zadorin's study of the enormous mass housing programmes of the Brezhnev era takes seriously the logistics of Khrushchev and Brezhnev's attempts to rehouse the entire union via mass production; Olga Kazakova's study of the Constructivist-trained designer Leonid Pavlov doubles as a tracing of the failures of Soviet cybernetics.[25] This work has important virtues in revealing how the apparently 'cosmic' constructions depicted in the coffee table books came about – and in filling in the void left by generations of western architectural critics and historians, for whom this work simply did not exist, and who paid no attention to it when it was actually happening, something which is also generally true of the western left. The work of many of these historians has often been highly critical of post-Soviet capitalism, and of the orientalist nature of western notions of Soviet socialism. For instance, in her recent collaboration with the photographer Alexei Bykov, the Kharkiv-based historian Ievgeniia Gubikina writes both of how for post-Communist authorities, these buildings are obstacles in the way of a parasitic project of, as she puts it, 'de-modernisation', an ideological impediment to national consolidation and a spatial impediment to the accumulation of capital. Meanwhile, the western interest is largely 'a new exoticism', where 'Soviet Modernist architecture is often portrayed as radical, futuristic, cosmic, optimistic, naïve, "mad" and exciting', and where the buildings 'have seemingly been taken over by nature, these "temples" overrun by "aborigines" and wild animals'.[26]

This sort of work has the potential to finally restore the subject matter of dreams and retroactive utopias, and the sourcebook for contemporary iconic architects, to historical materialism. But it tends to leave open, as the historian generally does, the question of what use all of these experiments might actually have in the present. One recent challenge to this comes in Mike Davis' essay 'Who Will Build the Ark', a dialogue between the dystopian and utopian potentials of the twenty-first-century conjuncture. When trying to find an affirmation of the modern city that can still point in a socialist – and, strikingly, ecological – direction, Davis turns to the Soviet avant-garde. Consider, for example, the Constructivists. El Lissitzky,

Melnikov, Leonidov, Golosov, the Vesnin brothers and other brilliant socialist designers – constrained as they were by early Soviet urban misery and a drastic shortage of public investment – proposed to relieve congested apartment life with splendidly designed workers' clubs, people's theatres and sports complexes. They gave urgent priority to the emancipation of proletarian women through the organisation of communal kitchens, day nurseries, public baths, and co-operatives of all kinds.[27]

These are not of merely retrospective value – they are a political intervention, which, for all their undoubted rooting in Fordist and Taylorist ideas of efficiency, constituted a project where 'social condensers' could help create 'a new proletarian civilisation', not merely make bourgeois civilisation more exciting. This has obvious practical application in countries that are as poor as the USSR was in the 1920s, as what the Constructivists were doing was not a dream work but 'a practical strategy of leveraging poor urban workers' standard of living in otherwise austere circumstances'. This is also of crucial importance 'in the context of global environmental emergency', as Davis puts it, meaning that 'this Constructivist project could be translated into the proposition that the egalitarian aspects of city life consistently provide the best sociological and physical supports for resource conservation and carbon migration'. Perhaps they really were the future after all.

Here, aesthetics is important, but it is secondary – the point is the Constructivist intervention into the urban crisis, and the specific typologies rather than shapes that they devised in the process. It's appropriate, then, that for one of the most convincing accounts of how these ideas can have an enduring socialist effect within a capitalist metropolis, we actually have to turn to a building from the Stalinist era, to which Davis otherwise rightly gives short shrift. The Anglo-Polish anthropologist Michal Murawski has worked for some years on a project about the Palace of Culture and Science in Warsaw, a sky-scraping neo-Renaissance edifice of the early 1950s, given as a 'gift' (of the sort you can't refuse) from Stalin and the Soviet people to the devastated Polish capital, and formally modelled on the aesthetics of the seven post-war neo-baroque skyscrapers Stalin had commissioned as a vainglorious victory gesture in the centre of Moscow, even using one of the same architects, Lev Rudnev (a former Constructivist), the same engineers, and a Soviet team of builders. Murawski argues in his book *The Palace Complex* that the result was actually the largest scale realisation of the 'social condenser' built anywhere.[28] At the convergence of all east–west and north–south routes in the capital, the Palace contains a youth centre, several cinemas, a swimming pool, a congress hall, several cafes, various public institutes, a Museum of Technology and a Museum of Evolution (!).

As his research makes clear, there is almost nobody in the Polish capital who has not used the building at some point. Moreover, the sprawling, complex plan of the building, and the parks and squares around it, have managed to confound nearly thirty years of capitalist attempts to replan the centre of Warsaw and erase its public spaces. Murawski argues, taking a line from the historian of Czechoslovak housing Kimberley Zarecor, that this is because the building remains, in a functional and continuing sense 'still-socialist'. It is within the capitalist city, but inherently, intrinsically against it, and a convincing, viable alternative to it. In Davis' phrase, then, it's upon this that we can build the ark.

NOTES

1   See Charlotte Higgins, 'Phil Collins – Why I took a Soviet statue of Engels across Europe to Manchester', *The Guardian*, 30 June 2017.

2   The description is taken from Evan Smith, 'Defend the Right to Strike', written for the inclusion of the banner in the Victoria and Albert Museum's 2014 exhibition 'Disobedient Objects', available at: www.vam.ac.uk/blog/disobedient-objects/defend-right-strike-grunwick-strike-banner.

3   Alexei Gutnov et al, *The Ideal Communist City*, New York: Braziller, 1968 [translated from the Italian].

4   See this useful obituary: David North, 'David King, 1943-2016 – Revolutionary socialist, artist and defender of historical truth', *World Socialist Web Site*, 14 May 2016, available at: www.wsws.org.

5   Reyner Banham, *Theory and Design in the First Machine Age*, Oxford: Butterworth, 1972, p. 177.

6   Ibid, p. 193.

7   Ibid, p. 297.

8   Kenneth Frampton, *Modern Architecture: A Critical History*, London: Thames and Hudson, 1980, p. 177.

9   Ibid, p. 180.

10   Manfredo Tafuri and Francesco Dal Co, *Modern Architecture*, London, UK: Faber, 1986 [first edition 1976], p. 175.

11   Ibid, p. 188.

12   Rem Koolhaas, *Delirious New York*, New York: Monacelli, 1994, p.307.

13   Ibid.

14   Ibid, p. 310.

15   Of particular importance: Catherine Cooke, *Russian Avant-Garde Theories of Art, Architecture and the City*, Hoboken, NJ: Wiley, 1995; and Selim Khan-Magomedov, *Pioneers of Soviet Architecture*, London: Thames and Hudson, 1987.

16   Catherine Cooke, 'Images or Intelligence?' in *Architectural Design*, 59(7/8), 1989, p. vii-viii.

17   One of the few systematic attempts to analyse this is in Pippo Ciora and Margherita Guccione, eds., *Zaha Hadid In Italy*, Rome: Quodlibet, 2017.

18   See: https://erickvanegeraat.com/project/russian-avant-garde.

19   For a recent special issue exploring this concept, see: *The RIBA Journal of Architecture*, 22, 2017.

20   Reinier De Graaf, 'Architecture is now a tool of Capital', *Architectural Review*, April 2015.

21   A more sympathetic interpretation of OMA's use of dialectics can be found in Hal Foster, 'Architecture and Empire', in *Design and Crime and Other Diatribes*, New York: Verso, 2003.

22   The text is online at https://www.dezeen.com/2010/07/12/zaha-hadid-and-suprematism-at-galerie-gmurzynska-zurich.

23   Oliver Wainwright, 'Zaha Hadid's Successor – scrap art schools, privatise cities and bin social housing', *The Guardian*, 24 November 2016.

24   For instance, in Agata Pyzik's *Poor but Sexy: Culture Clashes in Europe, East and West*, London: Zero Books, 2014; and Jamie Rann, 'Beauty and the East', *Calvert Journal*, 31 July 2014, available at: www.calvertjournal.com.

25   Most of these are discussed by the author in: Owen Hatherley, 'Designing the Soviet Union', *Jacobin*, 15 August 2016, available at: www.jacobinmag.com.

26   Alex Bykov and Ievgeniia Gubkina, *Soviet Modernism, Brutalism, Postmodernism: Buildings and Structures in Ukraine 1955-91*, Berlin: Dom Publishers, 2019, p. 7.

27   Mike Davis, 'Who Will Build the Ark?', in *Old Gods, New Enigmas*, New York: Verso, 2018, p. 219.

28   Michal Murawski, *The Palace Complex: A Stalinist Skyscraper, Capitalist Warsaw, and a City Transfixed*, Bloomington: Indiana University Press, 2019; and 'Actually Existing Success: Economics, Aesthetics, and the Specificity of (Still) Socialist Urbanism', in *Comparative Studies in Society and History*, 60(4), 2018.

WHAT SHOULD SOCIALISM MEAN IN THE TWENTY-FIRST CENTURY?

NANCY FRASER

'Socialism' is back. For decades the word was considered an embarrass-ment – a despised failure and relic of a bygone era. No more! Today, politicians like Bernie Sanders and Alexandria Ocasio-Cortez wear the label proudly and win support, while organizations like Democratic Socialists of America attract new members in droves. But what exactly do they mean by 'socialism'? However welcome, enthusiasm for the word does not translate automatically into serious reflection on its content. What exactly does or should 'socialism' signify in the present era?*

In this lecture, I provide some preliminary thoughts in search of an answer. Drawing on an expanded conception of capitalism, I shall suggest that we need an expanded conception of socialism, which overcomes the narrow economism of received understandings. Disclosing the capitalist economy's contradictory and destructive relations to its 'non-economic' presuppositions, I contend that socialism must do more than transform the realm of production. Over and above that *desideratum*, which I wholeheartedly endorse, it must also transform production's relation to its background conditions of possibility – namely, social reproduction, state power, non-human nature, and forms of wealth that lie outside capital's official circuits, but within its reach. In other words, as I shall explain, a socialism for our time must overcome not only capital's exploitation of wage labour, but also its free-riding on unwaged carework, public goods, and wealth expropriated from racialized subjects and non-human nature.

The result, as I said, will be an expanded conception of socialism. But expansion is not mere addition. The point is not to add more features to received understandings while leaving the latter unchanged. It is rather

* This is the text of the 2019 Solomon Katz Distinguished Lecture in the Humanities, delivered at the University of Washington, May 8, 2019 under the sponsorship of the Simpson Center for the Humanities

to revise our views of both capitalism and socialism by incorporating into them structural accounts of matters that are usually considered secondary – above all, gender/sexuality, race/ethnicity/nationality/empire, ecology, and democracy. The effect will be to cast a new light on all the classical topoi of socialist thought: on domination and emancipation; on class and crisis; on property, markets and planning; on necessary labour, free time, and social surplus.

Certainly, I won't be able to give anything close to a full accounting of these matters in the present lecture. But I shall have something to say, however preliminary, about three of these topoi: institutional boundaries, social surplus, and markets. In each case, I shall try to show that the problem assumes a different guise once we view capitalism as something more than an economy – and socialism as something more than an alternative economic system. The view of socialism that emerges from this exercise differs sharply from Soviet-style Communism, on the one hand, and from social democracy, on the other.

I shall begin, however, with capitalism. This is the necessary starting point for any discussion of socialism. Socialism, after all, is no 'mere ought' or utopian dream. If it is worth discussing now, it is rather because it encapsulates real, historically emergent possibilities: potentials for human freedom, well-being, and happiness that capitalism itself has brought within reach but cannot actualize. Equally important, socialism is a response to capitalism's impasses and injustices: to the problems that system generates non-accidentally and cannot solve; and to the forms of structural domination built into it, which cannot be overcome within it. More generally, socialism claims to remedy capitalism's ills. And so, it is there that we must begin. Only by identifying capitalism's constitutive dynamics and institutional structures can we grasp exactly what it is that must be transformed. And only by proceeding on that basis can we envision the positive outlines of a socialist alternative.

So: what exactly is capitalism? And what is wrong with it?

WHAT IS CAPITALISM?
AN EXPANDED VIEW

Often, capitalism is understood as an economic system, whose defining components are private property and market exchange; wage labour and commodity production; credit and finance; profit, interest, and rent: all elements denominated in money and combined in such a way as to institutionalize economic growth as a system imperative. On this view, capitalism coincides with the range of activities, relations, and objects that are monetized, held to embody or produce economic value. Call this the narrow or restricted view of capitalism. Assumed by most business men/women and by mainstream economists, it is also the unreflective common sense of society at large. So much so that it dominates the thinking of some of capitalism's critics. They, too, often subscribe to the narrow view of it.

What I shall call 'traditional Marxism' is a case in point. It views capitalism as a system of class exploitation centered on the relation between capitalists and workers at the point of production. The key relation, on this view, is between those who own the means of production as their private property, on the one hand, and those who own nothing but their capacity to work and must therefore sell that 'peculiar commodity' to a capitalist in order to live. This relation is crystallized in a market transaction in which labour power is exchanged for wages, but it is not an exchange of equivalents. On the contrary, the capitalist pays only for the worker's socially necessary labour time (the hours needed to produce a sum of value that covers the costs of the worker's subsistence) and appropriates the rest of the worker's labour time as 'surplus value'. The relation is therefore one of 'exploitation'. Exploitation is the very crux of capitalism on the traditional Marxian view. It is the secret of surplus value; the driver of technological innovation and rising productivity; but also the source of poverty and class inequality; the motor of wholesale irrationality, of non-accidental bouts of mass unemployment and periodic outbreaks of economic crisis.

Clearly, the traditional Marxian view of capitalism is a big improvement over mainstream apologetics. And yet it, too, remains overly narrow. This view focuses single-mindedly on the 'hidden abode' of production, while failing to interrogate the latter's conditions of possibility. These must be sought elsewhere, in other, 'non-economic' abodes, more hidden still. While traditional Marxism captures what we can think of as front story of capitalist society, it glosses over the backstory, which makes it not so much wrong as incomplete. To complete the picture, and thereby to arrive at a full understanding of capitalist society, we need to go beyond not only the mainstream conception but also the traditional Marxian alternative. Plumbing the more hidden depths beneath production, we need to disclose the non-economic conditions that make production possible. Let me mention four such non-economic conditions for the possibility of a capitalist economy.

The first is a sizeable fund of unwaged labour devoted to 'social reproduction'. This labour includes housework; the birthing and rearing of children; the care of adults, including wage workers, the elderly, and the unemployed – all aimed at the making and sustaining of human beings. These activities of 'people-making' constitute an indispensable precondition for 'profit-making'. Without them there could be no 'workers', no 'labour power', no necessary or surplus labour time, no exploitation, no surplus value, no accumulation of capital, no profit. Yet capital accords them no value, is unconcerned to replenish them, and seeks to avoid paying for them insofar as it can.

The second 'non-economic' precondition for a capitalist economy is a large fund of wealth expropriated from subjugated peoples, especially from racialized peoples. This wealth includes dependent, unfree, and unwaged or under-waged labour, but also expropriated land, looted mineral and energy deposits, human bodies and bodily organs, children and reproductive capacities – all serving as inputs to capitalist production for which capital pays little or nothing. Expropriated wealth was an indispensable source of capital stockpiling at the start of capitalism's history, as Marx maintained; but it did not cease with the system's 'maturation'. On the contrary, the capitalist economy relies even now on a continuing stream of free or cheap inputs as a major source of accumulation, alongside and inter-imbricated with exploitation. Absent such expropriation of subject peoples, the exploitation of 'free workers' would not be profitable. Yet capital disavows its reliance on such wealth and refuses to pay for its replenishment.

A third 'non-economic' precondition for a capitalist economy is a large fund of 'free gifts' and/or cheap inputs from non-human nature. These supply the indispensable material substratum of capitalist production: the raw materials that labour transforms; the energy that powers machines and the foodstuffs that power bodies; hence, arable land, breathable air, potable water, and the carbon-carrying capacities of the earth's atmosphere. Absent these natural-ecological conditions, there could be no economic producers or social reproducers; no wealth to expropriate or free labour to exploit; no capital or capitalists. Yet capital treats nature as a source of free or very cheap gifts to which it helps itself but fails to replenish or repair.

A fourth and final 'non-economic' precondition for a capitalist economy is a large fund of public goods supplied by states and other public powers. These include legal orders that guarantee property rights, contracts, and free exchange; repressive forces that ensure order, put down rebellions, manage dissent, and enable expropriation both within and beyond state territory; a money supply that stores value and enables transactions across broad swaths of time and space; transport and communications infrastructure; and a variety of mechanisms for managing system crises. Absent these public goods, there could be no social order, no trust, no exchange – hence no sustained accumulation. Yet capital tends to resent public power and seeks to evade the taxes that are necessary sustain it.

Each of these four conditions represents an indispensable presupposition of a capitalist economy. Each harbours social relations, social activities, and forms of social wealth that together form the *sine qua non* for accumulation. Behind capitalism's official institutions – wage labour, production, exchange, and finance – stand their necessary supports and enabling conditions: families, communities, nature; territorial states, political organizations, and civil societies; and not least of all, massive amounts and multiple forms of unwaged and expropriated labour. Fundamentally integral to capitalist society, they too are constitutive elements of it.

Capitalism, in other words, is no mere economy, but something larger. It is an *institutionalized social order* in which an arena of economized activities and relations is marked out and set apart from other, non-economized zones, on which the former depend, but which they disavow. A capitalist society comprises an 'economy' that is distinct from (and dependent on) a 'polity' or political order; an arena of 'economic production' that is distinct from (and dependent on) a zone of 'social reproduction'; a set of relations of exploitation that is distinct from (and dependent on) background relations of expropriation; and a socio-historical realm of human activity that is distinct from (and dependent on) a putatively ahistorical material substratum of non-human nature.

Here, in effect, we leave behind the narrow view of capitalism as an economy. Conceiving it, rather, as an institutionalized social order, we arrive at an expanded view. This new, expanded view of capitalist society has major consequences for the project of reimagining socialism. It changes – indeed enlarges – our sense of what is wrong with capitalism and of what must be done to transform it.

WHAT IS WRONG WITH CAPITALISM?
AN EXPANDED VIEW

On the narrow view, there are three main wrongs built into capitalism: injustice, irrationality, and unfreedom. Let us look at each point in turn.

On the narrow view, capitalism's core injustice consists in the exploitation by capital of the class of free propertyless workers. The latter work many hours for free, producing enormous wealth in which they have no share. The benefits flow rather to the capitalist class, which appropriates their surplus labour and the surplus value generated by it, reinvesting the latter for its own purposes, namely, to accumulate ever more of it. The larger consequence is the relentless exponential growth of capital as a hostile power that dominates the very workers who produce it. That is the core injustice on this view: the class exploitation of waged labour at the point of production. Its locus is the capitalist economy, specifically the sphere of economic production.

Likewise, on the narrow view, capitalism's chief irrationality is its built-in tendency to economic crisis. An economic system oriented to the limitless accumulation of surplus value, appropriated privately in the form of profit, is inherently self-destabilizing. The drive to increase profit by increasing productivity through technical advances results in periodic drops in the rate of profit, in the overproduction of goods, and the overaccumulation of capital. Attempted 'fixes' like financialization only postpone the day of reckoning, while ensuring it will be all the more severe when it does arrive. In general, the course of capitalist development is punctuated by periodic economic crises: by boom-bust cycles, stock market crashes, financial panics, bankruptcy chains, mass liquidations of value, and mass unemployment.

Finally, the narrow view entails that capitalism is deeply and constitutively undemocratic. Granted, it often promises democracy in the political realm. But that promise is systematically undercut by social inequality, on the one hand, and by class power, on the other. Then, too, the capitalist workplace is exempt from any pretence of democratic self-governance. It is a sphere where capital commands and workers obey.

On the narrow view, therefore, capitalism non-accidentally entrenches three chief wrongs. First, this system lives by exploiting and dominating wage labourers; second, it is structurally primed to spawn periodic economic crises; and finally, it is constitutively non-democratic. The trouble arises, in every case, from the inherent dynamics of capitalism's economy. Built into the DNA of that system, the wrongs of capitalism reside, on the narrow view, in its economic organization.

Once again, the picture is not so much wrong as incomplete. While correctly disclosing capitalism's inherent *economic* ills, it fails to register a range of *non-economic* injustices, crisis tendencies, and forms of unfreedom that are equally constitutive of this mode of social organization. These come clearly into view when we adopt the expanded conception of capitalist society.

Consider, first, that the expanded view of capitalism discloses an expanded catalogue of systemic injustices. Far from residing exclusively *within* its economy, many of these are grounded rather in the divisions *between* the capitalist economy and its non-economic conditions of possibility. The division between economic production, where labour is remunerated in cash wages, and social reproduction, where it is often unwaged, sentimentalized, and recompensed in 'love', is a case in point. Historically gendered, this division entrenches a fundamental gender asymmetry at the heart of capitalist societies and grounds the subordination of women, gender binarism and heteronormativity.

Similarly, capitalist societies institute a structural division between free 'workers', who can exchange their labour power for the costs of their reproduction, and dependent 'others', whose persons and assets can simply be seized. Unable to access rights, protections, or the full costs of their own reproduction, the latter group provides capital with a stream of free or cheap inputs that swell the tide of profit. This status division between the 'merely' exploitable and the downright expropriable is fundamental to capitalist society. Coinciding roughly but unmistakably with the global colour line, it undergirds a range of structural injustices, including racial oppression, imperialism (old and new), indigenous dispossession and genocide.

Then, too, capitalist societies institute a sharp division between human beings and nonhuman nature, which cease to belong to the same ontological universe. Reduced to a tap and a sink, nonhuman nature is opened to brute extractivism and instrumentalization. If this is not an injustice against 'nature' (or against nonhuman animals), it is at the very least an injustice against existing and future generations of human beings who are left with an increasingly uninhabitable planet.

Finally, capitalism institutes a structural division between 'the economic' and 'the political'. On one side stands the private power of capital to organize production, using 'only' the lash of hunger and need; on the other the public power of the state, which monopolizes legitimate violence and makes coercively enforceable law. The effect of this division is to truncate the scope of the political, expelling from the public agenda a range of life-and-death questions, as I shall explain. Devolving these matters to capital, capitalist societies offer only a poor and shrunken facsimile of democracy. Subjecting supposedly self-governing citizens to capital's arbitrary rule, they are veritable cauldrons of political injustice.

In general, then, an expanded view of capitalist society makes visible an expanded catalogue of structural injustices. As deep-seated and non-accidental as class exploitation, these injustices really *are* structural. A socialist alternative to capitalist society must remedy them too. Far from 'merely' transforming the organization of economic production, it must also transform the latter's relation to social reproduction, and with it, the gender and sexual orders. Likewise, it must end capital's freeriding on nature's 'free (or cheap) gifts' and its expropriation of the wealth of racialized populations. Finally, it must expand the scope of democratic self-rule beyond their current miserable limits. In sum, if socialism is to remedy capitalism's injustices, it must change not 'just' the capitalist economy, but the entire institutionalized social order that is capitalist society.

But that is not all. The expanded view of capitalism also enlarges our view of what counts as capitalist crisis. This view discloses some built-in self-destabilizing propensities, above and beyond those internal to its 'economy'. It discloses, first, a structural tendency to crises of social reproduction. Insofar as capital tries to avoid paying for the unwaged carework on which it depends, it periodically puts enormous pressure on the chief providers of that work: families, communities, and, above all, women. The current, financialized form of capitalist society is generating just such a crisis today, as it demands both retrenchment of public provision of social services and vastly increased hours of waged work per household and from women.

The expanded view also discloses an inherent tendency to ecological crisis, insofar as capital works overtime to avoid paying anything close to the true replacement costs of the inputs it takes from non-human nature. Depleting the soil and befouling the seas, this system floods carbon sinks and overwhelms the carbon-carrying capacity of the planet. Helping itself to all these things while disavowing their repair and replacement costs, it periodically destabilizes the metabolic interaction between the human and non-human components of nature. I don't need to belabour how acute is our present ecological crisis.

Capitalism's tendencies to ecological and social-reproductive crisis are inseparable from its constitutive reliance on expropriated wealth from racialized peoples: its reliance on stolen lands, coerced labour, and looted minerals; its dependence on racialized zones as dumping grounds for toxic waste and as suppliers of underpaid carework, increasingly organized in global care chains. The result is an entwining of economic, ecological, social crisis with imperialism and racial-ethnic antagonism. Neoliberalism has upped the ante here as well.

Finally, the enlarged view of capitalism discloses a deep-seated tendency to political crisis. Here, too, capital tries to have it both ways, living off public goods for which it tries not to pay. Primed to evade taxes and to weaken state regulatory capacities, it tends to hollow out the very public powers on which it depends. The current, financialized form of capitalism takes this game to a whole new level. Mega-corporations outgun territorially tethered public powers, while global finance disciplines states, making a mockery of elections (as in Greece) and preventing governments from addressing popular claims, even if they wanted to. The result is a major crisis of governance, now reflected in a crisis of hegemony, as masses of people across the globe defect from established political parties and common sense.

In general, then, the expanded view discloses that capitalism harbours multiple crisis tendencies above and beyond the 'economic'. Following Polanyi (and James O'Connor), I understand the former as 'inter-realm' contradictions, lodged at the joints that separate, and connect, the capitalist economy to its non-economic background conditions of possibility. In a nutshell, capital has a built-in tendency to erode or destroy or deplete (but in any case, to destabilize) its own presuppositions – which is to say, to eat its own tail. This, too, is part and parcel of what is wrong with capitalist society – and of what socialism must overcome.

Finally, the expanded view of capitalist society discloses an enlarged view of its democratic deficits. The problem is not 'only' that economic inequality and class power thwart the possibility of equal democratic voice in the political realm. Nor is it 'only' that bosses command on the factory floor. Equally if not more important is the pre-emptive removal of the most consequential matters from the scope of democratic-decision-making altogether. How should we organize the production of goods, of use values that satisfy needs? On what energic bases and through what sort of social relations? How should we relate the production of goods to the reproduction of persons, on the one hand, and to that of non-human nature, on the other? And perhaps most important of all: How shall we dispose over the social surplus we collectively produce? In capitalist societies, we have virtually no say in these matters. Investors bent on maximal accumulation decide them behind our backs.

In general, then, an expanded view of capitalist society discloses an expanded view of the system's ills. If socialism aims to remedy capitalism's wrongs, it faces a very big job. It must invent a new social order that overcomes not 'only' class domination but also asymmetries of gender and sex, racial/ethnic/imperial oppression and political domination across the board. Then, too, it must de-institutionalize multiple crisis tendencies: not 'just' economic and financial but also ecological, social-reproductive, and political. Finally, a socialism for the twenty-first century must vastly enlarge the purview of democracy to encompass not 'just' decision-making within a pre-defined 'political' zone, but more fundamentally, it must democratize the very definition and demarcation, the very frames, that constitute 'the political'.

WHAT IS SOCIALISM?
AN EXPANDED VIEW

Clearly, the project of rethinking socialism for the twenty-first century is itself a pretty big job – far too big for a single person or even a single group of persons engaged in theorizing. If the job gets done (which is a big 'if'), it will be through the combined efforts of activists and theorists, as insights gained through social struggle synergize with programmatic thinking and with political organization.

Nevertheless, I want to offer three sets of brief reflections that seem to me to follow from what I have already said. These have to do with institutional boundaries, social surplus, and the role of markets.

Boundary questions are at least as important as questions about the internal organization of supposedly given 'spheres' (such as 'the economic' and 'the political'). Instead of focusing exclusively or one-sidedly on the organization of 'the economy', socialists need to think about the 'economy's' relation to its background conditions of possibility: to social reproduction, non-human natural, non-capitalized forms of wealth and public power. If socialism is to overcome *all* institutionalized forms of capitalist irrationality, injustice and unfreedom, it must re-imagine the relations between production and reproduction, society and nature, and the social and the political.

I am not suggesting that socialism should aim simply to liquidate these divisions. The Soviet effort to abolish the distinction between 'the political' and 'the economic' can stand as a general warning against liquidation. But we can and must re-envision the institutional divisions that comprise a capitalist society. We might consider, for example, relocating them so that matters once relegated to the economic now become political or social. We might also contemplate softening institutional boundaries, rendering the various domains more responsive, indeed less antagonistic, to one another. Surely, a socialist society must overcome capitalism's tendency to institute zero-sum games, which take away from nature and social reproduction what they give to production.

Even more important, we must reverse current priorities among those domains: whereas capitalist societies subordinate the imperatives of social and ecological reproduction to those of commodity production, itself geared to accumulation, socialists need to turn things right-side up: to install the nurturing of people, the safeguarding of nature, and democratic self-rule as society's highest priorities, which trump efficiency and growth. In effect, it must put squarely in the foreground those matters that capital relegates to its disavowed background.

Finally, a socialism for the twenty-first century must democratize the very process of setting and revising institutional boundaries. Henceforth, the 'metapolitical' work of 'redomaining' must itself be made subject to collective democratic decision-making: democratic publics and *demoi* must themselves decide which matters will be addressed within which first-order arenas of political participation. One implication is that, while historically sedimented territorial units ('national' states) need not (and perhaps should not) be simply abolished, they do need to be articulated with new functionally demarcated political units, which operate at different scales and base participation on the 'all subjected principle'. In general, socialist redomaining should be constrained by the principle of non-domination – applied along all the major axes entrenched in capitalist societies – as well along any other axes of domination that we may discover or create in the future.

Moreover, redomaining must be guided insofar as possible by the principle of 'pay as you go'. Eschewing freeriding and 'primitive accumulation', socialism must ensure the sustainability of all the conditions of production, which capitalism has so callously trashed. In other words: a socialist society must undertake to replenish, repair, or replace all the wealth it uses up in production and reproduction. It must replenish care- and people-making work as well as work that produces use values or commodities. It must replace all the wealth it takes from 'the outside' – from peripheral peoples and societies as well as from nonhuman nature. It must replenish the political capacities and public goods it draws on in the course of meeting other needs. In other words: no free riding on matters relegated to a disavowed background. This proviso is a *sine qua non* for overcoming the intergenerational injustice endemic to capitalist society. Only by observing it can a socialism for the twenty-first century overcome capitalist irrationality and de-institutionalize its built-in proclivities to crisis.

This brings me to a second set of reflections, concerning the classical socialist question of surplus. Surplus is the fund of wealth, if any, that society generates in excess of what it requires to reproduce itself at its current level and in its current form. In capitalist societies, as I already noted, surplus is treated as the private property of the capitalist class and disposed of by its owners as they see fit, generally reinvested with the aim of producing yet more surplus – on and on, without limit. This, as we saw before, is both unjust and self-destabilizing.

A socialist society must democratize control over social surplus. It must allocate surplus democratically, deciding via collective decision-making exactly what to do with existing excess capacities and resources – as well as how much excess capacity it wants to produce in the future, indeed whether it wants to produce any surplus at all. In other words, it must de-institutionalize the growth imperative hard-wired into capitalist society. This does not mean we must institutionalize 'de-growth' as a hard-wired counter-imperative, but rather that we must make the question of 'growth' (how much, if any; what kind, how, and where) a political question. In fact, a socialism for the twenty-first century must treat *all* those questions I mentioned before as political questions, subject to democratic resolution: what and how much to produce; how many hours to devote to surplus production over and above what is needed to reproduce society at its current level.

Surplus can also be thought of as time: time left over after the necessary work of meeting our needs and replenishing what we've used up; hence, time that could be free time. The prospect of free time has been a central pivot of all the classical accounts of socialist freedom, including that of Marx. In the early stages of socialism, however, I doubt that free time would loom very large. The reason lies in the enormous unpaid bill that socialist society would inherit from capitalism. Although capitalism prides itself on its productivity, and although Marx himself considered it a veritable engine for producing surplus, I have my doubts. The trouble is, Marx reckoned surplus pretty much exclusively in the labour time that capital takes from waged workers after they produce value sufficient to cover their own costs of living. By contrast, he paid much less attention to the various 'free gifts' and 'cheaps' that capital expropriates and appropriates, and still less to its failure to cover *their* reproduction costs. What if we included *those* costs in our reckoning? What if capital had had to pay for free reproductive work, for ecological repair and replenishment, for wealth expropriated from racialized people, for public goods? How much surplus would it have really produced? That's a rhetorical question, of course. I wouldn't know how even to begin constructing an answer. But I am sure that a socialist society would inherit a hefty bill for centuries of unpaid costs.

It would also inherit a hefty bill for massive unmet human needs across the globe: needs for health care, housing, nutritious (and delicious) food, education, transportation, and so on. These too should not be counted as surplus investment, but rather as matters of absolute necessity. The same holds for the pressing and enormous job of de-fossilizing the world economy – a task that is in no way optional. In general, the question of what is necessary and what is surplus assumes a different guise in view of the expanded view of capitalism.

The same is true for the question of the role of markets in a socialist society. The answer suggested by what I have so far said here can be condensed in a simple formula: no markets at the top, no markets at the bottom, but possibly some markets in the in-between. Let me explain.

What I mean by the top is the allocation of social surplus. Assuming there is a social surplus to be allocated, it must be considered the collective wealth of the society as a whole. No private person, firm, or state can own it or have the right to dispose of it. Truly collective property, surplus must be allocated via collective processes of decision-making and planning – planning that can and must be organized democratically. Market mechanisms should play no role at this level. Neither markets nor private property at the top.

The same holds for the bottom, by which I mean the level of basic needs: shelter, clothing, food, education, health care, transportation, communication, energy, leisure. I have no illusion that we can specify once and for all exactly what counts as a basic need and exactly what is required to satisfy it. That too must be a subject for democratic discussion, contestation, and decision-making. But whatever is decided must be provided as a matter of right, and not on the basis of ability to pay. This means that the use values we produce to meet these needs cannot be commodities. They must rather be public goods. This is why, incidentally, I am not a fan of Universal (or Unconditional) Basic Income (UBI). That project involves paying people cash to buy stuff to meet their basic needs, thereby treating basic need satisfactions as commodities. A socialist society should treat them rather as public goods. Effectively, then, no markets at the bottom.

So, no markets at the bottom or the top. But what about the in-between? I don't have a worked-out view about this question. But I imagine the in-between as a space for experimentation with a mix of different possibilities – a space where 'market socialism' could find a place, along with cooperatives, commons, self-organized associations and self-managed projects. I suspect that many traditional socialist objections to markets would dissolve or diminish in the context I envision here, where their operation would neither feed into nor be distorted by mechanisms that drive capital accumulation and by the private appropriation of social surplus. Once the top and the bottom are socialized and decommodified, the function and role of markets in the middle would be transformed. That proposition seems clear enough to me, even if I cannot say exactly how.

In fact, I realize how generally thin and rudimentary is the view of socialism I have been sketching here. What I have offered is only the barest of outlines on a very small subset of relevant questions. But I hope that even this poor beginning can have some worth. I hope specifically that I have convinced you that the socialist project is worth pursuing in the twenty-first century – that far from remaining a mere buzzword, 'socialism' must become the name for a genuine alternative to the system that is currently destroying the planet and thwarting our chances for living freely, democratically, and well. I hope too that I have convinced you that socialism cannot today be understood in the old-school way. Only by starting with an expanded view of capitalism can we proceed to develop an expanded view of socialism that can speak to our full set of needs and hopes in the twenty-first century.

Also Available

Socialist Register 2019: A World Turned Upside Down?
Edited by Leo Panitch and Greg Albo

Since the Great Financial Crisis swept across the world in 2008, there have been few certainties regarding the trajectory of global capitalism, let alone the politics taking hold in individual states.

This has now given way to palpable confusion regarding what sense to make of this world in a political conjuncture marked by Donald Trump's 'Make America Great Again' presidency of the United States, on the one hand, and, on the other, Xi Jinping's ambitious agenda in consolidating his position as 'core leader' at the top of the Chinese state.

Contents:
Leo Panitch/Sam Gindin: Trumping the empire
Marco Boffo/Alfredo Saad Filho/Ben Fine: Neoliberal capitalism: the
        authoritarian turn
Ray Kiely: Locating Trump
Doug Henwood: Trump and the new billionaire class
Nicole Aschoff: America's tipping point: between Trumpism
        and a new left
Elmar Altvater/Birgit Mahnkopf: The Capitalocene: permanent capitalist c
        ounter-revolution
Alan Cafruny: The European crisis and the left
Aijaz Ahmad: Extreme capitalism and 'the national question'
Jayati Ghosh: Decoupling is a myth: Asian capitalism in the global disarray
Sean Starrs: Can China unmake the American making of global capitalism?
Lin Chun: China's New Internationalism
Ana Garcia/Patrick Bond: Amplifying the contradictions:
        the centrifugal BRICS
Adam Hanieh: The contradictions of global migration
David Whyte: 'Death to the corporation': a modest proposal
Umut Ozsu: Humanitarian intervention today
Colin Leys: Corbyn and Brexit Britain: Is there a way forward for the Left?

ISBN 9780850367355 paperback

Socialist Register 2018: Rethinking Democracy
Edited by Leo Panitch and Greg Albo

This volume seeks a re-appraisal of actually-existing liberal democracy today, but its main goal is to help lay the foundations for new visions and practices in the development of socialist democracy. Amidst the contradictions of neoliberal capitalism today, the responsibility to sort out the relationship between socialism and democracy has never been greater. No revival of socialist politics in the 21st century can occur apart from founding new democratic institutions and practices.

Contents:

ISBN. 978-0-85036-733-1 paperback

www.merlinpress.co.uk